Productive Men, Reproductive Women

Productive Men, Reproductive Women

The Agrarian Household and the Emergence of Separate Spheres during the German Enlightenment

Marion W. Gray

Berghahn Books
NEW YORK • OXFORD

First published in 2000 by
Berghahn Books

© 2000 Marion Gray

All rights reserved.
No part of this publication may be reproduced in any form or by any means without the written permission of Berghahn Books.

Library of Congress Cataloging-in-Publication Data

Gray, Marion W.
    Productive men, reproductive women : the agrarian household and the emergence of separate spheres during the German Enlightenment / Marion W. Gray.
       p.   cm.
    Includes bibliographical references and index.
    ISBN 1-57181-171-0 (hbk. : alk. paper)
    ISBN 1-57181-172-9 (pbk. : alk. paper)
      1. Sex role—Europe, German-speaking—History. 2. Europe, German-speaking—Rural conditions. 3. Europe, German-speaking—Economic conditions. I. Title.
HQ1075.5.E8525G73   1999   99-19028
305.3'094—dc21   CIP

British Library Cataloguing in Publication Data

A catalogue record for this book is available from the British Library.

Contents

List of Illustrations		vii
Preface		ix
Acknowledgments		xi
Introduction	Gender Norms and the Language of Economics	1
Chapter 1	The Historical Context: Hierarchy, Patriarchy, and Community (1600-1800)	25
Chapter 2	The Household as Economy: Dominance, Subordination, and Interdependence in Seventeenth-Century Economic Thought (1600-1720)	49
Chapter 3	The New Economics of Cameralism: Redefining the Male World by Separating It from the Household (1720-1780)	89
Chapter 4	The Enlightenment: Civil Society and Middle-Class Males as the Arbiters of Social Norms (1750-1790)	120
Chapter 5	The Enlightenment and the "Character of the Sexes" (1750-1790)	145
Chapter 6	The Household Ideal Caught in a Changing World (1750-1790)	173

Contents

Chapter 7	The Primacy of the Public Sphere: The Era of the French Revolution and Napoleon (1790-1815)	214
Chapter 8	"Scientific Agriculture" and the Sexual Division of Labor (1810-1830)	258
Conclusion	"Every Man is King in His House"	297
Works Cited		304
Index		361

Illustrations

Figure 2.1
Title page from Hohberg, *Georgica curiosa* (1695).
Courtesy of National Agriculture Library,
Washington, D.C.   57

Figure 2.2
Illustration of the household as economy from
Thieme, *Haus-, Feld-, Artzney-, Koch-Kunst und
Wunder-Buch* (1687). Courtesy of National
Agriculture Library, Washington, D.C.   60

Figure 2.3
Stylized garden and orchard from Hohberg,
Georgica curiosa (1695). Courtesy of National
Agriculture Library, Washington, D.C.   62

Figure 2.4
Working with horses as a strictly male activity.
Illustration from Thieme, *Haus-, Feld-, Artzney-,
Koch-Kunst und Wunder-Buch* (1687). Courtesy
of National Agriculture Library, Washington, D.C.   64

Figure 2.5
Medicine and physical care as female economic
responsibilities. Illustration from Hohberg,
Georgica curiosa (1695). Courtesy of National
Agriculture Library, Washington, D.C.   66

Illustrations

Figure 2.6
Table of contents of Thieme, *Haus-, Feld-, Artzney-, Koch-Kunst und Wunder-Buch* (1687). Courtesy of National Agriculture Library, Washington, D.C.   72

Figure 2.7
Harvest scene from Thieme, *Haus-, Feld-, Artzney-, Koch-Kunst und Wunder-Buch* (1687). Courtesy of National Agriculture Library, Washington, D.C.   75

Figure 5.1
Frontispiece from Campe, *Väterlicher Rath für meine Tochter* (1791). Courtesy of Bayerische Staatsbibliothek, Munich.   157

Figure 6.1
Depiction of the newest techniques of silk production in *Baierischer Ökonomischer Hausvater* (1785). Courtesy of Bayerische Staatsbibliothek, Munich.   183

Figure 6.2
The Hausvater's study, illustrated in Münchhausen, *Hausvater* (1764-1774). Courtesy of Bayerische Staatsbibliothek, Munich.   186

Figures 8.1a and 8.1b
Illustrations of plows and their use from Thaer, *Beschreibung der nutzbarsten neuen Ackergeräthe* (1803-1806). Courtesy of Kenneth Spencer Research Library, University of Kansas, Lawrence.   263-264

Figure 8.2
Depiction of women in the domestic sphere from *Neues Nürnberger Kochbuch* (1820). Courtesy of Bayerische Staatsbibliothek, Munich.   280

Preface

Some years ago, when working on a project which had nothing to do with gender, I was using Friedrich Benedict Weber's *Handbuch der ökonomischen Literatur* (Handbook of Economic Literature, 1803-1842) in the Spencer Research Library at the University of Kansas. Weber was a professor of Cameralism, the branch of the so-called State Sciences dealing with economics and public finance. He was active in formulating and disseminating the economic ideals of the early nineteenth century. My purpose in consulting his valuable bibliography was to locate primary published sources concerning the agrarian reform debates going on during Weber's lifetime. However, I was struck by Weber's extensive bibliographies on *Hausmütterliteratur* – literature for the mistresses of households – to which he devoted an exclusive section in each of the eight successive editions of the handbook. This was a genre I had not previously known.

Weber's exhaustive lists of books about female roles in the rural economy suggested to me that he and his contemporaries were preoccupied not only with the changing construction of the German economy but also with the place of women in the emerging nineteenth century. Later research proved my intuition to be right. The crucial transitional period spanning the end of the eighteenth century and the beginning of the nineteenth – the so-called *Sattelzeit* – witnessed a redefinition of the economy and a corresponding reconstruction of gender. Academics and publicists were preoccupied with these themes. Knowing how rapidly the socioeconomic conditions were changing, they felt compelled not to let women's and men's defined roles go adrift. They were rushing to prescribe new gender norms.

The questions arising from my initial discovery shaped my project, a study in the social history of ideas. Colleagues who knew my research often asked me why I confined my investigations to normative sources. They wanted to know if the changing ideals found a resonance in the social conditions of everyday life. The question is a natural one, and I want to know the answer myself. Testing how the emerging model of separate spheres impacted the everyday life of rural people is a research project that I have already begun to pursue. However, I found it important to delineate first the *normative* shift in gender construction, which is the purpose of this book. During the Enlightenment, leading thinkers in German-speaking Europe came to believe in a system of separate spheres for men and women. The notion of the productive market economy as a male realm and the reproductive, but devalued, domestic sphere as the female domain was new in the late eighteenth century. It replaced the older ideal of the "household economy." I have tried to document this transition in the writing and thinking about the agricultural and rural society. I am grateful that Friedrich Benedict Weber led me to this project of interpreting the establishment of the modern construction of gender in rural German-speaking society.

Acknowledgments

It is humbling to recall the extensive collegial and institutional support that made this project both possible and pleasurable. I am especially grateful for the many friends and colleagues who, along the way, provided sounding boards for my plans by reading drafts of parts of this work, or research proposals, and discussing these with me. Some have contributed to the shape of the work simply by discussing ideas. Those who knew of and supported the project in its earliest stages included Jean Quataert, Jürgen Schlumbohm, and Richard Raack. Many colleagues in History and Women's Studies at Kansas State University contributed to the project as it took shape. I am especially grateful to Sue Zschoche, Nupur Chaudhuri, and Jim Sherow who went out of their way to stay in touch with my work and to challenge me to be clear in my interpretation. I presented papers based on this work at professional meetings and received supportive criticism from many, including Hans Erich Bödeker, Gerald Soliday, and Heide Wunder.

I had the advantage of being associated with research institutes that supported me both materially and intellectually. The earliest was the Max-Planck-Institut für Geschichte, in Göttingen. Rudolf Vierhaus, the Director, was gracious in making facilities available to me, and I found him to be a challenging and helpful discussant. The collegial atmosphere in Göttingen brought me into contact with scholars from Germany and other parts of the world whose influence is felt in the pages of this book.

Acknowledgments

The Institute for Advanced Research at Indiana University provided an ideal atmosphere for writing as well as delightful opportunities to discuss my research with scholars in disciplines other than my own, for example Gerald Baldasty and Robert Netting. Henry Remak, Director of the institute, flattered me with his deeply personal interest in my interpretation of Enlightenment thought. His successor, James M. Patterson, and the Assistant Director, Ivona Hedin, went out of their way to ensure that I had ideal working conditions.

The Max-Planck-Arbeitsgruppe Ostelbische Gutsherrschaft, in Potsdam, gave me the opportunity to return to Germany as I was finishing my research and writing. This cordial group of scholars under the directorship of Jan Peters is intensely interested in the history of rural people's lives. They invited me to share with them some of my findings on gender history, but the gain was mine more than theirs. They delightfully listened to my presentations, challenged my thinking, and, most important, shared their expertise with me. Out of my experience with this group has grown my new research agenda, dealing with everyday life, gender, and the changing natural environment in the late eighteenth century.

My research benefited from financial support from the two German institutions mentioned above. I am also grateful for a Fulbright Senior Research Grant, which made possible a year's research in Munich and Göttingen. Stipends from the President's Faculty Development Fund, the University Small Research Grants Program, the History Department, and the Women's Studies Programs, all at Kansas State University, assisted in my travel and other research expenses.

I published several papers that grew out of the project and helped it take its eventual shape. I am thankful for the encouragement of Frances Richardson Keller to publish a paper on female education in the eighteenth century in a book she edited, *Views of Women's Lives in Western Traditions*. An article in *History of European Ideas*, an article in a book edited by Konrad Jarausch and Larry Eugene Jones, and several papers published in the *Proceedings* and *Selected Proceedings* of the Consortium on Revolutionary Europe helped me toward my goal. Silke Lesemann urged me to submit an article on Cameralist thought and the separate spheres to the journal *Werkstatt Geschichte*, which was published in 1998. Charles Ingrao invited me to participate in a project that led to the publication of a volume of essays on Germany in the transition era, 1750-1850. This book, edited by Heinz Duchhardt and Andreas Kunz of the Institut für Europäische Geschichte at Mainz, contains an article by me on the Enlightenment Law Codes and the reconstruction of gender.

My former graduate assistant, C. Todd Stevenson worked tirelessly, assisting in the initial stages of the preparation of the bibliography. Much later in the process, Jeff Howard, copyeditor for Berghahn Books, rendered invaluable professional expertise, resulting in a more precise prose. I appreciate his thoughtful suggestions made in a spirit of respect for my stylistic choices.

Finally I express appreciation to the numerous staff members at libraries who made my research possible. I received professional assistance from the following institutions: Bayerische Staatsbibliothek, Munich; Niedersächsische Staats- und Universitätsbibliothek, Göttingen; Staatsbibliothek-Preußischer Kulturbesitz, Berlin; Universitätsbibliothek der Freien Universität Berlin; Österreichische Nationalbibliothek, Vienna; Württembergische Landesbibliothek, Stuttgart; Herzog August Bibliothek, Wolfenbüttel; Economisch-Historische Bibliotheek, Amsterdam; National Agricultural Library, Washington, D.C.; Farrell-Hale Library at Kansas State University; Watson Library and Kenneth Spencer Library at the University of Kansas; the University Library and Lilly Library at Indiana University, Bloomington; and the University Library at the University of Wisconsin, Madison. I also located important, and sometimes rare, published works at several institute and seminar libraries at the universities of Göttingen, Munich, and Berlin.

This work is based almost exclusively on published sources; but for one small part of it, I consulted the papers of Theodor von Schön in the Geheimes Staatsarchiv Preußischer Kulturbeistz in Berlin-Dahlem. Here, too, I received invaluable professional help.

For the generous support I received, I am grateful.

This book is dedicated to Esther, Ben, and Antje, who unconditionally supported my work on this project. Their love sustained me throughout the research and writing. Long before I began the project, Esther helped me learn new ways to understand gender.

Introduction

Gender Norms and the Language of Economics

This book is about ideas that people in German-speaking Europe employed in order to give structure to their lives. It investigates a process through which society came to accept the belief that it was normal for men to be economic producers and for women to be active only in nonproductive activities, those often labeled "reproductive." These norms were essentially new in the nineteenth century, and they became deeply rooted. They accompanied the evolution of the phenomenon of the bourgeois housewife, who was economically dependent on her husband and confined to the private domain of the household. The nineteenth century witnessed the development of a cult of domesticity, an ideology decisive in anchoring the lives of women in the nonproductive household. Although rarely articulated systematically, this canon became powerful in configuring the lives of women and men.[1]

Modern Gender Norms

Bourgeois gender norms of the nineteenth century prescribed strict roles for both females and males. Men were to be leaders in the public sphere, directing the affairs of the state, the new private enterprise economy, and the religious, military, and educa-

Notes for this section begin on page 18.

tional systems. While the new standards divided life between the home and the public arena, they granted males alone the ability to move between the two. As fathers, husbands, and owners of family property, men enjoyed, according to the new ideals, a presiding role in private life. The law also usually granted them the ultimate authority in the rearing and education of children, although the task of carrying out these responsibilities belonged in large part to females.[2]

Middle-class gender norms denied women the ability to move between the two spheres. They limited the life-options of most bourgeois women to wifehood. (However, material conditions of life never conform completely to norms, hence not all women of this class were wives.) Under these standards, women could not be employed or self-employed. They lacked access to higher education. Civil law defined women as second-class citizens who could not generally represent their own interests in court. They did not enjoy fundamental political and civic rights and usually did not even possess legal guardianship of their own children. Many spent their days presiding over their husbands' households, supervising governesses, cooks, and servants. If they were of the less affluent middle class, they did the domestic work that servants performed in wealthy households. They entertained business and family associates. They derived their status, first, from their fathers and, second, from their husbands.[3]

The domestic woman was to be pious, submissive, and pure. Her life was devoted to ensuring the harmonious family life. An unmarried middle-class woman was a misfit, yet women often had little choice about their own marriages. Matrimony was often a matter arranged for the sake of family status. Divorce was hardly an option for women; those in unrewarding or abusive relationships had little choice but to endure them.

Such bourgeois norms also impacted the lives of working men and women. With the dissolution of traditional peasant communities and artisan households that accompanied the introduction of capitalist agriculture and manufacture, the workplace, for the first time in human history, became separated from the home on a large scale. Working-class people often accepted the dictates of their social superiors, which dictated that women should stay at home while men should be breadwinners. However, they frequently were unable to afford the luxury of having wives and mothers in economically unproductive roles, hence the pattern worked itself out differently for laborers than it did in the propertied classes. Working-class women typically earned wages during certain periods of their life courses, especially prior to marriage and as widows. But wives of workers also took employment in times when their husbands' earnings failed to support their households, and such occasions were frequent. In early industrial society, families commonly sent children to work in mills and factories with the goal of enabling wives and mothers to remain in the private sphere, devoted to reproductive activities.[4]

Working women earned paltry income. Under the assumption that women were not the primary supporters of their families, employers frequently paid them below-subsistence wages. In the nineteenth century it was virtually impossible for women to lead independent lives. Unmarried mill and factory workers, for example, could not afford individual lodging and were obliged to live in boarding houses where landlords often strictly supervised their personal affairs. Domestic servants, the largest single group in the women's workforce, lived in situations of economic, social, and psychological dependence. Often, young women's paternal families expected them to deliver part of their earnings home, a situation that less often applied to young men.[5] Even among the working classes, for whom life was often an economic struggle, nineteenth-century gender norms attributed independence and directive power to males and prescribed subservient roles to women. The nineteenth-century paradigm for social stability was the family consisting of a breadwinning husband and a homemaking wife.

By the end of the nineteenth century, the service sector of the economy was expanding dramatically. This created more paid work for women and for the first time, for daughters of the propertied classes. However, the established norms prevailed, resulting in conditions such as low pay for female employees, poor job security, and the demand that wives and mothers who earned wages bear the burden of second, unpaid, careers at home. Young, middle-class women were expected to quit their jobs if they married. Influential clerks' associations, established in order to improve the status of their members, often carried on their activities with the assumption that the most desirable path available to young women was to marry and leave the permanent workforce.[6] The employment open to females by the turn of the twentieth century was always associated with the notion of domesticity. Women could be nurses, servants, clerks in increasingly complex businesses, retail sales clerks, or teachers of young children; but the laws, the educational establishment, and private expectations prevented women from becoming supervisors or managers in business, or from entering the professions or the world of politics. Female schoolteachers in Imperial Germany lost their positions if they married. Legal, social and cultural norms were designed to keep women in the domestic domain of life and males in the public realm.[7] The reality of the separate spheres made women economically, politically, legally, and psychologically dependent on their fathers or husbands.

In the last decades of the century, growing numbers of feminists criticized double standards with regard to gender and the exploitation of women. Socialist feminists aspired for a completely new socioeconomic order in which altered material conditions would place men and women on equal footing. Liberal feminists worked for political, educational, legal, and cultural changes that would gradually end discrimination and make it possible for women to use their talents in the public or private sphere, according to their desires. Many women interested in strengthening the place of females in society chose not to strive for a breakdown of the barriers between the two spheres but rather to enhance roles for women by stressing the importance of maternity, the home, and charity organizations. In some circles motherhood became a metaphor for feminine strength.[8]

Introduction

The revolutions at the end of the First World War brought significant political innovations, such as the right for women to vote in the new Weimar Republic and the Austrian Republic, but the prevailing social imperatives – women's work is reproductive and men's is productive – did not change. In the wildly unpredictable market economy of the postwar era, women who sought places in the workforce often were more frustrated than rewarded, and they encountered major barriers to functioning in the public arena. The National Socialist regime that came to power following the Great Depression imposed policies discriminatory toward women, based on its romanticized ideals of separate and unequal places for the sexes. Ironically, the expanding economy and wartime needs brought more women into the workplace than ever before, yet National Socialism also introduced a degree of manipulation of women and men for the benefit of the state never before experienced, curtailing personal, economic, and political choices.[9]

After the Second World War, women enjoyed statutory guarantees of equality in the republics of West Germany and Austria, but factors such as unequal education, ghettoization of female work, cultural beliefs about motherhood and breadwinners perpetuated the gender hierarchy. State policies consistently reinforced the notion of the separate spheres, dissuading women from choosing life courses other than motherhood and housewife. The laws of East Germany promised gender equality, and the state's policies in the realms of education, maternity leave, employment, child care, reproductive choice, and women's health care were among the most far-reaching in the world. However there were discrepancies between the culture and the requirements of the new laws, and these worked to the disadvantage of women, ensuring that women faced the double burden of earning and homemaking. After reunification of the two German states, East German women found that the price for political freedoms was loss of the economic and social rights they had come to accept as normal. The separate-spheres ideology reasserted itself in law and policy in the new eastern states of the Federal Republic, resulting in disproportionate female unemployment, different wage scales for men and women, curtailment of social services such as child care, and loss of right to obtain abortions legally. Rights that had allowed women in East Germany to seek employment on a footing more nearly equal to that of men were lost when the western legal and constitutional system prevailed.[10]

Switzerland did not grant its female population the right to vote in national elections until 1971. In spite of recent legal and constitutional guarantees of equal rights for women and men, the familiar patterns of separate spheres prevailed, resulting in ghettoized female employment, unequal professional opportunities for the sexes, and a devaluation of housework.[11]

In German-speaking Europe – as in the rest of the Western world – educational systems, laws, economic forces, inherited cultural patterns, and simple misogyny have contributed to maintenance of the modern gender systems based on masculine superiority. Women have had to battle for the opportunity to function in the public world. Organized feminists and some individuals have fought to free men from the position as sole breadwinners and women from domestic bondage. Though gender relations have changed markedly, men are still disproportionately represented in the professions, in managerial positions, in political life, and in the leadership of social, educational, cultural, and religious institutions. The ideology of domesticity dominates women's lives. Females bear the largest responsibility for keeping households in order, and they suffer from ghettoization in the workforce. Males have been unwilling to relinquish their dominant roles in the public sphere afforded them by the economic, social, and political norms inherited from the previous century. Many women, subject to powerful socialization processes, have not welcomed changes toward a society that is not divided into a private, female sphere and a public, male sphere. Above all, women do not share in the wealth of society. They own a tiny fraction of society's total property, and poverty is largely a female and children's problem.[12]

Introduction

For two centuries powerful gender norms have contributed to the division of society into two unequal halves. Men have dominated the realms of government, the economy, the law, education, the military, and religious institutions. Usually women have been able to leave the private sphere only in situations in which deviation from the norm was deemed necessary. Often when they have functioned in the public sphere, they have carried with them the heritage of domesticity, as in the professions of nursing, clerking, and teaching. Important work in the modern world has often been devalued because women performed it. Men have enjoyed greater freedom of movement and freedom of choice than women. Laws have favored males over females, for example, in the ownership of wealth and property. The gender hierarchy has constituted a cornerstone of the culture not only in German-speaking Europe but across the Western world.

Researching Gender Norms through the Language of Economics

Early-modern gender systems were based on very different normative economic values than those which came to prevail after the era of the Enlightenment and the French Revolution.[13] Before the eighteenth century, predecessors of modern economists held the household to be the basic social and economic unit, and they assigned productive roles to men and women alike. Economic theorists conceived of productivity as an activity of the household under the custody of both sexes. Furthermore, they understood what has come to be termed reproductive work as the responsibility of both women and men.

This is not to say that gender roles were undefined. If anything, they were more strict than in the modern era. Certain jobs were men's work, and specific tasks belonged to women; society rigidly enforced these rules. The goals of the pre-Enlightenment era definitely did not include gender equality, for the society was based upon strict notions of hierarchy that applied to sex as well as to social status. Within each social stratum, men enjoyed privileges denied to women. Males held political, legal, and personal dominion over their daughters and wives. Men controlled the churches. They held jurisdiction over most property. However, everyone's task was economically vital to the functioning of the household. The very definition of "economy" was, as it is today, context dependent. Before the eighteenth century, the economy and household were synonymous. Women and men who worked to provide the basic needs of their households were, in effect, producers of food, clothing, shelter, and services for society as a whole. By the middle of the nineteenth century this conception had changed.

A goal of this book is to document a profound transition in the social understanding of gender between the early-modern era and the nineteenth century. Thus the main focus of the book's inquiry consists of ideas rather than the material conditions of life. It is based on the postulate that "male" and "female" are cultural constructions, and it seeks to interpret the meanings that men and women of preindustrial society in the German-speaking realm invested in these constructions.[14] Ideas are important to historians because they are the medium that allows societies to name their beliefs and practices. Every society creates its norms, rules that tell people how to organize their lives under both constant and changing conditions. These norms constitute an essential element in the cultural construction of gender and are as real as the so-called material conditions of history. It is imperative to know them if one is to understand gender as a historical phenomenon.

Some question this approach, for it can be argued that economic structures, rather than ideas, shape people's existence. It is true that the shift in lifestyles during the period covered by this study were forced by the transition from semifeudal to capitalist modes of production.[15] My position is that while it indeed is necessary to analyze changing material conditions in order to understand the origins of modern gender systems, it also is essential to interpret equally real ideas about masculinity and femininity. The latter task is the object of this book.[16]

The social construction of gender, broadly conceived, includes not only the language of the written and spoken word, but also the language of human actions, such as day-to-day work, interpersonal relations, festivals, and property-holding patterns.[17] In transitional chapters of the book, such as those on the Enlightenment, I have sometimes regarded material conditions as part of the language of gender. The core of the book, dealing more specifically with agricultural and economic thought, relies more strictly on language in a traditional sense. As people give meaning to words, the words themselves become icons that shape human perceptions and actions. It is this independent power of language that provides the rationale for the methodology utilized in this book.[18]

The economy and society of the early-modern period were undergoing sharp transitions, and social architects, sometimes intentionally and sometimes unconsciously, invented words for their lexica and advice books, new canons designed to help people make sense of altered circumstances and adapt to them. The study of new and changing norms helps explain the society out of which they grew and which they also shaped. While factors beyond people's control, such as population growth, the market economy, and the power of the state, profoundly transformed human relationships, the ways in which people adapted to these changes – often with the objective of maintaining a sense of personal or social security – were conditioned by social norms. These norms are an essential element in an understanding of any human nexus.

Some historians have associated the separation of the private and public spheres with the Industrial Revolution.[19] My research suggests that the norms that came to characterize the nineteenth century were actually in place in German-speaking Europe before industrial capitalism, in conjunction with the increased power of the state, disrupted traditional living and working conditions, and institution of new ones. While the Industrial Revolution was responsible for the establishment of the roles "housewife" and "breadwinner" as widespread social phenomena, the *ideals* fostering this development circulated widely before industry altered the social and economic landscape. An analogous transition helps illustrate this point: The concept of a free labor market existed before economic conditions and governmental reforms coincided to destroy the guild system and the household agrarian economy, facilitating the transition of artisans and peasants to a new status as wage earners. The existence of the idea of free labor helped guide the historical process. Similarly, the conceptualization of a society divided into public and private spheres separated by gender influenced the course of change with regard to men's and women's places. People use norms to construct the patterns of their social existence and especially to restructure society at times of transition.

My research methodology is indebted to the historiographical tradition *Begriffsgeschichte*, the social history of ideas. This approach differs from conventional intellectual history, because the ideas themselves are not the ultimate object of importance in the investigative process. Rather it is the interaction between ideas and society that is of primary interest. Ideas are significant as reflections of or shapers of the social polity.[20] The research rests on the premise that the normative concepts that societies employ to describe themselves and their institutions change fundamentally over time. Concepts such as "economy," "estate," "household," "property," "work," "gender," and "industry" are constructions rooted in specific historical contexts. When the historical environment changes, the meaning is recast; hence the vocabulary is meaningful only in relation to the setting in which it was articulated. The language is a key to understanding the historical conditions in which it was coined. *Begriffsgeschichte* focuses on political vocabulary in the broadest sense, encompassing private as well as public life. It seeks to understand multiplicities of ideals that serve the social needs and aspirations of particular cultures and hence shape collective perceptions of the world. It is thus a means of viewing social phenomena such as community relationships, work patterns, leisure, celebrations, gender systems, and family organization, as well as micro- and macroeconomic structures.

The authors whose works constitute the sources for this book were members of social and political elites. As state and university officials, and even as published authors, many were outsiders to the world they sought to change. They articulated visions that they hoped to implant in the rural society. Their writings normatively presented the world as they believed it ought to have been, not as it was. Yet the distinction between "is" and "ought" is not always clearly separate in the written word.[21] Those who hope to impose a certain structure on society almost always root their vision in some part of material reality. It is widely recognized, for example, that Adam Smith's *Wealth of Nations*, published in 1776 as a model for the future, drew heavily on examples of specialized labor and market competition that Smith found about him. It is not a work that could have been based on imagination alone.

The seventeenth-century German authors communicated their views in a genre called "Household Books," intended as guides to conducting the business of the household, synonymous with the economy. They hoped to restore a social order that they perceived was disappearing. Their prescriptions were rooted in historical imagination that had ties to a real past. Their successors, the Cameralists, of the following century, shifted the normative emphasis from the household to the state and the public sphere. They were dissatisfied with the pace of change and sought to accelerate it. Their models, likewise, were not invented from thin air. They could see emergent examples of the more streamlined economy they hoped would prevail. Thus, while the visions of the normative writers were by no means mirrors of absolute reality, they were nevertheless entwined with the social fabric of their past and present.

Feminist scholars such as Joan Scott and Catherine Hall have emphasized the subjectivity of language and demonstrated ways of deconstructing historical concepts in order to unveil very real meanings hidden beneath the literal ones. Scott emphasizes that "'language' does not reflect a reality external to it" but rather is "constitutive of that reality."²² In my work, I have sought to discover how the meanings that writers constructed themselves *became* a history rooted in the changing world out of which they grew. Language contains strongly gendered messages in many cases where the writer does not mention men, women, or their roles. For example Albrecht Thaer, the agricultural reformer of the early nineteenth century, defined a place for women by assuming a completely male readership and by imagining men, exclusively, in the roles of the modern agriculturist. In social discourse, silence about a particular group can denote a potent power relationship between that group and those who own the tools of scholarship and thus control the parameters of the discussion.

Scholars who work with the methods of *Begriffsgeschichte* have identified the revolutionary era, 1750-1850, as the age of birth of the modern social and political vocabulary in German-speaking Europe. A researcher attuned to language will notice that two writers a generation apart may have been using the same words to communicate quite different meanings; new definitions had grown up inside the old terminology, and the changes accelerated in the unique era spanning the late-eighteenth and early-nineteenth centuries. The transitions nevertheless were often halting and sometimes occurred in erratic spurts; the old and new definitions frequently existed side by side, competing for acceptance. Only by noticing changes that take place over decades, generations, and sometimes centuries can one discern clear configurations of change and successive ideologies. By the middle of the eighteenth century, concepts previously restricted to specific social groups were becoming more universally descriptive, because their meanings changed as journalists and political philosophers began to apply them to society as a whole. The concept "freedom," for example, changed radically. Before the middle of the eighteenth century, it was used in relation to specific individuals or groups to whom privileges or "freedoms" had been granted. A guild might hold the "freedom" to craft a product because it possessed a charter bestowing this right. Aristocratic estate owners might hold the "freedom" to assemble and to approve or veto new taxes. By the beginning of the nineteenth century, however, "freedom" had become a term of universal application, a right that, in theory, belonged to all rather than a privilege of a limited few. Political language also gained an ideological character during the transition from the eighteenth century to the nineteenth. Like the word "freedom," terms such as "industry" and "industrious" became slogans of social change. Thus language was a mirror of social conventions and also a formative influence on institutions.[23]

My research seeks to interpret changes in the written prescriptions about material life through a reading of the changing discourse about economics. This discourse itself possessed a social, gendered character. The vocabulary crucial to my analysis includes key words that describe people in their economic roles, including "household," "economy," and "work." Gender is a constant category of my analysis.[24] The concept of gender changed over time, as did the social constructions "male" and "female." Continuity of terms does not denote constancy of meaning.

There are other situations in which the terminology itself changes, manifesting new conceptualizations. For example, economists in the period of transition between the eighteenth and nineteenth centuries began to use new words to name the heads of agrarian households. Between the sixteenth and the eighteenth centuries, the common terms were *Hausvater* and *Hausmutter* (literally, "father of the household" and "mother of the household"). By the nineteenth century this nomenclature had fallen into disuse and had been replaced by the terms *Landwirt* (farmer or agricultural proprietor) and *Hausfrau* (housewife). The earlier idioms connoted economic interdependence of male and female estate managers. The nineteenth-century language, indicating proprietor and housewife, reveals a new cultural conceptualization of sexual differences and a new style of male-female hierarchy in conformity with the bourgeois notion of separate spheres.

This study rests on economic thought relating to agriculture. The normative, prescriptive sources on which it is based fall into one of two categories. Either they are representative of established genres, which means that they belonged to an accepted cultural milieu, or they themselves were in some way demonstratively popular in their own times, as indicated, for example, by numerous successive editions.

I have chosen to emphasize rural norms because until well into the nineteenth century German-speaking society remained overwhelmingly agrarian. Two of every three inhabitants spent their lifetimes extracting food and fibers from the soil. Even though many social architects of the eighteenth and early nineteenth centuries anticipated a time when the population would move to the cities and engage in manufacture or commerce, their ideals were visionary and not wholly representative of the society in which they lived. Germany's Industrial Revolution did not occur until after the middle of the nineteenth century. Thus it was agricultural strategists whose thought was the most relevant to my analysis, which concludes in roughly the fourth decade of that century. I have asked two simple questions: what did Germany's pre-industrial economists tell their contemporaries about gender? And how did their notions of gender change over time?

Before the middle of the eighteenth century, "economy" *(Ökonomie, Wirtschaft,* or *Haus- und Feldwirtschaft)* and "agriculture" *(Landwirtschaft)* were synonymous terms. Moreover, the concept "the economy" was often interchangeable with "the household." By the 1840s, the field of economics had assumed a radically different orientation under the influences of the Enlightenment, including the work of the Scottish philosopher and economist Adam Smith. By this time the bourgeois economic ideals, with corresponding gender norms, were firmly established. Economics had embraced its modern meanings, with emphasis on nation-states, commercial markets, domestic and world trade, and emerging manufacturing systems. In contrast to a century earlier, agriculture had become but one facet of a complex set of systems. This transition turned out to be profound in terms of the social organization of sexual difference.

Introduction

The old set of ideals prescribed a place for both females and males in the productive household economy. In the emerging conceptualization, agriculture was a capitalist enterprise rather than a household system, and as in other market-oriented undertakings, prescriptive writers largely disregarded females. The new economists often relegated women's work to the household and frequently defined it as "unproductive" because it was not associated with wages or marketplace.[25] In place of the traditional household literature, there sprang up a new prescriptive creed for women that focused on reproductive activities: cooking, sewing, child rearing, cleaning, and pleasing husbands.[26] The study of language – simply noticing when old idioms assumed new meanings and when new words replaced traditional terms – helps to document the ideals on which modern gender hierarchy took root and flourished in the late eighteenth and early nineteenth centuries.

The economy is a critical realm in which to examine gender, for the cultural constructions "male" and "female" are inexorably bound together with work, and work provides a framework for daily life. The notions "men's place" and "women's place" often refer to spheres of labor, earning, production, or reproduction. A great discontinuity existed between the old society's economic norms and those of the latter nineteenth century. The household in the early modern era was the assumed locus of important economic activities, including production, reproduction, and consumption. The relationship between these functions and the house changed significantly over time.[27] While old-regime ideals divided politics, education, and even religion, into two spheres – the male (public) and the female (private) domain – the early-modern normative economy assumed a male-female interdependence. New notions of "economy" that took firm root in the era of France's revolution tore apart this gender affiliation, giving men and women new, separate statuses and a distinctly modern kind of inequality.

It is not my intention to argue that the everyday life of rural women and men changed simultaneously with the reconceptualization of gender of the late eighteenth and early nineteenth centuries. The majority of the populace, the rural lower classes, probably knew relatively little of the economists' writings. Even though the state, through its civil servants, was very interested in reshaping village life, the peasantry often ignored the reformers.[28] Moreover, the writers on whom I have depended directed their attention to the propertied classes. In the seventeenth century they wrote primarily for the landed nobility, and in the eighteenth, increasingly for the rising bourgeoisie. However, I do not claim that even these groups were directly affected by the transition in gender norms at the time of its articulation. Rather, my argument is that the metamorphosis in economic ideals and the corresponding reformatting of gender established a cultural tradition that lasted far into the nineteenth century. The effects on people's lives showed up haltingly and unevenly. But there was a correlation between the reconstruction of gender in the period saddling the eighteenth and nineteenth centuries and the gender systems that prevailed decades later.

This book's linguistic history of economic and agricultural ideals from the beginning of the seventeenth century to approximately 1830 is contained in the core chapters, two, three, six, and eight. Chapter two provides the starting point by depicting the gendered nature of the household economy of the seventeenth century, which rested on the norm of an unequal male-female partnership. Material conditions at that time were undermining the ideals of the household economy, and chapter three portrays the eighteenth-century perspective that the economy was a masculine enterprise centered in the state. Chapter six explores the struggle of those interested in agriculture at the end of the eighteenth century to either use the old language of the "household" to preserve a world perceptibly in decline, or to make the most of changing conditions. Those who prided themselves in being modern, however, were unable to completely abandon the traditional vocabulary. Chapter eight illustrates how in the early nineteenth century the new, bourgeois construction of gender became a part of the language describing rural life. Users of the new discourse postulated for men a life in the public sphere of the productive economy and for women a domestic existence defined by the ideals of reproduction and domesticity.

Other chapters place this thought in historical context and contribute to a broader understanding of the cultural constructions of gender. These chapters are not so tightly focused on the vocabulary of the written word, but the emphasis is still on the cultural construction of gender. Chapter one depicts the social realities of the early-modern hierarchical society. Chapters four and five describe the emerging bourgeois ideals of the Enlightenment, many of which were not strictly focused on agriculture and rural life. Chapter seven documents ways in which transformation of the Napoleonic era strengthened the state, widening the gap between the public sphere and the private. These contextual chapters offer a means of connecting the normative concepts of the core chapters to the social realities in which those norms circulated. By the 1830s, the modern gender ideals of domesticity and productivity were part of a collective ideology that remained a formative part of the culture into the late twentieth century.

Notes

1. Sherry B. Ortner and Harriet Whitehead, eds., *Sexual Meanings: The Cultural Construction of Gender and Sexuality* (Cambridge, England: Cambridge University, 1981), 1-27. Veronica Beechey, *Unequal Work*, Questions for Feminism (London: Verso, 1987), 7-9, 51-52. Wally Secomb, "The Housewife and Her Labor under Capitalism," *New Left Review* 83 (1974): 3-24. Mary O'Brien, *The Politics of Reproduction* (Boston: Routledge & Kegan Paul, 1981), 19-64, 93-115. Catherine Hall, "The History of the Housewife," in *White, Male and Middle-Class: Explorations in Feminism and History* (Cambridge, England: Polity, 1992), 51-68. Catherine Hall, "The Early Formation of Victorian Domestic Ideology," in ibid, 75-92. These sources primarily analyze circumstances in Great Britain, not in Germany. Conditions differed between these two cultural areas, and therefore many of the situations specific to Britain may not be applicable to Germany. These sources and others named in this chapter that do not deal specifically with Germany I cite not for their historical data, but as examples of ways to analyze the sexual division of labor. American scholars were the first to systematically explain the doctrine of separate spheres. The classic works by Barbara Welter and Aileen Kraditor have been supplemented by a generation of historians. See Barbara Welter, "The Cult of True Womanhood, 1820-1860," *American Quarterly* 18 (1966): 151-74 and Aileen S. Kraditor, ed., *Up From the Pedestal: Selected Writings in the History of American Feminism* (Chicago: Quadrangle, 1968).
2. Barbara Maas, "Idealisierung und Domestikation: Das bürgerliche Frauenbild in der frühviktorianischen Publizistik," in *Frauen in der Geschichte III: Fachwissenschaftliche und fachdidaktische Beiträge zur Geschichte der Weiblichkeit vom frühen Mittelalter bis zur Gegenwart mit geeigneten Materialien für den Unterricht*, Geschichtsdidaktik: Studien, Materialien, vol. 13, ed. Annette Kuhn and Jörn Rüsen (Düsseldorf: Schwann, 1983), 139-66. Susan Moller Okin, *Justice, Gender and the Family* (New York: Basic Books, 1989), 8-9, 92, 110-33.
3. Theodor Fontane's novel *Frau Jenny Treibel* (1893) realistically portrays nineteenth-century bourgeois domesticity. I have used the Reclam edition: Theodor Fontane, *Frau Jenny Treibel oder "wo sich Herz zum Herzen find't,"* Universal-Bibliothek No. 7635 (Stuttgart: Reclam, 1973). See also *Das häusliche Glück: Vollständiger Haushaltungunterricht nebst Anleitung zum Kochen für Arbeiterfrauen*, Herausgegeben von einer Commission des Verbandes "Arbeiterwohl," 11th ed. (Mönchengladbach: Riffarth, 1882). On gender relations in the nineteenth century, see Ute Frevert, ed., *Bürgerinnen und Bürger: Geschlechtsverhältnisse im 19. Jahrhundert*, Kritische Studien zur Geschichtswissenschaft, vol. 77 (Göttingen: Vandenhoeck & Ruprecht,

1988). On women and the law, see Dirk Blasius, "Bürgerliche Rechtsgleichheit und die Ungleichheit der Geschlechter: Das Scheidungsrecht im historischen Vergleich," in ibid., 67-84. See also Ursula Vogel, "Property Rights and the Status of Women in Germany and England," in *Bourgeois Society in Nineteenth-Century Europe*, ed. Jürgen Kocka and Allan Mitchell, (Oxford: Berg, 1993), 241-69. Outstanding depictions of nineteenth century domesticity outside of Germany include: Leonore Davidoff and Catherine Hall, *Family Fortunes: Men and Women of the English Middle Class, 1780-1850*, Women in Culture and Society (Chicago: University of Chicago, 1991); Bonnie Smith, *Ladies of the Leisure Class: The Bourgeoises of Northern France in the Nineteenth Century* (Princeton, NJ: Princeton University, 1981); and Nancy Cott, *The Bonds of Womanhood: Woman's Sphere in New England, 1780-1835* (New Haven, CT: Yale University, 1977).

4. Ute Frevert, *Women in German History: From Bourgeois Emancipation to Sexual Liberation*, trans. Stuart McKinnon-Evans et al. (New York,: Berg, 1989), 83-93; Barbara Duden and Karin Hausen, "Gesellschaftliche Arbeit – geschlechtspezifische Arbeitsteilung," in *Frauen in der Geschichte: Frauenrechte und die gesellschaftliche Arbeit der Frauen im Wandel: Fachwissenschaftliche und fachdidaktische Studien zur Geschichte der Frauen*, Geschichtsdidaktik: Studien, Materialien, vol. 6, ed. Annette Kuhn and Gerhard Schneider (Düsseldorf: Schwann, 1979), 16-17. Karin Zachmann, "Männer arbeiten, Frauen helfen: Geschlechtsspezifische Arbeitsteilung und Maschinisierung in der Textilindustrie des 19. Jahrhunderts," in *Geschlechterhierarchie und Arbeitsteilung: Zur Geschichte ungleicher Erwerbschancen von Männern und Frauen*, Sammlung Vandenhoeck, ed. Karin Hausen (Göttingen: Vandenhoeck & Ruprecht, 1993), 71-96.

5. Barbara Franzoi, *At the Very Least She Pays the Rent: Women and German Industrialization, 1871-1914*, Contributions in Women's Studies, vol. 57 (Westport, CT: Greenwood, 1985), 19-20, 91-98. Frevert, *Women in German History*, 87-89. Marlene Ellerkamp and Brigitte Jungmann, "Unendliche Arbeit: Frauen in der 'Jutespinnerei und -weberei Bremen,' 1888-1914," in *Frauen Suchen ihre Geschichte: Historische Studien zum 19. und 20. Jahrhundert*, Beck'sche Schwarze Reihe, vol. 276, ed. Karin Hausen (Munich: Beck, 1983), 128-43. Dorothee Wierling, "'Ich hab meine Arbeit gemacht – was wollte sie mehr?' Dienstmädchen im städtischen Haushalt der Jahrhundertwende," in ibid., 144-71.

6. Carole Elizabeth Adams, *Women Clerks in Wilhelmine Germany: Issues of Class and Gender* (Cambridge: Cambridge University, 1988), 112. Edith Rigler, *Frauenleitbild und Frauenarbeit in Österreich vom ausgehenden 19. Jahrhundert bis zum Zweiten Weltkrieg*, Sozial- und wirtschaftshistorische Studien, vol. 8 (Munich: Oldenbourg, 1976), 54-80.

7. Richard J. Evans, "Liberalism and Society: The Feminist Movement and Social Change," in *Society and Politics in Wilhelmine Germany*, Evans, ed., (London: Croom Helm; and New York: Barnes and Noble, 1978), 197. In spite of the normative gender hierarchy, working-class women often were able to establish power in the household through their control of consumption. Lynn Abrams, "Martyrs or Matriarchs? Working-class Women's Experience of Marriage in Germany before the First World War," *Women's History Review* 1 (1992): 357-76.
8. Jean H. Quataert, *Reluctant Feminists in German Social Democracy 1885-1917* (Princeton, NJ: Princeton University, 1979). 4-14 and passim. August Bebel, *Die Frau und der Sozialismus* (Stuttgart: Dietz, 1893). Evans, "Liberalism and Society," 186-214. Frevert, *Women in German History*, 107-30, 138-48. Barbara Greven-Aschoff, *Die bürgerliche Frauenbewegung in Deutschland 1894-1933*, Kritische Studien zur Geschichtswissenschaft, vol. 46 (Göttingen: Vandenhoeck & Ruprecht, 1981), 22-147. Ann Taylor Allen, *Feminism and Motherhood in Germany, 1800-1914* (New Brunswick, NJ: Rutgers University, 1991).
9. Karen Hagemann, "Ausbildung für die 'weibliche Doppelrolle': Berufswünsche, Berufswahl und Berufschancen von Volksschülerinnen in der Weimarer Republik," in Hausen, *Geschlechterhierarchie*, 214-36. Christiane Eifert, "Geschlechterhierarchie in der Wohlfahrtspflege: Der sozialdemokratische Verband 'Arbeiterwohlfahrt' in den Zwanziger Jahren," in ibid, 193-213. Renate Bridenthal and Claudia Koonz, "Beyond *Kinder, Küche, Kirche*: Weimar Women in Politics and Work," in *When Biology Became Destiny: Women in Weimar and Nazi Germany*, ed. Bridenthal, Atina Grossmann, and Marion Kaplan (New York: Monthly Review, 1984), 33-65. Claudia Koonz, *Mothers in the Fatherland: Women, the Family, and Nazi Policy* (New York: St. Martin's, 1987), 175-219. Rigler, *Frauenleitbild und Frauenarbeit*, 81-151.
10. Robert G. Moeller, *Protecting Motherhood: Women and the Family in the Politics of Postwar West Germany* (Berkeley: University of California, 1993) 38-209. Hans-Peter Blossfeld, "Labor-Market Entry and the Sexual Segregation of Careers in the Federal Republic of Germany," *American Journal of Sociology* 93 (1987): 89-118. Susanne Rouette, "Nach dem Krieg: Zurück zur normalen Hierarchie der Geschlechter," in Hausen, *Geschlechterhierarchie*, 167-90. Dorothy J. Rosenberg, "Shock Therapy: GDR Women in Transition from a Socialist Welfare State to a Social Market Economy," *Signs: Journal of Women in Culture and Society* 17 (1991): 129-51. Friederike Maier, "The Labor Market for Women and Employment Perspectives in the Aftermath of German Unification," *Cambridge Journal of Economics* 17 (1993): 267-80. Ursula Beer and Ursula Müller, "Coping with a New Reality: Barriers and Possibilities," *Cambridge Journal of Economics* 17 (1993):

281-294. Hannelore Scholz, "East-West Women's Culture in Transition: Are East German Women the Losers of Reunification," *Journal of Women's History* 5 (1993/94): 108-116. Karin Maria Schmidlechner, "Frauen in Österreich seit 1945," in *Über Frauenleben Männerwelt und Wissenschaft: Österreichische Texte zur Frauenforschung*, ed. Beate Frakele, Elisabeth List, and Gertrude Pauritsch, Österreichische Texte zur Gesellschaftskritik, vol. 29 (Vienna: Verlag für Gesellschaftskritik, 1987), 213-24. Silvia Ulrich, "Die Bedeutung des Gleichheitsgrundsatzes für die rechtliche und faktische Gleichstellung von Frau und Mann in Österreich," in ibid., 225-39. Monika Gimpel-Hinteregger, "Arbeitsplatz Haushalt – Kann die Ehe als materielle Existenzgrundlage dienen?" in ibid., 240-50.
11. Isabell Mahrer, "Die Frau im Erwerbsleben," in *Les femmes et la Suisse en évolution – Die Frauen im Wandel der Schweiz*, ed. Than-Huyen Ballmer-Cao, (Aarau: Sauerländer, 1989), 57-65. Rita Gassmann, "Frauen und Gewerkschaften," in ibid., 56-70. Ruth Hungerbühler, "Haus- und Familienarbeit," in ibid., 71-77. Claudia Kaufmann, "Die Gleichstellung von Frau und Mann," in ibid., 101-106. Susanna Woodtli, *Gleichberechtigung: Der Kampf um die politischen Rechte der Frau in der Schweiz* (Frauenfeld: Huber, 1975), 110-222.
12. Rainer Geißler, *Die Sozialstruktur Deutschlands: Ein Studienbuch zur gesellschaftlichen Entwicklung im geteilten und vereinten Deutschland* (Bonn: Bundeszentrale für politische Bildung, 1992), 237-63.
13. Heide Wunder, "Gender Norms and their Enforcement in Early Modern Germany," in *Gender Relations in German History: Power, Agency, and Experience from the Sixteenth to the Twentieth Century*, ed. Lynn Abrams and Elizabeth Harvey (Durham, NC: Duke University, 1997), 39-56. Karin Hausen was one of the first scholars to call attention to the profound change in gender norms associated with the late eighteenth century in Germany: Karin Hausen, "Die Polarisierung der 'Geschlechtscharaktere' – eine Spiegelung der Dissoziation von Erwerbs- und Familienleben," in *Sozialgeschichte der Neuzeit Europas: Neue Forschungen*, Industrielle Welt, vol. 21, ed. Werner Conze (Stuttgart: Klett, 1976), 363-93. For examples of this interpretation outside Germany, see Smith, *Ladies of the Leisure Class*, and Davidoff and Hall, *Family Fortunes*. Some scholars question this thesis. See Amanda Vickery, "Golden Age to Separate Spheres? A Review of the Categories and Chronologies of English Women's History," *The Historical Journal* 36 (1993) : 383-414. Vickery, however, misrepresents the main scholarship on this subject by asserting that it rests on the argument that a supposed "golden age" of gender relations existed prior to the eighteenth century. Careful scholars do not engage in this oversimplification.
14. On gender as a category of historical analysis, see Joan Wallach Scott, *Gender and the Politics of History*, Gender and Culture (New York: Columbia

University, 1988), 2, 28-50. On feminist epistemology, see Sandra Harding, "Conclusion: Epistemological Questions," in *Feminism and Methodology: Social Science Issues*, ed. Harding (Bloomington: Indiana University; 1987), 181-90.
15. Annette Kuhn, "Das Geschlecht – eine historische Kategorie?" in *Frauen in der Geschichte IV: "wissen heißt leben ... ." Beiträge zur Bildungsgeschichte von Frauen im 18. und 19. Jahrhundert*, Geschichtsdidaktik: Studien, Materialien, vol. 18, ed. Ilse Brehmer, Juliane Jacobi-Dittrich, Elke Kleinau and Annette Kuhn, (Düsseldorf: Schwann, 1983), 34-47. Kuhn stresses that for several centuries before the transition to an industrial economy, ongoing processes, including the dissolution of the feudal hierarchy and the advancement of the capitalist economy, led to the establishment of the modern woman-centered household and the new gender systems. Her interpretation rests on material conditions rather than ideas, and she stresses a gradual transition rather than a marked change at the end of the eighteenth century. Jane Humphries, "The Sexual Division of Labor and Social Control: An Interpretation," *Review of Radical Political Economics* 23 (1991): 269-96. Humphries stresses biology (breast-feeding) as well as economic circumstances.
16. I do not concur with those who hold that a language-based history calls into question a materialist approach. See Lynn Hunt, review of François Furet, *Penser la Révolution Française* [Paris: Editions Gallimard (1978)], *History and Theory* 20 (1981): 313-23.
17. See, for example, Lynn Hunt, *Politics, Class, and Culture in the French Revolution* (Berkeley: University of California, 1984).
18. See, for example, Donald Worster, *Nature's Economy: A History of Ecological Ideas* (Cambridge, England: Cambridge University, 1994), 191-93.
19. Ann Oakley, *Woman's Work: The Housewife, Past and Present* (New York: Random House, 1976), 10-60. In the nineteenth century Marx and Engels systematically articulated the modern inequality of the sexes. They argued that industrial capitalism required two discrete units of labor: one domestic and one industrial. Both were essential for maintenance of the bourgeois society, but the split resulted in the oppression of women. See Friedrich Engels, *The Origin of the Family, Private Property and the State* (1884), ed. Eleanor Burke Leacock (New York: International Publishers, 1972). See also Secomb, "The Housewife and Her Labor," 3-24. Beechey, *Unequal Work*, 57. Janet Thomas, "Women and Capitalism: Oppression or Emancipation? A Review Article," *Comparative Studies in Society and History* 30 (1988): 534-49.
20. Reinhard Koselleck, *Futures Past: On the Semantics of Historical Time*, trans. Keith Tribe, Studies in Contemporary German Social Thought (Cambridge, MA: MIT, 1985), 73-91. For example, see Otto Brunner, Werner

Conze, and Reinhard Koselleck, eds., *Geschichtliche Grundbegriffe: Historisches Lexikon zur politisch-sozialen Sprache in Deutschland* (Stuttgart: Klett, 1972-92); and Rolf Reichardt and Eberhard Schmitt, eds., *Handbuch politisch-sozialer Grundbegriffe in Frankreich 1680-1820*, Ancien RJgime, vol. 10 (Munich: Oldenbourg: 1985-88). This approach in some ways parallels the work of François Furet, who in the 1970s and 1980s articulated techniques of using language as a tool of analysis. See his *Interpreting the French Revolution*, trans. Elborg Forster (Cambridge, et al.: Cambridge University, 1981). See also François Furet and Mona Ozouf, eds., *A Critical Dictionary of the French Revolution*, trans. Arthur Goldhammer (Cambridge, MA: Harvard University, 1989). Scholars of the French Revolution have taken a language-based approach much further by interpreting "language" broadly to include festivals and other communicative symbols. See Hunt, *Politics, Class, and Culture*. See also Hans Medick and David Sabean, "Emotionen und materielle Interessen in Familie und Verwandtschaft: Überlegungen zu neuen Wegen und Bereichen einer historischen und sozialanthropoligischen Familienforschung," in *Emotionen und materielle Interessen: Sozialanthropologische und historische Beiträge zur Familienforschung*, ed. Medick and Sabean, Veröffentlichungen des Max-Planck-Instituts für Geschichte, vol. 75 (Göttingen: Vandenhoeck & Ruprecht, 1984), 30-32. These two scholars contend that language ("speech") is too universal a medium to use in understanding the "material interests" of families. One must seek "codes," including the idioms of human-property relations and "rituals" such as the preparation and consumption of food. Other examples of language as a source of historical meaning: William H. Sewell, Jr., *Work and Revolution in France: The Language of Labor from the Old Regime to 1848* (Cambridge: Cambridge University, 1980); Gareth Stedman Jones, *Languages of Class: Studies in English Working Class History, 1832-1982* (Cambridge, England: Cambridge University, 1983); Joan Scott, "On Language, Gender, and Working-Class History," in *Gender and the Politics of History*, 53-67; and Ruth Bloch, "The Gendered Meanings of Virtue in Revolutionary America," *Signs: Journal of Women in Culture and Society* 13 (1987): 38-58.
21. Carolyn Merchant, *The Death of Nature: Women, Ecology and the Scientific Revolution* (New York: Harper Collins, 1989), 4-5.
22. Scott, "On Language, Gender, and Working-Class History," 53-67. Catherine Hall, "Feminism and Feminist History," in Hall, *White, Male and Middle-Class: Explorations in Feminism and History* (Cambridge, England: Polity, 1992), 22-34. Catherine Hall, "Competing Masculinities: Thomas Carlyle, John Stuart Mill and the Case of Governor Eyre," in ibid, 205-54.
23. Irmline Viet-Brause, "A Note on *Begriffsgeschichte*," *History and Theory* 20 (1981): 61-67. Helmut Berding, "Begriffsgeschichte und Sozialgeschichte,"

Historische Zeitschrift 223 (1976): 98-110. Reinhard Koselleck, "Sprachwandel und sozialer Wandel im ausgehenden Ancien Régime," in *Deutschlands Kulturelle Entfaltung: Die Neubestimmung des Menschen*, ed. Bernhard Fabian, Wilhelm Schmidt-Biggeman, and Rudolf Vierhaus (Munich: Kraus, 1980), 15-30. On the concept of "freedom," see Jürgen Schlumbohm, *Freiheit – die Anfänge der bürgerlichen Emanzipationsbewegung in Deutschland im Spiegel ihres Leitworts (ca. 1760-ca. 1800)*, Geschichte und Gesellschaft: Bochumer Historische Studien vol. 12 (Düsseldorf: Schwann, 1975). On "industry" see Focko Eulen, *Vom Gewerbefleiß zur Industrie: Ein Beitrag zur Wirtschaftsgeschichte des 18. Jahrhunderts* (Berlin: Duncker und Humblot, 1967).

24. On the social character of economic knowledge, see Marianne A. Ferber and Julie A. Nelson, "Introduction: The Social Construction of Economics and the Social Construction of Gender," in *Beyond Economic Man: Feminist Theory and Economics*, ed. Ferber and Nelson (Chicago: University of Chicago, 1993), 1-22; Janet Seiz, "Feminism and the History of Economic Thought," *History of Political Economy* 25 (1993): 189-93; Diana Strassmann, "The Stories of Economics and the Power of the Storyteller," ibid., 150-54; Michèle A. Pujol, *Feminism and Anti-Feminism in Early Economic Thought* (Hants: Edward Elgar, 1992), 1-11; and Nancy Folbre, "The Unproductive Housewife: Her Evolution in Nineteenth-Century Economic Thought," *Signs: Journal of Women in Culture and Society* 16 (1991): 463-84.

25. Pujol, *Feminism and Anti-Feminism*, 16. Folbre, "The Unproductive Housewife," 470. Joseph Schumpeter, *History of Economic Analysis* (New York: Oxford University, 1954), 628-30.

26. For example, see the advice book for working-class women *Das häusliche Glück.*

27. Heidi I. Hartmann, "The Family as the Locus of Gender, Class, and Political Struggle: The Example of Housework," in Harding, *Feminism and Methodology*, 109-134.

28. Gerd Spittler, "Abstraktes Wissen als Herrschaftsbasis: Zur Entstehungsgeschichte bürokratischer Herrschaft im Bauernstaat Preußen," *Kölner Zeitschrift für Soziologie und Sozialpsychologie* 32 (1980): 574-604. Reinhart Siegert, "Nachwort," in Rudolph Zacharias Becker, *Noth- und Hülfsbüchlein für Bauersleute oder lehrreiche Freuden- und Trauer-Geschichte des Dorfes Mildheim*, ed. Siegert (Gotha: Deutsche Zeitung; and Leipzig: Göschen, 1778; repr. Dartmund: Harenberg, 1980), 461-80. Rudolf Schenda, *Volk ohne Buch: Studien zur Sozialgeschichte der populären Lesestoffe 1770-1910*, Studien zur Philosophie und Literatur des neunzehnten Jahrhunderts, vol. 5 (Frankfurt am Main: Klostermann, 1970). 142-227.

Chapter One

The Historical Context
Hierarchy, Patriarchy, and Community (1600-1800)

Multiple factors, including social rank, gender, religion, place of birth, marital status, and age, determined every individual's place in the stratified society of early-modern, German-speaking Europe. According to accepted norms, two of these factors, estate and gender, were fixed qualities, established by birth. (For practical purposes, religion was also established by birth.) Some people were born to preside over others; these were situations not supposed to change during individuals' lifetimes or over generations. Members of this society believed that differences between people were caused by unalterable attributes bestowed by God.

In the more than three-hundred territorial states loosely bound together as the Holy Roman Empire of the German Nation, tradition and law recognized three strictly separated estates: aristocracy, peasantry, and townspeople. Each of these contained a countless number of tiers. Social mobility between estates was severely limited; it was highly difficult even to move between the tiers within one's estate. Economic fortune or misfortune might alter an individual's or a household's material standard of

Notes for this section begin on page 43.

living, but this normally would not result in a changed social standing under law and custom.¹

Aristocracy

The nobility, descended from medieval knights, comprised 1 to 3 percent of the population, depending on the region, and were the acknowledged superior estate. The complex gradations within the first estate differed from province to province. Yet dress, language, and demeanor distinguished all aristocrats from the remainder of the population. They enjoyed economic, social, legal, and political privileges deriving from their hereditary association with the land. In theory it was not possible to be a member of the aristocracy without belonging to an inherited familial manor. So important was the protection of this relationship between the upper estate and the land that in some German-speaking principalities it was illegal for non-nobles to be in possession of rural estates. By definition, aristocrats engaged in agriculture as a profession, although many who served the state, either in the military or in the civil service, were at least one step removed from farming. In the Holy Roman Empire's counties, grand duchies, duchies, princely bishoprics, electorates, and other principalities, noblemen commonly assembled periodically to share with princes the responsibilities of diplomatic and domestic affairs. In large, absolutist states like the Hohenzollern monarchy (Prussia), the assemblies met infrequently and had relatively ceremonial functions, although they still shouldered remnants of their ancient authority such as the "freedom" to approve or disapprove of new taxes. Nobles themselves were exempt from paying many taxes to royal or princely treasuries. Collectively, this minuscule estate comprised the most important political constituency of any ruler and in the eyes of society was the locus of social and political authority.²

Manorial jurisdiction, or *Grundherrschaft*, gave the aristocrats varying degrees of legal, economic, and personal powers over the rural population. A severe form of authority, *Gutsherrschaft*, existed on many sprawling estates east of the Elbe River and north of Habsburg territories. Since the end of the Middle Ages, as monarchs had usurped the traditional political privileges of the aristocracy and transferred them to centralized bureaucracies, they had recompensed the lords with tight control over local lands and people. In a context of agrarian crisis following the Thirty Years War, many seventeenth-century landlords had appropriated much of the peasant land, cultivating it for themselves and increasing the personal dependence of the workers. In the Duchy of Mecklenburg, where the process was especially prevalent, a lawyer, David Mevius, declared that it had become "almost common practice to trade and deal in serfs in the same way as was done with horses and cows." West of the Elbe, and in the south, where seigniorial properties were generally smaller, the bonds between lords and peasants had grown relatively weaker in the early-modern era. Here the noble families sometimes resided away from their lands, often at the princely court. In such circumstances, the main relationship between lord and subject consisted of the obligatory rent, a specified percentage of the annual production from peasant lands. Some collected rents in monetary payment rather than in kind. Under the *Grundherrschaft* system, these lords required fewer personal services of their tenants than did their peers in the east.[3]

The early-modern period experienced a growth of centralized state power that undermined aristocratic privileges. Early capitalist trade and production of the sixteenth to the eighteenth centuries altered the relationships among social ranks and the connections between people and the land. In certain rural regions, proto-industrial manufacture rivaled agriculture as the main economic activity. Textile products and metal wares produced under such circumstances often found worldwide markets. In spite of these changes, aristocratic entitlements – although they varied widely in nature throughout the German-speaking territories – assured the traditional first estate control over land and populace in the countryside.[4]

Both men and women of this estate enjoyed prestigious inherited connections through their linear families and their relationships with the land. Although their social station placed aristocrats of both sexes above the rest of the population, gender was a powerful and complex demarcation of rank and power. The medieval canons, which still prevailed into the late eighteenth century, set men above women. Unmarried women were wards of their fathers and, as the thirteenth-century code *Sachsenspiegel* stipulated, "the husband is guardian of his wife as soon as she marries him." Julius Bernhard von Rohr (1688-1742) wrote in his commentary on household law in the early eighteenth century:

> A master is allowed to direct all things in his household, so long as he does not contradict God's law, the statutes of his appointed government, and the customs of his locality, [or does not violate] justice, respectability, and the general welfare. Therefore the common saying, "Every man is king in his house" is very correct.

Rohr specified that the divine and human laws that placed a husband in a superior position over his wife also stipulated that she was the "helper" of her husband, a "comrade," and a subordinate. She was not entitled to pay for her work; instead she was guaranteed "a living." She was obliged to live in her husband's residence, no matter where he moved, unless he was a "vagrant," in which case the intent of the law was ambiguous. A husband was entitled to discipline his wife so long as he was "moderate" in doing so. If he overstepped this bound, he was subject to punishment.[5]

A Passau civil code of the thirteenth century stipulated that no secular court had the right to intervene in the way a husband treated his wife, although it granted that religious rules might be applicable. Only in rare instances did women represent their husbands in such realms. When women had business before a legal court, for example in inheritance questions, they normally had to be represented by husbands or male relatives.[6]

Marriages were contractual economic relationships between the paternal families of the couple, and their purpose was to perpetuate the holdings of the groom's family and, when possible, enhance the status of the woman's parental lineage. If the latter goal was not obtainable, the marriage should at least assure a noble daughter economic security and a social status appropriate to her heritage. Thus prudent matrimonial alliances among the aristocratic estate were always of highest priority in order to ensure the success of agricultural production and family reproduction. The chances of a union with a prestigious partner depended on the status and wealth of the respective eligible partners. In theory the dowry the woman brought into the marriage remained her possession; but as long as her husband lived, it was his prerogative alone to manage it as an integral part of the estate. He could not sell or otherwise disengage her property from the manor. If she were widowed, it would bring her a livelihood or serve as collateral for a new marriage.[7]

It was hardly imaginable for adults of aristocratic status to remain unmarried, and the only respectable place for those who did was in religious orders. Once a marriage was formed, it was next to impossible to dissolve it. Canon Law did not recognize divorce, and annulment was extremely rare. There were socioeconomic reasons for this. The marriage was a union of property from two families, and dissolution of a marriage would bring into question the status of the united properties. In exceptional cases when marriage annulments were enacted, they usually were achieved under the supervision of males – husband, father, and civil or ecclesiastical judges. They always contained provisions to safeguard the male inheritance.[8] Thus patriarchal rules required that men and women live in intimate relationships with one another and protected their social status above the rest of society, while ensuring that women of the highest rank were legally, culturally, and economically subservient to their male relatives, including their husbands.

Peasantry

At the other end of the social hierarchy stood society's largest hereditary estate, the peasantry. Their status, like that of their superiors, was inherited, and it, too, presupposed attachment to the land. In simplest terms, peasants were non-noble farmers who, through contractual arrangements, enjoyed rights to cultivate the soil and otherwise use its produce. The farms they occupied and tilled were typically enveloped within aristocratic estates, although peasants could live on the lands of, and work for, a prince, a monastery, or a municipality. In certain areas there were free peasants who maintained a degree of self-determination; but even their lives were organized through covenants with employers or landlords, which gave them a place in the social hierarchy and some economic security. Freedom of movement was not a universally valued objective in this society that lived by compacts and pledges. Peasants' contracts guaranteed them rights as well as obligations. These typically included the privileges of gathering fuel and food from estate forests; grazing animals on the common lands of the estates; receiving protection in time of warfare; securing relief during emergencies such as fire; and obtaining assistance during natural disasters such as flood and drought.[9]

Should peasant lands transfer from possession of one noble, ecclesiastical, municipal, or royal owner to another, the peasant household passed with it. Those who lived under *Gutsherrschaft* endured an especially strict form of hereditary servitude. Villagers also had commitments to work manually or with their draft animals in the fields and barnyards, or on the roads and bridges, of their lords. In some situations, the contracts specified a certain number of days a week of required labor, but sometimes this was not a written agreement so much as one regulated through a set of traditions and cultural values expressed through the concept of "domestic necessity" *(necessitas domestica* or *Hausnotdurft)*. Every household was due its "subsistence," and it was accepted that persons of higher social standing had greater "needs" than their inferiors. Lords could invoke the principle of "necessity" to justify the services they received from peasants. Lower estates, on the other hand, could claim that too much work for the manor house deprived them of "necessity." Either case could be brought to court. Normally peasants were not free to terminate their contractual arrangements with their lords. While they often "owned" or "leased" their houses and farms, they could not dispose of or leave these at will, because the property was held cooperatively by two partners – the manorial household and the peasant household.

Under a principle called *Flurzwang* the partners were compelled to maintain existing relationships between people and the soil. *Flurzwang* was associated with the manorial proprietor's obligation to grant to the peasants tillable fields of equal width or calculated equal yield and to ensure mutual rights to the meadows and forests, as well as with the peasants' obligation to cultivate these alone. In addition to these economic arrangements, the proprietor of the estate may have been not only the landlord but, especially in the eastern regions, also the political and judicial master of the peasantry. The institution of patrimonial jurisdiction established the landlord as the judicial authority over the inhabitants of the estate. Under many circumstances, peasant marriages took place with the approval of the lord, and the peasant families of the bridal couple had to pay wedding fees to the lord.[10]

Subsistence farming was the norm among the peasants, but the standard of living ranged from impoverished to wealthy, depending on the nature of the villagers' contracts, the size of their holdings, the quality of the soil they cultivated, and the ever-changing agricultural products market. An example of the prosperous peasantry *(Großbauern)* were the *Köllmer* of East Prussia, an independent estate comprising about 12 percent of the population but controlling 20 percent of the land. Economically these peasants stood closer to their aristocratic neighbors than to their poorer peers.[11]

While this system was arranged so as to ensure continuity, it was constantly undergoing change. In the early-modern period, many villages expanded, resulting in larger, irregularly arranged conglomerate communities *(Haufendörfer)*. These villages often consisted of new settlers, called *Seldner* in the south and *Kötter* or *Kossäten* in the north and east, who had much less secure contractual rights than families who had been on the land for longer times. As the population grew and economic conditions changed, the social and economic security of increasing numbers of peasants became precarious. By the eighteenth century, many in the countryside occupied the lowest rungs of the peasant estate.[12]

There were also the landless, who belonged to no formal social estate at all. These "subpeasant" estates *(unterbäuerliche Schichten)* included gardeners, handworkers, day laborers, cottage workers, harvest hands, and servants. They usually worked with short-term and insecure contracts for aristocrats or better established peasants. By the end of the eighteenth century, this group constituted between one-third and one-half of the total population. In 1767 in the Hohenzollern province of Silesia, they made up 78 percent of the rural inhabitants.[13]

The eighteenth century was a time of increased socioeconomic differentiation among the peasants, who produced the preponderance of the food and fibers in Germany. The patterns varied widely from region to region. Some villagers improved their economic circumstances, but large numbers became poorer and poorer. The causes for this were complex, but lower standards of living were associated with a population rise in German cultural areas, likely propelled by declining infant mortality. In the last half of the eighteenth century, the total populace within the borders of the Holy Roman Empire grew from approximately 18 million to 24 million. This placed pressure on households with fixed amounts of land by increasing the number of persons who had to be fed, even though resources remained relatively constant. An increasingly market-oriented economy frequently led to product shortages and surpluses, which threw the equilibrium of peasant life out of balance. Since the seventeenth century, the tightening of manorial control in the east – *Gutsherrschaft* – restricted peasants' personal freedom and economic security.[14]

Peasants were bound together closely by familial, social, and economic relationships. Groups often performed their work collectively, with the entire community planting, cultivating, or harvesting one another's fields. Together they celebrated occasions such as weddings and religious holidays. In many villages there were communally owned buildings such as meeting halls, stalls, mills, schoolmasters' residences, and baking ovens. The unique social organization of the peasant community, the *Gemeinde,* was medieval in origin and had been in a state of transition since at least the fifteenth century. In peasant life, the *Gemeinde* was a more defining institution than the state. The modern concept of individualism did not belong to the peasants' vocabulary or to the legal and canonical traditions under which they lived. Community solidarity gave peasants control over their own destinies. Villages possessed institutions of self-rule, including assemblies under the leadership of an elected leader (*Schultheiß, Bauermeister,* etc., depending on region) and courts to enforce customs and settle disputes. These enabled them to regulate collectively their economic circumstances and deal with landlords from positions of strength. In the areas of Germany east of the Elbe and Saale Rivers, the communal institutions were, generally speaking, weaker than in the west, for here aristocratic authority often undermined the self-regulating institutions. In many German-speaking areas, the growth of centralized state powers and a market economy since at least the sixteenth century placed the peasant *Gemeinde* under stress and in some regions almost completely destroyed their vital institutions. Nevertheless, in many cases the farmers were able to use their inherited traditions to resist changes that affected them negatively. Although if not with their full medieval strength, peasant communal organizations continued to govern the lives of rural people in the eighteenth century.[15]

Inheritance patterns varied widely among peasant cultures but can be classified in two broad schemas, impartible and partible. Under the first, prevalent in northern and central Germany, farms passed intact to the "principal heir" – often, but not always, the oldest son. In some areas the law prescribed the youngest son as the heir; and in a small but significant number of regional examples, daughters inherited farms. One socioeconomic purpose of this tradition was the maintenance of the farm's integrity through successive generations. The impartibility of familial land took precedence over the economic welfare of individuals, for siblings of the heir might be left with very insecure positions in life, and it placed females at a statistical disadvantage. In many southwestern provinces of Germany, by contrast, the practice of partible inheritance prevailed, under which equal amounts of land and property were passed down to all children in a family, often of both sexes. While partible inheritance did not distinguish between males and females or between older and younger, its continual division led to small, overly stressed plots, so that many heirs inherited only tiny patches and lost the opportunity to take over a viable farm. Population growth added to the strain among peasants who lived under either inheritance convention.[16]

If marriage was an economic partnership of production and reproduction among the aristocracy, it was essential to peasants for the same reasons. Work in rural life was strictly divided according to gender, hence unless a household had both male and female partners present, half of the tasks would remain undone. In some regions a peasant farm could pass to a new generation only after the heir was married; in other areas the marriage could occur only after inheritance. Both schemes sustained the close connection between property and matrimony. Widows and widowers often sought to remarry quickly; in one parish of northwestern Germany, 29 percent of the marriages involved persons who had lost a spouse through death. Marriage was also necessary to produce children who would be helping hands and become heirs, both of which were essential to the peasant culture. Wives derived status from their reproductive function and from their dowries. Beginning in the sixteenth century, religious and civil authorities were relatively successful in imposing a requirement of official marriages, as opposed to the informal unions peasants often had found acceptable prior to the Reformation.[17] Villagers themselves – especially the privileged members of the communities – often willingly cooperated with higher authorities in enforcing new normative standards. The alliance of church, state, landlords, and village elites to control people's reproductive lives helped ensure the patrimonial culture. Not merely children, but legal heirs, were necessary for an orderly transmission of property from one generation to the next.

Like aristocrats, peasant families normally arranged marriages for their children, and their economic circumstances determined the nature of the alliance. Although couples of the lower estates were more likely than their superiors to know one another before marriage, the institution was not based on love or personal choice. The peasant family was patriarchal. The husband and father presided over the household, controlled the common property, including the wife's dowry, arranged children's marriages, and participated in the village assemblies and courts. This patriarchal authority rested on custom and law and was enforced by magistrates.[18]

The cultural norms of rural life seem to have been designed to give continuity to peasant life generation after generation. But numerous and frequently unforeseen circumstances often destabilized peasants' lives. Disease, warfare, and natural disasters interrupted the routine of life and inflicted crises on households. Changing economic conditions – especially the growth of market capitalism in the early-modern era – forced peasants to adapt to new conditions. For example, many began to work in rural manufacturing establishments, while at the same time relying on their small plots and gardens to keep their income at the subsistence level. The growth of proto-industry in some areas forced peasants to adjust their notions of appropriate gender roles, producing the beginnings of a "dual economy" in which men devoted more of their energy to commodities for market and women produced non-market goods. Too many children in a family could make it difficult to feed and clothe the household and to arrange marriages. Too few offspring could lead to a shortage of hands to complete the work of house and field. Injury and infirmary could instantly turn a family member from an economic asset to a liability. Regardless of strong rules governing relations between kin and neighbors, cheaters and thieves could unsettle a village economy or bring disaster to a household. Despite these many disruptive factors, early-modern society possessed powerful coping mechanisms, and from a twentieth-century perspective the intergenerational continuity was remarkable.[19]

Townspeople

Although agriculture nourished, clothed, and housed Europe's people, approximately one-fifth of the populace lived in towns and cities, segregated from those who worked the land. Born into their status like their rural neighbors, townspeople were an estate unto themselves. The name of this social rank, *Bürgertum*, is related to the word *Burg*, signifying the walled towns; it is etymologically akin to the French, *bourgeoisie*, and the English, "burgess." In the Middle Ages it carried the connotation of propertied nonaristocratic urban dwellers. Although to modern eyes early-modern urban conditions would appear decidedly agrarian, with gardens, animals, and even woods inside their parameters, what distinguished this "middle estate" from the remainder of society was the fact that it did not engage in agriculture as a profession. Custom and law forbade its members to do so. They earned their livelihoods from trades, crafts, commerce, and performing services for others.[20]

The law recognized these people as belonging to an estate. They were distinguished from the remainder of the population primarily because they belonged to neither of the two ranks of agriculturists. In spite of their common legal classification, the *Bürger* comprised a wide spectrum of social positions, ranging from patrician merchants, who practically governed their municipalities through hereditary oligarchies, to the poorest of servants, who were tied by contracts to households of the more prosperous. Between the extremes of the patricians and the servants were the artisans, the producers of consumer products such as clothing and tools of daily life, who themselves could be either secure property owners or lead lives on the thin line between well-being and poverty. While all of these people belonged to the urban estate, only the male heads of households – merchants, artisans, and the few professionals – possessed the "freedom" to properly call themselves *Bürger*. Property ownership was an understood precondition of heading a household. So the formal citizenship of a town was an oligarchy of privileged males. Others, including the entire female population as well as male servants and wage earners, belonged by virtue of their attachment to these men's households. Occupation was a mark of personal identity, and many professions maintained the status of exclusive corporations, through which their members enjoyed unique political and social privileges. University faculties, for example, comprised such closed groups within their respective towns. So distinct were the individual ranks within urban society that cities had "clothing ordinances" specifying what apparel each category of persons was entitled to wear. Frankfurt am Main's ordinance of 1731 precisely designated the apparel allowable for five different classes of its inhabitants.[21]

Like their counterparts in the country, town dwellers lived and worked in corporate institutions designed to ensure stability. The guilds, organizations of both merchants and workers, not only regulated trade and manufacture but also typically served as the source of political, social, and even religious authority in the community. Free trade was antithetical to the guilds' codes of regulated work and contracted markets. In the guild economy, each chapter, organized around a single trade or craft, held a charter granting it the right to serve as the single producer and seller for a defined clientele. Guilds' economic objectives were to provide for the well-being of each member through a regulated and balanced system. Like village associations, guilds were experiencing stress in the early-modern era because of the growth of capitalism and the movement of manufacture into rural areas. Not all urban workers belonged to guilds, and often there was tension between these independent workers and the guild members. In spite of the dislocation their members were experiencing, guilds remained definitive for the lives and identities of great numbers of urban people.[22]

If heredity determined one's social standing, relationship to property further defined it. Even the wealthiest and most powerful merchants could not approach the status of those who presided over agricultural estates, for the practice of agriculture was considered the noblest of all professions. City dwellers were by definition of lower standing because their assets were not related to agriculture. But ownership of property – urban real estate, liquid capital, or the tools of one's trade – was also a distinct manifestation of rank in urban society. Skills were in some ways analogous to property, and both were requisite to guild membership.

Servants, who lived and served in the households of their superiors, derived their security and station from their contractual relationships with their masters. Every city had an entire population of servants *(Dienstmägde* and *Knechte)*, and this status, like that of journeyworker, was as often a stage in a person's life course as it was a mark of social position. Female servants, for example, were young, unmarried women whose parental families could not support them or provide endowments for marriage. A maid's hope was to assemble her own dowry from her meager earnings in order to make herself an attractive marriage prospect for an artisan and thus establish herself as a partner in a household.[23]

As in the countryside, there were many among the urban populace who, because of their low positions, legally belonged to none of the defined social estates; others were outsiders because they practiced "dishonorable" trades. These included not only vagabonds, paupers, and prostitutes but also those who performed what even contemporaries must have realized were socially useful functions: day laborers, migrant workers, clowns, actors, and grave diggers. In some localities even barbers, shepherds, and flax weavers were among the outcasts. The vocation of village schoolmaster placed those who practiced it curiously close to the outcasts because, although educated, they had no fixed "place." They were not organized into guilds. The outsiders usually lacked both property and contracts guaranteeing them places in a household.[24]

Everyone – husbands, wives, servants, apprentices, children, unmarried adult relatives – derived his or her status from attachment to households. In the public realm of politics and law, one person, the male head of household, usually represented the entire membership. His wife, although placed above everyone except her husband, was his subordinate; he was her "guardian." This was true in the city just as it was in the countryside. At only one stage in a woman's life course – widowhood – might she be exempt from this rule. Some widows managed businesses and administered property that their husbands had formerly controlled. Many early-modern book publishers, for example, were widows who carried on the business after their husbands died. Women often stepped into their deceased husbands' places, sometimes assuming full membership in guilds.[25]

Within this patriarchal arrangement, however, urban households normally were gendered partnerships of work. The law favored the male head of the household, but he could not function without a mate. In the city, as in the country, each profession had its male and female roles. Each partner brought both property and skills into a marriage, and these sustained the household. Thus women played vital roles in the economy at all levels of urban society. This naturally changed with time and varied according to local conditions, but the economic needs of households ensured women productive economic roles.[26]

Religious and Patriarchal Authority

The church was a primary locus of authority in old-regime society, including both post-Reformation Catholicism, predominant in the south and west, and the Protestant confessions, centered in the north and east. Although the clergy was not a constitutionally separate estate as in neighboring France, it exercised political authority in an age that made little distinction between secular and religious rule. The religious wars of the sixteenth and seventeenth centuries had ended with a series of treaties, which made the Holy Roman Empire's princes the authorities over the churches in their respective territories. They often used the churches as instruments of social control. The empire's twenty-nine archbishops – in Salzburg, Regensburg, and Bamberg, for example – were political governors as well as religious leaders in their own localities. The Archbishops of Trier, Mainz, and Cologne were among the eight powerful electors of the Holy Roman Empire. The church frequently upheld the authority of the secular princes, and the admonition to obey established authority lent legitimacy to political institutions. Rulers, in turn, often exercised some authority over ecclesiastical properties, sometimes giving governments and churches common agendas. After the Reformation, German churches acted as instruments of orthodoxy over their subjects. Other than the princes, lay persons exercised little influence over religious practice or church affairs, and even princely authority hardly reached into the realm of theology or religious practices. At all levels from the village school through the university, the theologically trained exercised nearly unlimited influence in education. The early-modern era was a period in which religion shaped men's and women's conception of the universe. In spite of theological disagreements, Lutheran, Calvinist, and Catholic clergy placed God at the center of their system of beliefs and agreed that the devil brought harm to people. Priests imparted to their parishioners a sense of an ordered universe sanctioned by a divine hierarchy. Only the empire's Jews stood outside one of the established churches, and for Christians there was no option but to accept one's ordained rank with deference.[27]

A patriarchal hierarchy determined the standing of men and women in society. Early-modern society lived with the paradoxical ideas that husbands and wives were equal to one another by virtue of social estate and unequal by virtue of gender. Gottlieb Siegmund Corvinus (1677-1746), a Leipzig attorney and author who published under the pseudonym Amaranthes, explained in his *Frauenzimmerlexicon* (Lexicon for Women) that a wife was:

> a married female ... subordinate to the will and command of her husband. [She] directs the household economy and ... supervises the servants. Whatever low ... heritage she may be descended from, she conjointly shares the rank of her husband, is entitled to the same legal status as he, and cannot be summoned to any court or jurisdiction except that in which her husband is resident.[28]

Comparing his own culture with several ancient and foreign ones, Corvinus asserted that women enjoyed a high status in Germany: the Jews of old, he said, had held women in contempt and had thanked God daily that they had not been born female; the Turks forbade women from attending religious services; the "foolish Persians" used the vulgar word "Harem" to describe women; and the "wild Sythians" regarded it as indecent to even utter the word "woman."

Proud of his society's high regard for women, Corvinus nevertheless was explicit about their subordination to their husbands. This prevalent and judicially based notion was one of the many that shaped human relationships in the changing society of early-modern Germany.

In early-modern Germany, the notion that society was divided into two sexes, male and female, was intersected by the twin ideals of social hierarchy and community. The word *Geschlecht*, which after the Enlightenment came to mean "sex," had many meanings, but none of them coincided exactly to the modern idea of male-female polarity. *Geschlecht* was an important mark of identity and usually meant "family" or social standing. In 1735 the encyclopedist Johann Heinrich Zedler defined *Geschlecht* first as a person's familial lineage and second as the "human race," indicating that all people belong to one *Geschlecht* because "all are descended from a single individual." In a third definition, Zedler associated *Geschlecht* with the linear family or "household." In Swabia, if a woman was described as "of *Geschlecht*," it indicated that she was of aristocratic status.[29]

Social status and a sense of honor often bound together women and men of the same estate, village, urban neighborhood, and household, thus rendering rank more important than sex in establishing bonds of allegiance. For example, in a manorial jurisdiction in Mark Brandenburg, peasant wives protected their husbands when maids accused the men of having impregnated them, even though community opinion accepted the maids' accusations as valid. A wife forced the maid to bear the responsibility of the pregnancy because it was in the interest of the guilty man's family *(Geschlecht)* to protect its honor by preventing his transgression from becoming officially acknowledged. Thus *Geschlecht*, a strong mark of personal identity, was not identical with masculinity or femininity so much as with family and status.[30]

A woman derived her place in society from her *Geschlecht*, her parental family and later her husbands' family. Such families were patriarchal in nature, for example, in inheritance practices. Whereas a family regarded it as a preservation of its lineage to bequeath an estate to a son, its obligation to a daughter was to provide her with a dowry so that she could be placed in a different *Geschlecht*, and parents often regarded this as a economic burden. An early-eighteenth-century lexicon advised fathers to bring up daughters well so that they "do not get into foolishness. In our western lands, daughters are endowed with a dowry at the father's expense and, when there are many, they are often a burden on the household."[31]

Early-modern Germany was a society in which order and stability were binding concepts. It was a culture that hardly knew the modern ideals of individualism, freedom, and social mobility. Although there were abundant exceptions to every rule – especially because of changing demographic and economic conditions – an individual's station in life was determined to a great degree by family heritage, the dictates of community, the rules of religion, and gender.

Notes

1. Richard van Dülmen, "Formierung der europäischen Gesellschaft in der Frühen Neuzeit," *Geschichte und Gesellschaft* 7 (1981): 20-30. Winfried Schulze, "Vom Gemeinnutz zum Eigennutz: Über den Normenwandel in der ständischen Gesellschaft der frühen Neuzeit," *Historische Zeitschrift* 243 (1986): 591-601. Günther Franz, *Geschichte des deutschen Bauernstandes vom frühen Mittelalter bis zum 19. Jahrhundert*, Deutsche Agrargeschichte, vol. 4, ed. Franz (Stuttgart: Ulmer, 1976), 33-35. Jürgen Kocka, "Stand – Klasse – Organisation: Strukturen sozialer Ungleichheit in Deutschland vom späten 18. bis zum frühen 20. Jahrhundert im Aufriß," in *Klassen in der europäischen Sozialgeschichte*, ed. Hans-Ulrich Wehler, Kleine Vandenhoeck Reihe, vol. 1456 (Göttingen: Vandenhoeck & Ruprecht, 1979), 138-39. Otto Gerhard Oexle, "Die funktionale Dreiteilung als Deutungsschema der sozialen Wirklichkeit in der ständischen Gesellschaft des Mittelalters," in *Ständische Gesellschaft und soziale Mobilität*, ed. Winfried Schulze and Helmut Gabel, Schriften des Historischen Kollegs, Kolloquien 12 (Munich: Oldenbourg, 1988), 19-51.
2. Friedrich Lütge, *Geschichte der deutschen Agrarverfassung vom frühen Mittelalter bis zum 19. Jahrhundert*, Deutsche Agrargeschichte, vol. 3 (Stuttgart: Ulmer, 1967), 119-58. Hans Rosenberg, "The Rise of the Junkers in Brandenburg-Prussia, 1410-1653," *American Historical Review* 49 (1943-44): 228-39. Hanna Schissler, *Preußische Agrargesellschaft im Wandel: Wirtschaftliche, gesellschaftliche und politische Transformationsprozesse von 1763 bis 1847*, Kritische Studien zur Geschichtswissenschaft, vol. 33 (Göttingen: Vandenhoeck & Ruprecht, 1978), 72-86. G. Benecke, *Society and Politics in Germany 1500-1750* (London: Routledge & Keegan Paul, 1974), 51-158, 181-225.
3. Lütge, *Geschichte der deutschen Agrarverfassung*, 116-200. Rudolf Vierhaus, *Deutschland im Zeitalter des Absolutismus (1648-1763)*, Deutsche Geschichte, vol. 6, Kleine Vandenhoeck Reihe, vol. 1431 (Göttingen: Vandenhoeck & Ruprecht), 31-36. Hans-Ulrich Wehler, *Deutsche Gesellschaftsgeschichte* (Munich: Beck, 1987-89), vol. 1, *Vom Feudalismus des Alten Reiches bis zur Defensiven Modernisierung der Reformära: 1700-1815*, 71-74. Hartmut Harnisch, "Probleme einer Periodisierung und regionalen Typisierung der Gutsherrschaft im mitteleuropäischen Raum," *Jahrbuch für Geschichte des Feudalismus* 10 (1986): 251-74. Herbert Knittler, "Between East and West: Lower Austria's Noble *Grundherrschaft*, 1550-1750," in *State and Society in Early Modern Austria*, ed. Charles W. Ingrao (West Lafayette, IN: Purdue University, 1994), 154-80. Recent findings call for a more differentiated interpretation of the rigidly different models traditionally thought to exist east and west of the Elbe. See Jan Peters, "Gutsherrschaftgeschichte in his-

torisch-anthropologischer Perspektive," in *Gutsherrschaft als soziales Modell: Vergleichende Betrachtungen zur Funktionsweise frühneuzeitlicher Agrargesellschaften*, ed. Peters, *Historische Zeitschrift* Supplement, 1995, 2-21.
4. Peter Kriedte, Hans Medick, and Jürgen Schlumbohm, *Industrialization before Industrialization: Rural Industry in the Genesis of Capitalism*, trans. Beate Schempp, Studies in Modern Capitalism (Cambridge, England: Cambridge University, 1981). Richard van Dülmen, *Entstehung des frühneuzeitlichen Europa 1550-1648*, Fischer Weltgeschichte, vol. 24 (Frankfurt am Main: Fischer, 1982). Dülmen, "Formierung der europäischen Gesellschaft," 5-41. Heinz Reif, *Westfälischer Adel: Vom Herrschaftsstand zur regionalen Elite*, Kritische Studien zur Geschichtswissenschaft, vol. 35 (Göttingen: Vandenhoeck & Ruprecht, 1979), 213-398.
5. Rudolf Hübner, *Grundzüge des deutschen Privatrechts*, 2nd. ed. (Leipzig: Deichert, 1913), 57-64. Marianne Weber, *Ehefrau und Mutter in der Rechtsentwicklung: Eine Einführung* (Tübingen: Mohr [Siebeck], 1907), 215-23. Julius Bernhard von Rohr, *Vollständiges Hauß- Haltungs- Recht, in welchem die nötigsten und nützlichsten Rechts-Lehren welche so wohl bey den Land-Gütern überhaupt, derselben Kauffung, Verkauffung, und Verpachtung als insonderheit bey dem Acker-Bau Gärtnerey, Viehzucht, Jagten, Wäldern, Fischereyen, Mühlen, Weinbergen, Bierbrauen, Vorwercken, Handel und Wandel mit anderen Oeconomischen Materien vorkommen, der gesunden Vernunfft, denen Römisch und Teutschen Gesetzen nach ordentlich und ausführlich abgehandelt werden* (Leipzig: Martini, 1716), 167-72.
6. Weber, *Ehefrau und Mutter*, 215.
7. Hübner, *Grundzüge des deutschen Privatrechts*, 104-106, 519-21. Richard Schröder, *Geschichte des ehelichen Güterrechts in Deutschland*, 2 vols., 4 sections (Stettin: Saunier, 1863; repr. Aalen: Scienta, 1967), vol. 2, section 2, 214-72.
8. Hübner, *Grundzüge des deutschen Privatrechts*, 522-43.
9. Franz, *Geschichte des deutschen Bauernstandes*, 33-38, 50-55. Wehler, *Deutsche Gesellschaftsgeschichte*, 1: 75-81.
10. Friedrich Wilhelm Henning, *Dienste und Abgaben der Bauern im 18. Jahrhundert* (Stuttgart: Fischer, 1969), 1-173. Friedrich Wilhelm Henning, "Bestimmungsfaktoren der bäuerlichen Einkommen im 18. Jahrhundert," *Jahrbuch für Wirtschaftsgeschichte* 1970, no. 1, 165-83. Renate Blickle, "Nahrung und Eigentum als Kategorien in der ständischen Gesellschaft," in *Ständische Gesellschaft und soziale Mobilität*, Schriften des Historischen Kollegs, vol. 12, ed. Winfried Schulze (Munich: Oldenbourg, 1988), 73-93. Renate Schilling, *Schwedisch-Pommern um 1700: Studien zur Agrarstruktur eines Territoriums extremer Gutsherrschaft, Untersucht auf der Grundlage des schwedischen Matrikelwerkes 1692-1698*, Abhandlungen zur Handels- und Sozialgeschichte, vol. 27 (Weimar: Böhlau, 1989), 17-38. Knittler, "Between East and West," 154-179.

11. Schissler, *Preußische Agrargesellschaft*, 81.
12. Franz, *Geschichte des deutschen Bauernstandes*, 224-33. Alan Mayhew, *Rural Settlement and Farming in Germany* (New York: Barnes and Noble, 1973), 123-30. Schilling, *Schwedisch-Pommern*, 30-31. Wolfgang Zorn, "Gewerbe und Handel 1648-1800," in *Handbuch der deutschen Wirtschafts- und Sozialgeschichte*, ed. Hermann Aubin and Wolfgang Zorn (Stuttgart: Union, 1971), 596-98. Jan Peters, "Ostelbische Landarmut – sozialökonomisches über landlose und landarme Agrarproduzenten im Spätfeudalismus," in *Deutsche Agrargeschichte des Spätfeudalismus*, Studienbibliothek DDR-Geschichtswissenschaft: Forschungswege Bilanz Aufgaben, vol. 6, ed. Hartmut Harnisch and Gerhard Heitz, (Berlin: Akademie, 1986), 213-44.
13. Dietrich Saalfeld, "Ländliche Bevölkerung und Landwirtschaft Deutschlands am Vorabend der Französischen Revolution," *Zeitschrift für Agrargeschichte und Agrarsoziologie* 37 (1989): 107. Vierhaus, *Deutschland im Zeitalter des Absolutismus*, 67-79. Josef Mooser, *Ländliche Klassengesellschaft 1770-1848: Bauern und Unterschichten, Landwirtshcaft und Gewerbe im östlichen Westfalen*, Kritische Studien zur Geschichtswissenschaft, vol. 64 (Göttingen: Vandenhoeck & Ruprecht, 1984), 25-26 Jan Peters, "Ostelbische Landarmut: Statistisches über landlose und landarme Agrarproduzenten im Spätfeudalismus," *Jahrbuch für Wirtschaftsgeschichte* 1970, no.1, 97-126.
14. Henning, *Dienste und Abgaben der Bauern*, 120-136. Wilhelm Abel, *Geschichte der deutschen Landwirtschaft vom frühen Mittelalter bis zum 19. Jahrhundert*, Deutsche Agrargeschichte, vol. 2, ed. Günther Franz (Stuttgart: Ulmer, 1962), 274-76. Hans-Heinrich Müller, "Bauern, Pächter und Adel im alten Preußen," *Jahrbuch für Wirtschaftsgeschichte* 1966, no. 1, 259-77. Saalfeld, "Ländliche Bevölkerung," 102-110. Peter Blickle, *Deutsche Untertanen: Ein Widerspruch* (Munich: Beck, 1981), 43-44. William W. Hagen, "Working for the Junker: The Standard of Living of Manorial Laborers in Brandenburg, 1584-1810," *Journal of Modern History* 58 (1986), 143-58. William W. Hagen, "Village Life in East-Elbian Germany and Poland, 1400-1800: Subjection, Self-Defense, Survival," in *The Peasantries of Europe From the Fourteenth to the Eighteenth Centuries*, ed. Tom Scott (London: Longman, 1998), 145-98.
15. Blickle, *Deutsche Untertanen*, 23-60. Heide Wunder, *Die Bäuerliche Gemeinde in Deutschland*, Kleine Vandenhoeck-Reihe, vol. 1483 (Göttingen: Vandenhoeck & Ruprecht, 1986), 7-11, 80-113. Manfred Riedel, "Gesellschaft, Gemeinschaft," in *Geschichtliche Grundbegriffe*, vol. 2 (1975), 801-62. Otto Brunner, "Europäisches Bauerntum," in *Neue Wege der Verfassungs- und Sozialgeschichte*, 3rd ed. (Göttingen: Vandenhoeck & Ruprecht, 1980). Blickle, *Deutsche Untertanen*. Hartmut Harnisch, "Die Landgemeinde der frühen Neuzeit und die Gemeindebauten," *Zeitschrift für Agrargeschichte und Agrarsoziologie* 40 (1992): 168-85. Thomas Robisheaux,

Rural Society and the Search for Order in Early Modern Germany (Cambridge, England: Cambridge University, 1989), 32-34. Thomas Robisheaux, "The Peasantries of Western Germany, 1300-1750, in Scott, *The Peasantries of Europe*, 111-44. Hermann Rebel, "Peasantries under the Austrian Empire, 1300-1800," in ibid., 191-225.

16. Ruth-E. Mohrmann, "Die Stellung der Frau im bäuerlichen Ehe- und Erbrecht: Ein historisch-volkskundlicher Vergleich," *Zeitschrift für Agrargeschichte und Agrarsoziologie* 40 (1992): 248-58. Ulrike Gleixner, *"Das Mensch" und "der Kerl": Die Konstruktion von Geschlecht in Unzuchtsverfahren der Frühen Neuzeit (1700-1760)*, Geschichte und Geschlechter, vol. 8 (Frankfurt: Campus, 1994), 10-12. Werner Rösener, *Bauern im Mittelalter* (Munich: R. Oldenbourg, 1991), 195-98.

17. Heidi Rosenbaum, *Formen der Familie: Untersuchungen zum Zusammenhang von Familienverhältnissen, Sozialstrukutr und sozialem Wandel in der deutschen Gesellschaft des 19. Jahrhunderts*, Suhrkamp Taschenbuch Wissenschaft, vol. 374 (Frankfurt am Main: Suhrkamp, 1982), 69-88. Lynn Abrams, "Concubinage, Cohabitation and the Law: Class and Gender Relations in Nineteenth-Century Germany," *Gender and History* 5 (1993): 82-83. Dieter Schwab, "Eheschliessungsrecht und nichteheliche Lebensgemeinschaft – eine rechtsgeschichtliche Skizze," *Zeitschrift für das gesamte Familienrecht* 28 (1981): 1151-54.

18. Rosenbaum, *Formen der Familie*, 69-88. Robisheaux, *Rural Society*, 32-34.

19. Dülmen, "Formierung der europäischen Gesellschaft," 5-41. Blickle, *Deutsche Untertanen*, 92-111. On the development of protoindustry and the adjustment of the rural populace to its new conditions, see Kriedte, Medick, and Schlumbohm, *Industrialization before Industrialization*, especially 41-73. Kuhn, "Das Geschlecht," 34-41, 49. David Warren Sabean, *Property, Production, and Family in Neckarhausen, 1700-1870*, Cambridge Studies in Social and Cultural Anthropology, vol. 73 (Cambridge, England: Cambridge University, 1990). Sabean's detailed multigenerational study analyzes human relationships in the village as they experienced enormous pressures of population growth, structural economic innovations, and cultural change. See also Robisheaux, *Rural Society*, 147-74, 201-26. Wilhelm Abel, *Massenarumt und Hungerkrisen im vorindustriellen Deutschland*, 3rd ed., Kleine Vandenhoeck Reihe, vol. 1352 (Göttingen: Vandenhoeck & Ruprecht, 1986), 46-54. Heide Wunder, "Die Ländliche Gemeinde als Strukturprinzip der spätmittelalterlich- frühneuzeitlichen Geschichte Mitteleuropas," in *Landgemeinde und Stadtgemeinde im Mitteleuropa: Ein struktureller Vergleich*, ed. Peter Blickle, *Historische Zeitschrift*, Supplement 13 (Munich: Oldenbourg, 1991), 385-402.

20. Manfred Riedel, "Bürger, Staatsbürger, Bürgertum," in *Geschichtliche Grundbegriffe*, vol. I (1972), 672-725. Günter Vogler, "Dorfgemeinde und

Stadtgemeinde zwischen Feudalismus und Kapitalismus," in Blickle, *Landgemeinde und Stadtgemeinde*, 39-64.
21. Vierhaus, *Deutschland im Zeitalter des Absolutismus*, 71-74. Peter Albrecht, "Die zunehmende Kleiderpracht der Mägde in den Städten des Herzogtums Braunschweig-Wolfenbüttel in der Mitte des 18. Jahrhunderts," *Braunschweigisches Jahrbuch* 60 (1969): 99-108. Richard van Dülmen, *Die Gesellschaft der Aufklärer: Zur bürgerlichen Emanzipation und aufklärerischen Kultur in Deutschland* (Frankfurt am Main: Fischer Taschenbuch 1986), 13-14.
22. Friedrich Lütge, *Deutsche Sozial- und Wirtschaftsgeschichte: Ein Überblick*, 3rd ed., Enzyklopädie der Rechts- und Staatswissenschaft (Berlin: Springer, 1966), 174-78, 256-64. Mack Walker, *German Home Towns: Community, State, and General Estates, 1648-1871* (Ithica, NY: Cornell University, 1971), 98-107. Wehler, *Deutsche Gesellschaftsgeschichte*, 1: 91-93. Michael Stürmer, ed., *Herbst des alten Handwerks: Quellen zur Sozialgeschichte des 18. Jahrhunderts* (Munich: Deutscher Taschenbuch Verlag 1979), 28-35. Wolfgang Zorn, "Handwerk und Verlagswesen im 18. Jahrhundert," in Aubin and Zorn, *Handbuch der deutschen Wirtschafts- und Sozialgeschichte*, 536-41.
23. Michael Mitterauer, "Gesindedienst und Jugendphase im europäischen Vergleich," *Geschichte und Gesellschaft* 11 (1985): 177-204. Richard van Dülmen, *Frauen vor Gericht: Kindsmord in der frühen Neuzeit* (Frankfurt am Main: Fischer, 1991), 76-80. Richard van Dülmen, *Kultur und Alltag in der frühen Neuzeit*, vol. 1, *Das Haus und seine Menschen 16.-18. Jahrhundert* (Munich: Beck, 1990), 121-32. Renate Dürr, *Mägde in der Stadt: Das Beispiel Schwäbisch Hall in der frühen Neuzeit*, Geschichte und Geschlechter, vol. 13 (Frankfurt: Campus, 1995), 145-265.
24. Carsten Küther, *Räuber und Gauner in Deutschland: Bandenwesen im 18. und frühen 19. Jahrhundert*, Kritische Studien zur Geschichtswissenschaft, vol. 20 (Göttingen: Vandenhoeck & Ruprecht, 1976), 13-29. Richard van Dülmen, "Der infame Mensch," in *Arbeit, Frömmigkeit und Eigensinn*, ed. van Dülmen, Studien zur Historischen Kulturforschung, vol. 2 (Frankfurt am Main: Fischer, 1990), 106-140. Anthony La Vopa, *Prussian Schoolteachers: Profession and Office, 1763-1848* (Chapel Hill: University of North Carolina, 1980), 11-22.
25. Lyndal Roper, *The Holy Household: Women and Morals in Reformation Augsburg*, Oxford Studies in Social History (Oxford: Oxford University, 1989), 27-35. Ulrike Prokop, *Die Illusion vom Großen Paar*, vol. 1, *Weibliche Lebensentwürfe im deutschen Bildungsbürgertum 1750-1770*, Psychoanalytische Studien zur Kultur (Frankfurt am Main: Fischer, 1991), 200-380. Silke Lesemann, *Arbeit, Ehre, Geschlechterbeziehungen: Zur sozialen und wirtschaftlichen Stellung von Frauen im frühneuzeitlichen Hildesheim*, Schriftenreihe des Stadtarchivs und der Stadtbibliothek Hildesheim, vol. 23

(Hildesheim: Bernward, 1994), 41-72. Daniel A. Rabuzzi, "Women as Merchants in Eighteenth-Century Northern Germany: The Case of Stralsund, 1750-1830," *Central European History* 28 (1995): 435-56. On widows as publishers, see Pius Dirr, *Buchwesen und Schrifttum im alten München 1450-1800*, Kultur und Geschichte: Freie Schriftenfolge des Stadtarchivs München, vol. 3 (Munich: Knorr & Hirth, 1921).

26. Merry E. Wiesner, *Working Women in Renaissance Germany*, Douglas Series on Women's Lives and the Meaning of Gender (New Brunswick, NJ: Rutgers University, 1986). Heide Wunder, *'Er ist die Sonn, Sie ist der Mond': Frauen in der frühen Neuzeit* (Munich: Beck, 1992)
27. Wunder, "Gender Norms and their Enforcement," 46-49. Vierhaus, *Deutschland im Zeitalter des Absolutismus*, 83-89. James D. Tracy, ed., *Luther and the Modern State in Germany*, Sixteenth Century Essays and Studies, vol. 7 (Kirksville, MO: Sixteenth Century Journal Publishers, 1986). Isabel V. Hull, *Sexuality, State, and Civil Society in Germany, 1700-1815* (Ithaca, NY: Cornell University, 1996), 53-106. Dülmen, *Die Gesellschaft der Aufklärer*, 13.
28. Amaranthes [Gottlieb Siegmund Corvinus], *Nutzbares, galantes und curiöses Frauenzimmerlexicon*, 2nd ed. (Leipzig: Gleditsch, 1739; repr. with epilogue by Manfred Lemmer: Frankfurt am Main: Insel, 1980), 571-72. On Corvinus, see the epilogue, 8-9.
29. Johann Heinrich Zedler, "Geschlecht," in *Grosses vollständiges Universal-Lexikon aller Wissenschaften und Künste Welche bißhero durch menschlichen Verstand und Witz erfunden werden* (Halle: Zedler, 1732-54; repr., Graz: Akademische Druck und Verlagsanstalt, 1961-64): vol. 10 (1735), 1222-23. Amaranthes, "Geschlechters Jungfern oder Frauen," in *Nutzbares Frauenzimmerlexicon*, 663-64. Jakob and Wilhelm Grimm, "Geschlecht," in *Deutsches Wörterbuch*, ed. Deutsche Akademie der Wissenschaften in cooperation with Akademie der Wissenschaften zu Göttingen (Leipzig: Hirzel, 1854-1971), vol. 4, section 1, part 2 (1897): 3903-12.
30. Gleixner, *"Das Mensch" und "der Kerl,"* 176-210.
31. *Compendieuses und Nutzbares Haußhaltungs-Lexicon, worinnen Alle beim Feld- Acker- Garten- und Weinbau, Wiesewachs, Holzungen, Jägerei, Fischerey, Bierbrauen, Vieh-Zucht, und sonst bei dem Haußhalten vorkommende Wörter und Redens-Arten gründlich und deutlich erkläret, Auch derer Thiere und Kräuter, Eigenschaft, Natur, Gebrauch und Mißbrauch auf das treulichste untersuchet worden sind; Daß man solcher sowohl in der Stadt als auf dem Lande, bey allen großen mittleren und kleinen Haushaltungen nützlich gebrauchen kan, In Alphabetischer Ordnung gebracht, mit sonderbaren Fleiß zusammen getragen von einem Liebhaber oeconomischer Wissenschaftler* (Chemnitz: Stößel, 1728), 960-61.

Chapter Two

—∞—

The Household as Economy

Dominance, Subordination, and Interdependence in Seventeenth-Century Economic Thought (1600-1720)

According to a prevalent seventeenth-century ideal, the economy was identical with the household. Prevailing norms held that the economy was a moral community composed of the humans, animals, plants, and natural resources of the noble estate. Economists combined ancient philosophical ideals with Christian teachings and agrarian folk wisdom to prescribe a structured, patriarchal order whose goal was the maintenance and reproduction of itself. Defined and articulated exclusively by men who possessed the power of education, social status, and property, this concept of the economy stipulated a gender and class hierarchy while it simultaneously made members of the ideal household mutually interdependent. This normative economy was a non-market system; it largely excluded the notion of commerce. It was not based on competitive ideals, and it did not strive for accumulation of wealth. Its objective was to be a self-sustaining unit that perpetuated itself in preparation for future generations.

Notes for this section begin on page 80.

The Concept of "Economics"

Many educated Europeans regarded their social world as modeled on Aristotelian ideals that included three branches of practical philosophy: ethics, or the doctrine of the individual; politics, the doctrine of government; and economics, the doctrine of the household. Each of these was thought to provide an exemplary prototype for human emulation. The latter, *Ökonomie*, derived etymologically from the Greek "*oikos*," meaning "house." The classical theory of the household, as articulated by Xenophon and Aristotle, held that the economy consisted of a master, a wife, children, and slaves. The objective of this small community was to work within a prescribed order to sustain itself. Concerned with maintaining a high quality of life, Aristotle did not link this goal with amassing wealth.[1]

The doctrine of the household had a venerable history in the Western world. Varro, Virgil, Cato, Columella, and Palladius reformulated it for their contemporaries in Roman society. Lost in the medieval West, the works of Aristotle and other classical authors survived in Islamic culture, and in the twelfth century medieval scholars translated them from Arabic to Latin, allowing the Scholastics of the Middle Ages to revive the Aristotelian tradition. Renaissance scholars, refocusing inquiry on the human condition, later revitalized the study of Aristotle's and Xenophon's economic theory. As late as the end of the eighteenth century, the Greek masters remained basic texts in the field, and they enjoyed new translations until the time of the French Revolution. Although early-modern German writers believed themselves to be mirroring Aristotle, their ideals were actually far from those of the ancient master. Seventeenth-century economic thought was an aggregation of three traditions: classical Greek economics, Christian teachings; and indigenous agrarian tradition.[2]

The German term *Wirtschaft*, used interchangeably with *Ökonomie*, denoted the activities of the *Wirt*, or caretaker. In its evolution, the word *Wirt* assumed many connotations, such as "host," "proprietor," "owner," "spouse," and "manager." In the agrarian culture, *Wirtschaft* was related solely to land and its products. By the sixteenth century, it was commonly understood to mean the science and art of managing the household. *Wirtschaft* encompassed the complex of human activities centered in the house, including relations between husband and wife, parents and children, masters and servants. According to this constructed view of the world, economics was a doctrine of the household and a theory of social intercourse.[3]

The Household Books

Following what they believed to be Aristotle's principles, the seventeenth-century conceptualizers of *Ökonomie* or *Wirtschaft* did not rule out commerce or exchange of goods and services, but trade was at most an ancillary activity in the sustenance of the household. For theorists and practitioners, economics pertained almost exclusively to agriculture. They often called their discipline *"Haus- und Feldwirtschaft"* (economy of the house and field). In this usage, *Haus* meant the people rather than the structure. Economic writings generally were in the form of comprehensive household manuals. They were massive, handsome, leather-bound folios written for aristocratic proprietors and designed to provide guidance for the rural life. These "household books" were addressed to the *Hausvater* – master or father of the household – and *Hausmutter* – mistress or mother of the household; both terms were approximate translations from the Latin *paterfamilias* and *materfamilias*, which signified less biological parents than persons who exercised authority over the property and the people of the house. The Latin *familia* included all people under the roof, dependents, relatives, servants, and, in antiquity, slaves. Yet, in addition to the managerial authority implied, the titles *Hausvater* and *Hausmutter* embodied reproductive connotations as well. The manuals, written in the vernacular German rather than in Latin, the language of scholarly treatises, combined theory with practical information about agriculture and thus dealt with wide-ranging matters that in modern terminology would be classified as morals and ethics, psychology, pedagogy, personnel management, engineering, and architecture. Handling money was not a forbidden activity as long as it contributed to the maintenance of the self-sustaining household. While estate proprietors often engaged in monetary exchange for goods and services, acquisition of wealth was not a purpose of the normative economy, and the concept of market trade had no place in the ideal household depicted in the manuals.[4]

This genre of economic literature took on its distinctive form at the end of the sixteenth century in Johann Coler's *Oeconomia Ruralis et Domestica* (Rural and Domestic Economy),[5] reached a pinnacle in Wolf Helmhard von Hohberg's definitive *Georgica curiosa aucta* (Careful Husbandry Improved: Guide to Noble Life in Land and Field), published in 1682,[6] and saw its last substantive reiteration in Franz Philipp Florinus' *Oeconomus Prudens et Legalis* (Prudent and Lawful Steward) (1702).[7] Dozens of seventeenth-century authors wrote similar works, many of which were issued in multiple editions, so that approximately every two years a new *Economics* appeared.[8] This literature was remarkably uniform in its language and ideals.

Traditions established by Martin Luther and other church reformers of the sixteenth century were formative for the household economists, who themselves held that the economy functioned under a religious mandate. Luther codified three categories of relationships in the household: husband-wife, parents-children, and masters-servants. Luther's influential follower, Justus Menius (1499-1558), popularized the concept "Christian economy" in his 1529 book *Oeconomia Christiana*, published "with a beautiful introduction by Dr. Martin Luther." Menius conveyed unequivocally that it was God, not humans, who commanded household members to work hard and obey the household master. Rejecting the Greek economists, who, he said, could not have known God's "statutes and rules," Menius rooted his philosophy in Biblical sources, reminding his readers of Psalm 127, which taught that if God did not build the house, its builders labored in vain. He asserted that the universe consisted of two realms, the spiritual and the physical; the latter was then divided into two spheres, *Oeconomia* and *Politica*. He wrote on the economy in order to inform people how to work well in the household; this would result in sound government. Luther and many of his contemporaries who wrote from theological perspectives emphasized the home as a private, affective, female sphere set apart from the public, economically productive male sphere of life. Indeed, they foreshadowed the nineteenth-century separate spheres.[9]

This ideal was not the one accentuated by the seventeenth-century writers interested in the notion of household as economy. They adhered to patriarchal religious views of the earthly household, thought to mirror the divine household, but they did not emphasize the separation of the domestic from the productive life. Both belonged to a single realm.

A little over a half century after Menius' work appeared, Coler's *Oeconomia Ruralis et Domestica*, combined Aristotelian models, as they were then understood, with the theory of the Christian economy. Although Johann Coler's (1566-1639) name stands on the title page, his father, Jakob (1537-1612), wrote much of the book; the son edited it and saw it through the publishing process. Jakob Coler was a Lutheran cleric, a professor of sacred languages at the University of Frankfurt an der Oder, and an ardent representative of Reform Orthodoxy, a movement that sought to preserve the purity of Lutheranism but also improve the quality of life. His father, Johann's grandfather, had also been a pastor and was a student friend of Luther's. When the book appeared, in installments (1593-1603), Johann had studied liberal arts, medicine and jurisprudence; afterward he studied theology and became a pastor. Contemporaries would not have been surprised to find theologians writing about economics. With their distinct religious perspective, the Colers specified that their 1,850-page book was written for the "secular household," that is, for people who were involved in the everyday business of farming. Having already published a shorter *Calendarium oeconomicum* (Economic Calendar) based on classical authors and the "farmers, shepherds, gardeners, and wine growers" of their region, the father-son team stressed their indebtedness to the classical Greek economic ideals of, Hesiod, Xenophon, Aristotle, and others. By the end of the sixteenth century it was no longer obligatory to reject the "heathen" Greeks as the religious reformer Menius had.[10] Johann and Jakob Coler also de-emphasized the authority of the state, as personified in the princely ruler that had been so important to Luther's and Menius' ordered society. They focused on the *oikos*, or household, as the central organizing principle of human interaction. They hoped their work would enhance people's lives by providing practical information, but this ideal was rooted in the Lutheran concept of the patriarchal household.

The *Oeconomia* was the prototype of the household books and remained extremely popular; no fewer than twelve reprinted and often revised editions were issued over a period of 106 years, four of which were issued during the disastrous Thirty Years War.[11] The book was written to show how to take care of all aspects of the estate. If their subject order is indicative of priorities in the economy, feeding the people of the household was a cardinal responsibility, involving both the activities of the field and those of the "inner household," the latter ranging from gardening to cooking. Taken as a whole, the economy included: cultivating, sowing, and harvesting fields; gardening; procuring wood; caring for horses; attending cattle; herding sheep; raising swine; overseeing dogs and cats; tending poultry; brewing beer, brandy, and vinegar; producing honey; hunting wild animals and birds; fishing; preparing herbs and medicines; and nursing the sick. The Colers instructed their readers on poisonous plants, fertilizing, weights and measures, and hedges.[12]

Hohberg's two-volume, 1,800-page *Georgica curiosa* had a similar format, and the author acknowledged indebtedness to Coler. It was richly illustrated with etchings depicting the countless activities of the household throughout the four seasons. Like its predecessor, it contained an opening "book" describing the estate, that is, the economy. This was followed by two books delineating the respective spheres of the master *(Hausvater)* and mistress *(Hausmutter)* of the household. Naturally Hohberg devoted the preponderance of the content of these volumes to the production of food and fibers. But he treated many other topics as well, including, for example, salt mining, milling, quarrying, the architecture of agricultural buildings, road and bridge construction, and the art of medicine. In an appendix, Hohberg described the respective "arts and crafts" of the master and mistress of the household, activities they might pursue in their leisure and to enrich their lives. Those of the master included copper etching; sculpting letters in marble; waterproofing boots; painting; procuring dyes from flowers; and papermaking. Among the mistress' crafts were the making of balsam; obtaining oil from nutmeg; wool dying; egg coloring; producing medicine from plants; bleaching and dying hair; working with precious stones; making translucent pictures; and soap making. Hohberg clearly idealized – even fantasized – many of the gendered responsibilities of the men and women who presided over the estate households. (How many *Hausväter* sculpted marble or crafted copper etchings?) Nevertheless his clearly demarcated economic responsibilities rested on an implicit economic interdependence of males and females essential to his prescribed values.

Hohberg (1612-1688) belonged to a Protestant noble family of modest rank and was a subject of the Austrian Habsburgs. As a non-Catholic, he was originally excluded from a role in the imperial court or the bureaucracy but not from a place in the military, in which he served as an officer during the Thirty Years War. His marriage to Anna Margaretha (Marusch) von Rohrbach raised his social standing and enhanced his economic status, although it brought with it the solemn responsibility of assembling dowries for four stepdaughters and later his own daughter. Following an appeal to Emperor Leopold, in 1659 Hohberg was able to claim the rank of baron in Bohemia, which enabled him to take a seat in the estates assembly. He was devoted to agriculture, and in the course of his lifetime owned and managed several different estates. Discrimination against Protestants in Austria forced him to sell his lands and move to Regensburg, where he was able to purchase new property; here he lived the last years of his life among other exiled Austrian Protestants of his class. A scholar and a prolific writer, Hohberg published both poetry and prose on themes of agrarian life.[13]

The *Georgica curiosa* was reprinted or revised at least five times between 1682 and 1716 when it was issued in an "expanded" edition under Hohberg's name, although he had died in 1688. In 1744 an abridged version appeared under the title *Austrian Book of Household Economy*, and the complete work came on the market again as late as 1749.[14] Hohberg's opus was exemplary of the prescriptive writing for noble proprietors of the late seventeenth and early eighteenth centuries. It must have served many as a reference work for a lifetime and may have been a guide for some families over several generations. Written for persons with a broad humanistic education, it was an orientation to one's life station and an instrument of cultural socialization. The book would certainly have been a central work of the aristocratic library.

Franz Philipp Florinus (died 1699), like many of the household book authors, was a Protestant clergyman. Before taking over the parsonage of Edelfeld and Kirmreuth in 1679, he had been the curator of the princely library of Christian August von Sulzbach, and in this post he had presumably enjoyed access to the books of the ancient and modern authors upon which he based his economics. Florinus was an active agriculturist, for he not only managed the estate attached to his parsonage but also a manor of his own. On the latter he enjoyed the privilege of a *Braurecht*, the bestowed "freedom" to brew beer for a specified consumer public. Between 1686 and 1689 this right was disputed by another party, but Florinus was able to win his case through a strong appeal to Duke Christian August. An active and versatile individual, Flori-

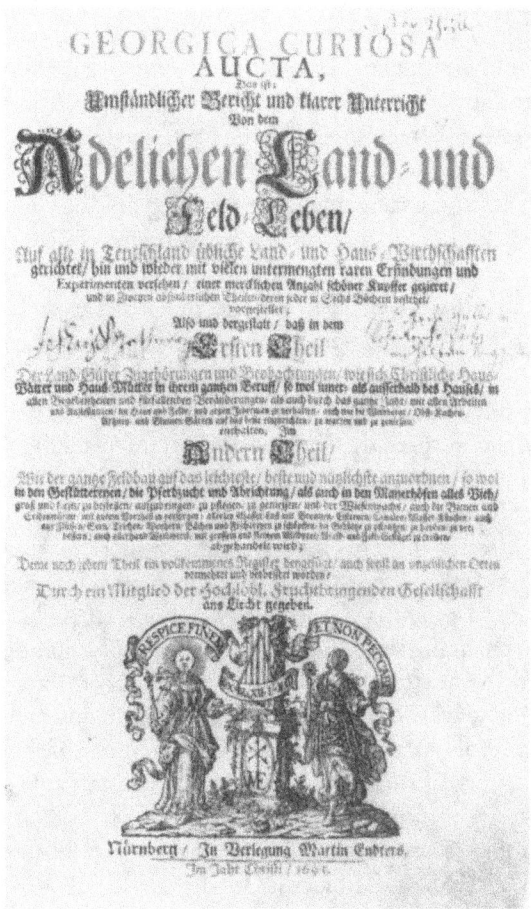

Figure 2.1 This title page from the 1695 edition of Hohberg's *Georgica curiosa* bears handwritten notes, presumably those of the estate owner – or owners – who used it. There are similar notes throughout the text, records made by the *Hausvater* about both his successes and his difficulties with Hohberg's prescriptive advice. The "household books" were essential sources of both theoretical and practical guidance.

nus brought together his scholarly and practical knowledge in his massive handbook, *Oeconomus Prudens et Legalis*, which was fifteen inches high, nine inches wide, and nearly five inches thick.[5]

The connection between theology and agriculture in the economic literature was reinforced by the Protestant custom of granting estates to pastors, on which they earned their livings. Unlike Catholic priests, the clergymen, as practicing heads of households with wives, children, and servants, were conscious role models for the secular society. Possessing the unique combination of academic training, religious perspective, and pragmatic experience, the pastor-authors played a significant part in defining the field of economics. Three traditions were almost equally evident in their pages: the ancient Greek doctrine of the household as handed down and reinterpreted; the new Protestant teachings on the "Christian economy"; and the centuries-old practices of agriculture of northern Europe.[16]

The seasonal rhythms stood beside Biblical teachings and ancient philosophy as conditioners of the norms of agrarian life. An agricultural calendar shaped every household book. Month-by-month, changing seasons determined the responsibilities of the master and the mistress, the children, the assistants, and the servants. Saints' days were usual markers for activities such as the planting of seedbeds, the gathering of the last honey of the year, or taking inventory of sheep herds. The short days and cold temperatures of winter required special attention to the welfare of animals and the proper storage of supplies so that they would sustain the household until the next harvest. In the spring, all hands were involved in their respective tasks to ensure that animals were taken from winter quarters and crops were set into the earth. Cultivation and restocking winter's hay, along with gathering fuel for the cold season and repairing roads and buildings belonged to the summer months. Fall harvests demanded great coordination and cooperation. They were also a time of celebration, stocktaking, and renewal of servants' contracts. Each month's calendar required both comparison with the previous year and looking ahead to the coming seasons to ensure that barns, kitchen, cellar, brewery, and spinning rooms were stocked and prepared for current and future tasks. Record keeping and projection enabled the economy to function in a sustained and regulated manner.[17] The economic tasks of life constituted an unending sequence of producing, harvesting, preparing, preserving, and consuming human necessities. The "household books" constructed a world in which the human agrarian culture stood in harmony with nonhuman nature.

While Jakob and Johann Coler emphasized the secular Greek heritage as the roots of the theory of the house, Hohberg, a half-century later, reinstated a strong religious bearing in the household doctrine. For him, successful *Haus- und Feldwirtschaft* rested on three prerequisites: First, God must bestow blessings on the estate; second, the master must possess an intimate knowledge of his land and its resources; and third, the master must pursue his work to the best of his capabilities and with pleasure. Hohberg insisted that the estate was a fief granted by God. The master was its custodian, charged to administer it in accord with divine plans for the universe.[18]

Work and Human Relationships in the Household Economy

The economists characterized the household as both a hierarchy and a team. With regard to the first of these qualities, the Colers drew upon an analogy between kings and *Hausväter* to assert the latter's authority.

> The economy is a monarchy, a regime in which a single person reigns and rules, namely, the head of the house. He alone must be the heart of the house … . [Under him stand] a wife, a company of children, and a company of male servants and maids. They must follow and obey the *Wirt*.[19]

With unselfconscious convictions about the weaknesses of women's character and the moral failings of servants, the Colers

Figure 2.2 The household *was* the economy. This illustration from Thieme's *Haus-, Feld-, Artzney-, Koch-Kunst und Wunder-Buch* (1687) depicts the wide variety of gender-specific facets of economic life, including harvesting wild foul, herding cattle, preserving food, keeping financial accounts, educating children, dairying, preserving family records, working in the kitchen, overseeing the poultry, storing harvested grain, working with horses, and gathering fuel.

made clear that this was a hierarchy of gender, class, and age. The household head must be wise, knowledgeable, and deliberate. He must know how to "govern his wife, children, and servants with great moderation." He should protect his wife; he should not burden her or insult her or strike her, for if the servants saw this happening they would lose respect for her. Because the devil made women want to look beautiful and attract attention through fancy clothing and jewelry, the master must teach his wife to be moderate and to avoid incurring debts.

As for the wife, she should be pious and God-fearing, love her husband, and "prepare the bed with pleasure." She must have a good upbringing and good education, "and just like the *Wirt* set a good example for the children and servants." Everyone in the household must work together. The master and the mistress should never exhibit pride or vanity. The wife had little reason to venture far from the house. Like a snail, she should be always in her house or ready to pull herself into it.

In this society of dominance and subordination, children should respect and obey their parents and taskmasters. They should help in the work of the estate at all times. They should not keep company with servants but should act authoritatively toward the persons of lower status so that the latter would be submissive in the absence of the parents. Parents and children should never discuss important matters in front of servants, for the common folk did not know how to be discrete.

The Colers asserted that a household could not be managed without male and female servants; but they emphasized that servants required strict discipline and were not to be trusted, for they would steal from their masters. Not only class, but also gender, determined that maids required special supervision. The common women of the household, according to the Colers, were prone to "thievery, gossip, roguery, quarrelling, swearing, and casting spells." They must be watched closely.

In addition to the servants, there were many other necessary members of the household: the manager *(Amtmann)*, a deputy to

Figure 2.3 This stylized garden and orchard from Hohberg's *Georgica curiosa* (1695) manual illustrates female economic responsibility. Though depicted here as a decorative part of the estate, the garden was essential to the production of food for the household. Workers in the background are harvesting fruit.

the master; the dairy woman *(Viehmutter)*, who assisted the mistress in supervising the maids and the cattle; the overseer *(Vogt)* of the male servants and horses, oxen, sheep, and bees; and various other persons, including record keepers and secretaries.[20]

While the Colers' arguments on first glance appear like those of the bourgeois era – the eighteenth century and later – the missing element is the nondomestic masculine sphere, which would develop a century later. In the stratified and authoritarian atmosphere of the Colers' ideal economy, the assignment of work roles established an interdependent male-female relationship of the household, although the mutuality of responsibilities was not always explicitly stated. The economists could write hundreds of pages without mentioning gender, often assuming that everyone knew the unyielding traditions: men and boys labored in the fields and with horses, oxen, and dogs; women and girls worked in the house, the garden, the poultry yard, and the dairy. The master supervised the male sphere; the mistress managed the female realm. It was as if work itself had two genders. The specificity of roles was never to be broken, although at times when the agricultural cycle demanded it – planting and harvesting, for example – males and females could labor side by side to accomplish essential tasks. Haying was traditionally a male-female cooperative activity. It belonged to both the masculine realm of fieldwork and the feminine sphere of the cattle and dairy.

The system depended on balance. The crop-rotation system rested on nature's replenishment of soil nutrients. A conception of sustaining diversity served as the basis for the maintenance of fields, orchards, and gardens for crops; woodlands for fuel, building materials, and wildlife; meadows to support animals; and ponds and streams for water and food. The patterned work of women and men fed and preserved the household.

Because one purpose of the household was to sustain itself over generations, the education of the young belonged to the wide spectrum of economic responsibilities. The economy thus included not only productive, but also reproductive activities,

Figure 2.4 Working with horses was strictly a male activity as shown in this illustration from Thieme's *Haus-, Feld-, Artzney-, Koch-Kunst und Wunder-Buch* (1687).

inculcating in the young the values of their heritage so that they would perpetuate them. Nannies cared for babies, but the master and the mistress held ultimate responsibility for the training of children and youth, including those of servants and their own. The economic writers exhorted mothers to nurse their own infants. Beyond infancy, education was gender-specific. Under the authority of the mistress of the household, girls learned the skills and values appropriate for women of their respective social standing. Under the master's supervision, boys gained the education that would equip them for their masculine responsibilities, whether as servants or as masters. Since the work that young people would later perform as adults would be within a household, so was their training. The prescribed instruction of youth consisted of supervised work on the estate. Teaching also was a reproductive task, for it continuously prepared coming generations to replace their parents in the household economy.

One of Hohberg's rich illustrations depicts a master-father seated, observing a tutor who has a book in hand standing before two boys. The youngsters' posture shows them to be dutiful, obedient learners. Hohberg provided guidance to the master and the mistress for education of their sons and daughters right into adulthood. At appropriate times the boys would accompany their father on trips. The daughters would work in the dairy, the garden, the kitchen, the cellar, and the weaving room to learn specific skills. Hohberg concluded his discussion of "education" with instructions on placing sons and daughters in appropriate places – marriage or monasteries – so that they could take their proper places in a stratified society. The household economy required the transmission of skills and values from one generation to the next.[21]

Interdependency and Masculine Language

Although there was much instruction for women in the seventeenth-century economic literature, there was no female voice.

Productive Men, Reproductive Women

Figure 2.5 Medicine and physical care were female economic responsibilities as illustrated here in Hohberg's *Georgica curiosa* (1695).

The male authors of the household books addressed their work to men in a highly stratified social context. The class and gender biases were probably invisible to readers because they were so widely accepted in this society, where people believed that observable dissimilarities in the character of groups – men and women, or masters and servants – were divinely endowed qualities indicative of inherent worth. The economic writers scoffed at women and even expressed fear of them; they often made women's presence unnoticeable at the same time they prescribed women's indispensable roles in the household economy. A gardening guide, *Sorgfältiger Hauß-Halter* (Attentive Householder), published in 1687 in Osnabrück, made no mention of women. Yet its three separate books contain information and instruction that can only have been intended for the household mistress: one on gardening; one on cooking, confection, and distilling; and one on household medicine – all female domains of responsibility. The etching on the title page depicts a master and mistress of the household jointly supervising estate activities, including a female gardener and a male servant tending a vineyard.[22] Like other books on economics, it addressed the male *Hauswirt* but described activities that everyone accepted as feminine. Its author also frequently employed the indefinite pronoun, *man*, meaning "one", as in "one prepares the soil early in the spring." This word's derivation from the masculine root is self-evident, and even if the writer meant it as gender-neutral, it is striking that books about women's work were written with masculine and neutral parts of speech and altogether without feminine references. The exclusively masculine perspectives represented in published literature tended to make women's work invisible.

Frequently the authors defined male and female roles in the opening passages of the manuals but employed ambiguous language in the practical sections. In controlling the public discourse of economics, men reflected the accepted hierarchy, by making women invisible, and they frequently attributed negative qualities to them. Yet at the same time the authors upheld women's essential role in society's work and insisted on their presence in the household, the economy. Moreover, in this stratified society, it was understood that some women, those of prestigious status, would occupy positions of power over many in the ranks of the household.

Hohberg was more explicit than many of the seventeenth-century authors in characterizing the discrete female and male spheres of the household. He specifically devoted Book Three of *Georgica curiosa* to the responsibilities of the household mistress, covering topics such as the education of daughters, the management of servants, the concerns of widows, the preservation and preparation of food, hospitality toward guests, the household apothecary, and hygiene and health care.[23] Hohberg often used masculine and feminine noun forms when addressing men and women respectively, but he was not consistent in this. While he sometimes used male constructions to describe female work, he never employed feminine language in relation to masculine activities.

Typical for his era, Hohberg accepted the rule of fathers and husbands as natural. He defended the convention of primogeniture on entailed estates, which, he said, had existed since the time of the Jews and was designed to keep families from falling into economic ruin. He expressed some concern about the practice's disadvantage to younger sons, but he was interested in the manor and the linear family rather than the individual person. When a father married off his daughter, with dowry, she renounced all rights to inheritance unless all male heirs should die. "One of the most consequential ... responsibilities [of] a Christian *Hausvater* is [assuring] in his own lifetime the good marriage of a son in order to perpetuate the family *(Geschlecht)*, or a daughter in order that she may be well taken care of." The regulation of family property, and the reproduction of the household for the next generation were fundamental objectives of the household economy.[24]

Despite his hierarchical conception of the economy, Hohberg regarded the house and its people, together with the fields, gardens, barnyards, forests, and waterways, as an ecological unity presided over jointly by the *pater familias* and *mater familias* and sustained by all of its members. Hohberg's sense of the integrated household led him to emphasize women's station. Joining in a debate about the inherent nature of woman that had been underway since the beginning of the Reformation, he posed the sensitive question, "Is it proper for a woman to become educated?" His answer rebuked those who wished to bar women from the world of learning:

> There are numerous men who are either so unreasonable or so unwise that they want to exclude female sex from humanity, to completely dispossess them ... . Those men who belittle women, however, deserve to be ridiculed rather than answered, because [their ideas] clearly contradict the [teachings] of Moses.

"Many people," Hohberg emphasized, "believe that women have the prerogative, the ability, the legal right to study and that they have the power of mind equal to that of men." After all, he argued, the ancient muses had been female. It would have been unnatural to exclude women from Mount Parnassus where Apollo, god of poetry and music, had presided over his poets.

> It is to be hoped that women educated in the philosophies of virtues and morals and in other honorable arts and sciences would thus fulfill their duties and their responsibilities toward both their husbands and the household economy more successfully and in a more harmonious manner. It is especially to be hoped that they would be more skilled in raising and educating their children. Otherwise they would have to entrust these tasks to a pretentious, poorly educated, ill-bred pedant.[25]

But the question of female education was troublesome in this male-dominated society. Hohberg acknowledged that authorities as venerable as the Roman philosopher Seneca had argued that erudition would detract women from their "normal household duties" and encourage them to mix into men's affairs. Hohberg agreed that "more harm than good" would occur if women marched off wholesale to study. If *all* women should study, this would lead to disorder because hardly one man in a hundred would want a woman who translated madrigals or wrote poems instead of helping in the household economy. Nevertheless, he asserted, it would be wrong to deny education to females of exceptional aptitude. Because the ideal household economy rested in part upon theological tradition, Hohberg could draw upon this heritage to assert the worth of women.

> Women, like men, are created in the likeness of God, and where there exists extraordinary talent and discerning judgement among them, and where these could be used to the praise of God and the service of the household, it would not only be without fault, but also praiseworthy and laudable [for them to gain an education].[26]

The "virtues and morals" Hohberg prescribed were not exclusively for females. They were the qualities required of all members of households to shape and sustain the economy. Hohberg's view that education would assist a woman in fulfilling her "duties" was not merely a way of preparing her for a subservient role. In his day it could be regarded as an empowerment, but one designed to enhance the household, not to offer independence to its members. In the values of this society, the highest calling – of either man or woman – was to fulfill one's duties toward God and the household.[27]

Hohberg' contemporary, Johann Christoph Thieme, emphasized reciprocal economic duties in his *Haus-, Feld-, Artzney-, Koch-Kunst und Wunder-Buch* (Book of the Arts and Wonders of the House, the Field, Medicine, and Cooking). He attributed one of his favorite phrases, "office and duties of the man and the woman," to Book Three of Aristotle's *Politics*. He prescribed the "office and duties" of all imaginable persons on the estate – master, mistress, children, steward, the (female) barnyard manager, male and female servants. Of nearly equal imperative were the duties toward God, toward work, and toward other members of the household. The master and father, for example, should keep God in mind in all of his work so that he would not be irritable or fault-finding; he should attend sermons and the sacraments regularly; he should inspect the animals' stalls – especially the horses' – morning and evening to see that they were well cared for; he should be the last in bed and the first to rise. The duties of the household members paralleled each other right down the hierarchy, including the impossible injunction that many different household members were to be the first to rise and last to bed. The lower in the social ladder, the more a person owed obedience and respect to superiors. The economy consisted of four components: duties between husband and wife; duties between parents and children; duties between masters and servants; and production of life's necessities.[28]

Marriage was a companionship of inequality. Thieme reminded the master that his wife was "like a weak and fragile vessel, who requires diligent and careful training and discipline. If you strike her, she will spring away; if you press her she will slip away like an eel; if you pressure her, she will leave; and if you are too mild, she will rule over you." In seeking a marriage partner, a man should not judge by the woman's property or beauty. Rather he should endeavor to find a reasonable, well-educated woman. Quoting Solomon, he said: "A sensible woman builds her house, but a foolish woman tears down the building with her own hands."[29]

Hohberg described the husband's jurisdiction over the wife as "equivalent to God's authority over humans." Characterizing the woman as the "weakest tool" in the relationship because of her "tender, mild, awkward temperament," he nevertheless stressed the importance of a relationship of "good understanding, love and unity." This was important because the woman's presence was essential: "A household without a woman is like a day without sunlight, a garden without flowers, a lake without fish. Without her assistance an economy can never be undertaken and carried on in proper order." The spousal team was like a yoke of oxen: if the two animals did not pull evenly, the cart or plow would go awry;

Figure 2.6 The table of contents of Thieme's "household book" illustrates the breadth of the economy. The chapters are: I. Householding in General; II. Field Production; III. Garden Production; IV. Wine Production; V. The House- Field- and Garden Calendar; VI. Brewing; VII. Cooking; IIX. Carving; IX. Candies and Pastries; X. Beekeeping; XI. Wild Game; XII. Care of Horses; XIII. Care of Cattle; XIV. Catching Wild Fowl; XV. Fishing; XVI. Medical Care for Both Men and Women; XVII. Distilling; IIXX. Healing Herbs; XIX. Unusual Occurrences and Miracles; XX. Decorative Activities. From Thieme's *Haus-, Feld-, Artzney-, Koch-Kunst und Wunder-Buch* (1687).

"likewise the household economy will malfunction if the marriage partners do not help one another harmoniously."[30] In the patriarchal culture, this harmony was a means of upholding the husband's authority over the household.

The Economy as Autarky

As a divinely granted fief, the moral economy of the household was intended to prosper without growing, expanding, or realizing a profit. Diligence and moderation were parallel and mutually compelling economic virtues. Thieme illustrated this with one of the many maxims that punctuated his book: "To do too little or too much, both [fulfill] the objectives of the Devil. Virtue's path is the middle way [of moderation]. Take this way and you will become a man."[31]

The normative organizing principle was that of "domestic necessity" *(Hausnotdurft)*, which was actually encoded into a Bavarian law of 1616. All households were entitled to meet their needs, that is, to sustain themselves at their appropriate and foreordained level. This ideal justified the labor services lords required of the peasants of their estates; it also prohibited masters from demanding too much work of their servants or from encroaching on the villagers' lands, for to do so would prevent the latter from obtaining their appropriate subsistence. Likewise, peasants had no grounds for complaint about the relative wealth of aristocratic households. The economic rule of needs naturalized gross disparity in living standards by defining out of existence luxury and profit. The goal was the maintenance of the bequeathed standard of living from one generation to the next. Seventeenth-century economists rejected commerce and trade in favor of autarky.[32]

Florinus underscored the integrated roles of the members of the hierarchical household with an organic metaphor to represent the economy. Like the human body, the household's welfare depended collectively on the health of each part. The master bestowed order and authority on the whole, but a healthy economy required that each member – heart, lungs, stomach, hands, feet – perform its essential role. The corporal metaphor emphasized the household's reproductive objectives, clearly placing the female role at the center. The household generated and gave sustenance to coming generations. Hierarchy and the organic model worked together to preserve order and stability. The whole was greater than the sum of its parts, and all were held together by moral imperatives. The household functioned only when each participant lived up to specified "household virtues." Importantly, there was similarity between the virtues prescribed for the master and those of the mistress. One of the paramount attributes was thrift, which "has ... a direct relationship to *'domesticity' (Häuslichkeit)* .... The *Hausvater* and *especially the Hausmutter should be ardently enjoined to [practice] domesticity.*" In his householding, "a master should at all times and places be ... *vigilant, careful, domestic, frugal, moderate, alert [and] diligent.*"³³

The early-modern construction of the economy included a division between "house" and "field," with the former having a greater affinity with women's activity and the latter with men's. This is why Florinus claimed that the virtue of domesticity was "especially" a female one. But, significantly, because of the shared nature of the responsibilities, it was not exclusively feminine. *"Haus- und Feldwirtschaft"* delineated two interconnected spheres of the economy, not two separate spheres. In theory, when production, reproduction, and consumption were carried on under one roof the one sphere could not exist without the other. Because duties were overlapping, so were the virtues, the guidelines by which people carried out their mandates. Hence domesticity was a male as well as a female quality. This would change with time, but for Florinus' readers it was inescapable that because women and men worked in coordinated capacities with the overriding goal of securing the "household necessity," they did not function with distinct male and female sets of virtues.

Figure 2.7 Because of the time-sensitive nature of the tasks it entailed, the harvest was one economic activity that brought females and males together to work in the same arena. Yet the work was almost always gender specific. From Thieme's *Haus-, Feld-, Artzney-, Koch-Kunst und Wunder-Buch* (1687).

Aristocratic Monopoly of the Language of Economics

The doctrine of the moral household economy was a property of the aristocracy. In an earlier century, the reformers Luther and Menius might have intended that their notion of the "Christian economy" apply to households at all levels of society, but the seventeenth-century economists wrote from class-specific perspectives. Hohberg's book was a philosophy and a guide written explicitly for noble proprietors. Others claimed ideally to be writing for broader spectrums of society. The Colers specified that their work was for all secular households – royal, princely, noble, urban, or peasant,[34] and Florinus suggested that his book was for economies "in the cities and those in the villages and estates."[35] But everything about these books – their expansiveness, their cost, their assumption of a high level of literacy, including some knowledge of Latin, suggests aristocratic culture. Their works were intellectually and physically inaccessible to peasants, and they were not about cities and guild life. While there were structural and normative similarities between households at the many different levels of society, the standards of the household literature were those of the small but powerful hereditary elite.

In the seventeenth century, the aristocratic philosophy of the Christian economy was a conservative ideal. It justified a worldview that was on the defensive because the material conditions on which it was based were undergoing a slow but unmistakable transformation. Since the sixteenth century, noble estate owners had been experiencing the gradual development of market trade. These empirical facts of economic life increasingly threatened the ideal of the autarkic household, which had never really existed but nevertheless remained a strong normative model. Overseas and domestic commerce had expanded significantly, and after the Thirty Years War their growth accelerated. Urban merchants and bankers were gaining increasing powers, and their resources offered the lure of enrichment to those who would participate in commercial ventures. Some rural landlords were boosting their production by demanding added services from their peasants. The lower classes did not accept these changes without challenge. They not only engaged in frequent revolts but also litigated their complaints in state courts, often carrying on these cases for years at great expense to themselves. These developments were detrimental to the ideal of the household, regardless of whether it had existed as a social reality.[36]

Economists emphasized the ideal of the moral household in defense against these perceived disorders. Johann Rist (1607-1667), a pastor in Holstein and translator of an Italian household book, reproached estate owners of his day who were placing their peasants in positions of greater bondage for the sake of material gain. He was especially critical of those of the northern Duchy of Mecklenburg, where conditions of servitude were becoming ever harsher under the *Gutsherrschaft* system. Rist feared that they were destroying the self-sustaining, divinely ordained *oikos*.[1]

Another potentially unsettling development was the dissemination of news about "scientific" discoveries that brought into question the philosophy on which the household economy was based. Educated German aristocrats were aware that astronomers, mathematicians, and philosophers were crafting new conceptions of nature as a rational order driven by precisely interlocking components. They knew of the discoveries of men like Johannes Kepler (1571-1630), court astronomer at Prague, who held the universe to be a celestial machine rather than a divine household. In Hanover, the philosopher Gottfried Wilhelm Leibnitz (1646-1716) accepted the new scientific epistemology that relegated Aristotle to the past and replaced traditional Christian theology with the notion of a transcendental, yet mechanistic, set of natural laws. Leibnitz carried on a public debate with the British scientist Isaac Newton (1642-1727) over the basic structure of the universe: The former argued the fundamental element to be "force"; the latter maintained it was "particles." With these developments under way, the household economists reaffirmed the Aristotelian, Christian, and folk traditions of the moral economy. Like other

Protestants of the Holy Roman Empire, the seventeenth-century economists rejected the Gregorian calendar, based on Copernican calculations, which Catholic princes had adopted in 1583.[38]

The early-modern household economists asserted the centrality of the patriarchal household in an era when many territorial rulers sought to expand their authority into the realms of private life. The authors of household books emphasized the duality of *Gottesvater* (God the Father) and *Hausvater*, but they avoided reference to the *Landesvater*, the territorial prince, regarded by many sixteenth-century reformers as the third corner of a trilogy of social authority. Ignoring the growing power of political rulers over private matters such as marriage and reproduction, the economic writers employed Aristotle and a theological heritage to profess the primacy of the household.[39]

Thus as the seventeenth century gave way to the eighteenth, Florinus reemphasized for his readers the familiar organic definition of economics, stressing the normative imperatives of sustenance and balance:

> The art of householding, also called economics *(Wirtschaft)*, is nothing other than the proper and orderly provision by the *Hausvater* of temporal and material goods and means of sustenance. The concept "economics" originates from two Greek words "house" and "order."

Florinus went on to specify that the economics of cities, estates and villages were practiced according to accepted cultural norms for the benefit of "the *Hausvater* and his faithful household and for the common good." [40]

Household as Economy

The household embraced the human activities of production, reproduction, and consumption. Seventeenth-century authors of household books were uninterested in issues that later economists would find important, such as the distinction between paid and unpaid labor, for their emphasis was on sustaining the community of the household and the generational family. Diverse activities, including educating the children, feeding and clothing the workers, and nursing the ill, all belonged to the *Oekonomie.* There was no differentiation between the private and the public sphere; the household was the nominal center of all human interaction. This economy was a matrix of power relationships in which social status and gender sometimes worked in tandem with one another and sometimes functioned as opposites. The ideal was harmony within hierarchy.

The economy was based on virtues, and all of its members, male and female, were enjoined to inculcate a subjective constellation of "economic virtues." Masculine virtues included dominance, authority, gentleness, thrift, attendance to duties, mindfulness of one's role as God's custodian, and domesticity. Feminine virtues included subservience, helpfulness; attendance to duties; frugality; cognizance of God's trust; wise management; and domesticity.

Although the ideals of the hereditary nobility faced increasing challenges in the seventeenth century, the nobility maintained a monopoly on the language of economics. Their principles may well have been reflected in the households of many social estates, for the model of the world that was framed around production and reproduction as a matter of survival would have made sense to those for whom survival was a primary focus of day-to-day life. Whether or not people lived up to the prevailing economic ideals, theory held that certain individuals were appointed stewards of the land and masters of other people in insulated hierarchical units. The economic goal was preservation of a self-sustaining and self-perpetuating community.

Notes

1. Johannes Burkhardt, Otto Gerhard Oexle, and Peter Spahn, "Wirtschaft," in *Geschichtliche Grundbegriffe* 7 (1992), 511-24. Dieter Schwab, "Familie," ibid., 2: 258-59. Irmintraut Richarz, *Oikos, Haus und Haushalt: Ursprung und Geschichte der Haushaltungsökonomik* (Göttingen: Vandenhoeck & Ruprecht, 1991), 19-25. Günther Bien, "Die Wirkungsgeschichte der aristotelischen 'Politik,'" in *Aristoteles "Politik": Akten des XI. Symposium Aristotelicum Friedrichshafen/Bodensee 25.8.-3.9.1987*, ed. Günther Patzig (Göttingen: Vandenhoeck & Ruprecht, 1987), 333-51. Scholars disagree about Aristotle's actual theory of economics. See M.I. Finley, "Aristotle and Economic Analysis," *Past and Present: A Journal of Historical Studies*, 47 (1970): 3-25; and Scott Meikle, "Aristotle and the Political Economy of the Polis," *Journal of Hellenistic Studies* 99 (1979): 57-73. Finley makes a distinction between "economic analysis," meaning the conceptualization of the economy, and "economics," the human and institutional activity surrounding the procurement and exchange of goods and services. I use "economics" in the former sense to mean the theory, doctrine, or discipline of economics.
2. Burkhardt, Oexle, and Spahn, "Wirtschaft," 524-59. Otto Brunner, "Das 'ganze Haus' und die alteruropäische 'Ökonomik,'" in *Neue Wege der Verfassungs- und Sozialgeschichte*, 3rd ed. (Göttingen: Vandenhoeck und Ruprecht, 1980), 103-27. Dürr, *Mägde in der Stadt*, 11-53. Julius Hoffmann, *Die "Hausväterliteratur" und die "Predigten über den christlichen Hausstand": Lehre vom Haus und Bildung für das häusliche Leben im 16., 17., und 18. Jahrhundert*, Göttinger Studien zur Pädagogik, vol. 37 (Weinheim: Beltz, 1959), 5-33. Sabine Krüger, "Zum Verständnis der Oeconomica Konrads von Megenberg: Griechische Ursprünge der spätmittelalterlichen Lehre vom Hause," *Deutsches Archiv für Erforschung des Mittelalters* 20 (1964): 475-561. Otto Gerhard Oexle, "Haus und Ökonomie im frühen Mittelalter," in *Person und Gemeinschaft im Mittelalter*, ed. Gerd Althoff et al., Karl Schmid zum 65. Geburtstag (Sigmaringen: Thorbecke, 1988), 101-22. On the Xenophon and Aristotle translations, see Friedrich Benedict Weber, *Handbuch der ökonomischen Literatur: Oder systematische Anleitung zur Kenntniß der deutschen ökonomischen Schriften die sowohl die gesammte Land- und Hauswirtschaft als die mit derselben verbundenen Hülfs- und Nebenwissenschaften angehen* (Berlin: Frölich; Berlin: Duncker & Humblot; Breslau: Holäufer; Leipzig: Hartman; Breslau: Max; Berlin: Grimma, 1803-42), vol 1, part 2, 185-86. On the incongruity between the Greek ideal of the *oikos* and the seventeenth-century iterations of it, see Hermann Rebel, "Reimagining the *Oikos*: Austrian Cameralism in Its Social Formation," in *Golden Ages, Dark Ages: Imagining the Past in Anthropology and His-

tory, ed. Jay O'Brien and William Roseberry (Berkeley, University of California, 1991), 61-62.
3. Burkhardt, Oexle, and Spahn, "Wirtschaft," 531-32, 550-59. Otto Brunner, *Adeliges Landleben und europäischer Geist: Leben und Werk Wolf Helmhards von Hohberg, 1612-1688* (Salzburg: Müller, 1949), 242-43. Hermann Paul, *Deutsches Wörterbuch*, 6th ed., ed. Werner Betz (Tübingen: Niemeyer, 1966), 804-805. Grimm, *Deutsches Wörterbuch*, vol.14, part 2 (1960), 629-48, 662-79. Schulze, "Vom Gemeinnutz zum Eigennutz," 595-600. In the nineteenth century, the conservative ethnographer Wilhelm Heinrich Riehl (1823-1897) popularized the term "*das ganze Haus*" (the whole house) to describe the totality of human activity in the preindustrial household. See his *Die Familie* (1855), which was issued as a part of his *Naturgeschichte des deutschen Volkes* (1869). I have used *The Natural History of the German People*, ed. and trans. David J. Diephouse, Studies in German Thought and History, vol. 13 (Lewiston, N.Y.: Mellen, 1990), 259-353, esp. 309-25. Like his French contemporary Frédéric Le Play (1806-1882), Riehl deplored the mobility and individualism of his era, and he used the term "whole house" to exalt not only the unity of the preindustrial household but also its patriarchy. Riehl's work was popular during the Third Reich because of its heroic glorification of the past. Riehl did not actually invent the term, *ganzes Haus*, for as Frühsorge points out, the seventeenth-century economists employed it themselves in various forms: Gotthardt Frühsorge, "Die Krise des Herkommens: Zum Wertekanon des Adels im Spiegel alteuropäischer Ökonomieliteratur," in *Ständische Gesellschaft und soziale Mobilität*, ed. Winfried Schulze and Helmut Gabel, Schriften des Historischen Kollegs, Kolloquien 12 (Munich: Oldenbourg, 1988), 97. Many modern historians continue to use the term, "whole house." Others argue that the whole house did not in fact exist or that it was an idealized form that did not conform to reality. See Kuhn, "Das Geschlecht," 44. Recently the work of Brunner and the concept of the "whole house" has again become a subject of debate. See Claudia Opitz, "Neue Wege der Sozialgeschichte? Ein kritischer Blick auf Otto Brunners Konzept des 'Ganzen Hauses,'" *Geschichte und Gesellschaft* 20 (1994), 88-98; Valentin Groebner, "Außer Haus: Otto Brunner und die 'alteuropäische Ökonomik,'" *Geschichte in Wissenschaft und Unterricht* 46 (1995), 69-80; Werner Trossbach, "Das 'Ganze Haus' – Basiskategorie für das Verständnis der ländlichen Gesellschaft deutscher Territorien in der Frühen Neuzeit?" *Blätter für deutsche Landesgeschichte* 129 (1993), 277-314; Gadi Algazi, *Herrngewalt und Gewalt der Herrn im späten Mittelalter: Herrschaft, Gegenseitigkeit und Sprachgebrauch*, Historische Studien, vol. 17 (Frankfurt am Main: Campus, 1996); Howard Kaminsky and James Van Horn Melton, "Translators' Introduction," in Otto Brunner, *Land and Lordship: Structures of*

Governance in Medieval Austria (Philadelphia: University of Pennsylvania, 1995), xiii-lxi. Dürr, *Mägde in der Stadt,* 11-144. Although as a normative concept "whole house" can be useful, because of the controversy it continues to engender I do not use the term. On Le Play, see John W. Shaffer, *Family and Farm: Agrarian Change and Household Organization in the Loire Valley, 1500-1900* (Albany: State University of New York, 1982), 15-17.

4. Historians of agriculture and economists of the "historical school" in the 1860s termed this genre *Hausväterliteratur.* See Wilhelm Roscher, *Geschichte der National-Oekonomie in Deutschland,* Geschichte der Wissenschaften in Deutschland: Neuere Zeit, vol. 14 (Munich: Oldenbourg, 1874; repr. New York: Johnson Reprint, 1965), 137-38. Writing from the perspective of the industrializing German nation-state, nineteenth-century scholars failed to recognize the centrality of agriculture to early-modern society and regarded the seventeenth-century writings as insignificant precursors to scientific economic thought because they dealt with the private and rural economy. In the 1950s Otto Brunner gave the term *Hausväterliteratur* a new currency for social historians by demonstrating the pivotal place of the genre in early-modern economic thought. See Otto Brunner, "Hausväterliteratur," *Handwörterbuch der Sozialwissenschaften* (Stuttgart: Fischer; Tübingen:. Mohr [Siebeck]; Göttingen: Vandenhoeck & Ruprecht, 1956-66), vol. 5: 92-93. Gotthardt Frühsorge has emphasized the problematic qualities of the expression and suggests the simple alternative "the old economic literature." I follow this recommendation in order to avoid anachronistic connotations incurred by using a subjective nineteenth-century term to describe seventeenth-century norms. See Gotthardt Frühsorge, "Die Begründung der 'väterlichen Gesellschaft' in der europäischen oeconomia christiana: Zur Rolle des Vaters in der 'Hausväterliteratur' des 16. bis 18. Jahrhunderts in Deutschland," in *Das Vaterbild im Abendland I: Rom, Frühes Christentum, Mittelalter, Neuzeit, Gegenwart,* ed., Hubertus Tellenbach (Stuttgart: Kohlhammer, 1978), 112-13, 205. See also Hoffmann, *Die 'Hausväterliteratur,'* 64. On the Latin and German terminology for house and family, see Mitterauer and Sieder, *Vom Patriarchat zur Partnershaft,* 18-23. Grimm, *Deutsches Wörterbuch,* vol 3 (1862), 1305. Schwab, "Familie," 2: 254-66. On commercial and market activity on noble estates see Irmintraut Richarz, *Herrschaftliche Haushalte in vorindustrieller Zeit im Weserraum,* Beiträge zur Ökonomie von Haushalt und Verbrauch, vol. 6 (Berlin: Duncker & Humblot, 1971), 114-88. This useful work depicts the material conditions of life on estates, as opposed to norms.

5. Johannes Colerus, *Oeconomia oder Hausbuch* (Wittenberg, 1593-1607). My references are to the edition *Oeconomia Ruralis et Domestica* (Mainz: Hayln, 1645). (In my text I use the common German spelling, Coler; in citations I retain the Latin Colerus, which is most often given on title pages of his

works.) Güntz regards Coler as a precursor rather than the originator of the tradition, which, he argues, assumed definitive form after the Thirty Years War. Max Güntz, *Handbuch der landwirtschaftlichen Literatur* (Leipzig: Vogt, 1897-1902; repr. Vaduz, Liechtenstein: Topos, 1977), vol. 1, 125.

6. Wolf Helmhard von Hohberg, *Georgica curiosa aucta, Das ist: Umständlicher Bericht und klarer Unterricht von dem Adelichen Land- und Feldleben, Auf alle in Teutschland übliche Land- und Hauswirtschafften gerichtet ... und in Dreyen absonderlichen Theilen, in Zwölff Büchern bestehende, vorgestellet; Also und dergestalt, dasz in dem Ersten Theil der Land-Güter Zugehörungen und Beobachtungen ... enthalten. Im Andern Theil, wie der gantze Feldbau auf das leichteste, beste und nutzlichste anzuordnen ... abgehandelt wird; Im Dritten Theil ist, was bevorab, in berührten 12 Büchern, gar nicht oder kürzlich enthalten, nunmehro vollständig ausgeführt zu finden; wobey ein bewährtes sehr nutzliches Koch-buch ... auch wie die Weinberge, Obst- Küchen- Artzney- und Blümen-Gärten auf das beste einzurichten ...* . (Nuremberg: Endters, 1682). My references are to the 1687 edition. See *Gesamtverzeichnis des deutschsprachigen Schrifttums 1700-1910*, ed. Peter Geils and Willi Gorzny (Munich: Saur, 1979-1984), 63:330.

7. Franciscus Philippus Florinus, *Oeconomus Prudens et Legalis: Oder Allgemeiner Klug- und Rechtsverständiger Haus-Vater* (Nuremberg: Riegels, 1702).

8. Following is a representative, though not complete, list of "household books" and related works published between 1593 and 1705, including revisions and reprints until 1750. It is based on bibliographies of Güntz (G), *Gesamtverzeichnis* (GV), Hoffmann (H), Roscher (R), and Stolleis (St), as well as the catalogs of the Bavarian State Library (BSB), the Herzog August Bibliothek (HAB), and the National Agriculture Library, Washington D.C. (NAL). One library collection or published source is indicated, using the acronyms above, where each work is located or cited, although many works are in more than one. Only those sources specifically cited elsewhere in footnotes are listed in the bibliography.

1591-1612	Colerus, Johannes, *Calendarium Oeconomicum et perpetuum*, Wittenberg (G)
1593-1607	Colerus, Johannes, *Oeconomia oder Hausbuch*, Wittenberg (GV)
1597-1607	Colerus, Johannes, *Oeconomia* (vols. 4, 6) Wittenberg (GV)
1605	Thumbshirn, Abraham von, *Oeconomia oder nothwendiger Unterricht* (R)
1615	Colerus, Johannes, *Oeconomia* (vols. 4, 6) Wittenberg (GV)
1617	Thumbshirn, Abraham von, *Oeconomia oder nothwendiger Unterricht* (R)
1617	Jugelius, Caspar, *Oeconomia oder nothwendiger Unterricht*, Leipzig (G)

1623	Colerus, Johannes, *Oeconomia*, Wittenberg (GV)
1632	Colerus, Johannes, *Oeconomia*, Wittenberg (GV)
1636-1645	Colerus, Johannes, *Oeconomia*, Magdeburg (St)
1645	Colerus, Johannes, *Oeconomia*, Mainz (GV)
1650	Rist, Johann, *Der Adeliche Hausvater*, Lüneburg (G)
1656	Colerus, Johannes, *Oeconomia*, Mainz (GV)
1665	Colerus, Johannes, *Oeconomia*, Mainz (GV)
1666	Böckler, Georg Andreas, *Nützliche Hauss- und Feld-Schule*, Nuremberg (F)
1669	Wündsch, Johann Wilhelm, *Memoriale oeconomicum politico-practicum: Das ist Unterrichtung eines haushaltischen Beambten*, Leipzig (G)
1669	Wegener, Johann Erasmus, *Neu Vermehrte Oeconomia Bohemno-Austriaca*, Prague (G)
1672	Colerus, Johannes, *Oeconomia*, Mainz (GV)
1673	Hermann, Christoph, *Haushaltungs-Buch*, Nuremberg (G)
1674	*Vermehrter und viel verbesserter Haushalter*, Osnabrück (G)
1675	Jugelius, Caspar, *Oeconomia oder nothwendiger Unterricht*, Leipzig (G)
1676	Agricola, Johann Jacob, *Schau-Platz deß Allgemeinen Hauß-Halten*, Nördlingen (G)
1677	*Vermehrter und viel verbesserter Haushalter*, Osnabrück (G)
1679-1683	Fischer, Christoph, *Oeconomiae Suburbanae*, Prague (GV)
1680	Colerus, Johannes, *Oeconomia*, Frankfurt (GV)
1682	Thieme, Johann Christoph, *Haus-, Feld-, Artzney-, Koch-Kunst und Wunder-Buch*, Nuremberg (GV)
1682	Hohberg, Wolf Helmhard von, *Georgica curiosa aucta*, Nuremberg (GV)
1687	*Ganz neu vermehrter Sorgfältiger Hauß-Halter*, Osnabrück (HAB)
1687	Hohberg, Wolf Helmhard von, *Georgica curiosa aucta*, Nuremberg (GV)
1687	Thieme, Johann Christoph, *Haus-, Feld-, Artzney-, Koch-Kunst und Wunder-Buch*, Nuremberg (NAL)
1692	Colerus, Johannes, *Oeconomia*, Frankfurt (GV)
1695	Hohberg, Wolf Helmhard von, *Georgica curiosa aucta*, Nuremberg (GV)
1696	Fischer, Christoph, *Fleissiges Herrn-Auge*, Nuremberg (GV)
1699-1701	Glorez, Andraes, *Vollständige Hauß- und Land-Bibliothek*, Regensburg (NAL)
1700	Thieme, Johann Christoph, *Haus-, Feld-, Artzney-, Koch-Kunst und Wunder-Buch*, Nuremberg (GV)

1701	Hohberg, Wolf Helmhard von, *Georgica curiosa aucta*, Nuremberg (GV)
1702	Florinus, Franz Philipp, *Oeconomus prudens et legalis*, Leipzig (GV)
1705	Jugelius, Caspar, *Oeconomia oder Unterricht von der Haushaltung*, Frankfurt (GV)
1705	Florinus, Franz Philipp, *Oeconomus prudens et legalis*, Nuremberg & Frankfurt (GV)
1711	Colerus, Johannes, *Neu, Verbesserter Colerus*, Leipzig (GV)
1715-1716	Hohberg, Wolf Helmhard von, *Georgica curiosa aucta*, Nuremberg (GV)
1719	Fischer, Christoph, *Fleissiges Herrn-Auge*, Nuremberg (GV)
1719	Glorez, Andraes, *Vollständiges Hauß- und Land-Bibliothek*, Nuremberg (GV)
1744	Hohberg, Wolf Helmhard von, *Österreichisches Hauswirthschaftsbuch*, Vienna (GV)
1748	Florinus, Franz Philipp, *Oeconomus prudens et legalis*, Basel (GV)
1749	Hohberg, Wolf Helmhard von, *Georgica curiosa aucta*, Nuremberg (GV)
1750	Florinus, Franz Philipp, *Oeconomus prudens et legalis*, Leipzig (GV)

9. Hoffmann, *Die "Hausväterliteratur,"* 42-45. Richarz, *Oikos, Haus und Haushalt*, 104-107. Ingrid Lies-Schindler, "Die Ehe als Gottgewollter Stand: Die Bedeutung der Ehe- und Hausstandslehre Martin Luthers für die Entwicklung bürgerlicher Framilienleitbilder vom 16. bis 18. Jahrhundert," in *Martin Luther: Ringvorlesung der Philosophischen Fakultät* (Saarbrücken: Universität des Saarlandes, 1983), 221-25. Merry E. Wiesner, "Beyond Women and the Family: Towards a Gender Analysis of the Reformation," *Sixteenth Century Journal* 18 (1987): 311-21. Merry Wiesner, "Luther and Women: The Death of Two Marys," in *Disciplines of Faith: Studies in Religion, Politics, and Patriarchy*, ed. Jim Obelkevich, Lyndal Roper, and Raphael Samuel, History Workshop Series (London: Routledge and Kegan Paul, 1987), 295-308. Scott H. Hendrix, "Christianizing Domestic Relations: Women and Marriage in Johann Freder's Dialogus dem Ehestand zu Ehren," *Sixteenth Century Journal* 23 (1992): 251-66. Krüger, "Zum Verständnis der Oeconomica," 531-34. Gerald Strauss, *Luther's House of Learning: Indoctrination of the Young in the German Reformation* (Baltimore: Johns Hopkins, 1978), 117-119. Justus Menius, *Oeconomia Christiana, dat ys, van Christliker hußholdinge* (Wittenberg: Ottinger, 1529), ch. 2, 3, and passim (unnumbered pages). Paul Münch, ed., *Ordnung, Fleiß und Sparsamkeit: Texte und Dokumente zur Entstehung*

der *"bürgerlichen Tugenden,"* DTV Dokumente, vol. 2940 (Munich: Deutscher Taschenbuch Verlag, 1984), 32-33

10. Johannes Colerus, *Calendarium oeconomicum & perpetuum: Vor die Haußwirt, Ackerleut, Apotecker und andere gemeine Handwerksleut, Kauffleut, Wanderleut, Weinherrn, Gertner und alle diejenige so mit Wirtschafft umbgehen*, epilogue by Gotthardt Frühsorge (Wittenberg: Axim, 1591; repr. Weinheim: Acta Humaniora, 1988). Colerus, *Oeconomia*. Hoffmann, *Die "Hausväterliteratur,"* 65-66. Günther Franz, "Pfarrer als Wissenschaftler," in *Das evangelische Pfarrhaus: Eine Kultur- und Sozialgeschichte*, ed. Martin Greiffenhagen (Stuttgart: Kreuz, 1984), 285-86. Manfred P. Fleischer, "The First German Agricultural Manuals," *Agricultural History* 55 (1981), 9-14.

11. See note 8. In the early eighteenth century, Julius von Rohr called Coler "certainly the first" German author to publish a systematic book on household economics: *Compendieuse Haushaltungsbibliotheck: Darinnen nicht allein die neuesten und besten Autores die sowohl von der Haushaltung sowohl überhaupt als auch insonderheit vom Ackerbau, Viehzucht, Jägerei, Gärtnerei, Kochen, Bierbrauen, Weinbergen, Wäldern, Bergwercken, usw. geschrieben, recensiert und beurtheilet* (Leipzig: Martini, 1716), 89. See Jutta Brückner, *Staatswissenschaften, Kameralismus und Naturrecht: Ein Beitrag zur Geschichte der Politischen Wissenschaften im Deutschland des späten 17. und frühen 18. Jahrhunderts*, Münchener Studien zur Politik, vol. 27 (Munich: Beck, 1977), 53.

12. Richarz, *Oikos, Haus und Haushalt*, 144-48.

13. Brunner, *Adeliges Landleben*, 11-59.

14. *Gesamtverzeichnis*, 63: 330.

15. There has been confusion among scholars about the authorship of Florinus' work. That more than one author was involved is made clear in the introduction, and the second volume or supplement, which appeared after Florinus' death, was of course the work of others. Heinz Haushofer, "Das Problem des Florinus," *Zeitschrift für Agrargeschichte und Agrarsoziologie* 30 (1982): 168-75. Gertrud Schröder-Lembke, "Protestantische Pastoren als Landwirtschaftsreformer," *Zeitschrift für Agrargeschichte und Agrarsoziologie* 27 (1979): 98. Ulrich Troitzsch, *Ansätze technologischen Denkens bei den Kameralisten des 17. und 18. Jahrhunderts*, Schriften zur Wirtschafts- und Sozialgeschichte, vol. 5 (Berlin: Duncker & Humblot, 1966), 38-44.

16. Schröder-Lembke, "Protestantische Pastoren," 94-95.

17. On the development of the notion of the calendar as a guide for economic life in the sixteenth century, see Gotthardt Frühsorge, "Nachwort," in Colerus, *Calendarium*, 1-32.

18. Hohberg, *Georgica Curiosa*, 1: 9-10. Frühsorge, "Die Begründung der Väterlichen Gesellschaft," 113-14.

19. Colerus, *Oeconomia*, 3.

20. Ibid., 3-11. On women's place in the old economic literature, Heinrich Schmidlin, *Arbeit und Stellung der Frau in der Landgutswirtschaft der Hausväter* (Heidelberg: Winter, 1941), contains useful information but is influenced by National Socialist ideology. The author draws conclusions about social reality based on prescriptive literature and should be used cautiously.
21. Hohberg, *Georgica Curiosa*, 1: 144-62, 273-90.
22. *Sorgfältiger Hauß-Halter, ganz neu vermehrter, betreffend einen nutz- und Lust- bringenden Baum- Küchen- und Blümen-Garten ... sambt einem Dreyfachen Koch- Condir- und Distillier-Buch nebst noch einem zwar kleinen doch auserlesenen Arzney-Büchlein* (Osnabrück: Distner, 1687).
23. Hohberg, *Georgica Curiosa*, 1: 273-455. Richarz, *Oikos, Haus und Haushalt*, 152-55.
24. Hohberg, *Georgica Curiosa*, 1: 11, 161, 284-85. On the imperative of the master to perpetuate the genealogical line, see Frühsorge, "Krise des Herkommens," 104 and passim.
25. Hohberg, *Georgica Curiosa*, 1: 280-81. See Wiesner, "Beyond Women and the Family," 311-12.
26. Hohberg, Georgica Curiosa, 1: 280-81.
27. On the "economic virtues," see Münch, *Ordnung, Fleiß und Sparsamkeit*, 22-25. Although Münch stresses the importance of the seventeenth-century household economists, he does not include excerpts of their writing in his collection of sources, thus implying greater continuity than I believe existed between sixteenth-century religious writers like Menius and late eighteenth-century authors who emphasized the normative distinction between the domestic and the productive realms. See Münch, 32.
28. Johann Christoph Thieme, *Haus-, Feld-, Artzney-, Koch-Kunst und Wunder-Buch, Das ist: Ausführliche Beschreib- und Vorstellung wie ein kluger Haus-Vater und sorgfältige Haus-Mutter wes Standes und Würden sie auch immermehr seyn mögen, mit vortrefflichem Nutzen und ersprießlichem Nahrungs-Aufnehmen ihr Haus-Wesen führen, und, durch Gottes reichen Segen auf ihre Nachkommen höchst glücklich fortpflanzen mögen: Alles um richtiger Ordnung Willen in zwantzig Abtheilungen enthalten* (Nuremberg: Hoffmann, 1687), 2, 43-83.
29. Ibid., 3. Citation from Proverbs 14:1 (Luther translation, "Die Sprüche Salamos").
30. Hohberg, *Georgica Curiosa*, 1: 142-43, 273. Wide-ranging prescriptive literature urged mutual respect and outlined mutual obligations between marriage partners. See Steven Ozment, *When Fathers Ruled: Family Life in Reformation Europe* (Cambridge, MA: Harvard University, 1983), 50-72.
31. Thieme, *Haus- ... und Wunder-Buch*, 41.
32. On the concept of household need, see Renate Blickle, "Hausnotdurft: Ein Fundamentalrecht in der altständischen Ordnung Bayerns," in *Grund- und*

Freiheitsrechte von der ständischen zur spätbürgerlichen Gesellschaft, ed. Günter Birtsch, Veröffentlichungen zur Geschichte der Grund- und Freiheitsrechte, vol. 2 (Göttingen: Vandenhoeck & Ruprecht, 1987), 42-62. Renate Blickle, "From Subsistence to Property: Traces of a Fundamental Change in Early Modern Bavaria," *Central European History* 25 (1992): 377-85. Blickle's research focuses on the peasant economy, but she demonstrates that the concept of household need applied to households at all levels of society. Schulze, "Vom Gemeinnutz zum Eigennutz," 601-602.
33. Florinus, *Oeconomus Prudens et Legalis*, 1: 1-2, 9, 132-33. Emphasis is Florinus'. See Richarz, *Oikos, Haus und Haushalt*, 162. The metaphor of the human body to represent society was common in the early modern era. See Winfried Schulze, "Vom Gemeinnutz zum Eigennutz: Über den Normenwandel in der ständischen Gesellschaft der frühen Neuzeit, *Historische Zeitschrift* 243 (1986): 598-99. See also Merchant, *Death of Nature*, 99-126.
34. Colerus, *Oeconomia*, 2-3.
35. Florinus, *Oeconomus Prudens et Legalis*, 534.
36. Frühsorge, "Die Krise des Herkommens, 104-09. Dietrich Rössler, Pfarrhaus und Medizin, in Greiffenhagen, *Das evangelische Pfarrhaus*, 243-46. William W. Hagen, "Seventeenth-Century Crisis in Brandenburg: The Thirty Years' War, the Destabliization of Serfdom, and the Rise of Absolutism, *American Historical Review* 94 (1989), 302-355. Sheilagh Ogalvie, "Germany and the Seventeenth-Century Crisis," in Geoffrey Parker and Lesley M. Smith, eds., *The General Crisis of the Seventeenth Century* (London and New York: Routledge, 1997), 57-86. Kriedte, Medick and Schlumbohm, *Industrialization*, 29-40.
37. Frühsorge, "Die Krise des Herkommens."
38. A. Rupert Hall, *The Revolution in Science 1500-1750* (London: Longman, 1983), 176-208. A. Rupert Hall, *Philosophers at War: The Quarrel Between Newton and Leibniz* (Cambridge, England, Cambridge University, 1980), 147-167. Frühsorge, "Nachwort" in Colerus, *Calendarium*, 2-8.
39. Joel F. Harrington, *"Hausvater and Landesvater:* Paternalism and Marriage Reform in Sixteenth-Century Germany," *Central European History* 25 (1992): 57-58. On the increased involvement of the state in private life, see Dülmen, *Frauen vor Gericht*, 8, 17-25. Dülmen, "Formierung der europäischen Gesellschaft," 30-41.
40. Florinus, *Oeconomus Prudens et Legalis*, 534.

Chapter Three

The New Economics of Cameralism
Redefining the Male World by Separating It from the Household (1720-1780)

At the close of the seventeenth century, when he wrote his comprehensive *Oeconomus Prudens et Legalis* (Prudent and Lawful Steward), Florinus could expect that readers would understand his definition of the economy as a household and a living organism. However, his ideals competed with an emergent and powerful constructed notion of the economy that brought into question the paradigm of the sustaining household. Not bound to aristocratic heritages, and working in the service of princes, competing economic theorists placed their confidence in the authority of secular rulers. Employing a language of money, property, and natural resources, but not questioning inherited patriarchal values, they sought to move the normative locus of the economy away from the household and into the princely court. These state servants conceived of economics as an enterprise practiced by academically trained specialists, and hence by an elite class of males. Redefining their world by separating it from the household, they naturally also recast the idea of the household, taking a step toward the privati-

Notes for this section begin on page 114.

zation of the domestic sphere. Their definition of the economy coexisted with that of the Aristotelian household – sometimes cooperating with it and sometimes competing with it and slowly becoming predominant.

Economists and a Changing World

For centuries theories of money and commerce had coexisted with the ideals of the self-sustained household. Like Xenophon and Aristotle, the Scholastics of the Middle Ages had recognized that the exchange of goods and services, while outside of the "economy," were important human activities. After the Greeks, these medieval scholars termed this the science of chrematistics, or "moneymaking." As commercial activity increased in the early-modern period, so did an interest in the theory of markets. Many contemporaries of Menius, Coler, and Hohberg believed that the ideal of the self-sustaining household failed to explain the expanding exchange of merchant capital between urban markets, between the city and countryside, and between European and colonial ports. As social and political theorists began to regard the state as an economic entity, they drew upon the medieval discipline of chrematistics to transform the notion of the economy.[1]

In his *Politische Discurs* Johann Joachim Becher (1635-1682) emphasized neither aristocratic agriculture nor individual households as the basis of the economy. He postulated an exchange economy based on specialization of tasks in three different estates: peasants, artisans, and merchants. Wilhelm von Schröder (d. 1689) pictured the economy as a large household but predicted that if its members consumed what they produced and did not engage in trade, the whole edifice would gradually decline and fall in upon itself. And Viet Ludwig von Seckendorff (1626-1692), advising his patron, Duke Ernst of Saxony-Gotha, about how to make their realms prosperous, emphasized not only stability and order but also increase of the population and the amount of economic property. His *Teutscher Fürsten-Stat* (Princely German State, 1655) was reprinted in many editions and was a classical text for Germany's seventeenth-century rulers.[2]

By the early eighteenth century, the economy of the state, of money, and of exchange was silencing the idea of household-as-economy. Growth in power of territorial rulers and changing philosophies of knowledge were driving a new construction of economics. Florinus died in 1699, but in 1719 unnamed collaborators published what they advertised as an expanded edition of his household book; in reality it signified that the notion of household was fading from the center of the picture. Only one out of seven divisions of the "revised" work dealt with the management of the estate as household. The remaining six addressed the princely court, giving instructions in the art of government, courtly administration, and the theological basis of politics.[3]

The new theory emphasized the princely household, administered according to the same moral principles as the noble estate, but the shift in emphasis from the local household to the princely realm had deep, transforming implications. This was occurring at the same time that some contemporaries were calling for the establishment of new university disciplines, the so-called Sciences of the State. In this context, King Frederick William I of Prussia established at the Universities of Halle and Frankfurt an der Oder professorial chairs of Cameral and Police Sciences *(Kameral- und Polizeiwissenschaften)*. The prefix *Kameral-*, derived from the Greek and Latin *camera* (room), signified the chambers of the royal or ducal household from which the ruler administered his domain, or the *Schatzkammer*, the treasure-chamber. Cameralism was the science of statecraft, and because it focused on ordered productivity in the princely realm, it incorporated what would come to be known as economics. *Polizei* (police), derived from the Greek *polis* (city-state or government), was the science of political administration. Its objective was to maintain order through such diverse realms as education, charity, the guarding of moral principles, and transportation. Cameralism, police, and economics were interrelated components of domestic government. The practitioners often were called, simply, "Cameralists." As other German monarchs followed Frederick William's lead, Cameral Science became an established curriculum in universities, including Vienna, Kaiserslautern, Heidelberg, Württemberg, and Gießen by the 1780s. University-educated Cameralists began to articulate the norms for human interaction surrounding productive activity. They disseminated their knowledge and views widely in textbooks, handbooks, scholarly treatises, and journals. Jurisprudence, political history, statistics, and Cameralism comprised the nucleus of the new State Sciences *(Staatswissenschaften)*.[4] Thus economics, as a branch of knowledge, was moving from the estate household to the chambers of the royal court.

Throughout Europe in this era of princely absolutism, the temporal rulers were expanding into new roles as overseers of the affairs of their subjects and as procurers of the well-being of their lands. The Dutch Republic, with its vast merchant fleet, presided over a new economy of global trade. Guided by the popular theories of mercantilism, French and British competitors were building empires of a new order and impressively enhancing their royal treasuries. Especially in the French monarchy of Louis XIV, these developments were accompanied by a shift of the locus of power from the manorial and provincial setting to the royal court. Mercantilist doctrine called for state promotion of economic activities such as mining and shipping that would stimulate the circulation of wealth and lead to full treasuries. Mercantilists measured a government's success in terms of favorable trade balances.[5]

German rulers, less involved in overseas trade than their neighbors to the west, nevertheless had presided since the sixteenth century over expanding markets, increasing regional economic specialization, and acceleration in trade. These princes welcomed theorists of absolutism. Men like Henning Arnisaeus (1575-1636), Viet Ludwig von Seckendorff (1626-1692), Samuel von Pufendorf (1632-1694), and Christian Thomasius (1655-1728) articulated the new principles of statecraft for Catholic and

Protestant German states. Johann Joachim Becher, a chemist and theoretician of mercantilism, traveled widely to study the Dutch and British commercial successes and encouraged German-speaking rulers to adopt the principles of mercantilism. These early scholars of absolutism still generally held the Aristotelian notion of the economy as separate from political theory.[6]

In consolidating their powers, German rulers embraced the principle of "public law," which rested not on the authority of written documents but on that of the dynastic leader. According to the doctrines of absolutism, monarchs were better equipped than aristocrats to ensure the welfare of their realms' subjects. Hence the establishment of public law and administrative law was in part an effort to wrest power from the nobles and place it in the hands of princes. The rulers sometimes accomplished this by gaining the support of urban groups, and even peasants, in the name of preserving traditional rights. The princes relied increasingly on middle-class civil servants to interpret and implement the new rules of political administration.[7]

While rulers were seeking new theories of governance, university scholars were redefining the academic disciplines. By the end of the seventeenth century, many questioned both the Aristotelian conceptualization of learning and the fusion of religious dogma with empirical studies. Reformers gave a new currency to the term *Wissenschaft* (science, scholarship), which the household economists had used informally to mean "knowledge." Now it came to signify systematic academic study, as opposed to traditional belief systems. This emphasis on academic experience resulted in the founding of new universities such as those at Halle (1694), Breslau (1702), Göttingen (1736), Erlangen (1743), Stuttgart (1781), and Bonn (1786). Emphasis on research and scholarship led to the establishment of academies of science, for example at Berlin (1700), Göttingen (1751), and Munich (1759). Older institutions sought to change their historic identification as centers of Protestant or Catholic theology. Among the new disciplines that interested academics were the State Sciences. To many

Germans, it was apparent that economics, as it was conceived by the authors of household book, was not subject to scholarly inquiry and was unequipped to address important topics such as trade and monetary circulation.[8]

The founders of Cameralism and the related State Sciences hoped that their efforts would bring German principalities into line with the increasingly powerful mercantilist states of Europe. Julius Bernhard von Rohr (1688-1742) published his 1712 dissertation, an argument for the institution of Economics as a university discipline, and he had in mind a definition of "economy" that was considerably more complex than that of his seventeenth-century predecessors. It consisted of two branches: that of "the princes ... the Cameral and State Sciences" and that of "private persons." The son of an aristocratic family of Saxony, Rohr studied law, mathematics, physics, chemistry, and economics, first at Leipzig and then at the new university of Halle. In his career as a civil servant, he utilized his academic skills to improve the effectiveness of state administration in several successive posts in the Duchy of Magdeburg (under jurisdiction of the King of Prussia), in the Niederlausitz, and at Merseburg (both in his native Electoral Saxony). At the same time his prolific publications – at least twenty-nine separate books – disseminated the new views of statecraft and economics.[9]

The Cameralists explicitly sought to de-emphasize the ancient moral theories of Aristotle, stressing instead practical, secular knowledge that would enable rulers to enhance their treasuries. The collection and evaluation of empirical data was a passion for many Cameralists. The modern word "statistics," evolved from the Latin derivation *Statist*, one who works in politics. An influential state scientist, Johann Peter Süßmilch (1707-1767) – although by profession a pastor, not a professor – specialized in population statistics. He not only counted people but also in his work, *Die göttliche Ordnung in den Veränderungen des menschlichen Geschlechts* (Divine Order in the Transformation of the Human Race), advocated that the state intervene in the reproductive lives of its subjects in order to increase their numbers. He believed that the greater the populace in a kingdom, the greater its prosperity. The early eighteenth-century thinkers were not moral philosophers but rather social engineers. They believed that experts, invested with the power of the state, should control both the natural and the human environments in order to make them serve society's goals. Rohr, in asserting his claim for the establishment of an academic chair of economics, warned that this must not be confused with the existing discipline, moral philosophy, which was based largely on the historic Aristotelian constellation of politics, ethics and economy. Cameralists argued that Aristotle's philosophy was inappropriate for training governmental officials, for the Greek philosopher and his German interpreters emphasized the relationships of household members rather than practical, productive activities.[10]

The Cameralists assigned a high moral value to the state, stressing its capacity to increase the prosperity and happiness of its people. Their use of the term "state" was not completely synonymous with "government," for what they really meant was civil society *(bürgerliche Gesellschaft)* in its most organized and responsible form. Yet they explicitly strove to separate ethics from economics and to define the latter as a science of the public realm, leaving the former as a private matter, perhaps appropriate for households. They also placed great faith in technology. New implements and machines, they were sure, would increase production in agriculture, mining, and manufacturing, augmenting the flow of capital and thus the welfare of society. These ideals had critical ramifications for gendered knowledge that Europeans used to give order to their world. If the Cameral Sciences were to be learned in university halls rather than from handsome household books, economic and technical knowledge was less accessible to women than it had been in the old economic manuals. Authoritative sources were physically removed from the households and belonged to institutions open exclusively to privileged males. In spite of Hohberg's genteel plea of the 1680s that talented women should be entitled to academic training, the noble academies of his day were exclusively a male arena. The universities and scientific academies of the eighteenth century were no different. If economics was an enterprise belonging to civil society rather than a household operation, it was a masculine venture. No woman ever held a civil servant position in old-regime Europe.

Household and Civil Society, Side by Side

The Cameralists did not succeed in definitively distinguishing their new science from the household literature. The interconnected nature of the three branches of the new university discipline – administration, economy, and police – is reminiscent of the holistic Aristotelian language, and it is hard to escape the conclusion that the state scientists were influenced by the paradigms they sought to reject. The Cameralists sometimes described the princely realm as the "household" of the father of the state *(Landesvater)*. They were carrying on a tradition of thought from the seventeenth-century household literature. And so long as territorial rulers had derived their incomes from the princely domain farms rather than from taxation, there was a logical and practical analogy between the economics of the household and that of the state, or civil society.[11] As a guide to the proper exercise of state power, Cameralism was a doctrine concerned with the ordering of productive activity, and in the eighteenth century it was difficult to imagine a productive economy without thinking of the aristocratic household.

By the 1740s, Georg Heinrich Zincke (1692-1769) had published his classification of the branches of the State Sciences. Typical for the Cameralists, Zincke was of the educated middle class, and he pursued an ambitious career, apparently one that involved risks. After studying first theology and then law, he held civil service positions in Prussia and in the principalities of Magdeburg, Weimar, Saalfeld, and Braunschweig-Wolfenbüttel. The Duke of Saxony-Weimar imprisoned Zincke for three years for allegedly involving himself in affairs beyond his competence. After recovering from infirmities caused by the incarceration, Zincke taught law, Cameral Sciences, and other subjects at Leipzig and Braunschweig. Cameralism was his passion, and he published widely in the field. His *Allgemeines Oeconomisches Lexicon* (General Economic Lexicon, 1731) was revised five times, with the last edition appearing in 1820.[12]

Zincke held Economics to be both an "academic and a practical" discipline that stood parallel to *Polizeiwissenschaft*. He asserted that, in both its scholarly and its applied forms, economics was an activity to be fostered by the civil society, represented by the state, with the design of ensuring temporal happiness *(Glückseligkeit)*. Acknowledging that economics *(Wirtschaft)* was a concept in transition that "today is used in various ways," he emphasized that the "private" economics of the household was different from that practiced at the level of the royal chambers. Implicitly devaluing the former, he nevertheless did not dissociate himself from its language. He comfortably employed the concepts *Hausvater* and *Hausmutter*, for example, and ascribed to them many of the traditional economic responsibilities. He even edited a book for use on estates, written by Heinrich Wilhelm Döbel, called *Geschickter Hausvater und fleissige Hausmutter* (Skilled Hausvater and Diligent Hausmutter, 1747). Yet his definition of the private economy contrasted significantly from that based on seventeenth-century Aristotelian concepts. Still equating the concept "household" with the word "economy," Zincke declared: "Householding means the conducting of those activities that have to do with money, monetary value, credit, and services. [It leads to] procurement of needs, comforts, and wealth." Thus the Cameralists, separating the economy into the public and private realms, nevertheless often regarded their work as complementary to, rather than discordant with, the literature of the moral household. But importantly, they saw the private economy in a new light, as a generator of wealth, not a sustainer of households and genealogies. Well-ordered households served the Cameralistic interests of the civil society through their productive activities.[13]

Rohr, who argued so persuasively for the establishment of the academic disciplines associated with Cameralism, published nearly a dozen books that were written for estate managers rather than for territorial rulers. His *Vollständiges Haußwirthschafts-Buch* (Complete Household Book) published in 1722, was of much smaller format than the traditional publications of Hohberg and Florinus (6.5 by 8.5 inches although 1,446 pages), presumably so that it could be carried around and used, rather than resting on the reading table of an aristocratic library. Another important difference was its decidedly secular bearing. It opened with traditional descriptions of the moral duties of persons of the household toward one another – *Hauswirt, Hauswirtin*, servants, administrators, and others – and then presented applied information about manorial agriculture. The book was aristocratic in orientation, although it contained occasional notations about practices of the peasant, for example: "There is hardly a peasant household so poor that it cannot support numerous chickens. The eggs that these useful animals lay serve the poor farmer as food, and what he has remaining he carries to the city and sells." Rohr maintained that both urban and agrarian economies included productive households but suggested that the agricultural economy was both more complex and more central to society's welfare.[14] This position his successors would soon reverse.

The Circulation of Money and the Public Economy

Johann Heinrich Gottlob Justi (1720-1771), writing thirty years later than Rohr, and still insisting on the "necessity of teaching economics and Cameral Sciences at universities," explained that "agriculture is of great importance to the state ... . The better private individuals practice economics *(Wirtschaften)*, the more the fortune of the state will be fostered."[15]

The careers of the Cameral Scientists disclose very different interests from those of the learned pastor-farmers who had written the economic manuals of the previous century. Justi led a colorful life. The son of a Thuringian civil servant, he studied Jurisprudence at several universities, pursued a brief early vocation as a lawyer, a writer and a councillor to the Duchess of Saxony-Eisenach. In 1751 he secured a post as professor at the Theresian Academy in Vienna, where he taught several subjects, including Cameral Sciences. He specialized in mining and assisted the Habsburg government under Maria Theresa in the improvement of its extraction operations. After three years, possibly because of failed investments in silver mining, he left Austria and went to the small Hanoverian city of Göttingen, where he became Commissioner of Polizei, a lecturer on Cameralism at the university, and Royal British Councilor of Mines (Hanover and Britain shared a monarch). But he left abruptly in 1757 amid unanswered questions about his finances and took a post in Copenhagen at the court of Frederik V of Denmark. He soon accepted the position of director of mines and superintendent of glass and steel works for Frederick the Great's government in Berlin. After five years he was dismissed and placed under arrest because of alleged irregularities in his accounts. Justi died in prison in Küstrin, protesting innocence of the charges against him. Although always on the move, he nevertheless published an impressive inventory of books dealing with the diverse topics such as statecraft, earth sciences, and mining, and through these he gained a reputation as one of the most systematic of all the Cameralist writers. He wrote under the name of "von Justi," indicating aristocratic status, although there is no evidence that he held a patent of nobility.[16] It was ambitious men like Justi who, by the mid-eighteenth century, were claiming the right to define Germany's social and economic norms. Ever on the lookout for new kinds of knowledge, Justi rejected the inherited wisdom of the *Hausväter* in favor of fresh, empirical learning.

Justi's language manifested the shift in the locus of the normative economy from the household to the public realm, which Justi often termed "the republic," a popular word in his day that had diverse connotations but often meant "common welfare." Justi used it as a synonym for "state" or "civil society," regardless of the constitutional form. He believed that while Christianity was an important cohesive force in society, it must be subordinated to civil authority, for "religion" – he meant the word to include all religions – could be a noxious as well as a positive influence on humanity. Like Florinus, who wrote eighty years earlier, Justi used the metaphor of the human body to describe the social order, but his image was strikingly different from that of his predecessor, who posited the *Hausvater* as the head, with the household members comprising the limbs of the economy. Justi employed the modern, scientific medical knowledge of his time to illustrate his analogy:

> If one compares the moral body of the Republic with the human body, so that business and the circulation of money represent the blood and its circulatory system – the internal life – one must regard the cities as the great cephalic vein and the aorta that constitute the most significant driving force of the whole process."[17]

In this pulsating society, economics was a subject hardly concerned with people and human relationships. It was the science of property *(Vermögen)*. The agricultural estate was not a sacred trust in the hands of a judicious custodian, as the authors of the household books had conceive it. "Property," Justi asserted, "is that over which we have power, or which we can control and manage ... . Property [consists of] all possessions and skills that we can employ in order to acquire the necessities and comforts of life." While some still described possessions in a "moral" sense, he said, "in relation to economics," property consisted of those things that could be assigned a value in terms of gold and silver. Credit was also an important component of economic property, as were skills, which could be put to use in occupations and professions. By using their property, people could produce "earnings, the profit we gain after calculation of our applied costs and efforts." Moreover, one should not be satisfied with small profits, for humans were entitled to have their needs and wants met in a satisfying manner.

In spite of Justi's fierce secularism and his emphasis on profit, he was a person of his era and could not escape the heritage of the moral economy, which taught that personal opulence was forbidden by the teachings of Christianity. While human necessities, satisfaction, and comfort were desirable goals, the simple amassment of riches was nevertheless inappropriate, he said, "because God and the natural laws he gave us entitle us to our needs and to the comforts of life but never to excess." He may even have agreed with Süßmilch's argument that luxury was an impediment to marital fertility. The importance of individual wealth was that it produced revenue for the state, which in turn ensured benefits to the citizens. Justi held the modern idea that everyone was obligated to pay taxes, and the affluent more than the poor, because "the person who has a large amount of property enjoys a great amount of protection and security."[18] The normative source of order and the foundation of social welfare were moving from the household to the state, the organizing institution of civil society.

Justi classified people in society by their functions in the economy rather than according to traditional philosophical or theological principles. He developed a socioeconomic taxonomy based on his observation of people working in their productive capacities. The urban and the rural populations played very different roles in society, according to Justi. A city was a "collection of corporations, families, and individuals" living in a protected or walled locale. Guilds brought order to cities and enabled them to produce products that society's needs. Cities had originated historically when "humans began to live with rational principles" and to recognize the "comforts and advantages" of urban life.[19]

Villages were different. Situated in the countryside, they produced raw agricultural products and were not arranged corporately but as "individual families." Justi insisted that peasants were the real proprietors of the land and criticized the unfree labor of semifeudal estates. He believed that excessive subdivision of land through inheritance was harmful, but he declared that modest farms were more efficient than large estates, because small proprietors were more industrious since they cultivated their own fields. He advocated transforming the *Gutsherrschaft* and *Grundherrschaft* systems into one of modern tenancy, whereby landlords lived from rents, not percentages of crops, for he felt that the tillers of the soil would labor more intensively if they stood to gain all the fruits of their toil.[20]

Moving in uncharted territory, Justi was searching for new ways of describing social and economic relationships. His vision was an aggregate of theory, observation, imagination, and inherited cultural values. His use of the word "family" was innovative in its time, but common among Cameralists, as the descriptor of the basic unit of society, replacing the older ideal, "household." Unlike its predecessor, "the family" was more of a conjugal arrangement than an economic one. It did not include the servants, animals, or lands of the living group. Families consisted primarily of one generation, not the genealogical heritage of forbears and heirs. This was the embryonic idea of the bourgeois family that would come more and more to dominate social thought about the natural social order. The visionary Justi retained a hierarchical sense of order and believed in strict order and discipline. Like the old economists, he mistrusted servants categorically and insisted that masters take strong measures to ensure that their domestic and field helpers not steal from them. Unlike his predecessors, he viewed servants as having a functional role – as employees – not an inherent one, in the family enterprise. He advocated incarceration of beggars in poorhouses where they should be forced to work as a deterrent to laziness.[21]

In staking claim to their own vocabulary, the State Scientists developed a new term for agriculture, *Landwirtschaft*. This expression was probably first used systematically in the 1720s and differed fundamentally from the common seventeenth-century phrase *Haus- und Feldwirtschaft*. First, the new word signified that agriculture was not equivalent to "the economy," as earlier authors had regarded it to be; agriculture was a single bough of the economic tree. Second, in comparison to the traditional conceptualization of Hohberg and Florinus, the new expression focused on the land, not on the people or the household. Third, *Landwirtschaft* carried an entrepreneurial connotation absent from *Haus- und Feldwirtschaft*. The linguistic break with the past was not a clean one, as Justi's explanation indicates, but this Cameralist made it clear that he supported the dissociation of the three elements – household, economy and farming – which in the old economists' language were interchangeable. "The science *(Lehre)* of agriculture is not a mere part of the art of householding, but [is], rather, of itself, a special discipline *(Wissenschaft)* that must be viewed, however, as subordinate to *Oekonomie*, although there are those who still wish to classify it by the latter name alone."[22] Justi did not completely devalue the rural economy, but he regarded it as an ancillary to the larger economic system, serving civil society and guided by government. In his hierarchy of values, agriculture was more than the household but was subaltern to the primary economy, that of the state.

Agriculture's purpose was no longer merely to sustain the household. Its two overriding functions were supplying produce to satisfy the needs and desires of all of society and fostering the commerce of the country. The ultimate goal of working the land, however, was "to convert the dispensable part of the produce and crops into money, to save part of this, and to earn income with it." Farmers were no longer stewards of the land; they were owners, and they deserved to use their property for human requirements and satisfaction. The way to do this was to extract earnings.

In describing the ecological relationship between people and the soil, Justi urged exploitation of the land to the fullest extent possible. Successful agriculturists, he argued, must have a thorough knowledge of market conditions; and the viability of a farm depended in part on its access to transportation links so that products could be shipped easily to distant trade centers. Justi was glad that he could detect more new land than ever before coming under the plow: "In many places one hears of the draining of lakes and bogs as well as old river beds [and] the conversion of the moors and [heathers] into arable soil."[23] Land was a commodity, a form of wealth that could be converted into money.

Cameralism, the Household, and Gender

The Cameralists redefined the economic world, and part of their way of lending it authority was to stress its separation from the old, the moral, and the domestic. Their assumption that the market belonged to men forced a reconceptualization of the house and the gender relationships within it.

Rohr, an early but important participant in the Cameralistic discourse, could not go so far as to represent the household as completely removed from economics. This was understandable in an era when household and economy customarily were still represented by the same word. Rohr argued, instead, that there were two economies, the new one of the state and the old one of the household. Striving to revise economic paradigms, he criticized the authors of the old household books for representing economic and moral responsibilities as identical, for example, a master's "duty and obligation toward his wife, children and servants." A *Hauswirt* should fulfill these charges "as a Christian and a reasonable human being," but they were not economic in nature, implicitly because they did not belong to the realm of the market.[24] Men were masters of the economy and rulers of the household, but increasingly their authority rested on different foundations in the two different spheres.

Regarding the private realm, Rohr emphasized the authority of the master over the people of the household: "A *Hauswirth* is allowed to do anything he pleases in his household, so long as it does not violate the laws of God, the laws of his appointed superiors, [and] the traditions of his locality ... . Thus one can well accept the common saying, 'every man is king in his own house.'" But the place of the wife was complex: she was at the same time a subaltern, a helper, and a partner. Her subordination rested on the authority of St. Paul's letters to the Ephesians and Colossians; in Genesis lay the source of the tradition of the wife as her husband's "helper." The concept of "partner" was based in Roman law, according to Rohr. Married people, he said, gain "common advantage through their work and toil … . According to these principles, a woman is bound to perform her services for the benefit of the husband and the household."[25]

A woman's responsibilities in the household included cooking and cleaning, but her status as wife entitled her to refuse jobs that were beneath her, such as those performed by maids, and exempted her from responsibilities that exceeded her expertise, such as business transactions. Her property belonged to the common possessions of the household and was managed by her husband, although there might be exceptional situations where she had special rights to administer it. Because she was a "helper," not a worker, she was not entitled to a wage for her efforts, as a maid would be; only widows might expect income from their work or property. A woman was mandated to live in her husband's house, even if he should move constantly, because she had promised before God to stand by him in all circumstances. But a husband was not allowed to step beyond the bounds of moderation in punishing his wife.[26]

This early Cameralist thus sought to distinguish between moral and economic responsibilities and presented a paradoxical explanation of gender relationships in the private realm. While Rohr reasserted the traditional ideal of the household community, to which all contributed and from which all benefited, he accentuated the moral and physical superiority of the husband. His representation of women as unqualified for business activity was an incremental step in segregating the private, female realm from the economy. The husband-master was the ultimate authority in both the economy and the household; the wife was partner-helper-subordinate, and only in the latter.

Most of the Cameralists were more concerned with processes than with people. Justi had less to say about gender than did Rohr or the authors of the household books. He employed nouns of a functional nature, rejecting the "moral" terms *Hausvater* and *Hausmutter*. (Justi used the adjective "moral" pejoratively to mean antiquated or useless.) In accord with his entrepreneurial concept of *Landwirtschaft*, Justi called the agriculturist the *Hauswirt*. This could be understood to mean "household manager," similar to the term *Hausvater*, but it lacked the reproductive connotation of the older word. When describing master-servant relations, Justi referred to the superior simply as *Herr* (master). The household patriarchy was not eradicated by the intended commercialization of agriculture.

In one short paragraph, contained in 175 pages on "householding" in his book on the State Sciences, Justi characterized the role of the estate wife. He wrote not about the *Hausmutter* but about the "marriage partner" *(Ehegenossin)*, easing toward the modern ideal of housewife. He also called her the *Landwirtin*, the female form of *Landwirt*. His trivialization of women's work amounted to a rejection of the normative role of the household mistress of the moral economy. Like his predecessors, he was interested in "good order" in society. He wrote that the wife of the *Landwirt* was no

> delicate lady who cannot bear the odors of the kitchen or who does not dare to leave her bedside table or her stateroom to go into the open air .... No, if a *Landwirtin* is to be a true assistant to her husband, she should at least help to bear and lighten the responsibilities for the kitchen, the cellar, and the cattle. However, these are no arduous tasks. If she maintains order in the kitchen on a daily basis, and now and again checks to see how it is being run, if she inspects the supplies, the behavior, and the faithfulness of the kitchen mistress, then she can utilize a few hours on Sunday afternoons to inspect the mistress's cattle account books, just as her husband does with all of the other accounts. Then she will have done her part as an honest helper.[27]

Still employing some concepts from the household economy, Justi transformed their meaning, casting a vision of his ideal wife of an entrepreneurial farmer. In the tradition of reformers of his time who prided themselves on their rejection of traditional and aristocratic values, he rhetorically contrasted his model with that of the alleged idle and delicate household mistress, depicting her as industrious and responsible. She was a helpmeet in traditional female spheres – but in no way the manager of former times. Thinking of the farm solely as a productive enterprise, Justi granted her no role in the productive part of the household or in the market economy. Unlike the normative *Hausmutter*, who presided over dairy, swine operations, clothing production, and the preservation and preparation of food, she was confined to the household. She lightened her husband's responsibilities in the "kitchen, cellar, and household."

Always experimenting with new ideals, Justi proposed the establishment of formal education for women, at least those of higher status. Early in his career he recommended the establishment of women's academies:

> For several years I have been of the opinion that it would be for the true betterment of the human race, that it would be uncommonly useful and beneficial, if one would establish a rational education system for the female sex. For this purpose [one should institute] a certain type of higher schools or academies ... . No one can deny that rational education of the female sex would have a great influence on the welfare and the happiness of the world. [28]

Justi justified this proposal with both philosophical and practical arguments. In the spirit of the Enlightenment, he declared: "finally they are just what we ourselves are, humans ... , who have the same rational mind that we have." A more concrete reason for the foundation of women's academies was to address the near total neglect of formal female education. In the finest houses, Justi asserted, daughters were, at best, allowed to be present when tutors taught their brothers. The tutors might teach them a few facts about Christianity and have them learn a few prayers by heart. In unusual circumstances, the daughters might have the chance to learn a little writing and arithmetic and have some music lessons. The way to improve on this, Justi proposed, was the establishment of formal schools.[29]

Justi's description of the staffing for the school illustrates some of his thinking about gender roles. "The teachers of this academy should consist largely of ladies. It would be necessary to select either widows or single women who are already of an age that is not so subject to passion for vain things and sensuous pleasures." (Justi's descriptions of the new male subjects in Cameralist studies in the universities contained no warning that young male professors would be subject to such temptations.) The female teachers could instruct the girls in "sewing, in all kinds of ladies' work, cooking, arithmetic, writing, music, dancing, and language." But these teachers would not be in a position to provide a complete education. It would be necessary that "two educated and honorable men" be employed at the academy. One could teach physics and history; the other, morals and economics. In spite of the fact that these latter subjects required male instructors, however, Justi went on to explain that the young women need learn them only in a passing manner. About physics he said "it would be enough [if they] would master just enough that they were not completely ignorant of the wonderful and magnificent works of nature." History should not be a "work of memorization" for the young ladies. Even moral philosophy and economics, two basic subjects of the old household economy, were to be learned casually: "Moral philosophy can be taught with some stipulations ... . One would teach these young girls those things about economics that would be important for all people," without emphasis on agriculture. "This would exhaust the knowledge that I would hold necessary for an educated lady."[30]

Justi stressed that the practical purpose of female education was to make women better wives: "Thousands of men have been deprived of their well-being and turned into unproductive members of society by foolish and simpleminded wives." Women, he said, were "leaders of the economy." The context, however, made it clear that he did not mean the economy of the civil society, or of markets, property, and profits. For the sake of clarity, he added "and the household *[Hauswesen]*." Female education would also help prevent women who never married from becoming burdens to society. Justi held up the Catholic Church, with its "ladies' cloisters, as a good educator of women."[31]

Like other Cameralists, Justi attached great importance to population growth. His contemporary, Süßmilch, argued that the state should encourage early marriages, dissuade alliances between partners of greatly dissimilar ages, train midwives, support medical science, discourage the use of home remedies, and give financial support to couples with large numbers of offspring. With similar motivation, Justi enthusiastically proposed a strategy to promote the birth of children. He professed concern about what he regarded as a large number of lower-class women who lacked dowries and therefore were unable to marry and bear offspring. This circumstance represented the loss of a potential economic resource, namely population. On the premise that ancient societies often had taken measures to ensure that women, whether rich or poor, beautiful or ugly, were able to marry, he proposed the establishment in each county of a government-supervised fund for dowries. This insurance program would procure its capital from a tax of one Reichsthaler, twelve Groschen per year for each girl under twelve years and double this for daughters between the ages of twelve and twenty-four. Fathers would pay the tax annually on the girls' birthdays. Justi calculated that if this were invested in solid securities paying five percent annually, each young woman could draw a fifty Reichsthaler dowry from it between her twenty-fourth and thirty-sixth year and still leave the principal in the account to accrue interest. If the woman was not married by the age of thirty-six, there was probably little hope of finding her a partner, so she could collect her fifty Thaler anyway, as her life support; so, like female education, the dowry insurance fund would keep single women from burdening the economy. Fathers of the propertied classes could contribute double the amount, and their daughters would have dowries of 100 Reichsthaler, as was befitting their estate.[32]

Enthusiastic about the powers of the state and the circulation of capital, Justi sought to develop principles that would enhance the well-being and happiness of society *(Glückseligkeit)*. One of his most important books was *Die Grundfeste der Macht und Glückseligkeit der Staaten* (The Foundations of Power and of the Happiness of States), and he explained its title this way:

> One cannot imagine a thorough and enduring happiness of a state that is not based on a sound administration of human affairs *[Polizei]*. How will a state ever achieve a secure and well-founded happiness if the welfare of individual families is not placed in appropriate union and association with the ... state?"[33]

In his fervor for new affiliations between individuals and governments, he reformulated his culture's gender hierarchy. His unique proposal for state-supervised dowries was based on the notion that women's economic role was to produce children who would enhance civil society's productive output of capital.

It was not new to regard women as childbearers; in the normative patrimonial household, reproduction had also been an economic function, through which women would gain status by bearing heirs and thus ensure the continuity of families *(Geschlechter)*. Novel in Justi's conception was the idea that women's duty to produce heirs was owed to the state, not to the moral household or the genealogical family. Otherwise Justi largely ignored the female half of the population; his formulaic words about the wife of the estate manager were patronizing, stressing the subordinate and helping function of women and discounting their expertise as well as the male-female reciprocity of responsibilities. Justi separated agriculture, where women worked, from what he specified as the main part of the economy; thus he excluded women from economic activity, although they were important as child bearers and directors of the household. He was working with ideas that would soon become widespread: that gender or sex *(Geschlecht)*, not family *(Geschlecht)*, determined one's place in life.

Justi, like his successor in Vienna, professor of Cameral Sciences Joseph von Sonnenfels (1733-1817), was influential in fashioning a language of economics that prevailed until after the French Revolution. Sonnenfels' *Grundsätze der Polizey, Handlung, und Finanzwissenschaft* (Principles of Polizei, Commerce, and Financial Sciences) was reprinted and used as a textbook until well into the nineteenth century. In this work, dedicated to Emperor Joseph II, Sonnenfels predictably defined the state as the central organ of society that brings security to its people, ensures their welfare, and expresses the common will. The government presided over the interests of civil society. A major theme was freedom of trade, through which these lofty goals were to be achieved. Through the powers of *Polizei*, the state's authority to ensure the well-being of its citizens, government agents, including schoolmasters and priests, would safeguard freedom of property and free commerce, while guaranteeing that people would not break civic rules. In a subsequent publication, *Politische Abhandlungen* (Political Essays,1777), Sonnenfels stressed that the state must foster both domestic and foreign trade. He pointed out how much conditions in his day had improved because governments wielded appropriate authority in such matters, as compared with previous eras when "commerce was left completely to private persons." One of Sonnenfels' key concepts, *ökonomischer Handel*, which he used to mean international trade – including one of his favorite types, re-exportation of previously imported goods – illustrates how much the definition of economics had changed in a century. The association of the economy with the household – *oikos* – had largely disappeared. Now the object of the economy was lively domestic and international market exchange under the watchful supervision of the prince.[34]

The eighteenth-century Cameralists set themselves apart from the moral household economists in several ways that intensified the impact of their ideas. They rejected Aristotelian models; they embraced a secular world view; they insisted that their disciplines could be plied only in universities or scientific academies; they intentionally separated the economy of the civil society from that of the private household; and they posited the state as the source of human order and prosperity. They also insisted that the objective of economic activity was making money, thus enhancing one's wealth and position. The Cameralists were a self-selected group of men with shared contextual and constitutive values. A world apart from the Christian-Aristotelian economists, they were cosmopolitans who believed that cities could contribute more to human welfare than agriculture could.

Repudiating the aristocratic value system, the Cameralists claimed for the middle classes the right to arbitrate society's economic and social norms. In disavowing Aristotelian ideals, they were not professing complete objectivity the way their positivist successors of a century later would. They were excited about the ways in which their science could serve dynastic rulers in the improvement of the whole of society. They emphasized the identity between the state and the doctrines of economics, and in contrast to their predecessors, they increasingly viewed private behavior as a matter of public concern.

In recasting the paradigms of economics, the Cameralists maintained androcentric values that transcended social class. Their combination of new economics and reformulated notions about gender magnified the normative distance between male and female. The Cameralists extracted economics from the realm that included females and made it a masculine undertaking. They linked the now male field of economics with the power of the ruling prince – with control, manipulation, exploitation, and profits. They defined the female economic role largely by omission, but they associated women with the private sphere, childbearing, and helping – in short, with an emerging, middle-class notion of domesticity. Their scientific, statistical approach would have been distasteful to the old economists, because it rejected the human, moral, and religious constructions that the latter believed gave form and integrity to economic life.

New Visions Competing with Old

If the Cameralists established new views of agriculture, the economy, and the household, they did not completely expunge the old economic ideals. The publishers who continued to reissue Coler's, Hohberg's, and Florinus' monumental works until the 1750s would not have done so if there had been no market for them. It is understandable that in a tradition-oriented agricultural culture, old tested beliefs would have enduring appeal. Hence, the idiom of the *Hausvater* and the *Hausmutter* endured tenaciously in the German vocabulary throughout the eighteenth century. It is easy to imagine young noble estate proprietors eager to make the seventeenth-century masters the cornerstone of their estate libraries, unaware of – or resistant to – the transforming language of the university-trained State Scientists and civil servants. Thus two visions of the ordered world rivaled one another for much of the eighteenth century,[35] and this competition was facilitated by the fact that the Cameralists, while insisting on their new conceptions, never completely rejected the language of the household. It served their objectives rhetorically to retain elements of the traditional vocabulary, lending an aura of familiarity to ideals that otherwise would have appeared extreme and severe.

Yet the Cameralists formulated new perspectives that would impact social norms for succeeding generations. Their ideals helped reshape the social construction of gender in the prevailing agrarian society. Some writers, such as the Saxon civil servant and economist Heinrich August Fischer (d. 1781), were enthusiastic about the gendered construction of the new economics. In the 1775 edition of his book on economic history, he pointed out that in the not too distant past, economics had been in the hands of "servants and women" *(Knechte und Weiber)*. However, this was changing, he happily declared, due to the work of the Cameralists. Economics was becoming a serious subject of study at universities where men were now sending their most capable sons to learn its principles. In the "hoary ... Middle Ages," he wrote, "Germans had been satisfied just to eat, and they did not even care about eating well. But recently, "the Germans have pulled themselves out of ignorance." What they need to do now is devote more attention to the study of *"Oeconomie- und Polizeywesen,* also called *Politico-Camerale* or *Domesticum."*[36]

Enthusiastic about their abilities to engineer social improvements, the Cameralists advocated new ecological norms, calling for governmental control over people's lives and human manipulation of land and natural resources. Exploitation of the soil for profit in order to achieve happiness for all *(Glückseligkeit)* replaced the idea of household need *(Hausnotdurft).* The Cameralists conceptualized humans as distinct from – and dominant over – nature. They redefined their own world by setting it apart from the female realm yet insisted on patriarchal dominance in the home, incrementally formulating a new type of gender hierarchy.

Notes

1. Herman Freudenberger, "Government and Economy: Introduction," in Ingrao, *State and Society,* 142-43. Finley, "Aristotle." S. Meikle, "Aristotle and Exchange Value," in *A Companion to Aristotle's "Politics"* ed. David Keyt and Fred D. Miller, Jr. (Oxford: Blackwell, 1991), 156-81. Carlo Natali, "Aristote et la chrématistique," in *Aristotles' "Politik": Akten des XI. Symposium Aristotelicum, Friedrichshafen/Bodensee, 25.8.-3.-9.1987* ed. Günther Patzig (Göttingen: Vandenhoeck & Ruprecht, 1990), 296-324. Burkhardt, Oexle, and Spahn, "Wirtschaft," 561-67. Dittmar, *Die deutschen Kameralisten,* 40-42, 44-46, 59-62, 66. Tribe, *Governing Economy,* 78-90. Brückner, *Staatswissenschaft,* 43-51. Vierhaus, *Deutschland im Zeitalter des Absolutismus,* 46. On early-modern trade and commerce, see the following: Dülmen, *Entstehung des frühneuzeitlichen Europa,* 364-67; Kriedte, *Spätfeudalismus und Handelskapital,* 100-115; Richarz, *Herrschaftliche Haushalte in vorindustrieller Zeit,* 67-188; Hermann Kellenbenz, "Gewerbe und Handel 1500-1648," in *Handbuch,* ed. Aubin and Zorn, 1:414-64. Zorn, "Gewerbe und Handel," in Ibid., 1:531-73.

2. Johnann Joachim Becher, *Politische Discurs, von den eigentlichen Ursachen des Auff- und Abnehmend der Stadt, Länder und Repbulicken in specie, wie ein Land volkreich und nahrhaft zu machen und ir eine rechte Societatem civilem zu bringen*, 3d ed. (Frankfurt: Zunner,1688; repr. Auvermann, 1972), 10, 101-102. Wilhelm von Schröder, *Fürstliche Schatz- und Rent-Cammer* (1682), excerpted in Krauth, *Wirtschaftsstruktur und Semantik*, appendix, 246-47. Viet Ludwig von Seckendorff, *Teutscher Fürsten Stat, Oder: Gründliche und kurtze Beschreibung welcher Gestalt Fürstenthümer Graff- und Herrschaften im H. Römischen Reich Teutscher Nation, welche Landes, Fürstliche und hohe obrigkeitliche Regalia haben von Rechts- und loblicher Gewohnheit wegen beschaffen zu seyn...* 3rd ed. (Hannau, 1665; repr. Auvermann 1976), vol 1, 222.

3. Franz Philipp Florinus, *Oeconomus Prudens et Legalis Continuatus: Oder Grosser Herren Stands und Adelicher Haus-Vatter* (Nürnberg, Frankfurt and Leipzig, 1719). Troitzsch, *Ansätze technologischen Denkens*, 42-44. Richarz, *Oikos, Haus und Haushalt*, 163-67.

4. David F. Lindenfeld, *The Practical Imagination: The German Sciences of State in the Nineteenth Century* (Chicago: University of Chicago, 1997), 11-45. Keith Tribe, "Cameralism and the Science of Government," *Journal of Modern History* 56 (1984), 263-284. Burkhardt, Oexle, and Spahn, "Wirtschaft," 569-573. Keith Tribe, *Governing Economy: The Reformation of German Economic Discourse 1750-1840* (Cambridge: Cambridge University, 1988), 35-54. William Bleek, *Von der Kameralausbildung zum Juristenprivileg: Studium, Prüfung und Ausbildung der höheren Beamten des allgemeinen Verwaltungsdienstes in Deutschland im 18. und 19. Jahrhundert*, Historische und Pädagogische Studien, vol. 3 (Berlin: Colloquium, 1972), 65-69. Vierhaus, *Deutschland im Zeitalter des Absolutismus*, 37. Erhard Dittrich, *Die deutschen und österreichischen Kameralisten*, Erträge der Forschung, vol. 23 (Darmstadt: Wissenschaftliche Buchgesellschaft, 1974), 30-34. Brückner, *Staatswissenschaften*, 60-91. Franz-Ludwig Knemeyer, "Polizeibegriffe in den Gesetzen des 15. bis 18. Jahrhunderts: Kritische Bemerkungen zur Literatur über die Entwicklung des Polizeibegriffes," *Archiv des öffentlichen Rechts* 92 (1967): 153-180, esp. 166-68. Hans Erich Bödeker, "Das staatswissenschaftliche Fächersystem im 18. Jahrhundert," in *Wissenschaften im Zeitalter der Aufklärung* ed. Rudolf Vierhaus (Göttingen: Vandenhoeck & Ruprecht, 1985), 143. Michael Stolleis, *Geschichte des öffentlichen Rechts in Deutschland*, vol. 1, *Reichspublizistik und Policeywissenschaft, 1600-1800* (Munich: Beck, 1988), 234-38, 366-83. Zorn, "Gewerbe und Handel 1648-1800," 1:571. Gerhard Stavenhagen, *Geschichte der Wirtschaftstheorie*, Grundriss der Sozialwissenschaft, vol. 2 (Göttingen, Vandenhoeck & Ruprecht, 1969), 23-28.

5. Dülmen, *Entstehung des frühneuzeitlichen Europa*, 321-66. Vierhaus, *Deutschland im Zeitalter des Absolutismus*, 45-46. Hans Rosenberg, *Bureaucracy,*

Aristocracy and Autocracy: The Prussian Experience, 1660-1815, Harvard Historical Monographs, vol. 34 (Cambridge, MA: Harvard University, 1958), 27-45. Anton Tautscher, *Staatswirtschaftslehre des Kameralismus* (Bern: Francke, 1947). Ingomar Bog, "Mercantilism in Germany," in *Revisions in Mercantilism*, ed. D.C. Coleman, Debates in Economic History (London: Metheun, 1969), 162-89. Hans-Joachim Braun, "Economic Theory and Policy in Germany 1750-1800," *Journal of European Economic History* 4 (1975): 301-22.

6. Brückner, *Staatswissenschaften*, 112-228. Horst Dreitzel, *Protestantischer Aristotelismus und Absoluter Staat: Die "Politica" des Henning Arnisaeus (ca.1575-1636)*, Veröffentlichungen des Instituts für Europäische Geschichte Mainz, vol. 55, Abteilung Universalgeschichte (Wiesbaden: Steiner, 1970), 170-259. Dittrich, *Die deutschen Kameralisten*, 52-55, 58-62, 68-72. Mikulá_ Teich, "Interdisciplinarity in J.J. Becher's Thought," *History of European Ideas* 9 (1988), 145-60. On the Cameralists' concepts of agriculture, see Sigmund von Frauendorfer, *Ideengeschichte der Agrarwirtschaft und Agrarpolitik im deutschen Sprachgebiet*, 2nd ed. (Munich: BLV, 1963), vol. 1, 126-41.

7. Rosenberg, *Bureaucracy*, 46-56. Stolleis, *Geschichte des öffentlichen Rechts*, 141-224.

8. Bödeker, "Das staatswissenschaftliche Fächersystem," 143-62. Fritz Hartung and Rudolf Vierhaus, eds., *Der Akademiegedanke im 17. und 18. Jahrhundert*, Wolfenbütteler Forschungen, vol. 3 (Bremen: Jacobi, 1977). Dreitzel, *Protestantischer Aristotelismus*, 1-12. Grimm, *Deutsches Wörterbuch*, vol 14, part 2 (1960): 781-98. Helmuth Kiesel and Paul Münch, *Gesellschaft und Literatur im 18. Jahrhundert: Voraussetzungen und Entstehungen des literarischen Markts in Deutschland*, Beck'sche Elementarbücher (Munich: Beck, 1977), 207-08. Notker Hammerstein, *Aufklärung und katholisches Reich: Untersuchungen zur Universitätsreform und Politik katholischer Territorien des Heiligen Römischen Reichs deutscher Nation im 18. Jahrhundert*, Historische Forschung, vol. 12 (Berlin: Duncker & Humblot, 1977), passim. Brückner, *Staatswissenschaften*, 56-60.

9. Rohr, *Compendieuse Haushaltungsbibliotheck*, 2. Troitzsch, *Ansätze technologischen Denkens*, 45-54. Brückner, *Staatswissenschaften*, 3, 56-60. Dittrich, *Die deutschen Kameralisten*, 76-81, 142-43. Inama, "Julius Bernhard von Rohr," in *Allgemeine Deutsche Biographie*, vol. 29 (1889), 62-64. Richarz, *Oikos, Haus und Haushalt*, 182-83.

10. Tribe, "Cameralism," 265-68. Bödeker, "Das Staatswissenschaftliche Fächersystem," 145-50. Paul, *Deutsches Wörterbuch*, 630. Dittrich, *Die deutschen Cameralisten*, 92. Johann Peter Sh8milch, *Die Göttliche Ordnung in den Veränderungen des menschlichen Geschlechts, aus der Geburt, dem Tode und der Fortpflanzung desselben erwiesen*, 3rd ed. (Berlin: Süßmilch, 1756). Johann Peter Süßmilch, "On Removing Obstacles to Population Growth,"

trans. Eileen B. Hennessy, *Population Development Review* 9 (1983): 521-29. On the advocacy of academic chairs of economics, see Simon Peter Gasser, *Einleitung zu den Oekonomischen Politischen und Kameralwissenschaften, worin für dieses mal die Oeconomico-Cameralia von den Domainen oder Cammer auch andern Gütern, den Administration und Anschlägen, so wohl des Ackerbaues als andere Pertinentien halber, samt den Regalien angezeigt und erläutert werden* (Halle: Wäydenhaus, 1729), 3-5.

11. Brückner, *Staatswissenschaften*, 54. Stolleis, *Geschichte des öffentlichen Rechts*, 340-41. Tribe, "Cameralism," 268.
12. Johann Georg Meusel, *Lexikon der vom Jahr 1750 bis 1800 verstorbenen teutschen Schriftsteller*, (Leipzig: 1802-16; repr. Hildesheim: Olms 1968), vol. 15 (1816), 418-24. P. Zimmermann, "Georg Heinrich Zincke," in *Allgemeine Deutsche Biographie*, vol. 45 (1900), 313-15. See Brückner, *Staatswissenschaft*, 80-91. Georg Heinrich Zincke, *Allgemeines Oeconomisches Lexicon* (Leipzig: Gleditsch, 1731; 3rd ed. 1744).
13. The articles, "Haushalten;" "Haushalter, Oeconomus;" "Haushälterin;" "Haushaltung;" "Haushaltungs-Buch;" "Haushaltungs-Geschäffte, Wirtschaffts- oder Nahrungs-Geschäffte;" "Haushaltungs-Kunst, oder die Kunst Hauszuhalten; Oeconomie, Oeconomische Wissenschaft;" "Haus-Mutter, Haus-Wirtin;" "Haus-Vater; Haus-Wirt;" "Wirtschafft", in Zincke, *Allgemeines Oeconomisches Lexicon*, 1093-1103, 1107-10, 3234-66. Heinrich Wilhelm Döbel, *Geschickter Hausvater und fleissige Hausmutter, oder kurze, doch gründliche Einleitung zur Haushaltung oder Landwirthschaft, nebst einer nützlichen Hausapothecke*, ed. G.H. Zincke (Leipzig, 1747; rev. ed., 1771).
14. Julius Bernhard von Rohr, *Vollständiges Haußwirthschafts-Buch, welches die Hauswirthschaffts-Regeln, die so wohl in Ansehung der Oeconomie überhaupt als insonderheit bey dem Feld-Bau, der Viehzucht, der Gärtnerey, den Jagt- und Först-Sachen, Fischereyen und Teichen, dem Kochen, Confitüren, Wein-Bau, Bierbrauen, und andern nöthigen Materien sich applieren Lassen, ohne Einmischung fremder Sachen gründlich und ordentlich vorträgt* ... (Leipzig: Gleditsch, 1722), 415. Rohr, *Compendieuse Hauushaltungsbibliothek*, 3.
15. Johann Heinrich Gottlob von Justi, *Staatswirthschaft: oder Systematische Abhandlung aller Oekonomischen und Cameral-Wissenschaften, die zur Regierung eines Landes erfordert werden*, 2nd ed. (Leipzig: Breitkopf, 1758; repr. Aalen: Scienta, 1963), vol. 1, xi, 61-62.
16. Erhard Dittrich, "Johann Heinrich Gottlob Justi, Cameralist," in *Neue Deutsche Biographie*, vol. 10 (1974), 707-709. Tribe, *Governing Economy*, 55-90.
17. Johann Heinrich Gottlob von Justi, *Die Grundfeste der Macht und Glückseligkeit der Staaten; oder ausführliche Vorstellung der gesamten Polizeiwissenschaft* (Königsberg: Hartung, 1760; repr., Aalen: Scienta, 1965), vol. 2, 19-46. Justi, *Staatswirthschaft*, 1:491. Wolfgang Mager, "Republik," in *Geschichtliche Grundbegriffe*, vol. 5 (1984), 571-618.

18. Justi, *Staatswirthschaft*, 1:438-44, 468-69. Johann Heinrich Gottlob von Justi, "Von Einrichtung der Steuern und Abgaben in einem Staat," in *Gesammelte politische und Finanz-Schriften über wichtige Gegenstände der Staatskunst, der Kriegswissenschaften und des Kameral- und Finanzwesens* (Copenhagen: Roth, 1761), vol. 1, 365-79, quotation from 367. Süssmilch, "On Removing the Obstacles," 526. Autorenkollektiv, *Grundlinien des ökonomischen Denken in Deutschland: Von den Anfangen bis zur Mitte des 19. Jahrhunderts*, ed. Akademie der Wissenschaften der DDR, Schriften des Zentralinstituts für Wirtschaftswissenschaften, vol. 3, (Berlin: Akademie, 1977), 189-94.
19. Justi, *Staatswirthschaft*, 1:491-96. Justi, *Grundfeste*, 1:302-52. Mack Walker, "Rights and Functions: The Social Categories of Eighteenth-Century Jurists and Cameralists," *Journal of Modern History* 50 (1978): 241-43 and passim.
20. Justi, *Staatswirthschaft*, 1:493, 523-24. Justi, *Grundfeste*, 148-70. Ingrid Mittenzwei, "Die Agrarfrage und der Kameralismus," in Harnisch and Heitz, *Deutsche Agrargeschichte des Spätfeudalismus*, 169-180.
21. Justi, *Staatswirthschaft*, 1:323-24, 521, 546-47.
22. Ibid., 1:522.
23. Ibid., 1:522-23, 533, 549-55. Frauendorfer, *Ideengeschichte*, 136-37. On reclamation of swamps, moors, and heaths in Justi's time, see Rudolf Berthold, "Wachstumsprobleme der landwirtschaftlichen Nutzfläche im Spätfeudalismus (zirka 1500 bis 1800)," in Harnisch and Heitz, *Deutsche Agrargeschichte des Spätfeudalismus*, 58-75; and Peter Kriedte, *Spätfeudalismus und Handelskapital: Grundlinien der europäischen Wirtschaftsgeschichte vom 16. bis zum Ausgang des 18. Jahrhunderts* (Göttingen: Vandenhoeck & Ruprecht, 1980), 132-33.
24. Rohr, *Vollständiges Hauß-Haltungs-Recht*, 83. Richarz, *Oikos, Haus und Haushalt*, 185-86.
25. Rohr, *Vollständiges Hauß-Haltungs-Recht*, 169.
26. Ibid., 169-72.
27. Justi, *Staatswirthschaft*, 1:546.
28. [Johann Heinrich Gottlob von Justi], "Vorschlag von Errichtung einer Akademie für das Frauenzimmer," *Ergetzungen der vernünftigen Seele aus der Sittenlehre und der Gelehrsamkeit überhaupt*, vol. 5, no. 1 (1747): 312-13.
29. Ibid., 314.
30. Ibid., 314-16.
31. Ibid., 322-25.
32. Süßmilch, "On Removing the Obstacles," 525-26. Justi, *Grundfeste*, 1:221. Johann Gottlob von Justi, *Grundsätze der Polizeywissenschaft in einem vernünftigen, auf den Endzweck der Polizey gegründeten, Zusammenhänge und zum Gebrauch akademischer Vorlesungen, abgefasset*, 3rd ed. (Göttingen: Vandenhoeck, 1782; repr., Frankfurt: Sauer & Auvermann, 1969), 76-106. On pop-

ulation policies in the absolutist states, see Ute Frevert, "Frauen und Ärzte im späten 18. und frühen 19. Jahrhundert – Zur Sozialgeschichte eines Gewaltverhältnisses," in Kuhn and Rüsen, *Frauen in der Geschichte* II, 179-82.

33. Justi, *Grundfeste*, 1:7. See Ulbrich Engelhardt, "Zum Begriff der Glückseligkeit in der kameralistischen Staatslehre des 18. Jahrhunderts (J.H.G. v. Justi)," *Zeitschrift für Historische Forschung* 8 (1981): 43, 49-64.

34. Joseph von Sonnenfels, *Grundsätze der Polizey, Handlung und Finanzwissenschaft* (Vienna, 1765-67); I have used the second edition (Vienna: Kurtzböck, 1768), 82-83 and passim. Joseph von Sonnenfels, *Politische Abhandlungen* (Vienna: Edlen, 1777; repr., Aalen: Scientia, 1964), 1-9, 82-92.

35. Rebel argues, in contrast to my interpretation, that the two traditions were more similar than different and that both contributed to a philosophical basis for a "police state." Rebel, "Reimagining the Oikos," 59-60, 71-75.

36. Heinrich August Fischer, *Versuch einer historisch-pragmatischen Beschreibung des alten deutschen Oekonomie und des in der Folge der Zeit, daraus erwachsen deutschen fürstlichen Cammerwesens* (Leipzig: Breitkopf, 1755); I have used the 1775 edition, 1-2, 7, 27. On Fischer, see Johann Georg Meusel, *Lexicon der vom Jahr 1750 bis 1800. verstorbenen teutschen Schriftsteller* 3 (1804), in *Deutsches Biographisches Archiv*, fiche 322, frame 410; Güntz, *Handbuch der landwirtschaftlichen Literatur*, 3:72

Chapter Four

The Enlightenment

Civil Society and Middle-Class Males as the Arbiters of Social Norms (1750-1790)

The changing economic thought of Johann Gottlob Justi and Joseph von Sonnenfels was but a single facet of a Europe-wide cultural phenomenon, the Enlightenment. This new constellation of values was characterized by an emphasis on rational problem solving and a belief that social change could bring increased happiness and prosperity to humans. Most Enlightenment thinkers advocated belief in the inherent worth and dignity of individual human beings. Yet there were many "Enlightenments," and the thought of those who saw themselves as partisans of this new intellectual movement was rife with contradictions. Many attacked the privilege of the nobility on the grounds that it was based on the irrational criterion of birth, but they continued to categorize people according to social and gender-based hierarchies. They did not regard as a problem the fact that they themselves constituted a privileged elite grounded on wealth, education, and masculinity. They advocated greater individual freedoms yet envisioned governments with coercive powers.

Notes for this section begin on page 140.

Enlightenment proponents were claiming the right to arbitrate the discourse about the fundamental nature of human society. It was in this context that new ideals about gender and the rural economy were developing. While this chapter does not deal explicitly with either gender or agriculture, it invites the reader to consider that by the mid-eighteenth century it was practically impossible to write about the place of men and women in agrarian life without confronting a compelling new language. This was the urban-centered vocabulary of rationality, of market trade, of social progress, and of new configurations of social hierarchy.

The Enlightenment and Natural Law

Like every new worldview, this one had a long evolution. It grew slowly from perspectives rooted in the Renaissance and Reformation that understood nature and society to be living entities rather than unchanging divine creations. The scientific revolution, beginning in the sixteenth century with discoveries such as those by Polish astronomer Nicolaus Copernicus (1473-1543), seemed to demonstrate that truth could be perceived through empirical observation and experiment and that the universe was governed by Natural Laws rather than by God's will. Copernicus' hypothesis that the sun, rather than the earth, was the center of the universe was just a beginning. There was more to be disclosed, and each new finding – for example, Galileo's moon craters (1609-10) and Newton's mathematical principles (1687) – convinced increasing numbers of educated people that science and change held the secrets to the present and future. It was becoming old fashioned to insist on the primacy of religion and tradition. An early Enlightenment philosopher, Christian Thomasius (1655-1728), stressed the power of reason as embodied in the human mind and rejected "prejudice," beliefs not based on rational principles. Nature itself was the organizing principle of the universe, according to philosopher Christian Wolff (1675-1754), and the decoding of Natural

Law was a corollary of the duty of fulfillment or self-realization, closely related to the idea of the pursuit of happiness.[1]

By the third decade of the eighteenth century, it was easy to identify the proponents and opponents of Enlightenment – *Aufklärung* – thought in German-speaking territories. After the middle of the century, the term *Aufklärung* was integral to the vocabulary of educated classes. By the 1780s multitudes of essays, books, and articles defining the new ways of looking at the world had been circulated. One of the most famous was a treatise by the celebrated Königsberg philosopher Immanuel Kant (1724-1804), "Beantwortung der Frage: Was ist die Aufklärung?" (In Answer to the Question: What is Enlightenment?), Kant claimed that his generation was not yet "enlightened" but that theirs was "an age of enlightenment," denoting the idea of progress always associated with the new views.[2]

The movement's emphasis on the worth of the individual led to the normative ideals of political representation and governmental responsibility to the governed. Its emphasis on Natural Law, rationality, individualism, and positive change reinforced a commitment to education as a means of improving the world. Enlightenment thinkers shared a growing commitment to the values of free markets, free labor, and economic competition. They often criticized religion, rejecting what they considered to be its dogmatic emphasis on unreasoned faith. However some Enlightenment philosophers sought to reconcile Christianity and rational thought. Many believed the ideals of civic freedom were based on Natural Law, but they called on the same principles to justify the rights of the sovereign state to intervene in human affairs.

None of the Enlightenment positions were considered self-evident in the eighteenth century, and much printer's ink was consumed by both the idealists who favored new social paradigms and those who feared the disorder that the new perspectives would bring. By the late Enlightenment, the word *Aufklärung* had assumed a polemical quality; it was hardly possible for a civil servant, a princely ruler, a teacher, a journalist, a merchant, or even a noble estate owner to avoid standing on one side of the Enlightenment debate or the other. Those who favored it had the advantage of the seductive appeal of "progress," but this was also an unsettling concept to a culture that for centuries had valued order more than change. Even ardent supporters of innovation – usually the members of a rising educated, urban elite – carried with them strict notions of social and gender hierarchy that endowed their ideals with a class-specific and gendered character.

Civil Society (bürgerliche Gesellschaft)

Alongside the concept of Nature, stood the notion of civil society, or citizenship *(Bürgertum),* one of the transforming ideas of Enlightenment thought. Prior to the Renaissance, the word "citizen" *(Bürger)* had been used restrictively as a mark of status of "free" (privileged) males, the heads of households. By the middle of the eighteenth century many Europeans, including educated Germans, had begun to employ the rhetoric of freedom as a right rather than a privilege and, hence, to argue that the people who lived in a political principality were citizens *(Bürger),* as opposed to subjects *(Untertanen).* This allowed the philosopher Leibnitz to describe "civil society" *(bürgerliche Gesellschaft)* as a "natural society" of urban and rural members whose goal was the achievement of the well-being of the public. The inclusion of both town and country in the definition embodied a rejection of the traditional notion that society consisted of three separate estates.[3]

While such claims often were intended as criticism of aristocratic privilege, they represented little danger to princely authority. In fact, the opposite often was true. The notion of citizenship implied responsibilities – civic duties – and in fulfilling these, citizens would strengthen the hand of the father of the state *(Landesvater).* In theories of absolutism, the prince was often called the "first citizen."[4]

Justi presented an excellent example of this kind of late-Enlightenment reasoning in his *Grundfeste der Macht und Glückseligkeit der Staaten* (Foundations of Power and Happiness of

States). He declared that a civil society must maintain "good order" in all of its parts: the classes of people must stand in suitable association to one another, for such an arrangement would allow the government to preserve the correct relationship with the governed. The "civic virtues" required of citizens were essential in all kinds of governments, monarchies included. They were neither moral nor religious in principle (but they must not contradict the rules of "true religion"). They constituted the "lawful behavior" of members of the polity in both the cities and the countryside, and they fell under the jurisdiction of *Polizei*. There were three orders of civic duties: those owed to the state; those owed to fellow citizens; and those owed to oneself.[5]

The first category comprised two classes, those imperative to all civil societies and those essential only under certain types of constitutions. Absolutely indispensable virtues in all civil societies, in order of importance, were: obedience; willingness to support the state with one's wealth; fidelity to the state; and placing the common good above one's personal well-being. Without these, a civil society could not exist. The situation-specific virtues were braveness, love of true honor, and industriousness *(Fleiß)*. The latter was required of states that engaged in commerce with others. Under modern conditions it was necessary that citizens "strive through industriousness and skills to increase their income, which itself constitutes the complete power and resources of the state."[6]

The second category of civic virtues, those that citizens owed to one another, included four that were essential: willingness to support the commonweal; justice; honesty; and civility. Some specific constitutional forms required other virtues. Democracies, for example, necessitated a love of equality, and democracies whose citizens engaged in commerce demanded thrift. Aristocracies required restraint. Justi argued that it was necessary to constitutionally establish such civic virtues because people, left to their own devices, were selfish and power-hungry. Nature had not endowed humans with a sense of social responsibility, so order must be achieved through rules.[7]

To the third category of virtues, those owed oneself, there belonged only one essential quality: good management of one's property. It was not that this was the only desirable virtue in this category, but this was the only one that the state could demand. Every state must have "rules of behavior" that applied to all of its subjects, but they were different from "civic virtues," which pertained only to citizens – property owners. In spite of his claim that "states have no authority over moral human virtues," only over "civic virtues," however, Justi felt it important to discuss vital moral virtues that applied to all inhabitants, not just citizens: temperance in food and drink; modesty; and chastity. He maintained that "neither Nature nor reason" dictated moderation and chastity or prevented promiscuity. Uncurbed, Nature would lead to capitulation to lust and desire, although Nature did provide its own "restraints," for example, pregnancy. Reason taught that habitual submission to passion was dangerous to health and would even cause early death. Although Nature did not prevent people from giving way to immoderation, civil law was not an appropriate mechanism of impeding immoderate behavior, because it was impossible for the state to supervise people's private conduct.[8]

Justi's theory of government was based on a new conception of society, one in which people bound themselves together as citizens, not as households. As in the old household, many of the new civic virtues were economic in nature. Unlike in the household economy, the virtues governing society were separate from the rules of morality; the public good was distinct from canons of personal behavior. Yet Justi was not quite willing to refrain from prescribing rules that applied to private conduct. While maintaining that the state did not have the responsibility to govern people's intimate lives, his discussion of such topics reveals an uneasiness about postulating a civic order in which the highest authority had no right to coerce persons to individual goodness.

Justi's rules of society excluded the concept of inherited privilege that had helped sustain the aristocratic culture. They also replaced the Aristotelian ideal of mutual responsibilities within the household with the "essential" civic virtues: support of the common good, justice, honesty and civility. While both the old and the new social orders equated property with entitlement, they differed significantly in their conceptualization of the social organism. The traditional patrimonial household had granted citizenship to the head only but nevertheless had included all members, even the propertyless – females, children, and servants. Varying widely in rank and privilege, they all held certain rights based on their membership in the household economy. Through this they gained status, even if a low one within the hierarchy of the home. Justi's more modern scheme was based on the axiom that those who possessed no property remained outside the civic order. Not surprisingly, Sonnenfels agreed and closely tied the notion of civil society *(bürgerliche Gesellschaft)* to business. He argued that free will and freedom of trade were the primary guarantees a state must offer its citizens, even though, he said, the goal of securing this for "every individual" was unobtainable.[9] The equation of property with citizenship later would become a sustaining feature of nineteenth-century bourgeois society.

The New Middle Class

Enlightenment ideas notwithstanding, the landed aristocracy retained a dominant position in eighteenth-century society. Neither escalating numbers of educated bourgeois civil servants at the German princely courts, nor the increasing contact between landed nobles and merchants (who for example, shipped the estate-produced grains oversees) softened the barriers between the estates. Agricultural property and the title in one's name still distinguished the aristocracy from the rest of society in real human intercourse. And agrarian production prevailed as the most important sector of the economy. But the university-educated civil servants, journalists, lawyers, authors, artists, doctors, and professors, through their acceptance of Enlightenment ideals, were adopting a sociopolitical vocabulary that gave them a certain social power. They were society's leading "citizens," in the new sense of the word. The Enlightenment idea of civil society accompanied the escalating economic and political importance of a new urban elite.

Study at Germany's new and reformed universities was becoming a key to success and professional standing for the sons of urban families. Academic training helped create almost a new estate of education, the so-called *Bildungsbürgertum*. They were joined in the last half of the century by a class of increasingly important leaders of business and commerce who no longer found their optimal interests to be within the tightly controlled guilds. These urban leaders thus rejected the estate-bound vision of society and endorsed an ideal of mobility, change, and citizenship. The growth of the absolute state contributed to the rise of the new middle class. Princes needed highly trained specialists to staff their administrative offices, and they often recruited nonnobles in sometimes conscious efforts to erode the traditional powers of the landed elite. Civil servants assumed a loose and informal corporate identity, the *Beamtenstand*. This group's demand for expertise, in turn, strengthened the hands of the universities, and rulers were pleased to put resources into the academic institutions that trained their staffs. Chances for social success sometimes were greater within the state and church bureaucracies than they were in entrepreneurship; nevertheless an important, growing class of retailers, shippers, bankers, grain exporters, and "manufacturers" occupied Germany's preindustrial landscape,[10] men who would constitute the civil society as envisioned by Justi and Sonnenfels.

As the new middle class assumed social prominence many cities were physically expanding (although some maintained a relatively stable population and others declined). While the centers of social power were shifting slowly from noble manors to princely courts, the capitals and trading centers of the territorial states were replacing some of the medieval "imperial cities" in importance. Berlin was a dramatic example. In 1709 this capital of the Hohenzollern lands extended its urban borders to include surrounding villages giving it a population of 57,000 inhabitants; by 1750 it had nearly doubled in size to 113,289. In 1790 its numbers had climbed to 150,803, making it – after Vienna, with 250,000 – the second largest city of German-speaking Europe. The Pomeranian seaport Stettin, on the mouth of the Oder River, which had come under Prussian jurisdiction in 1720 with 6,000 inhabitants, had more than tripled in size, to 23,000, by 1800. Bonn, a princely residence, expanded from 4,000 in the first half of the century to 10,000 by 1790. Many university towns flourished as well. Göttingen numbered 4,506 people in 1735, just as its university was founded. Fifty-one years later it had grown to nearly twice this size, to 8,144. Königsberg, not only a university city but a lively seaport and a military garrison, doubled its size between 1722 (24,990) and 1785 (48,692). Both figures exclude the military personnel stationed there and the estimated 700-800 inhabitants of the city's "Great Hospital." The growth of the cities was often erratic, and some of the medieval trading and administrative centers of the old Holy Roman Empire, such as Augsburg, were in decline; new hubs of culture and trade, such as Frankfurt am Main and Leipzig, were expanding. In general, the size and dynamism of towns and cities was on the rise in the eighteenth century. This was a development related to the enhanced position of the educated urban elites. The Enlightenment found its strongest centers of support in the bustling commercial cities, and in some princely courts, far more than on the landed estates of the powerful nobles.[11]

Hamburg, situated on a naturally protected harbor, the wide estuary of the Elbe, was a city of expanding commercial importance whose ships traversed the globe. With an advanced banking system modeled in part on that of Amsterdam, Hamburg exhibited a stunning example of capital accumulation in the eighteenth century. This was due in significant measure to the growth of three unique branches of manufacture: calico printing, sugar refining, and cigar manufacturing – all based on complex networks of world trade. Hamburg's new wealth was concentrated in the hands of enterprising families but typically not those of the old merchant guilds, many of whom were experiencing hard times. The thriving pre-industrial manufacture depended on a flexible supply of wage earners unbound by guild regulations. Hamburg became an unusually mobile society in the eighteenth century and grew to a population of 100,000, making it Germany's third-largest city.[12]

Expansion in the publishing business in the eighteenth century was an outward sign of the dynamism of the newly educated middle classes. Possibly four times as many books were coming into the readers' market at the end of the century as at the beginning. The part of the population that possessed the education, the economic resources, and the leisure to form a reading public was still a fraction of the whole, perhaps no more than 15 percent. Nevertheless Germany's new civil servants, lawyers, educators, and business leaders were avid readers, seeking to know more about the political, economic, social, and natural world about them. The "moral weeklies," inspired in part by Addison's and Steele's *Spectator* of London, were the first German publications designed and marketed for a widespread, popular readership. As the name of the genre implies, they sought to establish values and manners for everyday life, implicitly replacing the "sermons on the Christian household" of an earlier century and were written for women as well as men. The number of titles grew to over one hundred between 1720 and 1770. Twelve to fifteen thousand individuals read Hamburg's *Patriot*. Leipzig, Germany's foremost publishing center, produced a large number of the weeklies, but many middle-sized and small towns throughout Germany published them as well. In the first half of the century, they were produced largely in Protestant areas, but after 1760 they also popularized Enlightenment ideas in Austrian and Bavarian cities as well as in the ecclesiastical principalities. This fashionable medium accustomed large numbers of the population to gaining information and values through the printed word.[13]

The hunger for reading materials, as well as for a forum in which to discuss the new ideas coming into vogue, led to the popularity of reading societies. Typically these associations built their own libraries and subscribed to newspapers and journals. Their memberships consisted primarily of male, middle-class leaders of their respective cities; some counted aristocrats among their members, although always in a minority. The groups commonly adopted bylaws that obligated them to meet on a regular basis in such a manner as to prevent their becoming mere social organizations; they saw themselves not only as engaging in enjoyable intellectual discourse but also as assuming responsible civic tasks. In 1780 there were about fifty reading societies – mostly in northern Germany – and in the next twenty years their numbers exploded. By the 1790s there were as many as two hundred throughout the German landscape, including Catholic regions. Before the fashion faded, approximately 430 reading associations had been founded in German-speaking lands.[14]

Reading associations were only one variety of middle-class societies that discussed a host of contemporary issues, including poverty, health care, prostitution, commercial affairs, agrarian production, hereditary servitude, and the German language. The academies of science were in many ways similar to the reading societies, except that their membership was restricted to academics who cultivated an exclusive and scholarly style. The international Freemason movement, a network of secret societies that included both middle-class and noble members, took root in German towns in the 1730s, and lodges sprang up rapidly by the 1760s. The Freemasons sought to promote Enlightenment goals and ostensibly remained secret to ensure their freedom of ideas.[15]

Additionally, a whole category of "patriotic and public-interest societies" dotted the maps of the towns and principalities of the Holy Roman Empire by the end of the century. "Patriotic" in this context indicated honesty, integrity, and a love of civic virtue, not necessarily allegiance to a nation-state as the term would soon come to mean, although the patriots of specific cities and principalities often insisted on the superiority of their own version of citizenship. Enlightenment proponents also associated the word "patriotism" with commerce, market exchange, economic growth, private property, and freedom. Sonnenfels, in Austria, wrote that "ownership of land and personal freedom make a land of farmers into patriots." The Hamburg Patriotic Society (officially, "the Hamburg Society for Promotion of the Arts and Practical Trades") was one of the most active and served as a model for many others. It grew from a membership of ninety-six in 1765 to 514 by the end of the century. Most members were merchants, and membership was almost a prerequisite to election to the city's governing bodies. The patriotic society sponsored public competitions in which contestants presented written treatises recommending solutions to social, economic, political, or social problems, a favored technique in the eighteenth century for stimulating and disseminating new ideas. It fostered the founding of new schools and supported the building of roads, bathing facilities, firehouses, and a savings bank. In the 1780s it took a leading role in the reorganization of the city's relief system for the poor.[16]

Germany's new "citizens" – enthusiastic to disperse new ideas and solve society's problems – were privileged males. Alongside the Enlightenment's normative claim of universal citizenship, the old-regime assumption that property ownership was a condition of "freedom" remained unchallenged. Only the sons of well-to-do families attended universities, and normally only sons inherited family businesses. Small cliques of property owners governed the growing cities. In late eighteenth-century Hamburg, 3-4 percent of the populace of 100,000 was eligible to elect the 300-350 members of the governing councils, which were dominated by merchant families and a few professionals. The Freemasons, the reading clubs, the science academies, and the patriotic societies were male associations. Most of their constitutions did not explicitly prohibit women, artisans, workers, or servants among their membership. However, it seldom occurred to anyone to admit persons of these categories into their numbers. Between 1759 and 1785, the Bavarian Academy of Sciences was composed of people belonging to the following groups: court officials, civil servants, professors, historians and archivists, doctors and natural scientists,

Catholic and Protestant theologians, and "other professions," clearly not classifications that included women or working men. Of the 282 honorary members and the 206 regular members of the German Society of Göttingen between 1738 and 1755, there were twelve females, 2.45 women for every hundred men. They were registered simply as "women," while other members were identified by their profession or estate. Possibly they were widows who were allowed to maintain memberships of their former husbands. Some of Berlin's less prestigious reading societies allowed females to join. This practice was controversial and often drew criticism from the male members.[17]

Attacking the "Problems" of Poverty and Ignorance

These privileged men of the Enlightenment were not oblivious to the fact that they lived among a larger population who were not members of the "civil society." This situation presented certain problems that the Enlightened were eager to solve. While they attacked the critical issue of hereditary aristocratic privilege by insisting on a society of civic virtue, they also debated the challenges of poverty, infanticide, harsh and arbitrary justice, and the place of women.

Patrons of the Enlightenment seized on poverty as one of many problems requiring a solution on the road to a society of happiness. Ranging from the philosophers who contemplated the poor in their libraries to members of city councils who encountered beggars as they traveled from their residences to the city halls, the men who believed in civil society regarded poverty as an unseemly blight to be eradicated. The visible increase of poor people in both city and countryside catalyzed debates on this issue. Many who sought solutions were motivated by simple fear of the potential disruptive behavior of unemployed "mobs." Poverty was a problem to be solved through good *Polizei*, an ordered governmental policy. The old, religious approaches of alms giving fell into disrepute. A wisely planned economy would have little indigence, because it would enable people to sustain themselves. The eighteenth century accepted the premise that it was a government's responsibility to ensure every willing worker a means of livelihood. Hence, regulation of business was essential.[18]

Cameralists, the Enlightenment figures whose specific calling was to formulate economic, social and political policies, often believed there were distinct categories of impoverished folk: the lazy or undeserving poor; the worthy poor who, though willing to work, had encountered misfortune; and the truly destitute, including the elderly, the infirm, and propertyless widows. The latter category should be helped for humane reasons. The undeserving should be left to their own resources. The most important category, the worthy poor, should be placed in workhouses, manufacturing institutions that lodged, fed, and minimally paid people until they could recover control of their own destinies. In Cameralist theory, the workhouses would teach discipline and skills and turn the impoverished into productive supporters of the economy and state. They also would deter those who might try to take advantage of the system and beg for a living when they could be honestly laboring. Workhouses would strengthen the state. This cause went hand-in-hand with a well-ordered taxation program and a sound business economy. Justi put it this way:

> There is only one single means ... of controlling begging .... One must without delay detain all young, healthy, and strong beggars ... and confine them to specific workhouses in order to compel them to work .... This method promises sure success, for if the strong beggars and vagrants know that they will be locked up and forced to labor, then they will either leave the land of their own volition or will choose to work and support themselves honestly .... Freedom is precious to every individual.[19]

While the Enlightenment concern with poverty was far removed from the medieval notion that God intended some to remain poor, the Cameralistic stratagem of workhouses was not entirely new. Workhouses had been part of the urban landscape in many European cities, since at least the sixteenth century. The main innovation in the era of Enlightenment was their more widespread acceptance. There was a double message in the workhouse solution to poverty. On the one hand it was based on the notion that individuals could improve their economic conditions if they had the right skills and attitudes; and on the other, it was built on the suspicion that impoverishment was itself a sign of culpability. The language of punishment and assistance was intertwined in the debates on poverty. In the 1780s the Royal Society of Sciences of Göttingen sponsored a contest, offering a prize for the best tract on the establishment of "work-houses and prisons." Many agreed with Justi that the punitive quality of the workhouse was a positive incentive. Correct demeanor in the workhouse would prove a pauper's right to regain "freedom."[20]

By the 1780s some Enlightenment thinkers sought to explain poverty as a factor of the larger economic system. Johann Georg Büsch (1728-1800), a Göttingen-trained theologian, economist, and mathematician who devoted his career to improving the civic life of his native city, Hamburg, did not regard laziness as the sole cause of mounting indigence in his bustling seaport. Büsch, well known throughout Germany as a pioneer in the theory of capital circulation and fiscal policy, was the most influential member of the Hamburg Patriotic Society as well as cofounder and director of the city's Academy of Commerce, founded in 1768. He was one of Germany's most sophisticated theorists of the market economy at the time the Scottish philosopher Adam Smith was composing his *Wealth of Nations*. Büsch argued that capital must not merely be present in a society but circulate through the hands of all classes, the prosperous and unpropertied alike. He believed Hamburg's poverty to be caused by the failure of wealth to circulate to those at the lower end of the economic ladder. Büsch proposed a four-part plan for reforming Hamburg's treatment of the poor: First, they should be provided medical care so that they would be healthy enough to be productive. Second, a system of neighborhood or district welfare organizations should be established to ensure that administrators of relief would be in personal communication with their clients. Third, there should be a factory for the poor to work in, but not a workhouse, for workhouses had a bad reputation because of their coercive conditions. And fourth, the city should establish an information-distribution system for the lower classes; knowledge of the world around them and of opportunities was a prerequisite to making the system work for themselves. Under the sponsorship of the Patriotic Society, Hamburg put some parts of this scheme into effect in its reforms of 1786-1788.[21]

Enlightenment proposals to deal with poverty were based on the assumption that the changes occurring in society were positive and merely needed to work better. Büsch's ideals were among the few that recognized poverty was systemic rather than due to individual sloth. The manufacturing and world-trade system of Hamburg and of many other cities constituted a shock to the agrarian-based economy and introduced competition into an order formerly regulated by guilds. Büsch's proposal was to make this system more benign. The empowerment of the new middle class would be more threatened by bands of beggars than by its transformation into wage laborers. Eighteenth-century designs for eliminating destitution romantically envisioned that the poor would eventually join "civil society." More concretely, the planners pictured a situation in which the poor were no longer an embarrassment, a menace, or a strain on the state or the republic. Bands of tramps were a sign that society was not "happy."

The Enlightenment placed great emphasis on education as a fundamental means of improving society. Reasoning that correct information and rational thought were the basis for intelligent behavior, eighteenth-century social planners, in a veritable flood of publications, advocated the establishment of schools and other institutions of learning. In response to this burst of enthusiasm, some commentators identified their age as the "pedagogical century." The philosopher Kant wrote: "The individual can become human only through education. A person is nothing except that which is created through education." Social progress was obtainable as individuals cultivated their minds through schooling:

> Perhaps education will continually improve, and every successive generation will come a step closer to the perfection of humanity .... People are just now beginning to understand correctly ... what a good education actually embodies. It is delightful to imagine that human nature can be continually improved through education .... This opens to us the prospect of a future greater happiness of the human race.[22]

The notion of training young people for adulthood is as old as civilization, but the German Enlightenment brought new meanings to both the idea of humanistic education *(Bildung)* and the notion of practical schooling *(Erziehung)* in German-speaking regions. Since that time, "education" has implied schooling outside the home. In the eighteenth century there was a marked escalation in the formal training of children in public, private, and religious institutions, and this went hand in hand with a rise in literacy and in the circulation of published materials. Territorial rulers founded increasing numbers of schools, and several principalities established rules of compulsory attendance.[23]

The century's most famous European pedagogical thinker, Jean-Jacques Rousseau (1712-1778), stressed education as means to develop the individual into the mature citizen. His pedagogical novel *Émile*, translated into German soon after it was published, was exceedingly popular among the middle classes, and for a generation Émile and Héloise (another Rousseau character) became fashionable children's names. *Émile* profoundly affected German educational thought. Rousseau emphasized that a young boy's intellectual curiosity, combined with a teacher's skill in the use of reason and logic, would lead the youngster to high levels of sophistication, personal development, and academic achievement. The lessons and laws of Nature, discovered as a result of following innate curiosity rather than through forced instruction, would

Enlightenment

bring the young Émile to a state of maturity. Implicitly, this kind of education would improve all of society by making youngsters into rational citizens.[24]

A generation of "Philanthropinists," as German educational reformers called themselves, echoed Rousseau's ideals as they developed concrete plans for schools. Johann Bernhard Basedow (1724-1790) disseminated Rousseau's philosophy in his pedagogical writings and gained the attention of Prince Leopold Friedrich Franz of Anhalt-Dessau (1751-1817), who appointed him to establish a model school in Dessau, which Basedow called the Philanthropin. This laboratory of the Enlightenment, attended chiefly by middle-class boys attracted notice throughout Germany, and over sixty schools patterned themselves after Basedow's experiment. Johann Heinrich Campe (1746-1818), who spent some time as a teacher in Basedow's Philanthropin, became superintendent of education in the Duchy of Braunschweig-Wolfenbüttel under Duke Karl Wilhelm Ferdinand (1780-1806), and Campe established a pedagogical publishing house in Braunschweig from which he produced scores of books stamped with Rousseau's philosophy. In 1789-1791 he published a new translation of *Émile*. Campe stressed the inherent virtue of individuals: "The human being is by nature good-tempered. That means, in the first place, that all of [a person's] abilities, strengths, and drives ... aim ... at goodness and the well-being of the individual, and of others in association with him." The renowned Swiss educator Johann Heinrich Pestalozzi (1746-1827) wrote about education for the peasants. His educational novel *Leinhard und Gertrud* (1781-87) chronicled episodes in the lives of a simple, but enlightened, farm couple who taught their children to learn by questioning what they found around them in their household, barnyard, and community.[25]

Pedagogical architects devised model curricula in language, history, geography, civics, physical education, and other subjects. The number of schools grew at a rapid rate. In spite of these developments, however, most German boys and girls did not spend their days in schoolhouses. The majority of urban children from the propertied classes in the eighteenth century prepared for adulthood under their parental roofs as their forbears had done. Lower-class and lower-middle-class children learned by performing jobs in their parents' households and workplaces as soon as they could be productive. Often left with little social supervision, they learned social skills from their peers. And if formal schooling played a minor role in the socialization of urban youth, it was even less important in the village, even though the schoolmaster was becoming a more familiar figure in the rural landscape by the end of the century.[26]

A favored project of the reformers was the creation of "industry schools" *(Industrie-Schulen)* designed to educate urban and rural children of the lower classes. "Industry" was a concept in transition. In its Greco-Latin origins, it meant simply "diligence" or hard work; and it came with this heritage into common usage in Germany, probably from the French in the seventeenth century, and was used interchangeably with the German word *Fleiß*. In the eighteenth century, whose most influential thinkers were excited about the new economics, the word came to be associated with the work done in manufacturing, but without losing its earlier connotations. Reference works in Germany published as late as the mid-nineteenth century still used the old, qualitative definition: diligent labor. When pedagogical reformers of the Enlightenment proposed and built "industry schools," they did so with lofty, romantic goals, like those of Campe:

> If one wishes to reform a nation, if one wants to form rational, clever, skilled, diligent and valiant human beings, then [one must] give up the old ways … . Nowhere but in schools can a nation be educated to *Industrie* and to every other moral and political virtue.

On a practical level the Philanthropists intended to teach youngsters how to be arduous or "industrious" workers. Industry schools sprang up throughout the German urban landscape. Campe in

Enlightenment

Braunschweig, the Göttingen pastors Ludwig Gerhard Wagemann (1746-1804) and Arnold Wagemann (1756-1834), and Friedrich Eberhard von Rochow (1734-1805), Cathedral Canon of Halberstadt, designed such institutions as answers to the pressures on the rural population, the breakdown of the household economy, and the growth of the landless class. Their desire was to turn otherwise unproductive young boys into industrious workers, and their model was wage earning.[27] The "enlightenment" of the lower classes was based on the expectation that the very poor would become day laborers rather than irrational bands of unemployed beggars.

Frederick the Great argued in an essay entitled "Über die Erziehung" ("On Education," 1769), that one of the most important responsibilities of a wise monarch was the education of subjects in order to produce "useful and virtuous citizens." The youth must be taught industriousness *(Fleiß)*. They must be educated so that they would learn to work independently. "I am convinced that [through education] one can make out of people what one wants," asserted the enlightened monarch. Eighteenth-century educational ideals often combined the new emphasis on the state with emphasis on the development of the individual, resulting in the ideal that education was to form obedient, productive, morally conforming "citizens."[28] Education might provide social stability in an age when ideals of individualism, freedom, and self-determination threatened the fabric of hierarchical society.

The Civil Society

Enthusiastic about Nature's laws, rationality, the powers of the state, economic growth in a commercial economy, and social mobility for themselves, the self-named citizens of civil society created a cultural arena in which the value system of the aristocracy and the ideal of the household were becoming increasingly irrelevant. However, they never envisioned a society that was not based on a class and gender hierarchy. In the name of the good of all society – but often meaning for the good of the educated and propertied – the state could coerce and restrain its people and involve itself in their private lives on a scale not previously envisioned. The new civil society represented an emancipation of some middle-class males from the constraints of an aristocratically dominated culture. The propertied, masculine citizens of civil society were appropriating for themselves the right to be the arbiters of society's normative values.

Notes

1. Werner Schneiders, *Die wahre Aufklärung: Zum Selbstverständnis der deutschen Aufklärung* (Freiburg: Alber, 1974). Werner Schneiders, *Aufklärung und Vorurteilskritik: Studien zur Geschichte der Vorurteilstheorie*, Forschungen und Materialien zur deutschen Aufklärung, Abteilung II: Monographien, vol. 2. (Stuttgart-Bad Cannstatt: Frommann-Holzboog, 1983), 92-120. Hans-Martin Bachmann, "Zur Wolffschen Naturrechtslehre," in *Christian Wolff 1679-1754: Interpretationen zu seiner Philosophie und deren Wirkung*, ed. Werner Schneiders, 2nd ed., Studien zum achtzehnten Jahrhundert, vol. 4 (Hamburg: Meiner, 1986), 161-70.
2. Rudolf Vierhaus, "Aufklärung als Emanzipationsprozeß," *Aufklärung als Prozeß*, Aufklärung: Interdisziplinäre Halbjahresschrift zur Erforschung des 18. Jahrhunderts und seiner Wirkungsgeschichte, vol. 2, no. 2 (1987), 9-18. Horst Stucke, "Aufklärung," in *Geschichtliche Grundbegriffe*, vol. 1 (1972), 243-342. Immanuel Kant, "Beantwortung der Frage: Was ist Aufklärung" (1784), in *Werke*, ed. Ernst Cassirer (Berlin: Cassirer, 1922-23), vol. 4, 167-76. Franklin Kopitzsch, "Einleitung: Die Sozialgeschichte der deutschen Aufklärung als Forschungsaufgabe," in *Aufklärung, Absolutismus, und Bürgertum in Deutschland*, ed. Kopitzsch. (Munich: Nymphenburg, 1976), 11-167.
3. Schlumbohm, *Freiheit*, 48-66. Manfred Riedel, "Gesellschaft, Bürgerliche," in *Geschichtliche Grundbegriffe*, vol. 2 (1975), 719-745. Christopher Link, "Rechtswissenschaft," in Vierhaus, *Wissenschaften im Zeitalter der Aufklärung*, 131-36.

4. Riedel, "Bürger," 681-87. Diethelm Klippel, "Von der Aufklärung der Herrscher zur Herrschaft der Aufklärung," in *Aufklärung als Mission: Akzeptanzprobleme und Kommunikationsdefizite/ La mission des Lumières: Accueil réciproque et difficultés de communication*, ed. Werner Schneiders, Das achtzehnte Jahrhundert, Supplementa, vol. 1; Colloques de Luxembourg, vol. 2 (Marburg: Hitzeroth, 1993), 159-74.
5. Justi, *Grundfeste*, 2:195-209. See Münch, *Ordnung, Fleiß und Sparsamkeit*, 19-21, 157-67.
6. Justi, *Grundfeste*, 2:210-23.
7. Ibid., 2:223-36.
8. Ibid., 2:236-50.
9. Sonnenfels, *Grundsätze der Polizei*, 82-83.
10. Rudolf Vierhaus, "Deutschland im 18. Jahrhundert: soziales Gefüge, politische Verfassung, geistige Bewegung," in Kopitzsch, *Aufklärung*, 179-83. Wehler, *Deutsche Gesellschaftsgeschichte*, 1:206-208. Rosenberg, *Aristocracy*, 57-74. Otto Hintze, "Der österreichische und preußische Beamtenstaat im 17. und 18. Jahrhundert, in Hintze, *Regierung und Verwaltung: Gesammelte Abhandlungen zur Staats-, Rechts- und Sozialgeschichte Preußens*, vol. 1 of *Gesammelte Abhandlungen*, ed. Gerhard Oesterreich (Göttingen: Vandenhoeck & Ruprecht, 1962), 321-58. Otto Hintze, "Der Beamtenstand," in Ibid, 66-125. Bleek, *Von der Kameralausbildung zum Juristenprivileg*, 61-82. Bernd Wunder, *Priviligierung und Disziplinierung: Die Entstehung des Berufsbeamtentums in Bayern und Württemberg*, Studien zur modernen Geschichte, vol. 21 (Munich: Oldenbourg, 1978). Waltraud Heindl, *Gehorsame Rebellen: Bürokratie und Beamte in Österreich 1780 bis 1848*, Studien zu Politik und Verwaltung, vol. 36 (Vienna: Böhlau, 1991), 21-52.
11. Harm Klueting, "Stadt und Bürgertum: Aspekte einer sozialen Typologisierung der deutschen Städte im 18. Jahrhundert," in *Stadt und Bürger im 18. Jahrhundert. Das Achtzehnte Jahrhundert*, Supplementa, ed. Gotthardt Frühsorge, Harm Klueting, and Franklin Kopitzsch, vol. 2 (Marburg: Hitzeroth, 1993), 17-39. See articles on middle-class culture of eight individual German-speaking cities and several non-German ones in ibid. Reiner Wild, "Stadtkultur, Bildungswesen und Aufklärungsgesellschaften," in *Hansers Sozialgeschichte der deutschen Literatur*, vol. 3: *Deutsche Aufklärung bis zur Französischen Revolution, 1680-1789*, ed. Rolf Grimminger, 2nd ed. (Munich: Deutscher Taschenbuch Verlag, 1980), part 1, 103-107. Fritz Gause, *Die Geschichte der Stadt Königsberg in Preußen*, (Cologne: Böhlau, 1965-71), vol. 2, 65-295. Heinrich Scheel, *Die Begegnung deutscher Aufklärer mit der Revolution*, Sitzungsberichte des Plenums und der Klassen der Akademie der Wissenschaften der DDR, 1972, no. 7 (Berlin: Akademie, 1973), 3-5, 22.
12. Mary Lindemann, *Patriots and Paupers: Hamburg 1712-1830* (New York: Oxford University, 1991), 39-47.

13. Estimates range from a doubling to a fourfold increase in book publishing. See Wolfgang von Ungern-Sternberg, "Schriftsteller und literarischer Markt," in *Hansers Sozialgeschichte der deutschen Literatur,* 133-135. Kiesel and Münch, *Gesellschaft und Literatur im 18. Jahrhundert,* 154-179. Rolf Engelsing, *Der Bürger als Leser: Lesergeschichte in Deutschland, 1500-1800* (Stuttgart: Metzler, 1974), 182-215. Johann Goldfriedrich, *Geschichte des Deutschen Buchhandels im Auftrag des Börsenvereins der Deutschen Buchhändler,* vol 3: *Geschichte des Deutschen Buchhandels vom Beginn der klassischen Literaturperiode bis zum Beginn der Fremdherrschaft (1740-1804)* (Leipzig: Börsenverein der deutschen Buchhändler, 1909; repr. Leipzig: Zentralantiquariat der Deutschen Demokratischen Republik, 1970), 248. Herbert G. Göpfert, *Vom Autor zum Leser: Beiträge zur Geschichte des Buchwesens* (Munich: Hanser, 1977), 47-62. Herbert G. Göpfert, "Bemerkungen über Buchhändler und Buchhandel zur Zeit der Aufklärung in Deutschland," *Wolfenbütteler Studien zur Aufklärung* 1 (1974): 69-83. Wolfgang Martens, *Die Botschaft der Tugend: Die Aufklärung im Spiegel der deutschen Moralischen Wochenschriften* (Stuttgart: Metzler, 1971), 15-403. Gause, *Die Geschichte der Stadt Königsberg,* 2:232-43.

14. Marlies Prüsener, "Lesegesellschaften im achtzehnten Jahrhundert: Ein Beitrag zur Lesergeschichte" *Archiv für Geschichte des Buchwesens,* special issue, vol.13 (1972), Frankfurt am Main: Buchhandler Vereinigung, 370-594, esp. 379-87. Herbert G. Göpfert, "Lesegesellschaften im 18. Jahrhundert," in Kopitzsch, *Aufklärung,* 403-11. Otto Dann, "Lesegesellschaften und die Herausbildung einer modernen bürgerlichen Gesellschaft in Europa," in *Lesegesellschaften und bürgerliche Emanzipation: Ein europäischer Vergleich,* ed. Dann (Munich: Beck, 1981), 9-28. Richard van Dülmen, *Die Gesellschaft der Aufklärer: Zur bürgerlichen Emanzipation und aufklärerischen Kultur in Deutschland* (Frankfurt am Main: Fischer Taschenbuch Verlag, 1986), 82-90. Engelsing, *Der Bürger als Leser,* 216-58. Göpfert, *Vom Autor zum Leser,* 76-85.

15. Rudolf Vierhaus, "Aufklärung und Freimaurerei in Deutschland," in *Das Vergangene und die Geschichte: Festschrift für Reinhard Wittram zum 70. Geburtstag,* ed. Rudolf von Thadden, Gert von Pistohlkors and Hellmuth Weiss (Göttingen: Vandenhoeck & Ruprecht, 1973), 23-41. Dülmen, *Gesellschaft,* 11-132, passim, esp. 70-72. Wolfgang Hartwig, "Verein, Gesellschaft, Geheimgesellschaft, Assoziation, Genossenschaft, Gewerkschaft," in *Geschichtliche Grundbegriffe,* vol. 6(1990), 791-801.

16. Rudolf Vierhaus, "'Patriotismus' – Begriff und Realität einer moralisch-politischen Haltung," in *Deutsche patriotische und gemeinnützige Gesellschaften,* ed. Vierhaus (Munich: Kraus, 1980), 9-29. Joseph von Sonnenfels, *Ueber die Liebe des Vaterlands* (Vienna, 1771), 46, quoted in Ernst Wangermann, "Joseph von Sonnenfels und die Vaterlandsliebe der Aufklärung," in *Joseph von Sonnenfels,* ed. Helmut Reinalter, Veröffentlichungen der Kom-

mission für die Geschichte Österreichs, vol. 13 (Vienna: Österreichische Akademie der Wissenschaften, 1988), 162. Franklin Kopitzsch, "Die Hamburgische Gesellschaft zur Beförderung der Künste und nützlichen Gewerbe (Patriotische Gesellschaft von 1765) im Zeitalter der Aufklärung: Ein Überblick," in Vierhaus, *Deutsche patriotische und gemeinnützige Gesellschaften*, 75-103. Lindemann, *Patriots and Paupers*, 100-34.

17. Dülmen, *Gesellschaft der Aufklärer*, 40, 49. Göpfert, "Lesegesellschaften," 406-407. Wolfram Suchier, "Die Mitglieder der Deutschen Gesellschaft in Göttingen von 1738 bis Anfang 1755," *Zeitschrift des historischen Vereins für Niedersachsen* 81 (1916): 44-124. Deborah Hertz, *Jewish High Society in Old Regime Berlin* (New Haven, CT: Yale University, 1988), 90-91.

18. Michael Doege, *Armut in Preußen und Bayern (1770-1840)*, Miscellanea Bavarica Monacensia, vol. 157: Neue Schriftenreihe des Stadtarchivs München (Munich: Kommissionsverlag UNI-Druck, 1991), 32-163 passim. Christoph Sachße and Florian Tennstedt, *Geschichte der Armenfürsorge in Deutschland* (Stuttgart: Kohlhammer, 1980), 125-39. Justi, *Grundfeste*, 1:264-71.

19. Justi, *Staatswirthschaft*, 1:323-24. Similarly, see Justi, *Grundsätze der Polizeywissenschaft*, 287-89.

20. See August Friedrich Rulffs, *Ueber die Preisfrage der königlichen Societät der Wissenschaften zu Göttingen: von der vortheilhaftesten Einrichtung der Werk- und Zuchthäuser* (Göttingen: Rosenbusch, 1783).

21. Erich Döhring, "Johann Georg Büsch," in *Neue Deutsche Biographie*, vol. 3 (1957), 3. Eulen, *Vom Gewerbefleiß*, 144-55. Zorn "Gewerbe und Handel 1648-1800," 571. Lindemann, *Patriots and Paupers*, 93-95, 100-35.

22. Helmut König, *Zur Geschichte der Nationalerziehung in Deutschland im letzten Drittel des 18. Jahrhunderts*, Monumenta Paedogogica, vol. 1 (Berlin: Akademie, 1960), 40-47, 69-71. Immanuel Kant, "Über Pädagogik" (1803), in *Werke* ed., E. Cassirer (Berlin: Bruno Cassirer, 1923), 8:459-60.

23. Rudolf Vierhaus, "Bildung," in *Geschichtliche Grundbegriffe*, vol. 1 (1972), 508-23. Hermann Lange, *Schulaufbau und Schulverfassung der frühen Neuzeit: Zur Entstehung und Problematik des modernen Schulwesens*, Pädagogische Studien, vol. 12 (Weinheim: Beltz, 1967), 260-72. Ulrich Herrmann, "Aufklärung als pädagogischer Prozeß: Konzeptionen, Hoffnungen und Desillusionierungen im pädagogischen Denken der Spätaufklärung in Deutschland," in Vierhaus, *Aufklärung als Prozeß*, 35-55. König, *Zur Geschichte der Nationalerziehung*, 51-71. Mary Jo Maynes, *Schooling for the People: Comparative Local Studies of Schooling History in France and Germany, 1750-1850* (New York: Holmes & Meier, 1985), 33-50. Kopitzsch, *Aufklärung*, 68-69.

24. Jean-Jacques Rousseau, *Émile, ou de l'éducation* (La Haye: Néaulme, 1762); I have used the Everyman's Library Edition, trans. Barbara Foxley (London: Dent, 1974). *Gesamtverzeichnis*, 120:138. Engelsing, *Der Bürger als Leser*,

327-28. Susan L. Cocalis, "Der Vormund will Vormund Sein: Zur Problematik der weiblichen Unmündigkeit im 18. Jahrhundert," *Amsterdamer Beiträge zur neueren Germanistik*, special edition: *Gestaltet und Gestaltend: Frauen in der deutschen Literatur*, Vol.10 (1980): 46-48.

25. Rudolf Biermann, "Erziehungsmittel oder Erziehungsmassnahme? Zur Wandlung der philanthropischen Pädagogik bei Basedow, Campe, und Salzmann," *Paedogogica Historica* 2 (1972), 342-69. Quotation from Campe's *Väterlicher Rath für meine Tochter* (Braunschweig: Schulbuchhandlung, 1790), in ibid., 354. Otto Friedrich Bollnow, "Johann Bernhard Basedow," in *Neue Deutsche Biographie*, vol. 1 (1953), 618-19. Herrmann, "Aufklärung als pädagogischer Prozeß," 38-51. Johann Heinrich Pestalozzi, *Leinhard und Gertrud: Ein Buch fhr das Volk* (1781; repr. Munich: Winkler, 1977).

26. Jürgen Schlumbohm, "'Traditional' Collectivity and 'Modern' Individuality: Some Questions and Suggestions for the Historical Study of Socialization: The Examples of the German Lower and Upper Bourgeoisies around 1800," *Social History* 5 (1980): 74-89. Anthony J. La Vopa, *Prussian Schoolteachers: Profession and Office, 1763-1848* (Chapel Hill: University of North Carolina, 1980), 11-37. Engelsing, *Der Bürger als Leser*, 137-62.

27. Dietrich Hilger and Lucain Hölscher, "Industrie, Gewerbe," in *Geschichtliche Grundbegriffe*, vol. 3 ((1982), 237-42. Ursula Aumüller, "Industrieschule und ursprüngliche Akkumulation in Deutschland: Die Qualifizierung der Arbeitskraft im Übergang von der feudalen in die kapitalistische Produktionsweise," in *Schule und Staat im 18. und 19. Jahrhundert: Zur Sozialgeschichte der Schule in Deutschland*, ed. Klaus L. Hartmann, Franz Wenzel, and Hans Waldeyer, Edition Suhrkamp, vol. 694 (Frankfurt: Suhrkamp, 1974), 43-46. Joachim Heinrich Campe, *Über einige verkannte wenigstens ungenützte Mittel zur Beförderung der Industrie, der Bevölkerung und des öffentlichen Wohlstandes* (Wolfenbüttel: Verlag der Schulbuchhandlung, 1786; repr. in series Paedagogica, Frankfurt am Main: Sauer & Auvermann, 1969), 16 and passim. See Gernot Koneffke, "Einleitung," in ibid, V-LXIX. Georg Christoph Hamberger and Johann Georg Meusel, *Das gelehrte Deutschland: Oder Lexikon der jetzt lebenden Schriftsteller*, 5th. ed. (Lemgo: 1796-1834; repr. Hildesheim: Olms, 1966), vol.1, 533-40, vol 8, 286-87, vol. 10:493. Binder, "Friedrich Eberhard Freiherr von Rochow," in *Allgemeine Deutsche Biographie*, vol. 28 (1889), 727-34.

28. Friedrich der Große, "Über die Erziehung," in *Die Werke Friedrichs des Großen in deutscher Übersetzung*, trans. Friedrich von Oppeln-Bronikowski, ed. Gustav Berthold Volz (Berlin: Hobbing, 1913) vol. 8, 257-62. See also Wilhelm Rasch, "*Mensch, Bürger, Weib:* Gender and the Limitations of Late 18th-Century Neohumanist Discourse," *The German Quarterly* 66 (1993): 22.

Chapter Five

The Enlightenment and the "Character of the Sexes" (1750-1790)

The eighteenth century's redefinition of human norms presented a special question to philosophers and social architects: did civil society include women? A few early Enlightenment writers, such as Johann Christoph Gottsched (1700-1766) called upon women, like men, to join the educated world of scholars. In his moral weekly, *Die Vernünftigin Tadlerinnen* (The Intelligent Women Critics) Gottsched criticized the foolishness of female fashions, which might limit women's scholarly pursuits. Nevertheless he could not free himself from the notion that women had "other duties" as well – motherhood, wifehood, neighborliness, and friendship.[1]

If the number of publications that discussed women's place is an indication of the intensity with which the topic struck contemporaries, the question of gender truly hit a nerve in these changing times. By the last quarter of the century, pamphlets, educational tracts, journal articles, sermons, novels, poems, plays, and philosophical treatises on the place of women in society circulated

Notes for this section begin on page 168.

in enormous numbers. In their zeal to understand and classify the human being, Enlightenment proponents embarked on a quest for the "character of the sexes." Observing differences between men and women, most assumed that these were to be explained by the Laws of Nature. As the discussion proceeded, Gottsched's encouragement of women to join the intelligentsia fell largely on deaf ears; the almost unanimous conviction of Enlightenment thinkers was that women did not belong in the public sphere. Philosophers, educators, and jurists held that the human world was naturally divided between a public and a private sphere and that women's place was in the latter. Very few disagreed.

Protofeminist Ideals and Strong Women

In 1774 the publishing house of Christian Friedrich Voß in Berlin issued an anonymous advice book entitled *Über die Ehe* (On Marriage). The work was an immediate success and was revised and reissued at least thirteen times over the next fifty years. The author, who kept his identity secret for over twenty years until his death in 1796, was the Prussian civil servant Theodor Gottlieb von Hippel. Only then did contemporaries learn that Hippel had anonymously published this work as a part of a literary outpouring of novels, poetry, plays, hymns, and essays on social and political themes, which, when posthumously collected, filled thirteen volumes.[2]

A disciple of the Enlightenment, Hippel was very interested in gender. He was also an unconventional personality. Following a precocious childhood in a devout, Pietist, middle-class household, he studied theology and law at the Enlightenment-influenced University of Königsberg. He then embarked on a career of rapid advancement in Frederick the Great's absolutist bureaucracy in Prussia, holding a series of distinguished positions in the Prussian royal court of law, the Königsberg municipal council, and the royal tax bureaucracy. A leader in the Masonic Lodge, he was also mayor of the city, a member of the prestigious commission that advised the king on matters under discussion for the famous Prussian General Law Code. In the spirit of the Enlightenment, he developed concrete plans for a "Citizens' School" in Königsberg but the school did not come to fruition because of conservative opposition from the royal bureaucracy in Berlin.[3]

Reportedly of shy temperament, Hippel nevertheless carried on an illustrious public life. Both the oligarchic merchant families of Königsberg and leaders of the provincial nobility maintained high respect for him despite the fact that in his appointed offices he was answerable to the royal government rather than local guilds and estates. A lifelong bachelor, he was a familiar figure among the literary circles in the city. He enjoyed friendships with the philosopher Kant and the essayist Johann Georg Scheffner.[4]

Scheffner acted as an intermediary between Hippel and the Voß publishing house, enabling Hippel to concealing his career as an author. He experimented with highly introspective forms of literature that were later definitive in the development of the modern German novel.[5] Much of his writing reflects the goal of popularizing the ideals of the Enlightenment, and in many genres he sought to define the meaning of "self." Hippel believed that the rationality of the Enlightenment was compatible with the tenets of Christianity.

In many ways the first edition of *Über die Ehe* is clearly an artifact of a male-dominated society. An advice book designed to tell readers how to be successful in marriage, it celebrated matrimony and affirmed husbands' authority over wives: "The business of ruling is that of men, and ... every husband is judge in his household ... . Nature itself has declared women unfit to rule." It depicted women as the bearers and protectors of purity and took for granted that they could not participate in public affairs.[6]

In spite of this juridical language, Hippel emphasized the human individuality of persons in such a way that women could have understand his work as an affirmation of their place in the human community. He denounced traditions associated with marriage that limited the partners' free will. He argued that matrimony was an institution based on mutual love and criticized arranged marriages, the norm of his day, on the grounds that they were effected for the benefit of parental families, not the bride and groom. According to Hippel, even the prevailing notions about the proper age for marriage were "prejudices" that could stand in the way of two persons' life decisions. In an era practically obsessed with justifying cultural norms by equating them with Nature, Hippel openly argued that definitions of puberty were cultural and had nothing to do with Nature. He stressed that the inner being of a person – not parental desires or society's standards – should determine an individual's destiny, be that person male or female, young or old.[7]

Hippel wrote playfully but with serious intent about the German word *Frauenzimmer*, that in Luther's day had denoted the room in which the mistress oversaw the activities of the women of the household but later came to stand collectively for the community of women in the house, and finally for the individual woman of rank. Hippel pondered whether this curious evolution was shaped by the fact that property was transferred to a household in marriage as the bride's dowry. Parents were misguided, he complained, when they required that potential spouses possess wealth. Hippel also criticized the social coercion to marry, arguing instead for freedom of choice. He protested that the state involved itself in marriages, making matrimony into a "political institution" rather than a contract between individuals. He could have been referring to the Cameralist goals of controlling marriage in order to increase population, or to Prussia's limitation of marriages between members of different estates, which were thought to threaten the hierarchical social stability. It was a tradition as ancient as Rome, Hippel said, for governments to force people to marry and "still in many parts of Germany one will find certain small punishments for those who do not marry within a few years after becoming [adult] citizens." Love, he insisted, was the appropriate basis for marriage. Love brought out people's humane qualities.[8]

Hippel's definition of marriage, a state into which two persons of opposite sex entered on the basis of individual choice, implied equality of the partners. He denounced social conventions that made wives appendages of their husbands, such as the custom of addressing them by titles based on their spouses' status. And he asked why women were forced to forfeit their names when they married, a practice he felt obscured their true identity. Thus Hippel protested that conventional marriage destroyed a woman's personhood.[9]

Hippel stressed the contractual nature of matrimony. He disputed the traditional axiom that marriage's purpose was to produce heirs. Neither procreation nor sexual consummation were indispensable ingredients of the consensual contract, he declared. Hippel proposed that the ultimate purpose of marriage was mutual, lifelong support, and he proclaimed that each couple should decide together how they wished to conduct its life affairs. He suggested that marriage, like any contract, had the possibility of dissolution should it be flawed. He insisted unequivocally that the contract must sustain a woman left in widowhood. A widow was economically vulnerable, and she should never have to subordinate her welfare to that of her heirs, who were younger and could make a new start for themselves. "A widow is always a cripple," he wrote.[10]

Thus in 1774 Hippel published a book that embodied formulaic patriarchal stereotypes characteristic of his era but nevertheless criticized the subordination of wives to husbands. He described marriage as a relationship that should be entered solely on the basis of individual will. Each marriage must rest on the firm foundation of a love and mutual pledge intended to sustain the two partners.

As Hippel was experimenting with the idea of marriage of equals, a few female writers suggested strong roles for women by creating dynamic, successful women as characters in novels. Sophie von Sternheim, the heroine of Sophie von La Roche's (1730-1807) novel *Geschichte des Fräulein von Sternheim* (The

Story of Fräulein von Sternheim), when faced with male manipulation, intrigue, and deception, responded with an inner strength of emotion and intellect. This empowered her to maintain dignity in otherwise victimized situations and even to help other unfortunate women. Within the confines that society set for females of her class, La Roche, Germany's first widely acclaimed female novelist, served notice that women could exhibit Enlightenment qualities of reason, learning, and altruism. La Roche remained active as a writer, and later in her life she founded and published *Pomona für Teutschlands Töchter* (Pomona for Germany's Daughters), the first woman's journal of wide circulation published by a woman. La Roche consciously produced a gender-specific message designed to empower women. A product of her age, she was caught in an increasingly prevalent tendency to characterize women as "different," but in this context she illustrated through her life and writing that women could function in a public sphere and could come to one another's support.[11]

Another important way in which some women participated in public life was as the illustrious hostesses of eighteenth-century salons, the regular meetings of prestigious scholars and dignitaries for the purposes of intellectual discourse. Salons were a part of the political world, often serving as arenas for the conduct of urban, provincial, or princely affairs away from the city halls or royal palaces. In Berlin, Henriette Herz (1764-1847), Rahel Levin (1771-1833), and Sara Levy (1761-1854) were respected as members of the city's intelligentsia, and all of these Jewish women contributed to a lively intercourse between the Jewish and non-Jewish elites of Berlin. Elizabeth Staegemann (1761-1835) of Königsberg hosted a salon, whose regular members included Kant, Hippel, and Scheffner. She earned the respect of many on the account of her intellectual and artistic talent, and her pleasant personality. Later in Berlin she reestablished her salon, which was a frequent meeting place of the philosopher Johann Gottlob Fichte, the poet Clemens Brentano, and Rahel Levin Varnhagen, whose collected works comprise ten volumes.[12]

Salon members took seriously the early-Enlightenment dictum that women should be educated in aesthetic and pragmatic arts as articulated by a female voice in Hamburg's moral weekly, *Menschenfreund* (Friend of Humanity): "Are we not rational creatures just as men are? And do we not have the same right as they to enlighten our understanding, to recognize beauty and virtue, and to learn from the fields of knowledge those things that can make us wiser, more congenial and more affable?" But intelligence, learning, and personality alone would not open the way for such a role for a woman. The right social standing, substantial financial means, and usually – though not always – an understanding and supportive husband also were necessary. Henriette Herz quickly lost her illustrious role when her husband died and left her with too few resources to continue the tradition. A woman's intellectual strengths – even those of a very capable woman – could gain no public voice unless she were economically and culturally supported by a man.[13]

The Sexes as Polar Opposites

In spite of Hippel, La Roche, and the illustrious salon leaders, the eighteenth century redefined gender norms in a way that divided the public from the private world more firmly than ever before and rigidly identified the former as a male sphere and the latter as a female one. The shift was apparent in the language itself. The economic term *Hausmutter* – mistress of the household economy – began to fall into disuse by the early eighteenth century. In its place grew the new term of respect for females of high status, *Frauenzimmer*, the word that Hippel found worthy of derision.[14] Generations of people used this word, certainly without considering its etymology or subjective meanings, but the connotations of ornamentation, confinement, and privacy are apparent; and the word represents a significant change from the older form of address, which implied a managing partner in the economy.

Other linguistic metamorphoses reflected the eighteenth-century evolution of the normative meaning of masculine and feminine. The word "gender" *(Geschlecht)* came to be understood in its polar definitions, denoting "male" and "female." Enlightenment philosophers, in their new, secular, rational manner, probed the anthropological purpose of the differences between male and female. The invariable assumptions were that the sexes were opposites and that their antipodal traits, rooted in Nature, were an unalterable part of the logical ordering of the universe. Unlike the household-book authors, who had described men and women in terms of status, economic virtues, and duties, the Enlightenment authors sought to depict the inherent, universal "character" of the two sexes.[15]

The celebrated Kant published his own philosophical explanation of gender differences in his *Anthropologie in pragmatischer Hinsicht* (Anthropology from a Pragmatic Point of View), a compilation of lectures he had used for twenty years or more. This treatise represented Kant's attempt to classify the attributes of the human mind. It was based on the premise that through reason humans had the ability to liberate themselves from a state of Nature in which they had to rely on physical strength to survive. Emancipated individuals relied, instead, on their minds to live together peacefully in civil society. In spite of his postulate that the goal of society was to progress beyond Nature, Kant believed that the opposites he observed in men and women were part of Nature's plan to balance opposing traits. Philosophically Kant regarded both sexes as members of civil society, with each making a unique contribution to its success. However, when he came to his specific discussion of the "character of the sexes," he argued that "strength" distinguished masculinity and "art" characterized femininity. "One can presuppose that Nature's foresight placed more art in the female part [of humanity] than in the male, because it endowed the man with greater strength than woman." Nature's purpose was to make possible the marriage union, for a marriage was not an alliance of equals: "one party must be *subject* to the other, and, reciprocally, one must be *superior* to the other," for otherwise, "self-love" would result in endless fighting between the partners.[16]

Kant believed that in the "raw circumstances" of Nature, women had been like servants or beasts of burden: "The man leads with weapons in his hand, and the woman follows him, loaded with the household belongings." But in civil society this situation had improved, so that women could use their "arts" to balance men's power. "In the *progress of culture*, one of the partners must, in its own way, be the superior; the man over the woman through his physical properties and his courage, and the woman over the man through her natural gift of mastering the man's desire for her."[17]

In contrast to Hippel's idea that marriage was a partnership between two individuals, Kant depicted marriage as a struggle between the sexes, but a struggle that could become civilized through the balance between strength and art. Kant insisted that there was an "equality" in the household and that it derived from an equilibrium of powers:

> The man loves *domestic peace* and readily submits to [the woman's] regime, if only to avoid being prevented from attending to his business. She does not shy from *domestic warfare*, which she wages with her tongue, for the purpose of which Nature gave her a propensity to talk and an emotional eloquence, with which she disarms the man. He relies on the right of the stronger in commanding the household, because he is supposed to protect against external enemies. She [relies] on the right of the weaker in order to have men's protection against men and disarms him with tears.[18]

Searching to justify his claim of civic equality of the sexes, Kant attributed to Nature the polar attributes of masculinity – strength, command, and business external to the household – and femininity – weakness, emotion, conniving, and manipulation. He believed intellect accompanied strength but not weakness: "The educated woman ... uses her *books* much in the same way she uses her *clock*: she carries it around in order that others see that she has one, whether or not it is running or is correctly set by the sun." Moreover, they had different economic roles: "Man's economy is *earning*, woman's is *saving*."[19]

Kant did not contemplate the notion of women outside the home. Kant's "civic equality" of the sexes was to be found only in the household, never in the political or professional world. In his "Metaphysik der Sitten" (Metaphysics of Morals) Kant identified women, servants, minors, and "underlings" *(Handlanger)* as persons who lacked status as citizens because "they have to be under the direction or protection of other individuals."[20]

Optimistic about the progress of his own age, Kant argued that males and females had never been more equal than they were during the Enlightenment. Kant's civil society of equality, based on the struggle between strength and weakness, in fact represented a normative separation of the male and female spheres. It was an attempt to explain humanity in terms of the differences between Nature's inherently masculine and feminine qualities.

In 1787 Ernst Brandes (1757-1810), published a more popular appeal, his essay *Ueber die Weiber* (On Women), because, he said, the intellectuals of his day did not know anything about "the other sex," and there was too much untruth being disseminated on the subject. Using the entire history of Western civilization as his context, the Hanoverian civil servant and publicist argued that women's venturing out of their natural, domestic sphere caused social and moral decay. He believed that the ancient Greeks has reached high cultural achievements by keeping women confined and that the fall of Rome was hastened by the prevalence of females in public affairs. All of this led up to the alarming declaration that the eighteenth century was repeating Rome's mistake. Asserting bluntly that women were naturally inclined to superficiality and lacked intellectual capacity, Brandes spoke for many of his generation, differing from some, however, due to his unwillingness to even consider the premise of equality of the sexes. Brandes had little patience for the principles of the Enlightenment, and in 1784-85 he forged close ties to the British conservative Edmund

Burke. It is significant that a publicist of Brandes' persuasion could have come to the same conclusion about gender as many contemporaries who sought to explain and reinforce Enlightenment ideals: male and female were polar opposites.[21]

Education: Socialization for Separate Spheres

The twin ideals of female domesticity and male superiority were especially formative in the Philanthropinists' ideals on education, most of whom drew their inspiration from Rousseau. In his influential novel *Émile*, Rousseau devoted book five to the appropriate education of Sophie, the future wife of the young man who learned through natural curiosity and experience. Instead of being allowed the freedom to discover the lessons of Nature under the wise guidance of a tutor, as Émile was, Sophie was "destined by the law of Nature" to be Émile's helper and servant. Motherhood and household duties were her calling. She needed to learn needlework but not geography or history. A little training in arithmetic would be useful in her future domestic responsibilities, but too much reading would be harmful. Following this example, the Enlightenment's educational planners without exception proposed separate educational experiences for boys and girls.[22]

Campe, who admired Rousseau, regarded it as "the undisputed will of Nature and human society that the man should be the protector and overseer." He wrote *Väterlicher Rath für meine Tochter* (Fatherly Advice for My Daughter), a young woman's guide to life, in which he emphasized her basic humanity and her uniqueness as a female: "Who are you? You are a *person* and are therefore destined for everything for which the general profession of humanity entitles you. You are a *Lady* ... . Thus you have a double calling, a *general one* and a *special one*, one as *person* and one *as woman*." The entire book stressed the "special" calling of women: motherhood and wifehood. Campe employed old rhetoric to prescribe the new, private, domestic role for women:

You and your sisters are not destined to be just "large children ... fools, or the furies; you are rather created ... to become *wives* who bring happiness, *educating mothers,* and *wise managers of the interior of the household.* Accept your venerable calling with thankful joy!" As wives, you should "sweeten life through tender ... love, care, and concern" for your husbands. You should be mothers "who not only bear children but also plant in them the first germ of human virtues." And as manager of the house, you should, through your "vigilance, order, cleanliness, industriousness, thrift, economic knowledge, and skills, assure the honor, the domestic peace, and the happiness of the earning husband." These wifely and maternal responsibilities were the bonds that would hold together the state and society. "[Although] this seems incredible – not only the domestic happiness of the family but also the public welfare of the state is to a large degree in your hands and depends ... on the manner in which the female sex fulfills its natural and civic role." Campe emphasized that he was writing for the "young of the happy middle class." Much of the book is devoted to the "female virtues": purity of heart, piety, chastity, modesty, friendliness, prudence, love of order, domesticity, and frugality.[23]

The Philanthropinists of the Enlightenment differed from the Cameralists in an important way: whereas the latter tended to devalue private life and moral issues, the educational reformers placed emphasis on the home. Although they supported the development of secular, publicly supervised education, they continued to regard the household as an important atmosphere for inculcation of values. For them the home and its values were important buttresses of the social order. They viewed fathers as educational custodians of the home and depicted mothers as caretakers who had little to do with pedagogy. They urged fathers as well as schoolmasters to adopt the Rousseauean ideal of inquiry and discovery in place of strict memorization. They always depicted schoolmasters as males.[24]

An exception to this pattern was Rousseau's devotee in German Switzerland, Pestalozzi, who idealized the life of the common people, romanticized the home and hearth, and placed the mother

Figure 5.1 Campe romanticized the father-daughter relationship, as illustrated in this frontispiece to *Väterlicher Rath für meine Tochter* (Fatherly Advice for My Daughter, 1786). In the text, he depicted women as having the calling of wifehood and motherhood.

at its center. Hardworking, self-sacrificing, and nurturing, Pestalozzi's fictional heroine, Gertrud, maintained order in the household when her husband was tempted by unwholesome worldly enticements that might have ruined the family. Gertrud's moral authority was something gained naturally through inherited tradition and sensitive intuition. She presided over the arithmetic and reading lessons of her children and others who worked within her family's shop. The village schoolmaster was impressed by this ideal learning atmosphere and employed a woman to assist in the instruction of children in school.[25]

If they disagreed about the relative importance of females and males in education, Campe and Pestalozzi nevertheless concurred that the female role was strictly domestic, and this in an age that increasingly valued activities and sources of authority outside the household. Spokesmen form the Enlightenment generation agreed that science, mathematics, history, and languages were not necessary for female education.[26]

In this view, women should be trained in the fine arts and should, above all, master the arts of domestic life. They were destined for the household life of motherhood, wifehood, love, nurturance, and frugality. Their calling consisted of pleasing their husbands and physically caring for their children. They were not to participate in public life or the world of learning.

The provocative ideals of the civil society, with their vast possibilities for change, must have been simultaneously alluring and unsettling to the male definers of the Enlightenment. Uncertain where their redefinition of human nature would lead, they sought assurance in the proclamation that the home was the enduring source of social order, and they insisted it must be undergirded. Having redefined men's role outside of the household, they charged women with the obligation of maintaining the family and sought to shield them from change. But making females alone accountable for the private sphere, while opening new horizons of mobility in the public and political world for men, did not amount to a maintenance of the status quo for women. It is not that the eighteenth century *invented* the connection between femininity and the home, for the pedagogical and economic literature of the sixteenth and seventeenth centuries clearly upheld this normative ideal.[27] What was new was the simultaneous insistence that the male world was external to the home – and the female world the converse. Relative to men, women of the Enlightenment faced a new type of confinement within the bourgeois society. The language of female inferiority embodied in centuries of misogynous culture was a ready – and perhaps unconscious – tool for the architects of the new civil society.

Changing Norms of Gender and Family under the Law

Not surprisingly, one of the great projects of the Enlightenment, the recodification of laws, reflected the philosophers' and Philanthropinists' debates about gender. Two large German states rewrote their law codes in the last half of the eighteenth century: Bavaria promulgated its Codex Maximilianeus bavaricus civilis in 1756 and Prussia its Allgemeines Landrecht in 1794. Each in its own way reinforced the authority of the male in the household while construing his principal sphere of interest to be external to it.

The Bavarian code was named for Elector Maximilian Joseph III (1745-1777), known as a champion of Enlightenment ideals and as patron of the Bavarian Academy of Sciences. Enacted while Justi was conceptualizing his views on the government and the economy, the Bavarian code had the goal of bringing rational order into the state's civil statutes and hence into the society. Its framers sought consciously to ground their work in the theories of Natural Law. Consciously or unconsciously, they worked to increase the authority of the state over the private lives of subjects. A product of the early Enlightenment, the code employed language reminiscent of the previous century. It named the head of the household the *Hausvater* and stipulated the *Hausmutter* as deputy in his absence. It defined the household as consisting of all who lived with the master, including children, servants, relatives, and relatives-in-law. Marriage was an economic institution whose purpose was mutual support of the spouses and provision for the children. For this reason, marriages were inseparable. Because the husband was head of the family, "his wife is not only subordinate to him in the household but is also obligated to [render] normal and appropriate personal and household services." The marriage brought her a legal and social status equal to that of her husband that she would retain after his death. The law required her to move with him if he changed his residence. And as his economic dependent, she had the right to claim a livelihood "[not] only from her husband, but from his heirs." The code allowed interesting exceptions to this: first, if she could support herself; and second, if the man was without resources. In the latter circumstance, the wife and her heirs must support him.[28]

The principal author of this code, Wiguläus Xaverius Aloysius von Kreittmayr (1705-1790), published an extended commentary interpreting these provisions for his contemporaries. He debated the question of male superiority in marriage, since the foremost Natural Law philosophers, including Christian Wolff, had posited the theory of equality of the two partners (although Wolff had also distinguished between the male virtue, "authority," and the female virtue, "obedience"). Even though Kreittmayr found in Natural Law no justification for male dominance in marriage, he felt obliged to point out that divine law unquestionably supported the principle. The legal scholar Kreittmayr simply could not conceive of an operative egalitarian marriage, although he acknowledged that according to Natural Law theory a couple could bilaterally agree who was to be the superior. Offering the curious parallel of "the so-called Scottish Highlanders who have no trousers," he entertained the idea that it was possible for the man to be not only *de facto* but also *de jure* subordinate. Nevertheless, Kreittmayr concluded, with reductionist logic:

> Because the male sex has been in possession of power for so long, this dispute seems more academic than practical, since the possessors [of authority] will certainly never be displaced from their traditional position by the female sex .... So the man is, and remains, the master of not only his wife but also the whole family. They are always subordinate [to the man].[29]

Kreittmayr offered the explanation that, despite the theoretical equality enunciated by Natural Law, the woman would always defer to the man "partly because she is in some ways subordinate to him, and partly because he has greater presumption, due to his more mature understanding." Since society could not exist without "authority and subordination ... the master is granted a certain type of dominion over the members of his household that is called *Jurisdictionem domesticam*." The Bavarian code affirmed the husband's right to exact corporal punishment.[30]

Bavaria's mid-century codification enhanced the state's role in protecting patriarchy in the household. When Natural Law, the proclaimed foundation of the Maximilian code, posited equality in marriage, its framers fell back upon canon law and mere custom to sustain male authority. The code declared marriage to be an economic contract; but by focusing on the question of authority in the family rather than on productivity and consumption, it disregarded the concept of a self-sustaining partnership, fundamental to the ideal economic household of the seventeenth century. Codification of the law, in itself, emphasized the legal superiority husbands had always enjoyed, at the expense of the economic ideal of shared responsibilities.

The other major codification of the century, the Prussian General Law Code (Allgemeines Landrecht für die Preußischen Staaten) was a venture that occupied judicial scholars for nearly a half century, including Johann Heinrich Casimir von Carmer (1721-1801), Carl Gottlieb Svarez (1746-1798), and Ernst Ferdinand Klein (1744-1810). This favorite project of Frederick the Great (1740-1786) was already in process before he took the throne. The code was finally in place, regulating the private lives of Prussian people, a decade after the famous king's death. This detailed document, which occupies more than seven hundred pages in a modern, small-print edition, enhanced the strength of Germany's second largest territorial government by placing the Hohenzollern's varied lands under a uniform code. It also contributed to a secularization of authority in Prussia. The debates that contributed to the final version often were aired publicly in print media. In true Enlightenment style, Chancellor von Carmer offered gold and silver prizes for constructive commentaries on controversial issues under consideration by the framers. The code embodied compromises between Enlightenment principles, on the one hand, and what was politically possible in the semifeudal society, on the other. By defining people as citizens, the code set out what was intended to be the foundations for the new civil society. However, it also maintained the concept of an estate-based order and helped halt erosion of the boundaries between semifeudal estates, an erosion that many Enlightenment idealists had hoped to foster.[31]

With regard to gender, it opened with language many Enlightenment proponents would have greeted enthusiastically: "The rights of both sexes are equal, insofar as exceptions are not established by specific laws or legally binding decrees." The subordinate clause was portentous, for major portions of the code dealing with marriage and family elaborated deviations from the proclaimed equality. The code declared marriage to have two possible purposes: first, the procreation and raising of children, and second, the mutual sustenance of the partners. It stipulated that matrimony was a free, contractual, monogamous agreement between a man and a woman. She received his name and social rank. The law forbade unions of persons from unequal social standing, except in rare circumstances, and these required royal sanction. Once the alliance was formed, "the man is the head of the marriage, and his decision prevails in common affairs." The husband was "required to support his wife according to [the family's] social standing," unless he lacked the means to do so, in which case she was to be satisfied with lower standing. The man was constrained to "defend the person and the honor of the woman in and outside of the courts." The woman was "obligated to preside over the household of the man according to his social rank" and was forbidden to engage in any business or to enter into any contract without his approval. The law protected a woman's dowry as her entitlement and as a component of the common household property, but it stipulated that whatever she earned "she acquires ... for the man." Thus this code established the principle in Prussian territories that property and business, both external to the household, were the husband's affairs and that the household, separate from the business of the estate, was the woman's responsibility.[32]

The framers intended to limit the rights of a husband to corporally punish his wife, but they nevertheless failed to abrogate this ancient tradition outright; Svarez later issued the opinion that, by not having expressly forbidden beatings, the code implicitly sustained the historic prerogative of husbands. It explicitly upheld the right of parents to whip their children and the right of masters to beat servants. The authors of Prussia's code were interested in maintaining patriarchal authority, even if they modified some of its severe means of implementation.[33] Prussia's law specified detailed tests to prove the legitimacy of births and the consequences of illegitimacy. Children born into proper marriages bore the name and social rank of the father. They were obliged to honor and obey both parents, "but primarily they stand under the father's authority." As the wife owed obedience to her husband, the children owed allegiance to the father. They were entitled to economic support from him:

> Both marriage partners must render sustenance and education for the children, as appropriate according to rank. Primarily, however, the father must provide the cost for care. The mother herself, or someone under her supervision, must contribute physical care and attendance. A healthy mother is obligated to nurse her child herself. However, how long she gives the breast to the child is determined by the father … . The determination of the type of education the child shall receive is primarily the responsibility of the father.[34]

The Prussian code secularized marriage, placing it under the authority of the state and establishing the possibility of divorce. Termination of a marriage could take place by virtue of "very grave" offenses, including adultery on the part of either partner; but if a wife engaged in infidelity, she forfeited her opportunity for divorce from a philandering husband. Other enumerated grounds for divorce included sodomy; malicious desertion; chronic neglect of marital obligations; insolvency; insanity; intention to kill the spouse or allow the spouse to die; felony; disorderly lifestyles of drunkenness, wastefulness, or fiscal disarray; failure of the husband to support the wife; and religious conversion. Childless couples could agree to divorce simply by mutual consent.[35] The latter provision certainly pleased the Cameralists, who would see unions without offspring as wasteful of potential population resources.

Although Frederick the Great himself declared that the state consisted solely of individual persons, the Prussian Code defined family, not the individual, as the basic unit of society. This represented a significant departure from the metaphysically based notion of the household, during a period in which the word itself, *Familie*, was becoming the judicial and cultural norm. As defined by the code, the family consisted of "persons who belong to one another by blood." Servants, who under the criteria of the household economy were integral to the sustaining unit, were in the new formulation more like hired hands. "The relationship between master and servant is based on a contract, through which the one party obligates itself to perform certain domestic services for a specified period of time, and the other to make a specified payment." The text of the code implied a continuation of a patrimonial household arrangement, specifying, for example, that the master was supervisor of the education of boy servants and the mistress the supervisor of the girls, and stipulating that masters clothed and fed their servants. Nevertheless, the clear vision of the jurists was the transformation of the relationship into one of hired labor. Slavery was expressly forbidden.[36]

This massive law code did not apply to all German-speaking principalities, only to the expansive Hohenzollern-governed territories. However as an expression of principle and a model articulation of civil legislation from the Enlightenment, it established the marriage contract as a secular institution and made the state the overseer of personal human affairs more methodically than ever before. The code established some new options for women as members of the civil society, for example, the right of divorce, but the clear intent of the legal scholars was to foster civic order rather than to grant individual rights to women. Like Bavaria's code, the Prussian law configured marriage as an economic institution and legally preserved the patriarchal household. It separated domestic affairs from economic concerns and assigned these two spheres according to sex roles. Taken together, the Prussian and Bavarian codes signified a transition between the old household and the modern bourgeois family, solidifying the authority the male had over his wife and children and at the same time establishing a bond between this patriarchal unit and the state.

Separate Spheres in Civil Society

The new civil society's implications for males and females of the middle class were personified in the double biographies of Cornelia Goethe (1750-1777), and her brother, Johann Wolfgang von Goethe (1749-1832), Germany's most celebrated author and poet. The two siblings, only a year's difference in age, grew up in a privileged bourgeois household in Frankfurt am Main. Their father, Johann Caspar Goethe, a successful attorney, was a learned man who valued education. Contrary to the popular teachings of Rousseau, he gave his daughter and son nearly equal schooling, stressing intellectual growth. Under his direction and that of tutors, both children learned history, philosophy, literature, religion, and languages – Italian, French, English, and a little Latin. Cornelia, in addition, received singing and piano lessons. The two siblings developed an intimate companionship based in large part on their mutual love of literature. They read passionately and spent days pondering the meaning of the fiction and poetry they shared. Both were intellectually talented, and both fantasized becoming authors themselves. When Johann was sixteen years of age, his father sent him to Leipzig to study law. Obliging his father, he nevertheless argued for the freedom to follow his passion, literature.[37]

While the father and son argued about Johann's future profession, no one thought of a career for Cornelia. Her destiny was to become a wife. She did not immediately grasp this, however. She continued to pursue her intellectual interests and tried to preserve her relationship with her brother through correspondence, writing him excitedly of what she was reading and soliciting his responses. His letters were condescending:

> The tragedy you referred to is by Voltaire and is called "Mohamet ou le Fantisme." No, sister, don't get into this game, it is unbecoming [1765] .... "Der Pitaval" [a famous collection of stories about trials] is not for you. It contains nothing but factual reports without moral considerations .... You would certainly be bored [1766] .... Good heavens, how learned you have become! ... You claim that

"Pitaval" is enlightening about the real world. Fine, I will admit that, but this enlightenment is not for you, but rather for a man, who contemplates ... and understands something of these matters [1766] ... . I find your ideas still jumbled. Indeed, you have fine sentiments like every lady *(Frauenzimmer)* ... but they are too lightly experienced and too little thought out. With all of my knowledge of girls, I sometimes cannot understand how a girl can say [the things you do] ... . I notice that certain readings have ruined your taste ... . Therefore I wanted to ask you to read, in the year during which we will still be separated, as little as possible ... and to study housework and ... cooking, and also as a pastime to diligently practice the piano ... . I request that you perfect your dancing, learn the usual card games, and come to understand cleaning with good taste [1767].[38]

Wounded, Cornelia wondered what a woman's place was. She fantasized about love, but found that men, including her brothers' scholar friends, treated her patronizingly, assuming that she lacked education and intellect. By the age of twenty-two, her future was becoming a concern to her family. She became engaged to Johann Georg Schlosser, a lawyer from another successful Frankfurt family and a writer and friend of her brother. A Freemason and avowed friend of the Enlightenment, Schlosser wrote excitedly in his diary, "I have found a girl who loves me and whom I love like my life." Cornelia wrote in hers, "Life is senseless. I cannot adorn the banality with words. What am I writing about? I am becoming uglier and uglier; my mind counts for nothing. I will marry – unloved. I do not want to love any more ... . I am not living, rather life is pushing me forward." Immediately after the marriage, Cornelia fell ill and never fully recovered. The jurist whom she had married participated in Chancellor von Carmer's public debates on the Prussian General Law Code. His published commentary strongly criticized the proposed law for granting too much authority to wives and potentially undermining the head of the household. Three and one-half years after the wedding, and four weeks after the birth of her second child – a second daughter – Cornelia died, perhaps still loath to be "pushed" by life any longer. Her brother had already successfully embarked on his literary career, having published the historical play "Götz von Berlichingen" and his famous novella *Die Leiden des jungen Werthers* (The Sorrows of Young Werther). He had written *Urfaust*, a version of what would become his greatest work. He had accepted an appointment at the princely court of Saxony-Weimar, the first of several distinguished governmental posts he would hold.[39]

The Enlightenment defined civil society and retained a hierarchical conception of gender. While some philosophers entertained suggestions of a greater equality between the sexes, the Enlightenment principle that masculinity and femininity were opposites rooted in Nature led many to construct new, sharp distinctions between the cultural realms of women and those of men. The Enlightenment increased literacy and for the first time produced popular material for women to read, the moral weeklies. It offered a very few women the opportunity to become writers or salon hostesses. For the most part, however, the new constructions of womanhood and manhood confined women to reproductive activity and excluded them from the productive economy, while they opened opportunities in the professions, in business, and in the academic world to males who already enjoyed an ample measure of privilege.

Notes

1. Dagmar Grenz, *Mädchenliteratur: Von den moralisch-belehrenden Schriften im 18. Jahrhundert bis zur Herausbildung der Backfischliteratur im 19. Jahrhundert*, Germanistische Abhandlungen, vol. 52 (Stuttgart: Metzler, 1981), 8-9. Adalbert von Hanstein, *Die Frauen in der Geschichte des deutschen Geisteslebens des 18. und 19. Jahrhunderts*, (Leipzig: Freund & Wittig, 1899-1900), vol. 1:75-157. Martens, *Moralische Wochenschriften*, 529-31.
2. Joseph Kohnen, *Theodor Gottlieb von Hippel: Eine zentrale Persönlichkeit der Königsberger Geistesgeschichte: Biographie und Bibliographie* (Lüneburg: Verlag Nordostdeutsches Kulturwerk, 1987), 9-207. Theodor Gottlieb von Hippel, *Über die Ehe* (Berlin: Voß, 1774). On the publishing history of the work, see Joseph Kohnen, *Theodor Gottlieb von Hippel 1741-1796: L'homme et l'oeuvre*, Publications Universitaires Européenes: Série I: Langue et litterature allemandes, vol. 727 (Bern: Lang, 1983), 1397-1402. On the Enlightenment in Königsberg, see Joseph Kohnen, "Aspekte der Frankreich-Rezeption in Königsberg," in Schneiders, *Aufklärung als Mission*, 279-94.
3. Hans W. Jäger, "Theodor Gottlieb von Hippel," in *Neue Deutsche Biographie*, vol. 9 (1972), 202-203. Paul Schwartz, *Der erste Kulturkampf in Preußen um Kirche und Schule (1788-1798)*, Monumenta Germaniae Paedagogica, vol. 58 (Berlin: Weidmann, 1925), 71, 467-71.
4. Kohnen, *Theodor Gottlieb von Hippel: Eine zentrale Persönlichkeit*, 91-160. E. Brenning, "Johann Georg Scheffner," in *Allgemeine Deutsche Biographie*, vol. 30 (1890), 685-88.
5. Hamilton H.H. Beck, *The Elusive "I" in the Novel: Hippel, Sterne, Diderot, Kant*, American University Studies, Series I: Germanic Language and Literature, vol. 46 (New York: Lang, 1987). Paul Peterken, *Gesellschaftliche und fiktionale Identität: Eine Studie zu Theodor Gottlieb von Hippels Roman "Lebensläufe nach aufsteigender Linie nebst Beilagen A, B, C,"* Stuttgarter Arbeiten zur Germanistik, no. 106 (Stuttgart, 1981). Kohnen, *Theodor Gottlieb von Hippel ... L'homme*.
6. Hippel, *Über die Ehe*, 72, 91-94.
7. Ibid., 1-17.
8. Ibid., 4-5, 18-20, 22-23. On Prussia's prohibition of interclass marriages to prevent a decline of the aristocracy, see Koselleck, *Preußen zwischen Reform und Revolution*, 105-115.
9. Hippel, *Über die Ehe*, 26-27, 33-34.
10. Ibid., 31-33, 52-57.
11. Sophie von La Roche, *Geschichte des Fräuleins von Sternheim* ed. Barbara Becker-Cantarino, Universal-Bibliothek 7934 (1771; Stuttgart: Reclam, 1983). Ruth-Ellen B. Joeres, "'That Girl is an entirely different character!' Yes, but is she a feminist? Observations on Sophie von La Roche's *Geschichte des*

Fräuleins von Sternheim," in *German Women,* ed Joeres and Maynes, 137-56. Not all scholars agree about La Roche; some portray her as unable to overcome the social norms of her times. See Jeannine Blackwell, "Sophie von La Roche," in *German Writers in the Age of Goethe: Sturm und Drang to Classicism,* vol. 94, *Dictionary of Literary Biography,* ed. James Hardin and Christoph E. Schweitzer (Detroit: Gale Research, 1990), 154-61. Helga Brandes, "Das Frauenzimmer-Journal: Zur Herausbildung einer journalistischen Gattung im 18. Jahrhundert," in *Deutsche Literatur von Frauen,* ed. Gisela Brinker-Gabler (Munich: Beck, 1988), vol 1, 455-59. Ulrike Weckel, *Zwischen Häuslichkeit und Öffentlichkeit: Die ersten deutschen Frauenzeitschriften im späten 18. Jahrhundert und ihr Publikum,* Studien und Texte zur Sozialgeschichte der Literatur, vol. 61 (Tübingen: Niemeyer, 1998), 29, 75, 81-103.

12. Hertz, *Jewish High Society,* 96-104. Heindl, *Gehorsame Rebellen,* 286-290. Fritz Gause, "Elisabeth Johanna von Stägemann, geb. Fischer," in *Altpreußische Biographie,* ed. Christian Krollmann, Kurt Forstreuter, and Fritz Gause (Königsberg: Elwert, 1941-1978), 688. Gause, *Geschichte der Stadt Königsberg,* 2:258.

13. Martens, *Botschaft der Tugend,* 520-42; quotation from *Der Menschenfreund von Ostern 1737 bis Ostern 1739 (1739),* cited in Martens, 525. Sylvia Bovenschen, *Die imaginierte Weiblichkeit: Exemplarische Untersuchungen zu kulturgeschichtlichen und literarischen Präsentationsformen des Weiblichen,* Edition Suhrkamp, vol. 921 (Frankfurt am Main: Suhrkamp, 1979), 138-49. Herz, *Jewish High Society,* 96-104.

14. Paul, *Deutsches Wörterbuch,* 211-12. Grimm, *Deutsches Wörterbuch,* vol. 4 (1878), 83-87.

15. Johann Heinrich Zedler, *Grosses vollständiges Universal-Lexikon aller Wissenschaften und Künste Welche bißhero durch menschlichen Verstand und Witz erfunden worden* (Halle: Zedler, 1732-54; facsimile repr. Graz: Akademische Druck- und Verlagsanstalt, 1961-64), vol. 10, 1222-23. Grimm, *Deutsches Wörterbuch* vol. 4 (1897), 3903-12. Karin Hausen, "Die Polarisierung der 'Geschlechtscharaktere' –Eine Spiegelung der Dissoziation von Erwerbs- und Familienleben," in *Sozialgeschichte der Neuzeit Europas: Neue Forschungen,* ed. Werner Conze, Industrielle Welt, vol. 21 (Stuttgart: Klett, 1976), 363-93.

16. Immanuel Kant, *Anthropologie in Pragmatischer Hinsicht* (1800), in *Werke,* ed. Ernst Cassirer (Berlin: B. Cassirer, 1923), vol. 8, 196-204. Ute Frevert, "Bürgerliche Meisterdenker und das Geschlechtsverhältnis: Konzepte, Erfahrungen, Visionen an der Wende vom 18. zum 19. Jahrhundert," in *Bürgerinnen und Bürger: Geschlechterverhältnisse im 19. Jahrhundert,* ed. Frevert, Kritische Studien zur Geschichtswissenschaft, vol. 77 (Göttingen: Vandenhoeck & Ruprecht, 1988), 20-25. According to date of publication, Kant's anthropology could be discussed in Chapter 7 dealing with the period of the French Revolution. I discuss it in this chapter, however, because Kant conceptualized

it as early as the 1770s. He used it for lectures delivered in the winter semester of 1772-73. Norbert Hinske, "Immanuel Kant," in *Neue Deutsche Biographie*, vol. 11 (1977), 110-25, esp. 122.
17. Kant, *Anthropologie*, 303-04. I am indebted to Mary J. Gregor's introduction and translation, although the translated passages are mine. Immanuel Kant, *Anthropology from a Pragmatic Point of View*, trans. Mary J. Gregor (The Hague: Nijhoff, 1974). See also Barbara Duden, "Das schöne Eigentum: Zur Herausbildung des bürgerlichen Frauenbildes an der Wende vom 18. zum 19. Jahrhundert," *Kursbuch* 47 (1977): 127-30.
18. Kant, *Anthropologie*, 304.
19. Ibid., 306-307.
20. Immanuel Kant, "Die Metaphysik der Sitten" (1797), in *Werke*, 7: 120-21. Frevert, "Bürgerliche Meisterdenker," 21.
21. Ernst Brandes, *Ueber die Weiber* (Leipzig, 1787). I have used the revised edition, *Betrachtungen über das weibliche Geschlecht und dessen Ausbildung in dem geselligen Leben* (Hanover: Hahn, 1802). See Claudia Honegger, *Die Ordnung der Geschlechter: Die Wissenschaften vom Menschen und das Weib 1750-1850* (Frankfurt: Campus, 1991), 46-54, 58-62. Erich Botzenhart, "Ernst Brandes," in *Neue Deutsche Biographie*, vol. 2 (1955), 518-19.
22. Rousseau, *Émile*, 321-444. Angelika Puhlmann, *Mädchenerziehung in der bürgerlichen Gesellschaft: Klassenspezifische Unterschiede in der Vergesellschaftung der Mädchenerziehung*, Pahl-Ragenstein-Hochschulschriften, Gesellschafts- und Naturwissenschaften 13: Series Studien zu Bildung und Erziehung, 2nd ed. (Cologne: Pahl-Ragenstein, 1980). Inge Baxmann, "Von der Egalité im Salon zur Citoyenne – Einige Aspekte der Genese des bürgerlichen Frauenbildes," in *Frauen in der Geschichte III*, ed. Kuhn and Russen, 123-129. Isabel Hull, "'Sexualität' und bürgerliche Gesellschaft," 57-60. Elisabeth Blochmann, *Das "Frauenzimmer" und die "Gelehrsamkeit": Eine Studie über die Anfänge des Mädchenschulwesens in Deutschland*, Anthropologie und Erziehung, vol. 17 (Heidelberg: Quelle & Meyer, 1966), 26-29.
23. Campe, *Väterlicher Rath für meine Tochter*, vii, 5, 14-15, 138-251. Grenz, *Mädchenliteratur*, 47-65. Blochmann, *Das "Frauenzimmer" und die "Gelehrsamkeit"*, 31-42.
24. Allen, *Feminism and Motherhood*, 20-22.
25. Johann Heinrich Pestalozzi, *Leinhard und Gertrud: Ein Buch für das Volk* (1781), Winkler Dünndruck Ausgabe (Munich: Winkler, 1977). Allen, *Feminism and Motherhood*, 22-26. Monika Simmel, *Erziehung zum Weibe: Mädchenbildung im 19. Jahrhundert*, Campus Paperbacks: Pädagogik (Frankfurt am Main: Campus, 1980), 67-82.
26. On other Philanthropinists and gender, see Grenz, *Mädchenerziehung*, 86-98; Biermann, "Erziehungsmittel," 342-69; Blochmann, *Das "Frauenzimmer" und die "Gelehrsamkeit,"* 89-102.

27. Cornelia Niekus Moore, *The Maiden's Mirror: Reading Material for German Girls in the Sixteenth and Seventeenth Centuries*, Wolfenbütteler Forschungen, vol. 36 (Wiesbaden: Harrassowitz, 1987), 9-56.
28. *Codex Maximilianeus Bavaricus civilis: Oder neu verbessert und ergänzt Chur-Bayerisches Landrecht* (Munich: Vötter, 1759), part I, chapter 4, pp. 1-2; chapter 6, p.1, chapter, 12, pp. 17, 36-37, 44-45. Hermann Conrad, "Die Rechtsstellung der Ehefrau in der Privatrechtsgesetzgebung der Aufklärungszeit," in *Aus Mittelalter und Neuzeit: Gerhard Kallen zum 70. Geburtstag* ed. Josef Engel and Hans Martin Klinkenberg (Bonn: Hanstein, 1957), 255-57. Helmut Coing, *Europäisches Privatrecht*, vol 1: *Älteres gemeines Recht (1500 bis 1800)* (Munich: Beck, 1985), 116. Helmut Coing, *Handbuch der Quellen und Literatur der neueren europäischen Privatrechtsgeschichte*, 3 vols., 9 parts, Ver'ffentlichung des Max-Planck-Instituts für europäische Rechtsgeschichte (Munich: Beck, 1960-1988), vol. 2, 410. Schlumbohm, *Freiheit*, 84-91.
29. Wiguläus Xaverius Aloysius von Kreittmayr, *Anmerkungen über den Codicem Maximilianeum Civilem: Worin derselbe sowohl mit dem Gemein- als ehemalig Chur-Bayrischen Land-Recht genau collationirt, sohin der Unterschied zwischen dem alt- und neueren Recht samt den Urquellen, woraus das letztere geschöpft worden ist, überall angezeigt, und dies dadurch in ein helleres Licht gesetzt wird,* 2nd unchanged ed. (Munich: Verlag der Königlichen Central-Verwaltung des Regierungs- und Intelligenzblätter, 1821), vol. I, p. 3, § ii note 1; vol. I, p. 6, § xlv notes 2, 3, 4. On Natural Law doctrine and marriage, see Dieter Schwab, *Grundlagen und Gestalt der staatlichen Ehegesetzgebung in der Neuzeit bis zum Beginn des 19. Jahrhunderts*, Schriften zum deutschen und europäischen Zivil-, Handels- und Prozessrecht, vol. 45 (Bielefeld : Gieseking, 1967), 125-137. Hans Schlosser, "Der Gesetzgeber Kreittmayr und die Aufklärung in Kurbayern," in *Wiguläus Xaver Aloys Freiherr von Kreittmayr 1750-1790: Ein Leben für Recht, Staat und Politik*, ed. Richard Bauer and Hans Schlosser, Festschrift zum 200. Todestag (Munich: Beck, 1991), 3-36. Christian Wolff, *Vernünnftige Gedancken von dem gesellschafftlichen Leben der Menschen: und insonderhiet dem gemeinen Wesen zu Beförderung der Glückseligkeit des Menschen Geschlechtes, den Liebhabern der Wahrheit mitgetheilt* (1721), in *Gesammelte Werke* (Frankfurt: Regner, 1721; repr. Hildesheim: Olms, 1975), vol. 5, 33. Cocalis, "Der Vormund," 39-42.
30. Kreittmayr, *Anmerkungen*, 128. *Codex Maximilaneus*, part I, chapter 4, § 4, p. 19; part I, chapter 6, § 12, p. 44.
31. *Allgemeines Landrecht für die Preußischen Staaten von 1794*, Textausgabe, ed. Hans Hattenhauer and Günther Bernert (Frankfurt am Main: Metzner, 1970). Uwe-Jens Heuer, *Allgemeines Landrecht und Klassenkampf: Die Auseinandersetzung um die Principien des Allgemeinen Landrechts Ende des 18. Jahrhunderts als Ausdruck der Krise des Feudalsystems in Preußen* (Berlin:

Deutscher Zentralverlag, 1960), 21-172. Günther Birtsch, "Zum konstitutionellen Charakter des preußischen Allgemeinen Landrechts von 1794," in *Politische Ideologien und nationalstaatliche Ordnung: Studien zur Geschichte des 19. und 20. Jahrhunderts: Festschrift für Theodor Schieder*, ed. Kurt Kluxen and Wolfgang J. Mommsen (Munich: Oldenbourg, 1968), 97-115. Reinhard Koselleck, *Preußen zwischen Reform und Revolution: Allgemeines Landrecht, Verwaltung und Soziale Bewegung von 1791 bis 1848*, Industrielle Welt, vol. 7, (Stuttgart: Klett, 1967), 23-51. Dirk Blasius, *Ehescheidung in Deutschland 1794-1945: Scheidung und Scheidungsrecht in historischer Perspektive*, Kritische Studien zur Geschichtswissenschaft, vol. 74 (Göttingen: Vandenhoeck & Ruprecht, 1987), 28.

32. *Allgemeines Landrecht*, part I, title 1, § 1-24, p. 55; part II, title 1-4, § 1-250, pp. 345-419; part II, title 7, section 1, § 1-7, p. 433; part II, title 8, section 8, § 1-12, pp. 452-53; part II, title 9, § 1-12, pp. 534-38.
33. Koselleck, *Preußen zwischen Reform und Revolution*, 641.
34. *Allgemeines Landrecht*, part II, title 1-2, § 1-85, pp. 382-85.
35. Ibid., part II, title 1, § 668-834, pp. 367-372. See Blasius, *Ehescheidung in Deutschland* 30-31.
36. *Allgemeines Landrecht*, section II, title 3, § 1-53, pp. 408-410; section II, title 5, § 1-208, pp. 419-426. On the reference to Frederick the Great and the Landrecht's conceptualization of the family, see Koselleck, *Preußen zwischen Reform und Revolution*, 62-65. On the concept family, see Dirk Blasius, "Familie," in *Geschichtliche Grundbegriffe*, vol. 2 (1975), 253-301. See Zedler's 1735 definition, in which the servants were included in the family: Johann Heinrich Zedler, "Familia," in *Grosses vollständiges Universal-Lexikon*, vol. 9 (1735), 205-208.
37. Ulrike Prokop, *Die Illusion vom großen Paar*, vol. I, *Weibliche Lebensentwürfe im deutschen Bildungsbürgertum 1750-1770*, Psychoanalytische Studien zur Kultur (Frankfurt am Main: Fischer Taschenbuch, 1991), 38-48.
38. Quotations from Goethe's correspondence, Prokop, *Illusion vom großem Paar*, ibid., 1: 49-54.
39. Ibid. 1: 38-60, 2:67-122. 1:13, 16, 27. Prokop calls Cornelia Goethe's condition "illness as protest." Jane K. Brown, "Johann Wolfgang von Goethe," *German Writers in the Age of Goethe: Sturm und Drang*, 46-67. R. Jung, "Johann Georg Schlosser," in *Allgemeine Deutsche Biographie*, vol. 31 (1890), 544-47. Koselleck, *Preußen zwischen Reform und Revolution*, 62.

Chapter Six

The Household Ideal Caught in a Changing World (1750-1790)

By the second half of the eighteenth century, the Cameralists had moved the normative locus of the economy away from the household and into the princely chambers, and they had relegated agriculture to a subsidiary role in the dominant culture of state and society. The ideas and people of the future allegedly belonged to the cities and to governments, not to the rural estates.

In terms of the social reality, however, the vast majority of people continued to procure their livelihood from the soil. At the end of the eighteenth century, approximately 85 percent of the German population lived in rural villages or in small towns of less than five thousand individuals.[1] In spite of the popular ideal of an economy driven by manufacture and commerce, agriculture remained the predominant sector of the economy. It is not surprising that many publicists and academicians wrote about agriculture. All who did sought to preserve the vitality of rural life.

Defenders of agriculture found themselves supporting something that seemed increasingly outmoded because it was identified with the "unproductive" moral household economy. They faced

Notes for this section begin on page 207.

two choices. Either they might attempt to restore values held by many to be archaic, or they might seek to bring agriculture up to date by empowering it with ideals of the Enlightenment. Every writer on the subject fell somewhere between the poles of rigid conservatism and wholesale modernization. No one could deny the Enlightenment's captivation of language and ideas in the age; even those who sought to sustain the household ideal endeavored to equip rural life with the new tools of science and rationality. On the other side, those whose worldview was shaped primarily by the Enlightenment found themselves unable to discuss agriculture without framing their discussion within the venerable household concept. Language and cultural norms change erratically.

The Economic Societies and the Technical Improvement of Agriculture

Between 1650 and 1740 the population of German-speaking Europe expanded from approximately 10 million to nearly 18 million, and beginning in the middle of the eighteenth century an even more dramatic upswing occurred. The population in the East-Elbian provinces of Prussia more than doubled between 1740 and 1805. This was the very thing that Cameralists like Süßmilch and Justi sought, for they regarded people as economic resources. These social engineers would not have considered it a problem that the increased numbers put pressure on the semifeudal socioeconomic structures that were based largely on a premise of stability, rather than growth. Nevertheless, the population increase, along with a general rise in prices, the causes of which were widely debated, generated concern among governmental officials, and these factors contributed to a widespread, renewed interest in agriculture among the absolutist rulers of the late eighteenth century. Their apprehension increased when periodic crop failures – often afflicting large areas of Europe – caused subsistence crises, including starvation. A disaster of this nature in 1770-71 caused epidemic suffering.[2]

The solution to this problem seemed to be improved agriculture, and rulers took it as their responsibility to create conditions under which famines would be averted. Frederick the Great of Prussia (1712-1786) spoke for many of his era: "Agriculture is the highest of all arts; without it, there would be no merchants, no poets, and no philosophers. Only that which is brought forth from the earth is pure wealth." Maria Theresa (1717-1780) and Joseph II (1741-1790) of Austria took personal interest in agriculture. Joseph symbolically took the plow in his own hand to demonstrate his commitment to farming as the source of the monarchy's well-being. Carl Friedrich, Margrave of Baden (1728-1811), borrowed ideas from the French school of Physiocracy to enhance the agrarian output of his principalities. Elector Karl Theodor of Bavaria (1724-1799) strove to secure peasants' tenure rights and to improve regulation of common lands. Duke Karl August of Weimar (1757-1828), Goethe's patron, established model farms to demonstrate the latest production techniques. Landgrave Frederick II of Hesse-Cassel (1720-1785) sought to introduce the cultivation of novel crops from outside of Europe, and he experimented with new kinds of rents designed to encourage farmers to produce greater yields.[3] Without exception, the rulers of German-speaking states shared a preoccupation with the "improvement" of agriculture.

"Economic societies" dedicated to enhancing rural life sprang up throughout German territories. They were part of a larger movement that sought to re-equate *Ökonomie* and agriculture after the Cameralists had separated the two. Counterparts to the civic associations and reading societies of the cities, these agrarian associations frequently enjoyed the support of princely governments; most were founded at rulers' behest. Purportedly designed to bring the Enlightenment to the farming populace, they were paternalistic like the parallel organizations of the cities. Typically under the leadership of agricultural reformers, the economic associations – also called "patriotic societies," to signify their dedication to the ideals of progress and civic virtue in rural settings – published periodical literature containing practical advice for daily life and work. For example, the Silesian Economic-Patriotic Society issued the *Schlesische Volkszeitung* between 1789 and 1803 under the sponsorship of the Prussian minister Count Karl Georg Heinrich von Hoym (1739-1807). As many as 33,000 copies in German and 10,000 in Polish reached the Silesian villagers annually.[4]

Typical of their age, the economic societies often borrowed ideas freely from abroad. Many were strongly influenced by the agricultural practices of Great Britain, which were renowned for technical innovations and increased crop yields. Having experienced an enclosure of peasant holdings into entrepreneurial estates since the sixteenth century, British agriculturists, often led by the rising gentry, had also slowly adopted new crops, such as red and white clover, vetch, turnips, beets, and beans. These high-yield plants, with an accompanying transition from the three-field system to crop rotation, produced increased returns from the soil. The legumes expanded animal fodder production, sometimes by as much as sixfold, while at the same time capturing nitrogen and returning it to the soil. Contemporaries did not understand this process in modern scientific terms, but eighteenth-century farmers and experimenters knew empirically that grain yields increased in fields previously sown in clover. Root crops like turnips and beets provided rich animal food in winter. These combinations made it possible for fields of fixed size to feed greater numbers of people and promised larger regional yields, which would nourish the increasing population. Publicists in the last half of the eighteenth century enthusiastically promoted "English" crops and practices, many of which had been known for centuries in Germany but were not widely used. German reformers translated a number of British agricultural reformers, including Jethro Tull, John Mills, Francis Home, and Philip Miller. Frederick the Great of Prussia and Margrave Carl Friedrich of Baden sent young farmers to Britain to learn English ways and bring them home.[5]

Innovators urged the introduction of Asian and American plants, for example, rice, sunflowers, tobacco, Indian maize, and potatoes. The latter were known in well-to-do households for their gourmet qualities before the eighteenth century. By midcentury, those who sought to strengthen agriculture promoted their use for their productive and nutritional qualities, but the "earth apple" was accepted slowly by common tillers of the soil. Contemporaries estimated that planting potatoes as opposed to the traditional grains would allow any region to nourish three times the usual number of people. But they had to overcome resistance, not only of peasants but also of estate owners, some of whom believed that potatoes could actually feed so many people that their cultivation would reduce rural incomes because of decreased sales. Traditionalists feared that potatoes would destroy the grain-producing culture of Germany. Nevertheless, potatoes were among the many new crops that became popular in the last third of the century.[6]

The periodic agricultural crises made the ideas of innovators more acceptable, and many wrote about not only new crops but new techniques of animal production. Due to complex economic conditions, meat and dairy items had become less profitable than plant products since the Thirty Years War. Leaders of the economic societies advocated introduction of new breeds such as merino sheep from Spain and even buffalo from Asia. The latter were never more than an exotic experiment, but the new species of sheep became important to the economy of certain areas, such as Electoral Saxony. Reformers especially sought to spread word of the advantages of stall feeding of cattle. They also eagerly disseminated information about new implements: plows, harrows, rollers, drills, cultivators, and threshers. German writers were delighted to discover as many as eleven different types of plows and three distinct harrows of British origin and to compare their advantages for German conditions.[7] The economic societies were common consumers and disseminators of the new ideas.

They also propagated the Physiocratic theories developed by the French scholar François Quesnay (1694-1774), as outlined in his *Tableau économique* (1758). An advocate of free trade, Quesnay sought to restore agriculture to a respected place in France after decades of Mercantilist theory that stressed that the welfare of the state, derived from taxation, required the growth of commerce, business, and manufacture. In Germany the economic societies had a similar task of restoring agriculture to the status of a science after the Cameralists had relegated it to secondary rung of the economy. Physiocracy belonged to the Enlightenment tradition whose advocates hoped to emancipate people so that they could realize a fuller human potential, but Quesnay and his followers argued that agriculturists were the productive members of society, while those in trade and industry were the "sterile classes." Their goal was to foster the establishment of a flourishing market economy in the countryside, and they criticized the French monarchy for thwarting the growth of free enterprise through export prohibitions on agrarian products in order to keep consumer prices low. The Physiocrats advocated abolition of feudal restraints on agrarian enterprise and championed private property and free real estate markets. Like Mercantilists in its own country and Cameralists in the Germanies, Quesnay's French school sided with the state in the power struggle between the feudal aristocracies and the absolutist regimes. They held that centralized authority was necessary in order to establish economic freedom for the farmers; only with such liberty could the state economy prosper.[8]

Quesnay's economic ideas found eager acceptance in the new societies established in the 1760s, such as the Royal Danish Agricultural Society (1762), the Thuringian Agricultural society (1763), and the Leipzig Economic Society (1764). The first of these in the tiny duchy of Glücksburg, in Schleswig, was the creation of the court pastor and provost Philipp Ernst Lüders (1702-1786). An enthusiastic farmer himself, Lüders experimented with new crops, including the celebrated clovers, beets, and potatoes. With support of the Royal Danish government, which ruled Glücksburg, Lüders published the *Oeconomisches Magazin* (Economic Journal) in which he disseminated news of his experiments. He also published brochures in local dialect for the peasants. He founded an "agricultural academy" *(Acker-Academie)* with a membership of thirty-nine, including fifteen pastors, whom he commissioned to farm in an exemplary manner in order to instruct the country folk who labored with "ignorance, prejudices, and obstinacy." He hoped to eradicate these "strongest hindrances that stand in the way of the real improvement of agriculture." Lüders encouraged agriculturists of all social classes to join his academy, including the "fair sex, who often is used to thinking in more noble terms than is the male sex." He appealed to Christian VII of Denmark for reforms and asked when farmers would be able to start regarding their lands as private property unencumbered by semifeudal institutions such as common lands."[9]

A similar initiative further to the south in the small town of Lautern (today's Kaiserslautern) followed Lüders' experiment seven years later (1769). Agrarian reformer and economic writer Johann Riem (1739-1807) founded the Physical, Economic, and Beekeeping Society that attracted a wide membership from the surrounding region, including many clergymen and other well-educated men of the social elites. The society established an "economic garden," a fruit orchard, and a farm to serve as models for agriculturists. It assembled and exhibited a collection of plows and other agricultural implements and established a library of periodical literature. Riem's reputation led to the offer of a position in the civil service in Electoral Saxony, and he became executive secretary of the Leipzig Economic Society, which prided itself on importing ideas, books, and seeds from Great Britain.[10]

In the sprawling Habsburg territories, Chancellor Rudolf von Chotek (1707-1771) initiated the establishment of provincial economic societies, including those in Tyrol, Carinthia, Styria, Bohemia, Hungary, Croatia, and Transylvania. These reform-minded associations enjoyed direct subsidies from the empress' treasury. In the north, in Hanover, an agreement between the Hanoverian Elector, British King George III, Minister Burchard Christian von Behr (1714-1771) in London, and local estate proprietor and reformer Jobst Anton von Hinüber (1718-1784) led to the founding of one of the famous "patriotic associations," the Celle Society and Agricultural Organization. The Celle Society explicitly adopted for itself the task of implanting British ideas and practices into the German landscape.[11] Thus the often state-sponsored "patriotic" and "economic" associations strongly influenced the norms of the overwhelmingly agricultural society of late-eighteenth-century Germany.

Surely many eighteenth-century agriculturists found liberation in the lively discussion of new techniques, new tools, new crops, and increased production. These promised the new possibilities of progress for the countryside that Cameralism held out for the cities. It encouraged the introduction of science and rationality to rural life. However, it also initiated a transition in ideas about gender, perhaps largely unnoticed, but with significant consequences for the gender systems of rural society. The discourse, conducted by men in the public realm – economic societies, patriotic societies, princely courts, and administrative offices – often overlooked or rejected the feature that earlier generations had seen as the sustainer of agriculture and society: the moral household. The household and its female members were becoming invisible in the predominant discourse about the direction of rural society. The discussions of drill machines, Marino sheep, fodder beets, and clover largely ignored women and reinforced a growing pattern of masculine dominance of all aspects of farm life. Emphasis was shifting from the ethical organization of the rural household to the technology and progress that excited the men of the eighteenth century. It also linked the ideals of farming to those of the state, the realm guided by the most privileged and powerful men.

The Household Ideal in a Changing World

The concept of the household did not disappear from the vocabulary of rural society, however. Old idioms remained alive and vital in the language of farming, as in the title of the periodical

Baierischer Ökonomischer Hausvater (Bavarian Economic Hausvater) a publication of the Moral and Economic Society of Altötting-Burghausen, seventy-five kilometers east of Munich. Bavaria's rulers guaranteed this assembly of noblemen, governmental officials, clergymen, professors, and journalists the right to publish without censorship in order to encourage them to spread the Enlightenment to local farmers of high and low social status. This society's journal, more in the category of advice literature than were the systematic and philosophical household books after which it named itself, ranged widely in subject matter, including subjects from soil quality to the lack of industriousness among modern peasants and the need for "rural economic schools" to teach the lower classes how to improve their farming skills. The young male farmers and shepherds who would attend these schools would gain advantage of the latest "scientific knowledge" from textbooks written by "enlightened agriculturists."[12]

The editors of this serial publication continued to remind readers of the structure of the conventional household economy, however. As if worried that the traditional fixed hierarchies of class and gender were being forgotten, they seemed enthusiastic to publish practical advice on the proper roles of the female servants, including the stewardess *(Hofmeisterin)*, head household servant *(Hausmagd)*, swine maid, and cattle maid. The author's commentary on the second of these – reminiscent of the household books – illustrated his conception of the gendered household economy: The *Hausmagd*

> is completely indispensable to the administration of the estate ....
> She is the right hand of the stewardess. She serves the steward, the hunting master, and the gardener. She ... keeps the house clean. When the master and mistress come, she has many responsibilities in the kitchen.

She is in charge of the poultry, the cattle, and the beer cellar. She takes garden and dairy products to market for sale. She sees that kitchen waste is properly delivered to the gardener as fertilizer. She is "irreplaceable." "When she is absent or sick, an important component of the internal economy is missing."[13]

At the same time they extolled the virtues of the household, the editors brought to their rural readers information about new technologies. They were concerned that a technological revolution in the cities was bypassing the agrarian population, contributing to its second-place position in the changing socioeconomic order. In an illustrated article, a writer for the Bavarian society explained the construction and operation of a modern silk spinner, picturing a young woman as the producer of the thread for the clothing of Europe's wealthy and prestigious. In this example of pre-industrial *Industrie* in the countryside, the illustrator placed a female at the machine.[14] Spinning was female work in the gendered household economy, and even the transition to market production would not alter this.

The men who sought to improve Bavarian agriculture while spreading their conception of the Enlightenment were not thinking in terms of the male civil society or the new confining ideal of female domesticity. In their minds, the rural economy would be enhanced through hard work of males and females employing innovative technologies in the patriarchal household. Their conception of the economy accorded with that of their landsman who three decades earlier had published an economic guide for Bavaria:

> *Ars oeconomica*, or *Haushaltung*, is the *Hauswirth's* special talent for conducting the affairs of his inheritance and property, both inside and outside the house. The *Hauswirth* must not only ensure that he himself, his woman, children, servants, and animals can procure their basic needs *(Notdurft)*. He must also be able to put aside something substantial throughout the year ... for emergencies, normal consumption, celebrations, and taxes.[15]

In northern Germany, Hanoverian estate proprietor and bailiff Otto von Münchhausen (1716-1774), contributed substantially to the discussion on the place of agriculture in society with his impos-

Figure 6.1 In this depiction of the newest techniques of silk production in the *Baierischer Ökonomischer Hausvater* (1785) the illustrator placed a woman at the work-stool. The continuity of certain gender-specific jobs gave the appearance that gender roles remained constant, although their meaning within the economy was changing significantly.

ing five-volume work *Der Hausvater* (1765-1770). A fellow of the Celle Society and a member of a prestigious aristocratic family whose members had served the Electors of Hanover (and monarchs of Great Britain), Münchhausen occupied an imposing manor, Schwöbber, one of several belonging to his relatives, which dominated the landscape along the Weser valley. He emulated the tradition of master household economists of a century earlier, yet he sought to help agriculture modernize. He drew upon his training at the British-oriented University of Göttingen, where he had studied natural sciences and mathematics, as well as his practical experience in government and on the land. It had been over a half century since Florinus had written the last great *Hausbuch;* and although his work had been republished as late as 1750, it was clear that modern estate owners would find it anachronistic.[16] An increasing number of small, practical agricultural instructional guides were appearing in the book trade,[17] but there were no comprehensive authorities like Hohberg or Florinus to codify agrarian values for the last third of the eighteenth century. Münchhausen's handbook was bound in five octavo volumes rather than as a single, beautiful, yet unwieldy folio edition as its forerunners had been. More importantly, his work incorporated the principles of a commercial economy and modern agricultural practices even as it upheld norms belonging to the aristocratic estate. A popular work, it went through multiple printings and several revisions within a ten-year period. Münchhausen attempted to fill a perceived void with a didactic, trend-setting publication, but he anchored it with the idiom of the early-modern household.

Münchhausen did not open his guide with Aristotelian philosophy or with a description of the Christian economy. True to his technology-conscious age, he used his first chapter to draw his reader into the pragmatic business of farming with a treatise on the plow. He filled the entire first volume, 198 pages, with utilitarian information on such topics as the sowing of grain fields; the layout of gardens; the use of manure as fertilizer; feeding milk cows; coping with hail damage; managing meadows and hayfields; protecting against rabid animals; and comparing European weights and measures. Münchhausen self-assuredly described traditional agricultural practices of his own region, Lower Saxony and Westphalia, as exemplary for other regions. The plow he held up as a model was the one common to the locality of his estate, Schwöbber, but Münchhausen urged his readers to compare the traditions of their own areas with those of others. He stressed agricultural techniques in both German and non-German regions. He cited the ancient authorities of Greece and Rome. Münchhausen's book was an attempt to bring the latest information on agriculture to the aristocratic farmer. He stressed new methods such as crop rotation and irrigation. In contrast to the seventeenth-century authorities, he favored an interventionist agriculture rather than one attuned to seasonal cycles. For example, he advocated cultivation of imported varieties of hay, instead of the harvesting of native grasses.[18]

With phrasing reminiscent of the Newtonian model of the universe, Münchhausen described the integrated household economy:

> The entire business of the household must hold together like clockwork. Every gear must mesh exactly with the others and contribute its part in order to keep the whole in motion. No wheel may remain still; otherwise the entire system suffers. If one places emphasis on a single wheel alone and lets the others rust, everything comes quickly to a halt.[19]

Unlike the old economists, Münchhausen depicted the estate master as a "patriot" who loved his fatherland, ensured that *Industrie* was practiced on his manor, and contributed to the economic wellbeing of society through "commerce, ... the soul of a country." Citing the French philosopher Montesquieu, Münchhausen explained that trades were established as small operations and that the proprietor gained courage to expand on the basis of early success. Trades must be conducted in the spirit of freedom and competition, yet in an orderly and measured manner. The monopolies of the great aristocrats must be broken, for they suppressed beneficial business transactions. "As soon as the right trading spirit finds its place in a nation, the inhabitants take on [a new] style of thinking, and everyone is guided to thrift, order, economy *(Wirtschaft)*, and caution." In order to promote the new knowledge of husbandry and economics among his peers, Münchhausen founded a learned society of *Hausväter*, which met monthly at his estate. Each

Figure 6.2 The Hausvater's study, as illustrated in Münchhausen's *Hausvater* (1764-1774), was full of scientific instruments and books, the tools of the Enlightenment. The agricultural operations of the estate are visible from the windows of the study.

member obligated himself to subscribe to a scientific journal, and at the meetings they discussed "the expansion of the sciences and scholarship" and "topics related to farming and agriculture."[20]

Münchhausen joined a serious debate of his era on the question of grain tariffs designed to protect domestic agriculture against international competition. This controversy lasted well into the nineteenth century and was by no means confined to

Germany; it was played out in Great Britain in the form of the debate over the Corn Laws, which did not end until 1846. Münchhausen stressed that while he, as an estate owner, personally stood to gain from protective import taxes on agricultural products, he nevertheless unequivocally supported free trade. He extracted a 172-page section of the *Hausvater* and reissued it in 1775 as a book entitled *Der freye Kornhandel als das beste Mittel um Mangel und Theuerung zu verhütten* (The Free Grain Market as the Best Safeguard against Scarcity and Rising Prices). Stressing the negative effects of mercantilist policies, he criticized a succession of grain tariffs that the Diet of the Holy Roman Empire had enacted over the previous thirty years. Rejecting customs barriers categorically, he illustrated their possible detriment with the example of Berlin, whose government officials had interfered with the free market by prohibiting the importation of Hamburg sugar, thinking they could procure the product cheaper from Bordeaux. They soon discovered that with the Hamburg competition eliminated, the French city increased its prices, and the citizens of Berlin faced higher consumer costs for the product they had attempted to obtain more cheaply through market manipulation.[21]

Some people, Münchhausen pointed out, erroneously believed that a land could not support more people than it could feed. If this were true, he asked, how could Holland or Hamburg exist? The key to large, prosperous populations was free circulation of wealth. States must learn to exist in a condition of interdependency. Those that tried to be autonomous would revert to the condition of the "wild people of America." Bringing the argument more directly to his agrarian reader, Münchhausen urged the German aristocratic proprietor to consider the potential commercial possibilities of brewing beer and distilling brandy, two rural products that many estates traditionally produced in high quality, but only for consumption within the household. There were great markets to be tapped in the cities, to the benefit of rural producers. Münchhausen understood that for this plan to become a reality, the urban monopolies of the brewing guilds would have to be broken, but this would be a positive development.[22]

The mistress of the household was an essential figure in Münchhausen's clockwork-estate. Not allowing himself to be tied to a specific age or social estate, he named her, interchangeably, *Mutterfamilias*, *Hausfrau*, and *Frauenzimmer*. To her roles he devoted a comprehensive bibliography and prescriptive instruction throughout the text, because "certain responsibilities in the house belong solely or primarily to the housewife." These should include the entire range of household affairs: cooking, butchering, preserving, confectionery, dyeing, washing, and sewing, among other activities. "The kitchen is one of the most important aspects of the internal economy," he noted. But "kitchen" was to be understood in an old and broad sense: "Essential to a good kitchen is a good physician and a good pharmacy." Münchhausen credited one of his female ancestors, "an exceedingly industrious *Hausmutter*," with the establishment of the household and estate ledgers more than a century earlier, and these still served as the models he presented for his readers.[23]

Gender roles were to be explicitly observed. "A nobleman in the country cares for his horses and dogs, and when necessary he takes a walk through the garden. But it would be improper for a person of his status to be found in the kitchen or the cellar, the bakery or the brewery." Münchhausen conceived of the estate as a household. He mentioned that on a normal day forty-eight to fifty persons ate at least two meals at his table.[24]

The patriarchal and religious language of the past blended with eighteenth-century notions of the clocklike universe to shape the author's ideal household:

> I exhort ... the pious *Hausvater* to recognize God ... and to ascribe to Him all the attributes ... of the highest being ... . God remains the most perfect reality who ... created the entire edifice of the world and set it into motion ... . God can love nothing that does not contribute to the maintenance of the supreme purpose, namely the promotion of the order of the whole.

Living in an increasingly secular world, Münchhausen instructed his reader to understand the attribute "pious" *(fromm)* to mean not merely God-fearing or religious, but, rather, "honest and sincere" *(rechtschaffen und redlich)*. These were exactly the adjectives Zedler had used to define "patriot" in his Universal Lexicon of 1740, a work that sought to codify the knowledge and ideals of the Enlightenment in its sixty-eight volumes.[25] With values in transition, Münchhausen, like many of his contemporaries, employed a traditional religious idiom to exhort his readers to take full advantage of opportunities for secular change.

Like his predecessors, Münchhausen prescribed specific qualities for the *Hausvater*. He should be a patriot; he should impart discipline; he should be a friend of humanity; and he should be frugal. A "patriot" loved his land, obeyed the law, paid taxes, made sacrifices for the good of the whole, strived to increase industriousness *(Fleiß)*, and promoted trade and commerce in his country. A patriot, unlike a "statesman" *(L'homme d'état)*, was not interested in the power of the state but rather in the good of the whole. Hence he was a citizen, a member of the new civil society. The master should maintain discipline over children and servants responsibly, not arbitrarily and not employing undue harshness. As a friend of humanity, a *Hausvater* was generous to others in need. In conducting his own affairs, he was conscious of the effects of his actions on neighbors and relatives. A good master was frugal but not miserly.[26]

In discussing "the *Hausvater* in his economy," Münchhausen intimated a modern ideal of gender-separated responsibilities by illustrating certain topics with parablelike examples of appropriate and inappropriate behavior. Under the subject of estate expenditures, he offered a vignette about the *Hausvater*, "Cyrus," who labored under several burdens, including great indebtedness to his brothers, responsibility for his sister's dowry, and support of his widowed mother. War damaged Cyrus' estates: disease struck his animals; the tenants could not pay their rents. He would have experienced complete bankruptcy had he not been married to an intelligent woman with a substantial dowry. She convinced him to reduce his operations so that they could live from their income and keep something in reserve for improvements, and this put him back on a solid economic footing. Hence it was the family wealth, always enhanced by a fortunate marriage, and the good sense of his female partner that helped the man prosper.[27]

Still under the heading "the *Hausvater* in his economy," Münchhausen discussed the virtue, thrift *(Sprarsamkeit)*, essential to the economy. Without indicating why, he offered female examples, to illustrate. "Lucia" presided over a large staff of servants with such a commanding overview of the spinning, weaving, cleaning, and preparation of food on the estate that neither human energy nor material goods were wasted. She cared for her eight children with precise planning, providing for each individual exactly what was needed, with no excess. Lucia personified not only thrift but also the twin virtues, "order and cleanliness," which must be attained in every realm of their household. In this regard, Lucia stood in stark contrast to "Sybilla," who kept clothing clean and neat but allowed disorder elsewhere, and to "Susanne," who maintained a tidy living room but allowed disarray in the guestroom, as well as to "Ursel," whose table was spotless but who allowed her cook to be slovenly in the kitchen.[28]

Thrift, cleanliness and orderliness were increasingly gender-specific female virtues. But they were not yet exclusively so. Münchhausen offered his readers negative examples of *Hausväter* whose disorderly behavior was not to be emulated: "Stephan" permitted his dogs to run around in the house and overlooked it when his servants allowed the animals to eat from fine china! In "Minutius'" household "there reigned everywhere order, beauty, gracefulness, stateliness, and cleanliness in complete harmony," but Minutius was so obsessed with these virtues that his spotless house was never used. This was contrary to the purpose of the household. With mixed metaphors Münchhausen moved between two ideal worlds, the household economy in which the domestic virtues of orderliness and cleanliness were not gender-specific, and the newer norm in which these qualities were exclusively feminine.[29]

The direction of Münchhausen's thought is clear. His prescriptions of quality essential to the proper functioning of rural economy, like those of the Bavarian Patriotic Society, stressed increased productivity through technology and the hard work of men and women in established roles, but with an emphasis on the male as businessman and the female as housekeeper. In place of the autarchic, morally based household promoted a century earlier, Münchhausen stressed the interrelationship between individual farming units and the markets of cities and distant lands, just as he emphasized the interdependence of princely states.

In spite of his emphasis on the household, Münchhausen valued, above all, participation of the male in the civil society as defined by the commercial economy. He did not envision a place in this sphere for the *Hausmutter*. He admonished her to work hard at female tasks. Seemingly without a conscious plan to do so, he entrusted to the woman the reproductive functions of the household: contributing her familial property; wisely supporting her husband when he encountered difficulties; rearing the children; and keeping the house clean and orderly. Despite his praise of his foremother's estate ledgers, he reported that on his own manor he entrusted household matters to a male administrator,[30] presumably because it was more businesslike to do so. It is significant that Münchhausen from time to time used the new word *Hausfrau* to indicate the spouse of the *Hausvater*. *Hausfrau* was the term that in the nineteenth century would come to be associated with the norms of bourgeois domesticity. Münchhausen, the Bavarian economists, and other reformers of the middle and late eighteenth century[31] were beginning to articulate middle-class values in connection with the rural household.

Attempting to Revive the Old Household Ideal

Christian Friedrich Germershausen (1725-1810), an enterprising pastor and enthusiastic agriculturist, was dissatisfied with Münchhausen's stress on commerce and his de-emphasis of the balance of gendered work in the rural economy. Germershausen occupied the parsonage of the Brandenburg village Schlalach, where his father had held the same post before him. Like the economic writers of the seventeenth century, Germershausen was prepared to discuss the household economy from both a theological and a practical perspective. He used the fields attached to his house as an experiment station. He also assisted the *Hausmutter* of the local aristocratic estate, whose husband had died at a young age, in the management of her household, and he claimed this helped him understand the female role in agriculture. He was interested in Münchhausen's encyclopedic work but contended that the Hanoverian nobleman had neglected the role of the *Hausmutter*. Setting out to correct this, Germershausen in 1778 published the first installment of a five-volume agricultural handbook designed specifically for the female partner as head of the household. Within four years, he had completed the reference work, *Die Hausmutter in allen ihren Geschäfften* (The Complete Guide to the Activities of the Mistress of the Household).[32]

Shortly thereafter, Germershausen published *Der Hausvater in systematischer Ordnung* (The Systematic Guide for the Master of the Household) and numerous other practical books for agriculturists, including an economic encyclopedia. Germershausen's practical books were extremely popular, but it was the *Hausmutter* that established his reputation. Many of his subsequent publications bore the simple annotation "by the author of *Die Hausmutter*." Publishers reprinted his books frequently, in complete and abridged editions. In 1789 a seven-volume composite edition of *Die Hausmutter* and *Der Hausvater* appeared in Russian, published in Moscow. Germershausen's works stayed on the market until as late as 1818, eight years after his death, forty years after the first appearance of *Die Hausmutter*. By dividing the prescriptive writings for the two sexes, Germershausen established a minor genre of literature addressed to women in agriculture at the very time when changing conditions were calling into question the traditional normative female role.[33]

Germershausen's *Die Hausmutter* gained acclaim in academic circles. Johann Beckmann (1739-1811), a Göttingen professor of economics, wrote that the work would correct a serious deficiency in economic literature. An Enlightenment-inspired believer that all new things would improve society, Beckmann contributed to the newly constructed notion of agriculture as an independent science, and he was an active member in numerous local "economic societies" as well as several of the new academies of science. He was also an enthusiastic proponent of innovative technologies and became known as the "father of technological sciences" in Germany. Beckmann agreed with Germershausen about the importance and diversity of the household mistress' role and was enthusiastic about the technological and scientific expertise the village pastor imparted to women who were partners in agriculture.[34]

Germershausen's intention was to bring to women new knowledge and technological expertise, which since the founding of the Cameral Sciences had been less and less accessible to them; at the same time he sought to revive the Christian household ideal. He looked back to the venerated notions of unity and self-sufficiency that predated Cameralism and the Enlightenment. Although conservative, he was no simple reactionary who rejected innovations of his own era. He stressed the science and technology that had given an important edge to the Cameralists and Enlightenment thinkers. Significantly, he also rejected the tradition that held the household economy to be the exclusive domain of the aristocracy. Germershausen addressed his works to "middle-class" householders, indeed to "all classes of the middle estate." He was aware of the new leadership emerging in the age of Enlightenment, and his concern was that rural people and the agrarian life not be bypassed. He regarded up-to-date information as their empowerment to preserve the eroding world of the moral household economy.

In accord with developments of his day, Germershausen chose the middle classes to lead agriculture to a higher level. Originating in the seventeenth century, the concept of "middle class" was seldom used in German-speaking Europe before the second half of the eighteenth century, when it rapidly gained popularity. Like many of his contemporaries, Germershausen employed the term heuristically in rejection of the idea of aristocracy. His emphasis was not on a hereditary group but rather on a rank of persons who stood between the powerful and the poor. His preferred term, *Mittelmann*, was the same as that used by the Cameralist Justi to designate those "separated on the one hand from the poor masses and on the other from the noble, the respected and the rich." While other writers of his day almost always meant urban people when they used the term "middle class," Germershausen insisted that the term belonged to the country. In his era most people not of the aristocratic or peasant estates were legally prohibited from owning agricultural lands. Germershausen sought a new gentry to guide Germany into the future. But, paradoxically, this new class was to take the lead by preserving the age-old tradition of the moral household.

Intentionally molding his work in the tradition of the household books of an earlier century, Germershausen represented economics as a practical science but one resting on a firm philosophical and theological basis. He devoted the preponderance of his ten volumes of economic handbooks to concrete information on subjects such as crop cultivation, animal husbandry, food preparation and preservation, and the production of nonfood products such as textiles. Two entire volumes of *Der Hausvater*, six hundred pages, dealt with the cultivation of crops, while 300 pages of *Die Hausmutter* pertained to the care of cattle and swine.[35] But like his predecessors, the author regarded the human relationships of the household as the foundation of a well-functioning economy. He emphasized the collaborative roles of the two presiding figures, who must:

> share a single, unified goal with regard to the household ... . If the *Hausvater* and *Hausmutter* are in agreement, so that each and every endeavor is undertaken ... for the common good of the household or the increase of productivity, then they can, with the support of the supreme *Hausvater* [God], who affords ... order and diligence to

humans, [stand assured] that they will not be guarding, caring for, and working [their estate] in vain.³⁶

Marriage was an economic contract with both productive and reproductive purposes: procuring the mutual necessities of the partners and the bearing and education of children. The household must provide for the needs of the present generation and ensure that the household would reproduce itself for the next. The strict division of labor was predictable. Fieldwork, construction, and the keeping of horses and dogs were masculine activities. The cultivation of vegetables, the dairy operations, the care of swine and poultry, the preparation of food, brewing, and textile preparation were female in nature. The *Hausvater* was to oversee the male servants, while the *Hausmutter* supervised the women. Haying and some other responsibilities were shared, as had been the case for centuries.³⁷

The household included a large number of servants *(Gesinde)*, and Germershausen stressed the economic nature of the master-servant relationship. For the sake of order in the affairs of the estate, he emphasized, it was the important to maintain within the household just the right balance of people, neither an excess nor too few. This included the field servants and cottagers *(Ackergesinde, Cossäthen and Häuseler)* who belonged legally to the household as well as the growing numbers of day laborers and other wage earners *(Tagelöhner, Arbeitsleute, and Handarbeiter)*.³⁸

Like Münchhausen, Germershausen joined the debate over the emerging free market in agriculture. Whereas the Hanoverian nobleman championed freedom in the grain trade, however, the Brandenburg pastor was more interested in troubling labor questions. During the 1780s wages on the estates were escalating; and to the puzzlement of many observers, this was the case not only for hired workers but also for contracted household and field servants who were bound by traditional contracts to the household economy. Because he did not adhere to the modern definition of economics, Germershausen did not seek an explanation for the rising cost of labor in terms of tangible inflationary phenomena of his day, such as population growth, higher prices for consumer goods, expansion of the international grain market, proto-industrial development, land speculation, or warfare. These phenomena, plus the fact that some landowners were gradually shifting from servant labor to wage earners, were certainly in part responsible for increased wages that had many contemporaries concerned.[39] However, Germershausen concluded that the root of the plight was decay of the moral household, and he asserted that the masters and mistresses could control this trend if they would merely uphold tradition and make good decisions rather than yielding to trendy pressures. Germershausen believed that a deterioration of patriarchal authority in the household, the school, and the church was allowing servants to become too materialistic and demanding. They sometimes even expected gifts from their masters, such as money with which to buy fancy clothing at fairs. The problem was not gratuities in themselves, which, if tendered in the right manner, would induce servants to be grateful and work diligently. Rather, the cause of disorder was that masters were giving presents at the *request* of their workers! The traditional master-servant codes *(Gesindeordnungen),* designed to preserve constancy in household operations, were becoming ineffective, for masters often increased wages in spite of them codes and seemed to be doing this in order not to incur the villagers' disfavor – indicating a deterioration of authority. Masters must simply put a stop to these modern practices, Germershausen warned, and "make a commitment neither to promise, nor to pay, higher wages to the servants than is customary in the region."[40]

Germershausen deplored the gradual shift from traditional household and field servants – unfree labor – to hired workers. This development might have short-term advantages, but in the long run it intensified a breakdown in household relationships and was a manifestation of the "increasing moral decay and irreligion" of the times. It enkindled a belief among the lower classes that they were in a position to give orders, rather than to obey their superiors' rules. Masters and mistresses should work for the restoration of a proper balance in which the estate servants could meet their responsibilities without oppression or arbitrary treatment. Revitalization of communal institutions in the villages, such as councils of elders, would "bring the people back to a better path" and induce the servants to work diligently and loyally rather than seek material gain. The elders might establish village libraries containing "economic books" to teach the people how to improve themselves. Contracts between masters and servants require the latter to "subjugate themselves to the household authority," Germershausen reminded his readers.[41]

The household, then, was an economic entity bonded by moral values. It was the basic unit of society and should be governed according to practices ordained by time. The mistress of the household, unlike her husband, who typically inherited an estate, often came to a household from a distant area by contractual arrangement. For the sake of continuity, it was her responsibility to familiarize herself with the local customs, culinary tastes, and norms of behavior. By incorporating these into her own routine, she would contribute to the preservation of order.[42] A wife's purpose was to perpetuate the heritage and lineage of her husband's family.

A successful economy was based on local tradition and was rural, not urban. To illustrate this, Germershausen described the ill fate of "Pastor Thorsander," a man raised in the city who came into possession of a country estate. Adding to the handicap of his origin, he made an enormous mistake by bringing a bride from town instead of marrying a daughter of his deceased predecessor on the estate. At the very least he should have married a woman from the countryside who could advise him about the ways of the land. Both master and mistress, cut off from the ancestral training of rural people, were ignorant about crops and animals. Thorsander committed another blunder by employing workers from villages outside his own estate. Unfamiliar with the local techniques of agriculture, they worked his lands improperly, and worse, they had no loyalty to the household, which led them to cheat Thorsander. Within seven years, the poor man was in financial ruin. Even the Seven Years War, "which helped so many household managers ... get on their feet, did not help him out of his problems." At Thorsander's death, the estate had sunk to a mere quarter of its original value. Thorsander's experience illustrated the woes of modern society, including the encroaching urban culture, the decline of tradition, the decay of community, and the loss of morals. Only restoration of the household economy could reverse this degeneration.[43]

Each estate was a regime unto itself and was to be administered according to a budget. The fiscal objective was the maintenance of an equilibrium from year to year, so that the household maintained its ordained status. There should always be a surplus at year's end, not for profit or reinvestment but for emergencies. Fiscal management was a joint responsibility of the master and the mistress. Each presided over a separate budget related to his and her respective responsibilities, although the budget of the *Hausmutter* was subordinate to that of her husband. By mutual agreement – not by arbitrary choice of the male – they would decide upon the appropriate proportion for the wife's budget. She, from her special vantage within the household, might have a better view of the whole estate than her husband, and for this reason, it was her responsibility to participate in budgetary supervision, despite the fact that her budget was a mere "branch" of his. This participation as a partner – though one of subordinate status – would keep her prepared to carry on business in his absence. She was always to exercise the "female virtue" of thrift. But "the master must not expect that she alone practice frugality; he must do the same ... . It is an error to expect this economic virtue from one partner more than from the other." The "economic virtues," tradition, hard work, frugality, and piety, would increase productivity and sustain the yearly rhythm of life.[44]

The mistress supervised the activities of two separate kitchens, one for the serving classes and one for those of her own status. Each required a distinct regimen because the masters and workers of the household consumed different foods, each prepared by its own methods and requiring unique expertise. Kitchens must be run according to scientific principles. The preparation of food was a specialized skill based on dietary principles, local tradition, and practical knowledge in physics and chemistry. For example, the mistress must know the special properties of metals so that she would not cook with those that would produce toxic effects. Mealtimes, like work times, were strictly regulated, and failure to conform was a moral default on the part of the mistress.[45]

In addition to being responsible for nutrition, the enlightened mistress directed the entire process of fiber production and textile preparation. Even though the actual growing of flax, as a field activity, belonged to the realm of the *Hausvater*, it was nevertheless necessary that she possess functional knowledge about planting, growing, and harvesting the plant, for female servants under her jurisdiction were involved in the fieldwork. Moreover, textile preparation was the women's sphere, and an enlightened mistress was a manager who needed an understanding of the complete operation, not a worker who followed instructions. Germershausen presented to her information on flax production processes in various regions, including Silesia, the Rhineland, Lüneburg, and England. One could learn how to improve one's own practices through such knowledge; and the *Hausmutter* must assume this responsibility, because "one cannot expect economic innovations of the common peasants. They are frightened of change and have little time and few resources for experiments. The middle class *(Mittelmann)* must be their guiding light."[46]

The household mistress was also a medical practitioner. Because she would need skill in matters such as pregnancy, delivery of babies, and childhood disease, Germershausen provided her with a composite of the latest applied medical science, based on the leading authorities. The mistress' own daughters, "future *Hausmütter*," were a special responsibility. The pastor guided his reader carefully through the education phases of daughters, from birth to marriage, giving pedagogical instruction on physical, spiritual, intellectual, and social development. Preparing daughters to carry on in their mothers' footsteps ensured that the reproductive side of the economy was well attended.[47]

Whereas the authors of the "household books" of the previous century latter often had assumed that their readers would be familiar with customary gender roles, Germershausen did not believe that this was the case. For this reason, and also because he wanted to insist on the centrality of the female position in the operation of the household economy, Germershausen was more explicit in ascribing responsibilities to the female head of the household than his predecessors had been.

He admonished the *Hausmutter* that the estate itself should produce the commodities of household consumption. In this era of growing manufacture and commerce, increasing specialized enterprise, and a diminishing female role in the productive economy, he instructed women to preserve old traditions and never purchase through the market the basics of life. At a time when rural industry was producing more and more textiles for domestic consumption and export trade, the *Hausmutter* should use only her home-woven fabric. Although garden products, beer, wine, and bread were increasingly for sale in markets, she should produce what the household consumed. While people like Münchhausen were pointing to the advantages of the commercialization of these rural products, Germershausen prepared explicit instructions for home brewing and distilling. Acknowledging that urban women would need fewer medical skills than rural ones who lived far from physicians, he nevertheless upheld the traditionalists' position in a widespread debate about home medicine versus professional practitioners.[48] Germershausen intended his five volumes of technical and scientific information, richly interspersed with cultural advice, to empower the female agriculturalist in a changing world. She must use her position to resist the transition to a household consumer economy.

Germershausen sought also to give the master a basis of support so that he might persevere authority in the moral household in a time when secular ideals of civil society and commercial economy were eroding the foundation of the old order. He strove to empower both the *Hausvater* and *Hausmutter* to maintain their gender-specific but mutually supportive roles of the imagined household economy.

By the turn of the century, guidebooks for the household mistress had gained acceptance as a subdivision of economic literature. Friedrich Benedict Weber (1774-1848), a professor of economics and cameral studies at Frankfurt an der Oder, and Theodor Christian Friedrich Enslin (1787-1851), a publisher and bibliographer, both followed the example of Beckmann in recognizing writings for household mistresses as a distinct genre. In his 1803 publication *Handbuch der ökonomischen Literatur* (Handbook of Economic Literature), Weber listed 168 titles pertaining to the activities of the "female agriculturist and *Hausmutter*," and in 1809, 160 newly published works in this category.[49] Beckmann reported that the Society of Sciences in Göttingen agreed with Germershausen's ideal that *Hausmütter* should use estate-produced, rather than "foreign" (meaning commercially marketed) products.[50]

Gender and the Rural Household in the Age of Enlightenment

In the last decades of the eighteenth century, the question of men's and women's roles in work and culture occupied a prominent place in the minds of many, especially those who cherished agriculture. Johann Georg Krünitz (1728-1796) addressed the issue of gender in his authoritative economic encyclopedia. A medical doctor by training, Krünitz had broad academic interests but was best known for his comprehensive economic reference work that was carried on by successors until completed in 1858, reaching a total of 247 volumes. Krünitz was a collaborator with Beckmann, who reportedly influenced him to change the name of the reference work after several volumes were published – from *Oekonomische*

Encyklopaedie (Economic Encyclopedia) to *Oekonomisch-technische Encyklopaedie* (Economic-Technical Encyclopedia) to signal its modernity.[51]

The article "Frauenzimmer" in Krünitz's imposing work addressed the topic of women's role in society and demonstrated that Theodor Gottlieb von Hippel was not entirely alone in attributing gender inequality to socialization rather than to Nature. Like many people of his era, the author of this article believed that the relative bodily strength of men and women was of importance in determining their respective work roles and status. While he said there was "no doubt" about female physical inferiority in his own day, he argued that this was due to human conditioning. In the original state of Nature, he theorized, men and women had been of equal stamina and had hunted side by side to procure life's necessities. As evidence of feminine strength, he described the case of a "wild girl," unspoiled by civilization, who had allegedly appeared in a French village in 1731. She had amazed local peasants and authorities with her strength and endurance, illustrating that a woman uninfluenced by civilization had capacities not commonly attributed to the female sex. It was modern culture that made women weak. Another indication of this was the robust working-class woman who often worked side-by-side with her husband, less enfeebled than women of the upper classes by civilization's norms. Among the rich and powerful, men had made women frail by placing them in seclusion and subjugation; men themselves had become "tyrants" over women. Contrary to the popular notion, women were "just as capable as men of thinking and acting." Women had the innate courage to bear arms and the talents to be scholars and poets. To develop their skills, they should be educated equally with men and "set to serious work." Following these prescriptions would lead to great progress, because society would gain the advantage of women's untapped talents. Giving women the authority they deserved would also engender happier marriages, because the partners would be equals. Thus at least one authority, publishing in the context of an "economic" encyclopedia, held out the possibility of male-female equality and rejected the notion that feminine worth was dependent on the restoration of the moral household.[52]

Such views, derived from Enlightenment convictions, were rare, however. Even Krünitz wrote contradictory commentary in his reference work that upheld the patriarchal ideal. The article "Hausvater" explained that a *Hausvater* "indisputably" exercised authority over his wife just as he did over his children. It belonged to "the nature of things" that the weaker party was dependent on the stronger and that the nurtured would be a ward of the nurturer. "Therefore the woman must be under the domestic authority of the man." And if inferior physical strength determined the status of the woman, so did the fact that "in pregnancy, childbearing, and other female conditions, Nature gave women many more liabilities in administering important affairs than it did men." The notion of sexual difference rooted in Nature led Krünitz to ignore the vision of gender equality articulated elsewhere in his encyclopedia in favor of patriarchy. How else could one define *"Hausvater"*?[53]

Almost all writers who viewed agriculture as the primary organizing institution of society employed the idiom of the household. It was for them a foundation stone of the language of the rural society. In spite of their common rhetoric, two primary ideals of gendered culture competed with one another in debates about the rural economy. According to the model shared by Münchhausen, the Bavarian economists, and numerous members of economic societies throughout German-speaking Europe, agricultural progress required commercialization and complex technology. Such reformers were concerned less about people and more about products than their intellectual predecessors had been. Yet they clearly envisioned males taking the lead in the agrarian changes.[54] They exhorted females to work diligently in the household, but they did so in a time when the household was losing its importance to the economy. They thus helped implant in the countryside a quiet, definitive shift in the normative culture, undergirding new ideals of public and private spheres. This linguistic innovation was probably invisible to most people because of the perception that the economic partnership between men and women had always been an unequal one. Moreover, the inequality was assumed to be natural and was reinforced by the newest law codes. To many, women's place must not have appeared to change at all; they were to occupy the places that had seemed to define women's work since antiquity: household, garden, dairy, spinning chamber, and nursery. The difference in women's roles, imperceptible to many, was a component of the new norm of a market economy, directed by men and holding no place for women.

Germershausen represented the opposing model. He perceived the erosion of the old gender ideals in the countryside and sought to reverse the process by reinforcing the moral concepts of the household. Germershausen's *Hausvater* and *Hausmutter* presided over a Christian, patriarchal system, but they also represented a rising middle class (for example in their use of science and technology to secure the ancestral agrarian values). In his best known work, the guide for the household mistress, Germershausen rejected the Enlightenment construct of female dependence and frailty. He refused to accept the growing distinction between the private and the public spheres.

Even this traditionalist, however, was unable to resist the lure of progress, for only a few years after completion of *Die Hausmutter*, when Germershausen turned to the role of the household master, he accommodated his vision much more to the new thought that was the foundation for this separation. Citing no less a reformer than England's Arthur Young (1741-1820), Germershausen defended agriculture against the encroachment of urban commerce. At the same time he emphasized that both "private welfare *[Privatglück]* and the general well-being *[allgemeine Glückseligkeit]* rest on the ever increasing yields of the soil," not the maintenance of the age-old ideal of household necessity. In the introduction to *Der Hausvater*, Germershausen pointed approvingly to the growing volume of "economic literature" as an auspicious sign of the times but warned his contemporaries not to be complacent that agriculture would progress without governmental leadership:

> One dare not even consider the idea that rural enterprise *[ländliche Industrie]* has progressed so far that it requires no further improvement ... and that national policies *[Staatspolitik]* are obligated to do no more than to see that countries preserve their current conditions and do not regress. Whoever presumes this has too little knowledge of agriculture ... and too limited a vision of the possible increased production.

In spite of his five-volume plea for the integrity of the old household in *Die Hausmutter*, Germershausen found himself attracted to economic development in the sense advocated by the Cameralists and free-market proponents. Citing Münchhausen, whose ideas had apparently become more attractive to him over time, Germershausen declared that Germans had much to learn from the British about manufacturing. In 1789-90, he published a book on sheep farming in which he depicted "patriotic economists" (males), producing wool for commercial markets. In this work he urged his readers to be alert to the supply and demand of markets and even used the example of profitably produced flax – a strictly female activity in his earlier work. The depicted producers and marketers were conspicuously male in this manual.[55] The lure of progress was seductive in the eighteenth century, and it did not escape even those who set out to fortify traditional cultures in the face of social and economic change.

With regard to normative gender roles, the debate about agriculture fostered a linguistic separation of the public and private spheres and an accompanying shift in the language of the household "virtues." Whereas domesticity, thrift, and obedience were virtues common to both women and men in the seventeenth-century, by the end of the eighteenth they were increasingly exclusive female attributes. The attribute of industriousness, as embodied in the word *Industrie*, also earlier shared by both sexes, was assuming a new meaning and a masculine character to accompany the cultural emphasis on acquisition and exchange of wealth through competition. The old word *Fleiß*, meaning hard work, still applied to women.

Even Germershausen's language was ambiguous when he described the virtues he so ardently sought to strengthen. As he strove to undergird the old ideals for the work of the *Hausmutter*, his own historical context led him to articulate something that sounded much like the nineteenth-century bourgeois notion of domesticity. He exhorted mistresses to teach their very young daughters – through age six – lessons in "orderliness and cleanliness." Mothers should instruct their seven- to twelve-year-old daughters to appreciate the simple ways of the country and to shun fancy clothing. They should train them at home rather than in trendy "French schools and boarding schools." Future mistresses should learn reading and arithmetic but no foreign languages; they should never read novels. They should enhance their skills in sewing. *Hausmütter* should help their older daughters, after the age of puberty, to focus on one, ultimate goal, marriage. The girls must remain pure and chaste and cultivate the "economic virtues," the chief of which was modesty.[56]

In a separate essay on woman's role in marriage, in 1782, Germershausen objected to the popular idea that a woman's role was to bring property into the partnership. Her part was more active than this. She was to enhance the household economy by practicing the virtue of "thrift."[57] While the pastor intended to emphasize the active economic role of the female partner who helped secure life's necessities, his rhetoric, modern in its rejection of the aristocratic institution of the dowry as the indication of a woman's worth, would later be used to stress that a wife was not a producer but merely a consumer.

The debate between the agrarian reformers who sought to foster progress and those who strove to shore up the household ideal assumed a dynamic of its own. The language of both sides ultimately contributed to the normative separation of the public, market sphere from that of the private household. Those who agreed with Münchhausen did not object to this; those who held views like Germershausen's were unable to resist it.

Notes

1. Lütge, *Deutsche Sozial- und Wirtschaftsgeschichte*, 421.
2. Abel, *Geschichte der deutschen Landwirtschaft*, 275. Abel, *Massenarmut und Hungerkrisen*, 46-54.
3. Quotation from Frederick the Great: Abel, *Geschichte der deutschen Landwirtschaft*, 277; see also 274-75. Frauendorfer, *Ideengeschichte der Agrarwirtschaft*, 184-85. Helen P. Liebel, *Enlightened Bureaucracy versus Enlightened Despotism in Baden, 1750-1792*, Transactions of the American Philosophical Society, New Series, vol. 55, no. 5 (Philadelphia: American Philosophical Society, 1965), 40-54. Charles W. Ingrao, *The Hessian Mercenary State: Ideas, Institutions, and Reform Under Frederick II, 1760-1785* (Cambridge, England: Cambridge University, 1987), 68-73.
4. Brückner, *Staatswissenschaften*, 291-92. John G. Gagliardo, *From Pariah to Patriot: The Changing Image of the German Peasant, 1770-1840* (Lexington: University Press of Kentucky, 1969), 106. On the meaning of "patriotic" in this context, see Vierhaus, "Patriotismus," 9-31.
5. Abel, *Geschichte der deutschen Landwirtschaft*, 306-12. Gertrud Schröder-Lembke, "Englische Einflüsse auf die deutsche Gutswirtschaft im 18. Jahrhundert," *Zeitschrift für Agrargeschichte und Agrarsoziologie* 12 (1964): 29-36. Hans-Joachim Braun, "Die Sozietäten in Leipzig und Karlsruhe als Vermittler englischer ökonomisch-technischer Innovationen," in Vierhaus, *Deutsche patriotische Gesellschaften*, 241-54.
6. Braun, "Die Sozietäten," 312-19. On potatoes and population growth, see Robert McC. Netting, *Balancing on an Alp: Ecological Change and Continuity in a Swiss Mountain Community* (Cambridge, England: Cambridge University, 1981), 159-68. See Amaranthes, *Frauenlexikon*, "Tartuffeln," and related entries, 1997-1981, and Lemmer, "Nachwort," ibid., 23.
7. Abel, *Geschichte der deutschen Landwirtschaft*, 314-21.
8. Stavenhagen, *Geschichte der Wirtschaftstheorie*, 35-46. Frauendorfer, *Ideengeschichte*, 159-62. Elizabeth Fox-Genovese, *The Origins of Physiocracy: Economic Revolution and Social Order in Eighteenth-Century France* (Ithica, NY:

Cornell University, 1976), 43-60. Brückner, *Staatswissenschaften*, 291-92. Mittenzwei sees more similarity than difference between the Cameralists and the Physiocrats: "Die Agrarfrage und der Kameralismus," 180-81.

9. Gertrud Schröder-Lembke, "Oeconomische Gesellschaften im 18. Jahrhundert," *Zeitschrift für Agrargeschichte und Agrarsoziologie* 38 (1990): 16-18. Güntz, *Handbuch*, 2: 39-40. Gottfried Ernst Hoffman, "Philipp Ernst Lüders: Ein landwirtschaftlicher Reformer Schleswig-Holsteins im 18. Jahrhundert," *Blätter für deutsche Landesgeschichte* 89 (1952): 134-52.

10. Schröder-Lembke, "Oeconomische Gesellschaften," 16-17. Christian Gottlieb Jöcher, "Johann Riem," in *Allgemeines Gelehrten-Lexikon*, continued and expanded by H.W. Rotermund 6 (1819), in *Deutsches Biographisches Archiv*, fiche 1037, frames 284-93. Hans-Joachim Braun, "Die Sozietäten in Leipzig und Karlsruhe als Vermittler englischer ökonomisch-technischer Innovationen," in Vierhaus, *Deutsche patriotische und gemeinnützige Gesellschaften*, 245-47.

11. Karl Dinklage, "Gründung und Aufbau der theresianischen Ackerbaugesellschaften," *Zeitschrift für Agrargeschichte und Agrarsoziologie* 13 (1965): 200-11. Norbert Schindler and Wolfgang Bonß, "Praktische Aufklärung – Ökonomische Sozietäten in Süddeutschland und Österreich im 18. Jahrhundert," in Vierhaus, *Deutsche patriotische Gesellschaften*, 263-82. Ludwig Deike, "Die Celler Sozietät und Landwirtschaftsgesellschaft von 1764," in ibid., 161-94. Ludwig Deike, *Die Entstehung der Celler Landwirtschaftsgesellschaft: Ökonomische Sozietäten und die Anfänge der modernen Agrarreformen im 18. Jahrhundert*, ed. Ilse Deike and Carl-Hans Hauptmeyer, Quellen und Darstellungen zur Geschichte Niedersachsens, vol. 113 (Hanover: Hahn, 1994), 74-104.

12. *Baierischer Ökonomischer Der Hausvater oder gesammelte Schriften der Kurfürstlichen Gesellschaft sittlich- und landwirtschaftlicher Wissenschaften in Burghausen* (Munich: Fritz, 1780-1786). See the articles: "Eines alten Freundes, und Gönners der Leipziger Sammlung eingeschickter Beytrag, von der Gesinden oder Ehehalten Noth," vol.1 (1780): 120-28; "Antwort auf die Frage des Münchnerischen Intelligenzblatts Nro. 38," vol. 1 (1780): 190-92; Franz von Paula Schranck, "Gedanken über die Erziehung der Bauernjugend," vol. 5 (1781): 130-175. Schindler and Bonß, "Praktische Aufklärung," 283-93.

13. "Auszug aus eines Freundes, und adelichen Landwirths sehr nützlichen, und praktischen Anmerkungen, über die Wirthschaft eines adelichen Gutes," *Baierischer Ökonomischer Hausvater* 2 (1780): 593-603, 669-70, 675-82, 738-52.

14. "Beschreibung eines Seidenhaspels," ibid., vol. 8 (1785): 246-48.

15. *Georgica Bavarica: Oder Oeconomische Auszüge und gründliche Nachricht wie sowohl Adeliche Land- als gemeine Bauern-Güther verbessert, und derselben*

jährliche Erträgnissen und ein Merkliches vermehrt werden können (Munich: Vötter, 1752), 3-4.
16. Otto von Münchhausen, *Der Hausvater* (Hanover: Helwing, 1764-74). The publisher, Nikolaus Förster, reissued various volumes with new dates frequently, so that it is difficult to identify individual editions. Each volume was published in two parts, sometimes bound together and sometimes separately. For volume six, only part one was published. Helwing also published a so-called "third edition" in 1774-75: *Gesamtverzeichnis 1700-1910*, 101:32. I have used the second edition, 1766-1770. C. Leisewitz, "Otto von Münchhausen," in *Allgemeine Deutsche Biographie*, vol. 23 (1886), 7-8. Gebhard von Lenthe and Hans Mahrenholtz, *Stammtafeln der Familie von Münchhausen*, Schaumburger Studien, vol. 36 (Rinteln: Bösendahl), 221-22. Richarz, *Herrschaftliche Haushalte*, 28-33.
17. Daniel Liberti, *Die in Churfürstenthum Sachsen und angräntzenden Landen approbirte Adeliche Hauß-Wirthschafts-Kunst in welcher diejenigen Sachen so in einer wichtigen Hauß-Haltung täglich vorkommen, absonderlich, was ein rechtschaffener Haußwirth und Verwalter jeden Monat durchs gantze Jahr zuthun und wie er endlich Jahres-Rechnung formieren und schlüssen soll, abgehaldelt werden* (Leipzig: Groschuff, 1701). Solomon Fischer von Azendorff, *Unterrichteter Hauß-Vater und kluger Gärtner, nebst dem verständigen Jäger-Meister oder gründliche Anleitung wie die Haußhaltungs-Kunst mit Nutz zu Begreiffen* (Hanover: Förster, 1705). *Der sorgfältige Hauß-Wirthschafts-Verwalter, welcher gründlich zeiget, was durchs gantze Jahr so wohl in Wirthschaffts-Rechnungen als im Haus-Wesen und Acker-Bau In acht zu nehmen, daß ein guter Nutzen daraus erfolge. Nebst wohl approbirten Vieh- Roß-Artzeneyen und dienlichen Hauß-Mitteln versehen* (Leipzig: Rohrlachs, 1712). Johann Joachim Becher [Sturm], *Kluger Haus-Vater, Verständige Haus-Mutter, vollkommener Land Medicus wie auch Wohlerfahrner Roß- und Vieh-Artzt, nebenst einem deutlichen und gewissen Handgriff die Haushaltungs-Kunst innerhalb von 24 Stunden zu erlernen* (Leipzig: Groschuff, 1714). *Sächsisch- und Brandenburgisches Land- und Hauß-Wirthschaftsbuch* (Nuremberg: Riegeln, 1730).
18. Münchhausen, *Hausvater*, 1:1-198.
19. Ibid., 1:337.
20. Ibid., 3:234-38; 4:71, 104-7.
21. Ibid, 4: 473-540. Otto von Münchhausen, *Der freye Kornhandel als das beste Mittel um Mangel und Theuerung zu verhüten: Zur Warnung auf künftige Zeiten aus der Erfahrung und aus neuen Gründen erwiesen* (Hanover: Försters, 1772), preface [n.p.]. On the debate over the grain trade, see Frank T.W.C. Schuurmans, "State, Society, and the Market: Karl Sigmund Altenstein and the Language of Reform 1770-1807" (Ph.D. diss., University of Wisconsin-Madison, 1995), 171-303. Frank Schuurmans, "Eco-

nomic Liberalization, Honour, and Perfectibility: Karl Sigmund Altenstein and the Spiritualization of Liberalism," *German History* 16 (1998): 165-84.
22. Frank Schuurmans, "Economic Liberalization," passim. Münchhausen, *Hausvater*, 2:594. On the "freedom" (privilege) of brewing for commercial purposes see Zedler, *Grosses Universal-Lexikon*, vol 3 (1733): 1794-1800. Jablonski, in describing the arts of brewing and distilling, assumed that it would be done by brewers who had been granted the privilege. See the articles, "Brantwein" and "Brauen" in Johann Theodor Jablonski, *Allgemeines Lexikon der Künste und Wissenschaften, oder Deutliche Beschreibung des Reichs der Natur, der Himmel, und himmlischen Cörper, der Luft, der Erde, sammt den bekannten gewächsen, der Thiere, Steine und Erzte, der Meers und der darinne lebenden Geschöpfe; Ingleichen Aller menschlichen Handlungen, Staats-Rechts- Kriegs- Policey- Haushaltungs- und Gelehrten-Geschäffte, Hanthierungen und Gewerbe, samt einer Erklärung der dabey vorkommender Kunst-Wörter und Redens-Arten*, rev. ed. (Königsberg: Hartung, 1748), 166-67.
23. Münchhausen, *Hausvater*, 1:425-27, 2:587-606. Richarz, *Herrschaftliche Haushalte*, 33.
24. Münchhausen, *Hausvater*, 1:426, 2:593.
25. Ibid., 4:8-49. Zedler, *Grosses Universal-Lexikon*, vol. 26 (1740): 1393. On Zedler, see Jürgen Voss, "Deutsche und französische Enzyklopädien des 18. Jahrhunderts," in Schneiders, *Aufklärung als Mission*, 238-41.
26. Münchhausen, *Hausvater*, 4:50-296. Deike, "Die Celler Sozietät," 176-78.
27. Münchhausen, *Hausvater*, 4:286-88.
28. Ibid., 373-77.
29. Ibid., 374-75. As always, the language and the values changed unevenly. Orderliness, for example, remained a masculine norm for a long time in some contexts. See Sabean, *Property, Production and Family*, 144-45, on *liederlich* [slovenly] as a term of contempt for men in the nineteenth century.
30. Münchhausen, *Hausvater*, 1:425-31.
31. For example: Johann Georg Leopoldt, *Nützliche und auf die Erfahrung gegründete Einleitung zu der Landwirtschaft* (Berlin: Günther, 1759). B. von Wichmannshausen, *Das Oeconomische Allerley* (Leipzig: Wendler, 1762); Johann Gottlob von Schönfeld, *Die Landwirthschaft und deren Verbesserung nach eigenen Erfahrungen beschrieben* (Leipzig: Breitkopf, 1773); [Johann Wiegand], *Der wohlfahrene Landwirth: oder vorläufige Anleitung wie die Landwirthschaftsökonomie, nämlich der Feldbau, die Waldungen, die Teiche, die Mayerhöfe und die Schäfereyen in einen viel verbesserten Stand gebracht werden könnte* (Vienna: Krauß, 1774-75); *Der Sächsische Landwirth in seiner Landwirthschaft, was er jetzt ist und was er seyn könnte oder: wie ein jeder seine Einkünfte in kurzer Zeit um mehr als die Hälfte sehr leicht erhöhen könne* (Leipzig: Hilscher, 1788-91). See Rudolf Jentzsch, *Der deutsch-lateinische Büchermarkt nach dem Leipziger Ostermeß-Katalogen von 1740, 1770 und*

1800 in seiner Gliederung und Wandlung, Beiträge zur Kultur- und Universalgeschichte, vol. 22, (Leipzig: Voigtländer, 1912), 141-45, 299-312. One agricultural guide that emphasizes commercial enterprise is conspicuous for its early date: Emanuel König, *Georgica Helvetica Curiosa, oder neu curioses Eydgenossisch-Schweitzerisches Haus-Buch* (Basel: König, 1706).

32. Christian Friedrich Germershausen, *Die Hausmutter in allen ihren Geschäfften* (Leipzig: Junius, 1777-81). Rainer Gruenter, "Die Hausmutter in allen ihren Geschäfften," *Euphorion: Zeitschrift für Literaturgeschichte* 57 (1963): 219-26. Rainer Gruenter, "Nachtrag zur Hausmutter," ibid., 61 (1967): 155-62. Gotthardt Frühsorge, "Die Einheit aller Geschäffte: Tradition und Veränderung des 'Hausmutter'-Bildes in der deutschen Ökonomieliteratur des 18. Jahrhunderts," *Wolfenbüttler Studien zur Aufklärung* 3 (1976): 137-57. Franz, "Pfarrer als Wissenschaftler," 287-88.

33. Christian Friedrich Germershausen, *Der Hausvater in systematischer Ordnung* (Leipzig: Junius, 1783-86). Christian Friedrich Germershausen, *Oekonomisches Reallexikon, worin alles was nach den Theorien und erprobten Erfahrungen der bewährtesten Oekonomen unsrer Zeit zu wissen nöthig ist*, (Leipzig: Feind, 1795-1799). Güntz, *Handbuch* 1:151-55. *Gesamtverzeichnis*, 45:367. Russian composite edition of *Der Hausvater* and *Die Hausmutter:* Germershausen, *Khoziain i khoziaika; ili dolzhnosti gospodina i gospozhi vo vsekh vidakh*, trans. Vasilii Levshin (Moscow: 1789). See Germershausen, "Nachricht von Herrn Pastor Germershausens Hausvater," in *Nützliche Sammlung von Aufsätzen und Wahrnehmungen über die Witterungen, die Haushaltskunde, das Gewerbe, die Naturkenntniß, Polizey, und andere damit verknüpfte Wissenschaften, welche die Fortsetzung des Wittenbergschen Wochenblatts ausmachen*, ed. Johann Daniel Titius (Leipzig: Junius, 1782-1792) vol. 1, 125-27. Germershausen was not the first to write separate handbooks for males and females. See companion volumes translated from the French: *Der wohl unterwiesene Landwirth, oder der Freund des Landmannes* (Nuremberg: Schwarzkopf, 1768); and *Die wohl unterrichtete Landwirthin, oder Anfangs-Gründe zur erlernung einer klugen und vernünftigen Haus- und Landwirtschaft zum besten des weiblichen Geschlechts gesammelt*, new ed. (Nuremberg: Schwarzkopf, 1774). Beckmann judged these publications of poor quality compared to those of Germershausen: Johann Beckmann, *Physikalisch-Ökonomische Bibliothek worin von den neuesten Büchern welche die Naturgeschichte, Naturlehre, und die Land- und Staatswirthschaft betreffen, zuverlässige und vollständige Nachrichten ertheilt werden*, (Göttingen: Vandenhoeck & Ruprecht, 1770-1808), vol. 9 (1778), 272.

34. Beckmann, *Physikalisch-Ökonomische Bibliothek*, vol. 9, 272-73; vol. 11, 36, 38-39. Ulrich Troitzsch, "Die Schriften von Johann Beckmann (1739-1811) unter dem Aspekt der 'Gemeinnützigkeit': Ein Diskussionsbeitrag," in Vierhaus, *Deutsche patriotische Gesellschaften*, 355-69. Hans- Peter Müller

and Ulrich Troitzsch, eds., *Technologie zwischen Fortschritt und Tradition: Beiträge zum internationalen Johann Beckmann-Symposium Göttingen 1989* (Frankfurt am Main: Lang, 1992). Brückner, *Staatswissenschaften*, 291-92.

35. Germershausen, *Der Hausvater*, 2: passim, 3: passim; *Die Hausmutter*, 4:535-872. On the concept of middle class, see Werner Conze, "Mittelstand," *Geschichtliche Grundbegriffe*, vol. 4 (1978), 51-62. Richarz, *Oikos, Haus und Haushalt*, 206.
36. Germershausen, *Der Hausvater*, 1:166.
37. Germershausen articles "Ehe" and "Ehestand," in *Oekonomisches Reallexikon*, 2:359-60. See also his *Der Hausvater*, 1:217-80 and *Die Hausmutter*, 5:63-149. In addition see the articles "Ehe," "Ehe-Geld," and "Ehe-Mann" in Georg Heinrich Zincke, *Allgemeines Oeconomisches Lexicon*, (Leipzig: Gleditsch, 1731), vol. 1, 604-605.
38. Germershausen, *Der Hausvater*, 1:280-83. The terms used here are Germershausen's and are common to his region. The terminology for various classes of rural workers varied widely between territories. For some eighteenth-century definitions see the following: Zincke's articles "Gesinde," "Gesinde-Lohn," and "Gesinde-Noth" in *Allgemeines Oeconomisches Lexicon*, 1:929-32. Friedrich G. Leonhardi, *Erdbeschreibung der preußischen Monarchie* (Halle: Schwettsche, 1791-98), 1:347-48, 359. *Allgemeines Landrecht*, part II, title 7, section 6, 433-51. See Miterauer, "Gesindedienst," 198, n. 65.
39. On inflationary trends, see Schissler, *Preußische Agrargesellschaft*, 59-104. See also Wilhelm Abel, *Agrarkrisen und Agrarkonjunktur: Eine Geschichte der Land- und Ernährungswirtschaft Mitteleuropas seit dem hohen Mittelalter*, 3rd ed. (Hamburg: Parey, 1978), 196-219; and Kriedte, *Spätfeudalismus und Handelskapital*, 127-42. On one estate's shift to wage labor, as a result of disputes with the peasants, see William W. Hagen, "The Junkers' Faithless Servants: Peasant Insubordination and the Breakdown of Serfdom in Brandenburg-Prussia, 1763-1811," in *The German Peasantry: Conflict and Community in Rural Society from the Eighteenth to the Twentieth Centuries* (New York: St. Martin's, 1988), 71-101.
40. Germershausen, *Der Hausvater*, 1:223-26. Germershausen, *Die Hausmutter*, 5:97-102. On perceived deterioration of authority of the *Hausvater* see Koselleck, *Preußen zwischen Reform und Revolution*, 62-70; and Hans-Heinrich Müller, "Der agrarische Fortschritt und die Bauern in Brandenburg vor den Reformen von 1807," *Zeitschrift für Geschichtswissenschaft* 12 (1964): 636-48.
41. Germershausen, *Der Hausvater*, 1:298-301, 304-306. Germershausen, *Die Hausmutter*, 5:133-34.
42. Germershausen, *Die Hausmutter*, 1:367-416.
43. Germershausen, *Der Hausvater*, 1:293-6.

44. Ibid., 166-213; quotations from pp. 200, 209. See also Germershausen, *Die Hausmutter*, 5:28-63. Münch, *Ordnung, Fleiß und Sparsamkeit*, 24-32.
45. Germershausen, *Die Hausmutter*, 1: passim, 2: passim, 3:1-356.
46. Ibid., 4:349-405; quotation p. 382.
47. Ibid., 5:149-656. See Marion W. Gray, "Educating for Domesticity: Pedagogical Ideals in the *Hausmütterliteratur* during the Age of Enlightenment," in *Views of Women's Lives in Western Tradition: Frontiers of the Past and the Future*, ed. Frances Richardson Keller, Women's Studies, vol. 5 (Lewiston, N.Y.: Mellen, 1990), 407-31.
48. On textile production see Kriedte, *Spätfeudalismus und Handelskapital,* 156-58. See Justi's comments on brewing, a commercial activity: *Staatswirtschaft*, 507-11. On garden products: Abel, *Geschichte der deutschen Landwirtschaft*, 220-22. On the debate on medicine: Frevert, "Frauen und Ärzte," 183-90.
49. Friedrich Benedict Weber, *Handbuch der ökonomischen Literatur, oder systematische Anleitung zur Kenntniß der deutschen ökonomischen Schriften die sowohl die gesammte Land- und Hauswirthschaft als die mit derselben verbundenen Hülfs- und Nebenwissenschaften angehen* (Berlin: Fröhlich, 1803; Berlin: Duncker und Humblot, 1809; Breslau: Holäufer, 1816; Leipzig: Hartman, 1823; Breslau: Max, 1832; Berlin: Grimma, 1842), vol. 2: 263-82; vol. 3, 286-304; vol. 4, 201-21; vol. 5, 218-35; vol. 6. 280-93. Theodor Christian Enslin, *Bibliotheca Oeconomica oder Verzeichnis aller brauchbaren in älterer und neuerer Zeit, bis zur Mitte des Jahres 1824 in Deutschland erschienen Bücher über Land- und Hauswirthschaft* (Berlin: Enslin, 1825), 34, 39, 43-44, 58-61.
50. Beckmann, *Physicalische-Ökonomische Bibliothek*, 11:172-73.
51. Wolfhard Weber, "Johann Georg Krünitz, Enzyklopädist," in *Neue Deutsche Biographie*, vol. 13 (1982), 110-11. Voss, "Deutsche und französische Enzyklopädien," 245. *Gesamtverzeichnis*, 81: 321-24.
52. Krünitz, "Frauen-Zimmer," in *Oekonomische Encyklopaedie*, 14:801-19.
53. Krünitz, "Hausvater," ibid., 22:414-15.
54. See for example, Leopoldt, *Nützliche Einleitung zu der Landwirthschaft.*
55. Germershausen, *Der Hausvater*, 1, preface, ix-xi. Christian Friedrich Germershausen, *Das Ganze der Schafzucht aus Beurtheilung und Berichtigung älterer und neuerer Theorien nach Grunden und eigener Erfahrung* (Leipzig: Junius: 1789-90).
56. Germershausen, *Die Hausmutter*, 5:444-45, 555-604, 626-30.
57. Christian Friedrich Germershausen, "Der Mann kann die Frau nicht reich machen, wohl aber die Frau den Mann: Denn der ersparrte Pfennig ist besser als der erworbene," in Titius, *Nützliche Sammlung*, 1:1-5. This essay was reprinted in *Hannoverisches Magazin* 21 (1783): 677-88.

Chapter Seven

The Primacy of the Public Sphere
The Era of the French Revolution and Napoleon (1790-1815)

In 1789 revolution broke out in France, and it brought lasting changes to all of Europe, including Germany. By the early nineteenth century a new middle-class ideology prevailed, making permanent the break between the old regime and the new. This constellation of ideas was often unsystematically articulated but was nevertheless widely accepted among the educated classes. It included the imperatives of private property and free markets and embraced the ideal of careers based on talent rather than on heredity. It stood for the Enlightenment concept of individualism, as opposed to the precapitalist norms of corporate and household identity. Strengthened states fostered the development of the new goals and public institutions. The bourgeoisie benefited directly from expanded bureaucracies, through which their educated sons gained profitable careers. In these roles the sons of the new middle class found it in their interest to continue the process of empowering the state and remaking society in their own image.

Notes for this section begin on page 250.

In this historical context, debates about the relative roles of women and men in society took on a new intensity. Enlightenment writers such as Kant, Hippel, and Humboldt rekindled intense debates about gender, sometimes with new perspectives, and sometimes insisting on the validity of old positions. This discourse was echoed at popular levels in society. In the context of uncertainty and threat embodied in the French Revolution, many sought security in familiar themes of an ordered gender hierarchy.

Governments increased control over their subjects in the name of citizenship, and the female half of the population, regardless of social class, could lay no claim to the new authority. States emerged from the revolutionary era with constituencies of male property owners. Women found themselves increasingly defined by middle-class notions of domesticity, separated from the civil society of the reformed and invigorated state governments.

The Increased Authority of the State

In France after 1789, the new leaders went about abolishing manorialism and old-regime absolutism and establishing modern institutions based on the ideals of a civil society in the hands of propertied males. The revolutionaries ensured the existence of an economy based on commerce, free labor, and free trade. Following a decade of upheaval, General Napoleon Bonaparte took over leadership of the government, reestablishing stability and consolidating many of the revolutionary changes. In 1799, 1806, and 1809, he led his armies against those of Austria and other German states, and the French brought with them the energy unleashed by the Parisian revolutions. By 1812, the political map of the Germanies had been completely altered. The Holy Roman Empire was dissolved; parts of western Germany were fused into the extended French Empire; other areas were under French control as the Confederation of the Rhine, which included the new Kingdom of Westphalia, ruled by Napoleon's brother, Jerome Bonaparte. Prussia had suffered a shattering subjugation in 1806-1807, and while King Frederick William III did not lose his crown as many German princes did, the French drove his court far from Berlin. It took up residence in the provincial city of Königsberg while French troops occupied two-thirds of the Hohenzollern territory and demanded massive reparations. Austria had endured the humiliation of having Vienna conquered by the French, had sacrificed significant territories, and had suffered bankruptcy of the state treasury. The Habsburg Monarchy faced an uncertain future.

In the 1790s, immediately after the French Revolution, many Enlightenment partisans in Germany held spirited hopes for radical change in their own society that they had dreamed of for longer than a generation. Pamphleteers and journalists raced to spread the good news of the revolution throughout Germany. Jacobin clubs sprang up not only in the French-occupied cities on the east bank of the Rhine but also in northern cities like Hamburg. Poets extolled the revolution's virtues, while newspapers carried the "revolutionary fever" to German villages. Peasants demanded "freedom and equality like in France." Reading societies increased in numbers as never before. At the University of Göttingen, the historian Ludwig Timotheus Spittler (1752-1810) lectured enthusiastically on the possibilities of "democracy," in which, he stressed, "the legislative authority [rests] with the entire folk and a ... majority rules."[1]

But by 1794, as news of events from across the Rhine brought reports of violence, including those about "the Terror" and the beheading of King Louis XVI, many were shocked. Even before Napoleon came to power, German princes and their civil servants had perceived the French events as a threat to the legitimacy of monarchical institutions and their own futures. Some of the intellectual activity sparked by the Revolution was unfriendly to the course of events in France and geared toward protecting home cities and towns from the chaos. The newly formed Literary Ladies Society in the small residence town of Oldenburg was one small example of ways in which intense political discussion may have fostered a greater public role for women than before 1789. But contrary to what its name might suggest, it was under the leadership of the prominent local male business and civic leaders and allowed women of prestigious families to be members, albeit passive ones. The club discussed contemporary authors whose works could by no means be considered revolutionary. Their biweekly meetings seemed to be focused on trying to ensure that Germany would not experience revolution. By the middle of the decade, enthusiasm for revolutionary ideas waned in Germany.[2]

However, defeat on battlefields in the Napoleonic encounters seemed to open up another kind of possibility for change. An impetus for restyling society began to come not from Jacobin clubs but from governments. Not only those directly established by Napoleon, such as in Westphalia, but those like Austria, Bavaria, and Prussia that attempted to respond to the challenges of the new era with their own reforms, sought to put new ideals into practice. In Germany's subjugation governmental reformers found seedbeds for their ideas. Rulers who previously had censored critical thought began instead to recruit innovators into their planning councils. In the summer of 1807, just weeks after the Peace of Tilsit had stripped Prussia of all of its territories west of the Elbe, Prussian administrator Friedrich Staegemann rejoiced about impending new freedoms: "Serfdom will be abolished, everyone will be able to purchase aristocratic lands, compulsory guilds will be destroyed, and all foreign products will become importable."[3]

The political leaders called in to save Germany were trained in the tradition of the Cameralists, and they regarded the locus of economic life and political authority to be in the halls of government, not in the household. They worked to strengthen the authority of the state in order to put into practice their ideals about society and the economy.

Karl August von Hardenberg (1750-1822), soon to become Staatskanzler of Prussia, expressed the consensus of Reformers in many corners of Germany in 1807:

The French Revolution, of which the present wars are a continuation, gave to the French, along with bloodletting and turmoil, a completely new energy. All the slumbering forces were awakened. Deplorable and weak conditions, old prejudices, and deficient institutions were destroyed – admittedly along with much that was good.[4]

The cause for the French Revolution's violence and excess, Hardenberg reasoned, was that the holders of power in France had foolishly tried to resist the changes. Prussia should not follow this example; rather it should seek

> a revolution in the good sense, leading directly to the grand purpose of the ennoblement of humanity through wisdom of the government and not through violent impulses … . That is our goal, our leading ideal. Democratic principles in a monarchic regime: this seems to me the appropriate form for the present spirit of the times. Pure democracy we should leave until the year 2440.[5]

Under such mandates, reformers drafted, debated, revised, and promulgated princely decrees, bringing constitutional change such as the Napoleonic Civil Code, peasant "emancipations," bureaucratic reforms, the abolition of guilds, and the establishment of citizen armies. Alongside the notion of civil society stood the ideals of duty and service to one's government. Government leaders in the non-occupied parts of Germany sought to arouse feelings of local pride as a way of turning the forces engendered by the French Revolution back against France and emancipating Central Europe. By 1814, they were successful in doing this. A coalition of European armies inflicted defeat on Napoleon in the so-called Wars of Liberation. Within months, European heads of state convened in Vienna to redraw the political map.

The experience of the French Revolution and Napoleon's Empire altered German-speaking Europe forever. Regardless of whether they were enthusiastic or alarmed, political leaders had to acknowledge that they were dealing with an unprecedented set of social, economic, and political conditions. The state was becoming something previously unknown. The middle-class ideal of civil society now guided rulers and their ministers, not their opponents. Citizenship became fused with the new notions of state and nation. Suffering at the hands of the French led many of Europe's German-speaking populace to place trust in their princely governments, and this development helped transcend old differences of region and estate. There even developed an early expression of German nationalism, as philosophers and publicists began to use the concepts "folk" and "nation" interchangeably in their attempts to heal Germans' wounded pride. Fichte delivered his famous "Lectures to the German Nation" in French-occupied Berlin in 1808 and used the opportunity of defeat to begin to chart the concept of a common origin of German culture that logically should lead to a unified state.[6] Such ideals remained ephemeral, while on a more concrete level the princely governments of Germany developed modern institutions and practices, including professional bureaucracies, new methods of taxation, constitutionals, citizenship, and market economies. These attributes coalesced with expanded involvement of government in the lives of citizens.

Post-1815 governments throughout Germany practiced state-building at the expense of decentralized authority. For example, in the newly created state of Nassau, situated where the Lahn River joined the Rhine, the Prime Minister, Baron Ernst Franz Ludwig Marschall von Bieberstein (1770-1834), strove to solidify the power of the princely government. He faced opposition from the territory's imperial knights, who previously had been virtual masters of their own lands, owing allegiance to no jurisdiction except the Holy Roman Emperor. The fact that there was no longer an emperor facilitated Marschall's efforts to dismantle the remnants of feudalism and make these proud aristocrats "citizens" of the Wiesbaden government like the newer citizens of lower heritage. Further up the Rhine, in the Grand Duchy of Baden, university-trained civil servants sought to implement the plans of Grand Duke Carl Friedrich (1738-1811), an avowed proponent of free trade and Enlightenment ideals. They encountered stubborn resistance from landed nobles and even from representatives of the old urban middle class, who correctly feared erosion of their local prerogatives. But the civil servants found allies in the new bourgeoisie, those who had long resented their disenfranchisement under the old regime and welcomed a role in the new order. Further to the east the old Kingdom of Saxony, which had lost territory and prestige as a result of the Napoleonic wars, was under the leadership of Prime Minister Detlev von Einsiedel (1773-1861), a self-proclaimed conservative and staunch opponent of reform. Nevertheless, he presided over changes similar to those in the western states of Nassau and Baden. Intent upon rationalizing the business of government, he replaced the semifeudal privy council, a body that had represented the interest of the provincial estates, with a modern ministerial cabinet, thus moving this kingdom toward a statehood of centralized authority associated with the ideals of civil society. Utilizing government-sponsored publications, ceremonial events surrounding the monarch, and a new green-and-white Saxon flag to replace the ancient dynastic colors of black and gold, Einsiedel strove to implant among Saxons a sense of allegiance to the government at Dresden.[7]

Germany's changing worldview ran much deeper than the respective partisan positions or the temperaments of its rulers and ministers. In all forty-one states that emerged from the Congress of Vienna as members of the German Confederation, both professed reformers and avowed conservatives solidified conditions that would represent the interests of the rising educated and propertied middle classes. The modern state gained a firm foundation in the post-Napoleonic era, gradually rooting out the remnants of feudal institutions. Professional civil services took command of everyday affairs of government and assured continuity of political tradition even as they enacted constitutions, established taxes based on business and capital, modernized educational systems, and strove to make agriculture a profitable enterprise. They sought to establish free markets, under which industry would take root and flourish.[8] Government leaders, preoccupied with strengthening states, did not concern themselves with the household economy.

Feminist Voices of the 1790s

In the initial years of the French Revolution, when there was both excitement and fear in the air about society's institutions and the future of humanity, a few individuals publicly insisted that the new ideals of citizenship and equality must apply to women as well as to men. In 1792, the publisher Voß issued the amazing 430-page essay *Über die bürgeliche Verbesserung der Weiber* (On Improving the Civic Status of Women) written anonymously by Theodor Gottlieb von Hippel. Moving far beyond his earlier book on marriage, Hippel resolutely criticized patriarchy. His new work was a document of revolutionary implications.[9]

Hippel was able to see women as persons in their own right, and his book argued the case. Like his contemporaries of the Enlightenment, he looked to Nature for answers to life's ultimate questions, and his belief in Nature's benevolence led him to the conviction that women could not possibly be subordinate to men, because no reasonable order would assign the important task of childbearing to inferior beings. Men, not Nature, he argued, had made women into "slaves," and Hippel sought a cultural-historical explanation for the gender hierarchy of his day: In society's ancient natural condition, men and women had enjoyed equal status, and Eve had even possessed greater rationality than Adam. In prehistoric times males and females had probably procured their food by hunting together. However, women, being detained from the hunt during the "last hours of pregnancy and six hours after delivery," had developed skills that allowed them to continue productive work close to the hearth. They invented methods of preserving food and domesticating animals, thus becoming the world's first farmers. This left males, the hunters, in control of weapons, and they began to regard themselves as "superior to everything that was not a man," their wives included. As society became more complex, men fashioned communities to protect their possessions, using their weapons against one another to do so, and they came to regard women as part of their property. The institution of the state emerged, and it made women wards, not citizens. Roman law formalized the inferior status of women; and in modern times, unequal education, the custom of marriage, and social conventions such as female modesty perpetuated women's subordination.[10]

This must change, Hippel argued, and the first step was the granting of citizenship to women. He solemnly denounced the French revolutionary constitution of 1791 which denied women – "half the nation" – citizenship. Hippel pointed out that this placed them on a level with criminals who had forfeited their citizenship by felonious conduct. "All human beings have the same rights. All French people, men and women alike, should be free and should be citizens." Citizenship alone, however, would not engender identical status, because established patterns of socialization perpetuated inequality. Hippel emphasized the necessity of educating females and males alike as a prerequisite to equal social status. "Let the wall that divides us come down! Let us raise citizens for the state without regard to differences in gender and leave that which women must know as housewives and mothers to separate instruction, and all will return to Nature's order."[11]

Hippel was one of the few of his era to perceive socialization as the cause of gender differences. He stressed that the convention of confining women to the home and barring them from the professions – modern domesticity – prevented them from achieving equal status. He argued that society handicapped itself by excluding women from public life. He believed that women possessed unique, beneficial attributes, including high moral standards, intuitive mathematical skills, linguistic talents, and poetic sensibilities. These special endowments should be put to use for the good of humankind: Society must open to women its council chambers, courts, lecture halls, businesses, and places of employment. Only then would humanity advance toward its ultimate goal. "The most basic principle of Natural Law, and one which cannot be challenged, is the mandate that the right to human perfection may not be limited."[12]

Thus the revolutionary context of the 1790s spawned Europe's first modern feminist ideals, based on the Enlightenment design of elevating all humanity.[13] Through education, as well as changes in law and culture, women could gain independence and equality. Hippel's ideas belonged to a tiny, international chorus. His fiery British contemporary, Mary Wollstonecraft – whose work he apparently did not know – was the most recognized writer of this era to have advocated gender equality. Her *Vindication of the Rights of Women* stressed the importance of equal education. In revolutionary France, the Marquis de Condorcet published "On the Admission of Women to the Rights of Citizenship." And the sharply outspoken Olympe de Gouges placarded her "Declaration of the Rights of Woman and Female Citizen" around Paris in response to the national assembly's "Declaration of the Rights of Men and Citizens."[14]

In the year following the appearance of *On Improving the Civic Status of Women,* Hippel published (still anonymously) the fourth and thoroughly revised edition of his advice book *Über die Ehe* (On Marriage). He had rewritten a pivotal chapter, "On Authority in Marriage," cleansing it of its patriarchal language and posing the question: "What should prevent women from participation in governing the household?" Instead of a hierarchy, he asserted, a marriage should be a companionship of shared responsibility: "Between married partners there should be unison." He severely criticized the existing culture that condemned wives to "lifelong slavery."[15]

Thus while some Enlightenment partisans were praising the Revolution and others were denouncing its excesses, Hippel emphasized its exclusion of women from the new civil society. During the last years of his life, although preoccupied with professional responsibilities for the state of Prussia, Hippel planned an even more sharply critical edition of his book on women's civic status, which he did not succeed in publishing before his death in 1796. To him it was clear that gender inequality was increasing in his age because of the new freedoms available to men only: "The most disastrous thing ... about the sad state of the other sex is that it has nothing to hope for! This contrasts with the male sex, for which so many opportunities have opened up, not only in regard to each individual, but also to society as a whole."[16]

In the aftermath of the Revolution, several female writers came forward to criticize the misogyny of their society. One of the most outspoken was Amalia Holst (1758-1829), born Amalia von Justi, a daughter of the Cameralist. She was thirteen years old when her father died in Küstrin Prison, and she maintained a life-long interest in her father's life and work. She was probably self-educated and as a young woman supported herself by teaching and later as director of a school. She married a Hamburg citizen, Ludolf Holst, a doctor of law and a businessman who belonged to the Hamburg Patriotic Society. Amalia Holst had two daughters and one son. As a writer she passionately defended the rights of women. Similar to Mary Wollstonecraft in England, she scoffed at those who alleged that relative physical weakness of women signified intellectual subordination. Holst argued that women were simply held down by inferior education. Within two years of the storming of the Bastille in Paris, Holst anonymously published her *Bemerkungen über die Fehler unserer moderner Erziehung* (Commentary on the Mistakes of our Modern Education, 1791). Just over a decade later she published, this time under her own name, *Über die Bestimmung des Weibes zur höheren Geistesbildung* (On Woman's Destiny for Higher Education 1802), in which she cited hundreds of authors ranging from those of classical antiquity to the erudite of her day. The book is a virtual guide to Enlightenment writers who addressed the subject of gender. She recommended Hippel warmly to her readers, while she fiercely disputed the misogynous ideas of authors such as Campe, Pockels, Rousseau, and Brandes.[17]

Holst accepted the norm of marriage and domestic roles for women. She sought to demonstrate that "higher academic education does not conflict with the more specific profession of woman as wife, mother, and housekeeper." She believed in a truly companionate marriage, "a contract ... between two free, equal [individuals] in order to enjoy, inwardly, the advantages of companionship, to respect humanity, and to raise useful citizens for the state." Marriage was an agreement between the partners to strive for a single goal. They owed one another "mutual and just appreciation of their respective strengths, ... patience concerning their flaws and weaknesses, help and support in danger and suffering, friendly assistance in the small necessities of life, and cheerful, intimate participation in [each other's] joys."[18]

Holst passionately believed in the equality of the sexes. Women and men shared the same capacities because they were humans. The characteristic that separated human beings from animals was the ability to reason and improve their minds. People had the capacity to strive for perfection.

> Are we excluded from this civility because we are women? ... Should we not, do we dare not, concern ourselves with the most important subjects of human knowledge? Should we not, ourselves, engage in research, analysis, and philosophical self-reflection ... in order to establish firm principles for ourselves, in order to stand safe in situations of danger? Who dares argue that we are not [entitled to these things]?

Although she wrote with optimism, she did not believe her own age had treated women well. They had not really been able to participate in the Enlightenment. The "pseudo-Enlightenment" *(Afteraufklärung)*, which was all females were allowed, was "more dangerous than no knowledge at all."[19]

During the revolutionary decade, Marianne Ehrmann (1755-1811), a pioneering female journalist, published periodicals for women, first *Amaliens Erholungsstunden* (Amalie's Hours of Recovery) and later *Die Einsiedlerinn aus den Alpen* (The Female Recluse from the Alps), through whose pages she hoped to "nurture, enlighten, and ennoble the reason, heart, and curiosity of my female friends." She accused men of leaving women's minds undeveloped so that they would be sensual and submissive rather than intellectual. "I want to cry when I see our sex eternally being led like a toddler, completely without culture." Ehrmann was oblique in her criticism of patriarchy, possibly because she was dependent upon sales of her journal in order to support herself and her husband. Many of the approximately one thousand subscribers were men, probably most of whom purchased the publication for their wives. Whether out of conviction or out of a sensed need to conform to social norms, Ehrmann openly criticized the French Revolution; she quoted Rousseau on the separation of the spheres and used accepted language depicting female qualities as determined by Nature. Though a successful professional herself, she did not directly appeal for women to practice public professions. But her enterprise was not a socialization tool for feminine weakness. Through subtle devices such as translations of foreign authors, she raised questions such as "Why should not women *[Frauenzimmer]* also be capable of mastering all branches of human knowledge?" Her personal circumstances and temperament may have had more to do with her journalistic efforts than did the revolutionary fever of the 1790s. However, she belongs to that decade as a strong woman who understood enough about the gender systems to be able to make a career for herself while encouraging women to examine their own life circumstances.[20]

Emilie Berlepsch (1755-1830), a poet and essayist whose work appeared in the prestigious *Teutscher Merkur*, lamented that misogyny had distorted marriage and that education socialized females into submission and vulnerability. She called upon women to develop independence and take control of their own affairs: "There is only one shield which can guard the soul and protect its delicate sensitivities against harm; and this shield is called – self-reliance .... We must learn to stand alone." Her vision, like that of many contemporary feminists, stressed female strength, but she envisioned them exercising it in domestic situations:

> The woman is no longer just the housekeeper of the man and bearer of his children; she is also an educator and a participant in his ... complicated affairs and has her own sometimes not unimportant role in society ... . The woman must know that ... she, supported by her own reason, must walk many a rough, steep, or slippery trail. When she knows this, she will work to train her understanding, sharpen her critical facility, and strengthen her character.[21]

Thus against the revolutionary backdrop of the last decade of the century, some female German writers insisted that the Enlightenment values of individualism and self determination be applied not just to men but to those of their sex as well. These critics of society tried to make clear to their contemporaries that the ideal of domesticity, in transition from the household economy to civil society, could be stifling to womanhood.

At the same time the Göttingen historian Spittler lectured his students that the new politics must involve the female half of the population, not just males. He pointed out that a real democracy had never existed in the history of the world, precisely because women had always been barred from the legislative process. Such was the case in France under the new revolutionary constitution, just as it was in Switzerland under the ancient Canton system, which was often proclaimed to be a democracy:

> This exclusion has no rational basis, for women are indisputably humans, and we have [already] acknowledged self-government as a human right. The countless arguments that male despots employ to attempt to justify the exclusion of women are indefensible.[22]

The common propositions that women's "monthly illness," pregnancy, or the nursing of infants should disqualify females were ridiculous, Spittler insisted, for no one ever considered excluding sick or weak men from participation in democracies. Furthermore, "a physical indisposition that does not harm our mental state cannot be used to deny us a basic right of our moral nature." To those who argued that women's mental capabilities were inferior to men's, Spittler retorted, "what irrationality!" Women often successfully ruled European states as queens, and if whole monarchies let themselves be governed by individual females, was it not untenable to refuse women, as members of society, the right of voting under democratic constitutions? Finally, Spittler added, lack of experience could not be held up as a ground for prevention of women's participation in politics, for this elitism "is completely contrary to the essence of a democracy." These, he asserted, were the same kinds of self-serving arguments that the nobility had often used to retain its exclusive privileged position of political power.[23]

Bourgeois Patriarchy:
Women Excluded from the Public Sphere

Spittler was a singular voice, seldom heard except by his students (his lectures were not published until nearly two decades after his death). And as the short-lived ideal of actually placing government in the hands of the people faded by the second half of the 1790s, so did the voices calling for female participation in political life. Spittler's career is symbolic of the path of revolutionary ideals in Germany. In 1806 he gave up his academic position in response to an invitation by Prince Ludwig Eugen (1731-1795) of Württemberg to join the top level of high civil service of his native principality. If Spittler's radical proclamations had not already ended, they did with this appointment. He even declined to prepare a new edition of his earlier acclaimed textbook on the history of European states, presumably out of fear that its radical perspective would impair his governmental work. Under Ludwig Eugen's successor, Friedrich (1754-1816), to whom Napoleon bestowed the title of king, Spittler accepted the positions of state minister and curator of the University of Tübingen, along with a personal patent of nobility. Spittler, who a decade earlier had called for democratic government including women, now could not see a way out of joining the elite he once deprecated.[24] Germany's transformation in the era following the French Revolution was decisive and dramatic, but clearly not radical. Voices calling for the equality of the sexes had faded quickly, and the era of the new civil society represented but a new kind of patriarchy.

The theme of gender relations, however, continued to generate heated discussion as Germany came into contact with the ideas of the French Revolution. The "character of the sexes" was a raw nerve of the transitional epoch. The scholarly elite could not resist joining the debate. Wilhelm von Humboldt (1767-1835), the renowned statesman and erudite philologist who traveled in the Berlin circles of salonière Henriette Herz and Rahel Levin, felt obliged to take up his pen on the subject of gender. Humboldt believed that the dichotomy between male and female was a necessary organizing principle, without which, "Nature would not be Nature; its clockwork gears would stand still." The secret of Nature rested on the "reciprocal action" of male-female. The two opposites found "harmonious union" in physical sex. "In the purely corporal aspect of his being, man finds expressed in unmistakable script that which he should strive to bring into his moral presence." In an interesting perspective on human reproduction, Humboldt described maleness as "generative power" and femaleness as "receiving power." Humboldt suggested, nevertheless, that individuals possessed both male and female qualities, and that it was impossible to find anywhere "pure masculinity" or "pure femininity." He wrote affirmatively of qualities he considered feminine and suggested that he, himself, was endowed with positive female attributes – openness, depth of feeling, and empathy for others. But, like Kant, he also postulated that men were strong and rational, while women were delicate and emotional. He contrasted the "the enlarged chest, the stronger skeleton, and less concealed play of muscles" of males with the softness and diminished strength of women. Femininity he characterized with the qualities of grace, charm, and beauty. "Charm and beauty converge no less in the male than in the female. But they are the law of the latter while in the former they seem to bring into being the law of reason." In order to understand the female sex in terms of its distinctive properties, Humboldt declared, one must begin with "moral character." "Sentiment is active and busy in women, like the mind [is] in men." Femininity required "elucidation before the power of intellectual or poetic production is possible." Absolutely unique and essential to women's character was the "feeling of motherhood, above all before the fruit is born." Another essence of femininity was "submission."[25]

Humboldt wrote in the spirit of Kant, who in 1798, at the age of 74, was moved to publish his lecture notes on anthropology from which he had been instructing his students for a quarter century and which contained his theories of gender differences. The scholar from Königsberg and the philosopher-statesman from Berlin believed passionately in the Enlightenment and proclaimed to value human dignity. Both set out to depict male and female equality in opposites, but neither was able to imagine the sexes in other than a hierarchical relationship to one another. Unlike Hippel, they were unable to bring themselves to a position that did not involve a male-female hierarchy. Every set of comparative descriptors they grasped embodied inequality of power, of mind, or of will. Like Kant's overt "strength" and "weakness," Humboldt's more subtle "reason" and "emotion" posited not only polarities but also asymmetry. Unlike Hippel, who believed that souls possessed no specific sex, Humboldt could not imagine that socialization accounted for observed distinctions in masculinity and femininity. He could only conclude that dissimilarities were inherent, genetic properties, rooted in Nature.[26]

Another influential philosopher, Johann Gottfried Fichte (1762-1814), whose reputation soared in the years following the French Revolution, enthusiastically entered the disputation on differences between woman and man. Predictably, he began with the premise that civil society elevated both sexes. Yet Fichte never even tried to imagine equality of the sexes. He simply accepted that women were inferior beings in need of protection and not entitled to the rights men could claim in civil society. He developed an elaborate explanation of the inequality of women and men based on his understanding of human sexuality. He approached the question of the character of the sexes through the institution of marriage, which he described as a "total union of two people ... founded on sexual instinct." Like many Enlightenment social philosophers, Fichte believed that human sexuality, powerful, dangerous, and requiring control, belonged to the essence of human nature. Significantly, sexual difference also was the basis of civil society. The man, more driven by sexual motivation – and yet more in control of it – was compelled to find gratification. The woman, in contrast, was driven to please him.

> All of the other differences of the sexes rest on this single difference ... . The woman cannot yield at all to sexual desire in order to satisfy her impulse, and since she, nevertheless, must surrender to a force, this force must be no other than that of satisfying the man.

Matrimony, the institution that allowed man and woman to realize their highest respective capacities, was founded not on mere legal or judicial statues but was based on "the more eminent legality of Nature and Reason." Originally, in the condition of Nature, men had simply satisfied their sexual desires. However, as they gradually brought civil society into being, they had invented marriage. Men had discovered that "love lived in woman" and had wanted it for themselves and had learned to love in relationships. Nature determined that sexual unions must be monogamous, for only through exclusive love could marriages elevate men and women. In simple terms, then, woman's role was to please man, and, indeed, this was her contribution to civilization. Women made men whole, enabling them to become participants in civil society.[27]

A purpose of marriage in civil society was to preserve "absolute freedom" of choice for the partners. No wedding should ever take place if the relationship was not based on love. It was in this regard that a woman needed the state's protection. Since she was subject to her parents' will, she could be forced to marry according to their wishes, and without love, which would mean degradation for her. The state must guard her "human rights" and prevent this from happening. For a man, this was not so important, for "it was against the nature of things" that he could be subject to force.[28]

Marriage thus protected and elevated women by granting them freedom through submission. The woman

> must subjugate herself for the sake of her own will .... The woman does not belong to herself but to the man. As soon as the state recognizes the marriage ... which ... a higher order has created, [the state] ceases to regard her as a juridical person. The man represents her completely. [From the perspective of] the state, she is entirely nullified through her marriage, as a result of her own inevitable will that the state has guaranteed.[29]

Having made this absolute pronouncement, Fichte raised the question, "Does the woman have the same rights in the state as the man?" He answered affirmatively, beginning with the observation that "this question could seem foolish in itself. If the sole basis of all legality is reason and freedom, how could there exist between the two sexes, who both possess the same rationality and the same freedom, a difference in rights?" The answer was simple: Since the beginning of human existence, women had enjoyed fewer rights than men, and such a universally accepted principle must have a profound basis. The reason for it was that when a woman married and became subject to her husband, she joined a household, and "regarding the *domestic* and *internal* relationship, *the tenderness of the man necessarily gives her everything she has lost, and more.*" Fichte argued that, although some complaining women and their male defenders – perhaps he meant Holst and Hippel – claimed that females enjoyed fewer rights than males, this was not true; women possessed everything men did. All they lacked was the "outward appearance" of rights and freedoms. "A reasonable and virtuous woman can be proud only of her husband and her children, not of herself, for she forgets herself in these."[30] A woman's way to civic freedom, then, was to forfeit her legal existence and personhood and to submerge her identity into that of her family. Fichte spoke for many of his generation when he identified women with the home and philosophically declared that they had no existence separate from it.

During the revolutionary era, the controversy over the character of the sexes raged among popular writers as well as among intellectual celebrities. Predictably, those who postulated inherent gender inequality outweighed the voices of Hippel, Holst, Berlepsch, and Ehrmann. Carl Friedrich Pockels (1754-1814), a proclaimed friend of the Enlightenment and a civil servant, teacher, and author in Braunschweig, published a five-volume work, *Versuch einer Charakteristik des weiblichen Geschlechts* (Essay on the Character of the Female Sex). He declared that "Nature in all wisdom" had determined that the "woman is bound to her house and to housework by chains ... where she may help her husband and her Fatherland raise her children [and] fulfill the great calling of her sex without distractions."[31]

Jakob Mauvillon, (1743-1794), military officer, professor at Braunschweig, member of the Masonic Order, and prolific essayist who was known as a supporter of the Enlightenment, joined the gender debate with a work entitled *Mann und Weib nach ihren gegenseitigen Verhältnissen geschildert* (Man and Woman Depicted According to their Opposite Characteristics). Mauvillon wrote in response to Ernst Brandes' book on the character of women, and his purpose was to defend the female sex. He began by pointing out women's many important contributions to culture. Mauvillon believed that "Nature [had] treated women poorly, compared to men." Yet, when it came to interpreting women's place in civil society, Mauvillon explained that while, under Nature's laws, each individual gained a sense of self through the uniqueness of personal character, a woman achieved her identity by "renounc[ing] her will" and identifying with her husband. Finally, he pointed to the advantage of having women in the home: "How greatly would the spirit of all working men be hindered, how much time would it rob from them if they had to concern themselves with household matters?" This defender of womanhood, it turned out, did not view married women as persons in their own right, and the idea of gender opposites led, in his thinking, to the practical situation of separate spheres. This all seemed natural to Mauvillon; he presumed it was designed to make men's lives easier.[32]

Fanning the fires of debate, Ernst Brandes revised and expanded his anti-feminine essay, *Ueber die Weiber* (On Women), which he published in 1802 under the title, *Betrachtungen über das weibliche Geschlecht und dessen Ausbildung in dem geselligen Leben* (Observations on the Female Sex and its Education in Sociable Life). Women's negative influence was just one of several alarming developments he commented on in print. Others included the French Revolution, the spread of the ideas of progress, and the spread of new ideas through the print media.[33] Once again, those Germans favorable to change and those hostile to it agreed on separate spheres and gender hierarchy.

The topic of sex roles preoccupied the literate public in the changing world of the turn of the century. In the unsettling times of the French Revolution, many rushed to confirm the reassuring idea of naturally determined gender differences. In their Thursday meetings after 1797, female members of Oldenburg's Literary Ladies Society listened attentively to the lectures of their husbands and other civic leaders who used the texts of authors like Fichte, Pockels, Brandes, Campe, and Ehrmann to justify the ideal of separate spheres. By the late 1790s the Enlightenment belief that Nature had destined women for the private sphere gained reinforcement in ever-widening circles. Journalists of that decade used womanhood rhetorically in depicting the threats facing society. Some published accounts of "female addicts of revolution" spreading their poison and attacking the church, the state, and the moral order of German society, thus mingling the fear of revolution with anxiety about changing gender roles. Some publications, on the other hand, emphasized stories in which women bravely resisted foreign intruders and even gave their lives in defense of their husbands, households, and Fatherland. Thus the threat many Germans felt in the revolutionary era led to newly imagined ways for women to become self-sacrificing caretakers.[34] With femininity and revolution often uttered in the same sentence, writers of the revolutionary era generally reinforced the female ideal of submission, domesticity, passivity, servility. As people's identity came to be associated with states, men's roles were within the civic realm while women's place was to support it by remaining in the private domain. A part of men's self-redefinition in the revolutionary era included assuring themselves that they were separate from women.

The Institutionalization of Public and Private Order

Predictably, many governments undertook revision of their domestic legal systems during the period of Napoleonic upheaval. The states of the Confederation of the Rhine, as well as those under direct French rule, adopted the famous Napoleonic Civil Code. Composed under the emperor's supervision between 1800 and 1804, it incorporated many provisions from the revolutionary legislation of the 1790s. In France this four-volume set of statutes regulating private life had represented a consolidation of Napoleon's authority, and in the Confederation of the Rhine its implementation helped solidify French rule. The thrust of the law was abolition of feudal privilege and the creation of a civil society. Conveniently this meant that the newly enfranchised would owe their acquired political prerogatives to the new authorities. The code's elimination of measures governing feudal relations, however, was uneven and allowed the German nobles to retain much of their ancient prerogative, although they now had to share political power with nonaristocratic property owners. In some principalities this code did not outlast the Napoleonic era, but once the extension of political enfranchisement to the middle classes was initiated, the process was not reversible. In some provinces, including the Prussian Rhineland, Rhine-Hessen, and Baden, the French civil code remained a basis of civil law until the beginning of the twentieth century.[35]

The code's provisions regarding marriage and the household established a systematic, legal separation of the male and female spheres. The new laws excluded all women, regardless of their status, from civil rights such as that of bearing witness to official documents or to be notary publics. Wives could appear before a court only with the consent of their husbands. The code was especially consequential when considered from the perspective of the household economy. Measures retained from the revolutionary legislation of the 1790s abolished primogeniture and required that estates be divided between all heirs, including daughters. In the main, the law codified the ideals of private property and individualism under a middle-class, patriarchal model. Based on the notion that a husband owed protection and economic support to his wife, while she owed obedience and fidelity to him, it granted the husband the right to control the joint assets of a couple and prohibited a wife from negotiating contracts without her spouse's consent. She would need his permission to sell, mortgage, or donate her own property. Except for those women certified as public vendors, wives could not engage in professions or become business proprietors on their own accord. The code required a wife to assume her husband's nationality and to live in his house. If she should leave, it would be under penalty of denial of economic support, and she would have to compensate her husband in the form of an indemnity.[36]

The French law imposed a double standard with regard to fidelity. A wife who had an extramarital affair could be imprisoned, and her conduct entitled her husband to seek a divorce. A husband, however, could engage in sexual liaisons without legal penalty unless he brought his mistress to live in the marital household. In that case the wife could demand a divorce and the husband could be fined – but not imprisoned, as she would have been for a less egregious offense.[37]

The code granted fiscal and legal guardianship of children to the father alone, whether he resided with the family or not. The mother had no authority in the financial affairs of a couple's minor children. The father retained the ancient "right of correction" which allowed him to imprison his children for up to six months without involvement of judicial authorities. His consent – not the mother's – was required for a child's marriage. Only widowed mothers could exercise some of these prerogatives, and if they remarried, they generally forfeited them to the new husband and stepfather. The code embodied precise rules designed to ensure the legitimacy of children and to provide for orderly inheritances. For example, a widow could not remarry until ten months after the death of her spouse, protecting the new husband from gaining heirs who were not his biological children. A widower was obliged to no such waiting period. If a woman were pregnant when her husband died, a male guardian would be appointed for the unborn child, safeguarding against improper conduct on the part of the pregnant woman. Interestingly, the mother could become guardian after the baby was born, establishing one of the few instances in which mothers had the right of legal responsibility for their own children. The Napoleonic Civil Code, while eroding feudal institutions in many German-speaking territories, anchored into law the new bourgeois family ideal.[38]

Making the husband and father legal and political warden over all members of the household, the code exceeded both the Bavarian and Prussian laws in replacing aristocratic paternalism with a bourgeois patriarchy and restricting personal individualism. It created a class of male clients indebted to the new states. While the code's reformed inheritance rules undermined the feudal inheritance structure, the Napoleonic system promised a new kind of stability by appointing men as heads of households and giving them ties to increasingly powerful governments. In this bourgeois order, the state belonged to men, and women belonged to men.

The Habsburg Monarchy, struggling to maintain its integrity and stay abreast of the times after Napoleonic defeats, also undertook a reform of its civil law. This effort, under the leadership of the jurist Franz A. Elder Zeiller (1753-1828), represented a continuation of processes underway throughout the eighteenth century. Zeiller was enthusiastic about the opportunity to systematically apply Enlightenment ideals, something that he said had only become possible in the revolutionary period. He acknowledged philosophical indebtedness to Kant and was committed to the principles of Natural Law.[39]

He was able to publish a revised code for the German Habsburg territories in 1811, which, from the state's perspective, had the merit of bringing marriage under increased civil jurisdiction. In doing so, it sought to respect religious traditions and to accommodate the diversity of the Habsburgs' subjects, allowing various practices for Catholic, Protestant, and Jewish citizens. For example, the code outlined four main grounds for divorce but stipulated that these did not apply in the case of Catholic marriages, which were terminated only by death of a partner. The four reasons for divorce were: the commission of adultery or a crime resulting in five years of incarceration; abandonment; endangerment of life or health; and extreme cases of mutual incompatibility, but in such circumstances only after a trial separation. The marriage itself was a contract: "Two persons of opposite sex declare their will to live in inseparable community, to produce children, and to give one another mutual assistance." New was the fact that the rules of the contract were encoded in civil law, making marriage an affair of the state.[40]

Zeiller stressed that the revised code eliminated the old idea of the husband's coercive powers *(Gewalt)* over the wife, a concept that had been reiterated in Austrian statutes as late as the 1780s. Instead, he attempted to write into the law the principles of common property, and reciprocal duties and respect, between marriage partners. When it came to specifics, he found it necessary to clarify this mutuality by emphasizing differences in roles:

> The man is the head of the family. In this capacity it is primarily his responsibility to direct the business of the household. It is also

incumbent upon him to provide the wife a reasonable living from his resources and to represent her in all situations.

The code thus made a woman's position entirely dependent upon her husband's, which from Zeiller's perspective was an advantage for her: "The wife receives the name of the man and enjoys the rights of his status." In return, she was obligated to reside at his residence, wherever that may be, and to "help him in household and business according to her abilities. Insofar as the domestic order allows it, [she] is required to obey rules established by him, as well as to see that they are heeded [by others]."[41]

The Austrian code instituted an explicit division of responsibility regarding parental roles. Although it granted to the couple joint responsibility to provide physically, educationally, and morally for the children, it granted "paternal power" *(väterliche Gewalt)* to the father, because he was head of the family. "It is fundamentally the responsibility of the father to furnish livelihood for the children until they can support themselves. The mother is primarily bound to give them physical care and take care of their health." Thus the husband-father was the economic provider for the household. The wife-mother was caretaker and nurse. The code's stipulations regarding guardianship and widowhood reinforced this principle. The law assumed a mother would not be able to provide economically for her children. If a father died, the wardship would devolve first to the paternal grandfather, then to the mother, then to the paternal grandmother, and finally to the closest male relative. However, mothers and grandmothers who found themselves in the position of guardians were required to have male "co-guardians." Except for the latter situation, "persons of the female sex, members of religious orders, and inhabitants of foreign states generally cannot be guardians." The only women to whom the law assigned economic responsibility for their children were unwed mothers, in cases where the father had not acknowledged his paternity. A woman's claim that a particular man had fathered her child had no legal validity. Under this set of rules, since there was no father and there were no paternal relatives, the mother had to provide for the children.⁴²

It was logical that the Austrian jurists specified that a mother could not normally provide for her children. She was not entitled to the estate of her husband, even though the marriage was to have been one of "inseparable community." If her husband died, a wife received the "usual maintenance of the estate" for six weeks or, if she were pregnant, until six weeks after the child was born. After that she received a "widow's allowance" every three months, presumably paid by a male relative of her deceased husband.⁴³ This code ensured that men would control property and economic transactions, while women took care of children in all ways except materially. With rare exceptions, women were economic dependents.

In the work of the judicial reformers of Napoleonic Germany it is difficult to distinguish between several coexisting motivations. The rhetoric of the Enlightenment, the slogans of the French Revolution, and the goal of consolidating political authority often mutually reinforced one another, leading to a codification of bourgeois patriarchy in the new civil codes. As they enhanced the powers of their respective states, they secured social order by granting propertied males a place in civil society and guaranteeing the males' authority over the women of their households. The reformers were following the ideals of their Enlightenment teachers, most of whom extolled human equality and then drew the conclusion that the inequality of the sexes was rooted in Nature.

Reformers of the Napoleonic era in Prussia did not attempt to write a new civil law; Prussia's General Law Code, completed in 1794, predated their own efforts at reform by only a few years and must have seemed as modern as many would have wanted. They did, however, undertake a serious discussion of the shape and role of the citizenship of the new state and actively debated the conditions under which they would establish local, provincial, and national representative assemblies. The reformers, under the leadership of Baron Heinrich Friedrich Karl vom Stein (1757-1831), generally agreed that entitlement to vote or stand for election would be a privilege of property owners and others who held some status such as membership in the clergy, the military officer corps, or the hereditary nobility. They always meant men, those who had been heads of households under the old regime, and their intent was to include the propertied, educated middle class in political life.[44]

One Prussian political reform measure mentioned women. This was the famous municipal ordinance of 19 November 1808, which structured urban government of Hohenzollern lands and remained in effect, with some revisions, until the twentieth century. By establishing city councils of prominent citizens, elected on the basis of their membership in civil society, rather than as spokesmen for guilds or corporate organizations, the reformers were able to streamline the lines of authority between cities and the monarchical regime. The ordinance stipulated that cities were comprised of two fundamental classes of people: "citizens" and "the protected." The former category consisted of property owners and business proprietors who earned more than 150 or 200 Thaler a year, depending on the size of their cities or towns. The latter were servants, laborers, and wage earners, those who did not possess the means to be "independent." Citizenship was not automatically conferred upon the eligible. They had to make application in order to attain the status, but citizenship was mandatory for business proprietors. Among those eligible for citizenship were "unmarried persons of the female sex" who resided in the city, otherwise met the qualifications, and chose to make application.[45]

This was not a measure designed to extend the benefits of civil society to females. It was, rather, a continuation of an old-regime practice of regarding widows and daughters as the bearers of their deceased husbands' or fathers' status. Under the new law, as under the old, marriage always eliminated females from the possibility of citizenship. Wives of citizens would enjoy the rank and protection of their husbands; other wives were simply categorized with their spouses as "protected" residents. Furthermore, female citizens were of a special class, the only citizens expressly denied the right to vote. When the ordinance was revised in 1831 to extend citizenship to all inhabitants of cities by abolishing the status of "the protected," the right of suffrage remained a privilege of those who would have met citizenship qualifications under the original delineation – and women were still excluded.[46]

In the city of Königsberg, a relatively high number of females petitioned for citizenship in 1809, the first year of reform. Of the 443 applicants, there were twenty-four women. (In this year three times the usual number of petitioners came forward, and the addition of their names brought the total number of citizens to 3,426 in this city of 50,000.) Some of these twenty-four women, like many men, may have come forward because the new law threatened proprietors with loss of property or business if they failed to join the rolls of citizenship. Nevertheless, the fact that the ratio of women to men, although still a small one, jumped by a factor of ten in 1809, suggests that the reform encouraged females who had previously held back from joining the roles of the elite. Of the twenty-four women who formally became citizens in 1809, almost every one was listed as a "widow and property owner," the primary exceptions being a few whose title, Baroness or Countess, must have seemed a more important designation. One applicant, Charlotte Albertina Grubin, an innkeeper, may have been a business-proprietor in her own right, instead of a widow, and Regina Rinckin was listed simply as a "property owner," originally from Königsberg Altstadt. She was possibly an unmarried daughter of a deceased citizen. The registration records show that the women who applied for citizenship often went to the government office in groups, perhaps to give support to one another. On 17 January 1809, five widows were written into the list, and approximately two weeks later, on 1 February, another five, so that these two parties represented nearly half of the total number of women for that year. Otherwise women tended to apply on the same day as a male relative.[47]

As a class, women were not welcome members of the new civil society. No reformers entertained the idea of enfranchising women at a level above the municipal community. The only opportunity a woman had to participate in the newly designed civic life of her city or town was to be left in charge of a deceased husband's or father's business, and this was with a muted voice, not a chance to vote.

Education: The Public and the Private Spheres

One of the most lasting changes to come to Germany in the transitional decades of the Napoleonic era was the establishment of the modern school system, conceptualized after Enlightenment ideals of "humanistic education." At the initiative of Minister vom Stein, Wilhelm von Humboldt became the director of the Division of Culture and Education of the Prussian Ministry of Interior. Humboldt, a former pupil of Campe, developed the design for the famous Berlin University as a replacement for the Prussian universities lost as a result of territorial changes in the Napoleonic wars, but also as an opportunity to bring into reality an institution formed according to Enlightenment thought. He presided over a reform of the entire educational system of Prussia. His leading ideal was that of "universal education," by which he meant the development of the complete potential of the human being through immersion in the study of ancient languages and classical studies. This was to be realized through the development of the *Gymnasium*, Germany's respected secondary school, which served as the training grounds of the intellectually talented before they entered the university. The reforms represented a chance for sons of nonaristocrats to have the same opportunities as young noblemen. The Prussian plans also led to separate educational tracks for the more and less intellectually talented, forming the basis for the system that came to typify modern formal German education. Humboldt's reforms also assured that the state, rather than the church, became the supporter and overseer of education, although his ideal of academic freedom included the principle that the state would not monitor or control thought. Humboldt and his colleagues brought into being these innovations, which proved extremely important for Prussia's young men, especially those of propertied families who could afford to take advantage of the new opportunities. It did not occur to the reformers to include women. Not until more than a half a century later, in the 1870s, did Prussian officials undertake a serious discussion of public education for women.[48] The educational reforms arising from the French revolutionary era, based on Enlightenment ideals, were for males.

Unlike the Prussian reformers, Betty Gleim (1781-1827) of the Free City of Bremen, also a German patriot of the Napoleonic era, had much to say about women's schooling. Gleim was the daughter of a middle-class family who saw to it that she received a good education. As a young woman she was betrothed, but the brief engagement was terminated, and Gleim decided to become a teacher. Her father's death in 1806, just as the French were driving deep into Germany, left her to help support her family, and at the age of 25 she founded in Bremen the School for Daughters of the Higher Classes, modeled after Pestalozzi's ideals. Her city came under foreign rule in 1810 as part of the French Empire, and like many of her era, she was interested in helping Germany improve in the tradition of the Enlightenment as it freed itself from foreign domination. She was a prolific writer, publishing as many as twenty books, including not only treatises on education but also German grammars, patriotic essays, and cookbooks.[49]

Gleim worked for progress in society, but unlike many male leaders, she placed emphasis on education of the individual rather than politics. She explained her position in her book *Erziehung und Unterricht des weiblichen Geschlechts* (Education and Training of the Female Sex, 1810). While many put their hopes for improvement in "political revolution, well designed constitutions, or generally in the context of the state ... they do not ... realize that all true improvement, freedom, and peace are, and must be, rooted in the innermost part of the human." It was education that would bring advancement, but slowly, step by step.

> Humanity cannot be led to its destiny through a sudden leap, through power and force, but rather through quiet, almost imperceptible efforts ... . Education is the mustard seed out of which a new race can arise. What is education? Education is stimulation and improvement of all powers of the human being ... for a harmonious unity and a common goal.[50]

Women, because of their humanity, were entitled to independence through education. But like almost all Enlightenment thinkers, Gleim was sure that Nature had made men and women to be different. "The man has his own gender characteristics, and the woman has hers." This is why separate education was required for the two sexes. The ultimate difference was that men would "hold public and civic offices, ... become doctors and lawyers and priests," while "a public life is hardly suited for the individuality of women." Females could scarcely accomplish anything worthwhile or achieve happiness in a position that "injures our individuality every moment." Those who, in the name of wanting to assist womanhood, suggested that women participate in the world of men were misguided:

> Nothing would be gained, but there would be infinite loss. What would happen to the children? Would they not become completely wild and spoiled? ... No, the proposals to allow women to participate in all public and civic offices of men are conceited and chimerical ... . [They] would turn things upside down and bring about a completely flawed world.[51]

Surely influenced by her own personal history, Gleim wrote that women should prepare themselves to earn a living. There would be situations in which widows and other single women should provide for themselves, rather than becoming a burden to their families. Moreover, the ability to earn a wage would free them from the untenable situation of having to accept a marriage proposition to an unsuitable partner merely for the sake of economic security. But in their training they must focus only on occupations that corresponded as closely as possible with "the true female profession." Women might become caretakers of children, teachers, or housekeepers. The kind of schooling required for this was "not an academic, but rather a basic one, not a one-sided, rather an all-round education." By schooling girls and young women in this way – and by implication giving boys and young men specialized, academic training – society would set itself on the path toward the "harmonious whole" that was the goal of humanistic education.[52]

Unlike her contemporary, Amalia Holst of nearby Hamburg, Gleim did not believe that the Enlightenment had been unkind to women. It offered them the chance to participate in making society whole by training them to be housewives. The publicist, educator, and friend of womanhood made it explicit in the dynamic days of educational reform – when the notion of "profession" was assuming an increasingly important meaning – that Nature determined women for one profession only and that their femininity prevented them from participating in public life. They were to support themselves with paid employment only when the normal shape of the bourgeois family was disturbed by the death of a husband or some other unfortunate circumstance that left a woman without a male partner and patron.

> The sphere of work for which most women are destined is that of marriage partner, mother, and housewife *(Ehegattin, Mutter,* and *Hausfrau),* and even those ladies who remain unmarried have duties to fulfill that are related to this profession. Therefore every girl should be specifically trained to fill such a role.

The jobs of wife and mother did not require special schooling other than acquiring general knowledge, training one's mental powers and keeping a pure heart. However,

> it is different with the housewife *[Hausfrau].* Here a careful preparation is indispensable. The lack of such has brought misery and a sense of dejection to thousands. Oh, it has filled the soul of many a woman with regret, with burden, with gnawing grief ... because she

wanted to do what she recognized as her duty, but could not do it. It has also often robbed the man of respect for his wife.

This profession of housewife was incumbent upon all women, not just the laboring classes. Even the daughters of the wealthy families never would know what might befall them. "There are many examples of rich people who have descended to begging .... Situations can arise in life that no mortal could have imagined: Just think of the French Revolution!"[53]

Gleim's prescriptions for female socialization belonged to a growing genre. Girls' training manuals embodying these values appeared frequently in the 1790s. The *Handbuch für Mädchen von reifem Alter* (Handbook for Girls of a Mature Age), published in Munich, taught that the destiny of girls was different from that of boys. Borrowing heavily from Campe's *Väterlicher Rath* (Fatherly Advice), the anonymous author, who claimed to be a woman, declared:

> The man makes himself useful and recognized in public affairs. As statesman he assists princes with his insights; as judge he administers the laws. As soldier he defends the state; his breast is the wall behind which the merchant and worker provide for the needs and the wants of fellow citizens and the farmer tills his land. The pastor and the doctor serve similar roles, each according to his specialty and gifts. The stage on which they play their roles is the world ... . Fame makes their names known. In good circumstances they earn ... riches and honors ... . The *Frauenzimmer* has quite a different nature. Her business is in her house, and her praise is limited to the small circle of her family and friends. Her vocation is *to become a wife who brings happiness, a mother who educates, and a wise manager of household affairs.*

The book included little songs for the girl to sing while she performed her domestic chores.[54]

The Prussian reformers were establishing state-supported schools for boys, and Gleim wished they would do the same for girls. She even agreed, in theory, with an idea proposed by Fichte that the state should take control of children's lives and educate them. However, since parents of girls would never make this sacrifice of parental love, and because the government has no right to coerce them to do so, the state should build "appropriate" schools for girls. These would consist of six types: seminars for upper-class daughters *(Frauenzimmer);* training schools for nursemaids; institutes to educate the staff of child care centers; "good elementary schools" that not only taught reading but focused on the whole child; "appropriately constructed girls' schools"; and "industry schools for the poorest classes," in which children would receive free education and "the mental powers of girl pupils would be awakened and exercised."[55]

Gleim's prolific literary career may have been as much a way of supporting herself as it was a commitment to her ideals. The importance of her writing is not its originality, for her work paraphrases well-worn Enlightenment ideals, and her book is full of lengthy quotations from Pestalozzi. What is significant, rather, is the fact that a woman who set out to help women participate in the Enlightenment through self-fulfilling intellectual development was completely bound to the new ideal of separate spheres. Gleim's lifelong efforts to enable women to participate in the Enlightenment through education were framed by the idea that women belong at home as helpmates. Their only reason to prepare for paid work was to prevent them from becoming burdens to society in the event of misfortune, such as the failure to become married or the death of a husband. Gleim called upon the state – the growing institution of control in society – to help women prepare for their domestic careers. She asked for more than the male reformers were willing to give, for they ignored girls and positioned the state to help boys. It is symbolic that Gleim's *Bremisches Kochbuch* (Bremen Cookbook) was by far her most popular work. She brought out a new edition in 1826, a year before her death, but the book was reprinted, reissued, and revised at least eleven more times, with the thirteenth edition appearing in 1892, symbolizing that her emphasis on domesticity struck a deep chord in nineteenth-century society. Gleim also published a Bavarian cookbook that went through seven editions between 1808 and 1840.[56]

Separate Spheres

In the era of the French Revolution, powerful feminist voices in German-speaking Europe appealed to society to apply the ideals of individualism and self-determination to both sexes. Yet the entreaties of Hippel, Holst Berlepsch, and Ehrmann were smothered by the avalanche of ideas, based largely on the Enlightenment concept of Nature that placed men and women in separate and unequal positions. The idea of civic emancipation for men and domesticity for women appealed to something deep in European culture. Even many who were impatient because the new order excluded women from the Enlightenment's benefits implicitly accepted women's "natural" relationship to the home. The construction of female domesticity in combination with inherited patriarchy created a new culture, and it was especially consequential in the context of the expanding notion of male citizenship. It separated women from men in work, excluded women from the productive economy, and placed husbands over wives in the home.

The Napoleonic era accelerated the transition in cultural values that had long been underway in German-speaking Europe. The idea that authority resided in the state gained greater precedence over the old norm that emphasized the moral household as the basic unit of society. In the name of civil society, governments took control of affairs that had belonged to the private, religious, and moral realms. New law codes defined the relationships of family members, granting what amounted to constitutional guarantees to males that they presided over their wives' and daughters' lives. During the Napoleonic era in German-speaking Europe, people's identities became tied more and more closely to states. New educational institutions for males and fashionable ideas on female education anchored for coming generations the Enlightenment notions of public spheres for men and domestic realms for women. The vocabulary of the Napoleonic era spelled the end of the moral concepts *Hausmutter* and *Hausvater,* replacing both with the modern designation "profession."[57] For many males this opened up worlds of new opportunities. For women it increasingly meant *one* profession: housewife.

Notes

1. Holger Böning, ed., *Französische Revolution und deutsche Öffentlichkeit: Wandlungen in Presse und Alltagskultur am Ende des achtzehnten Jahrhunderts,* Deutsche Presseforschung, vol. 28 (Munich: Sauer, 1992). Quotations from Rolf Reichardt, "Probleme des kulturellen Transfers der Französischen Revolution in der deutschen Publizistik 1789-1799," in ibid., 24. Jürgen Voss, ed., *Deutschland und die Französische Revolution: 17. Deutsch-französisches Historikerkolloquium des Deutschen Historischen Instituts Paris (Bad Homburg 29. September-2. Oktober 1981),* Beihefte der Francia, vol. 12 (Munich: Artemis, 1983). Heinrich Scheel, *Süddeutsche Jakobiner: Klassenkämpfe und republikanische Bestrebung im deutschen Süden Ende des 18. Jahrhunderts,* 2nd ed., Schriften des Zentralinstituts für Geschichte, Series I: Allgemeine und deutsche Geschichte, vol. 13 (Berlin: Akademie, 1962). Walter Grab, *Norddeutsche Jakobiner: Demokratische Bestrebungen zur Zeit der Französischen Revolution,* Hamburger Studien zur neueren Geschichte, vol. 8 (Frankfurt am Main: Europäische Verlagsanstalt, 1967). Helmut Berding, ed., *Soziale Unruhen in Deutschland während der Französischen Revolution, Geschichte und Gesellschaft,* Special Issue, 12 (1988). Friedrich Eberle and Theo Stammen, eds., *Die Französische Revolution in Deutschland: Zeitgenössische Texte deutscher Autoren,* Universalbibliothek, vol. 8537 (Stuttgart: Reclam, 1989). Ludwig Timotheus von Spittler, *Vorlesungen über Politik,* ed. Karl Wächter (Stuttgart: Cotta, 1828), 51-52.
2. Helga Brandes, "Die 'Literarische Damen-Gesellschaft' Oldenburg zur Zeit der Französischen Revolution," in Böning, *Französische Revolution,* 439-51. Arno Herzig, Inge Stephan, and Hans G. Winter, eds., *"Sie und nicht wir": Die Französische Revolution und ihre Wirkung auf Norddeutschland und das*

Reich: Politik und Recht, Literatur und Musik (Hamburg: Dölling und Galitz, 1989).
3. Staegemann to Elisabeth von Staegemann, 20 Aug. 1807, in *Aus der Franzosenzeit: Ergänzungen zu den Briefen und Aktenstücken zur Geschichte Preußens unter Friedrich Wilhelm III., vorzugsweise aus dem Nachlaß von F. A. von Staegemann*, ed. Franz Rühl (Leipzig: Duncker und Humblot, 1904), 30.
4. Hardenberg, "Über die Reorganisation des preußischen Staats," Riga, 12 September 1807, in *Die Reorganisation des preußischen Staates unter Stein und Hardenberg*, Publikationen aus den preußischen Staatsarchiven, vol. 93, Part I: Allgemeine Verwaltungs- und Behördenreformen, vol. 1: Vom Beginn des Kampfs gegen die Kabinettsregierung bis zum Wiedereintritt des Ministers vom Stein, ed. Georg Winter (Leipzig: Hirzel, 1931), no. 261, p. 305.
5. Hardenberg, "Über die Reorganisation," 305. "The year 2440" is a reference to Louis Sebastian Mercier, *Das Jahr 2440: Ein Traum aller Traeume* (London, 1772; Leipzig: Schwickert, 1782).
6. Fichte, "Reden an die deutsche Nation" (1808), *Werke in sechs Bänden* ed. Fritz Medicus, Philosophische Bibliothek, vol. 127 (Leipzig: Meiner, n.d.), vol. 1, 357-64. Reinhard Koselleck, "Volk, Nation, Nationalismus, Masse," in *Geschichtliche Grundbegriffe*, vol. 7 (1992), 325-35.
7. Barbara C. Anderson, "State-Building and Bureaucracy in Early Nineteenth-Century Nassau," *Central European History* 24 (1991): 222-47. Loyd E. Lee, "Baden between Revolutions: State-Building and Citizenship, 1800-1848," ibid., 258-67. Lawrence J. Flockerzie, "State Building and Nation-Building in the 'Third Germany': Saxony after the Congress of Vienna," ibid., 268-92.
8. Lindenfeld, *The Practical Imagination*, 46-88. Eberhard Weis and Elisabeth Müller-Luckner, eds., *Reformen im reinbündischen Deutschland*, Schriften des Historischen Kollegs, Kolloquien 4 (Munich: Oldenbourg, 1984; Eberhard Weis, *Mongelas* (Munich: Beck, 1988-89), esp. vol. 2: *1799-1838: Der Architekt des modernen bayerischen Staates*; Bernd Wunder, *Priviligierung und Disziplinierung: Die Entstehung des Berufbeamtentums in Bayern und Württemberg (1780-1825)* Studien zur modernen Geschichte, vol. 21, (Munich: Oldenbourg, 1978); Marion W. Gray, *Prussia in Transition: Society and Politics under the Stein Reform Ministry of 1808*, Transactions of the American Philosophical Society, vol. 76, no. 1 (Philadelphia: American Philosophical Society, 1986); and Barbara Vogel, *Allgemeine Gewerbefreiheit: Die Reformpolitik des preußischen Staatskanzlers von Hardenberg (1810-1820)*, Kritische Studien zur Geschichtswissenschaft, vol. 57 (Göttingen: Vandenhoeck & Ruprecht, 1983). Helmut Berding, *Napoleonische Herrschafts- und Gesellschaftspolitik im Königreich Westfalen 1807-1813*, Kritische Studien zur Geschichtswissenschaft, vol. 7 (Göttingen: Vandenhoeck & Ruprecht, 1973). Marion W. Gray, "'Modifying the Traditional for the

Good of the Whole': Commentary on State-Building and Bureaucracy in Nassau, Baden, and Saxony in the Early Nineteenth Century," *Central European History* 24 (1991): 293-303. For focus on a later part of the nineteenth century see David Blackbourn and Geoff Eley, *The Peculiarities of German History: Bourgeois Society and Politics in Nineteenth-Century Germany* (Oxford, England: Oxford University, 1984), 176-205.

9. Kohnen, *Theodor Gottlieb von Hippel: Eine zentrale Persönlichkeit* 9-207. Theodor Gottlieb von Hippel, *Über die Bürgerliche Verbesserung der Weiber*, ed. Ralph-Rainer Wuthenow (Berlin: Voß, 1792; Frankfurt a. M.: Syndikat, 1977).

10. Hippel, *Über die Bürgerliche Verbesserung*, 51-78. Rasch, *"Mensch, Bürger, Weib,"* 21-22. Ruth Dawson, "Theodor Gottlieb von Hippel und seine Schrift, 'Über die bürgerliche Verbesserung der Weiber,'" *Jahrbuch für internationale Germanistik* 8 (1980): *Akten des VI. Internationalen Germanisten-Kongresses*, 65-69. Ruth Dawson, "The Feminist Manifesto of Theodor Gottlieb von Hippel (1741-96)," *Amsterdamer Beiträge zur neueren Germanistik*, 10 (1980): *Gestaltet und Gestaltend: Frauen in der deutschen Literatur*, ed. Marianne Burkhard, 13-32. Hull, *Sexuality, State, and Civil Society*, 323-32.

11. Hippel, *Über die bürgerliche Verbesserung*, 115-145; quotations, 121, 132-33.

12. Ibid., 150-240; quotation, 196-97.

13. My use of the word "feminist" is not meant to imply that Hippel or his contemporaries employed this term or that there was a conscious political movement on behalf of women's rights. I use it descriptively, signifying persons critical of patriarchy and seeking to improve the position of women. The word itself did not come into use until the second half of the nineteenth century.

14. Timothy Sellner, "Introduction," in Theodor Gottlieb von Hippel, *On Improving the Status of Women*, trans. Timothy F. Sellner (Detroit: Wayne State University, 1979), 35-37, 39-42. "Appendix: Rauschenbusch-Clough on Hippel and Wollstonecraft," ibid., 219-21. Mary Wollstonecraft, *Vindication of the Rights of Women*, ed. by Carol H. Poston, Norton Critical Editions in the History of Ideas (London: J. Johnson, 1792; New York: Norton, 1975). Marie Jean Antoine Nicholas de Caritat, Marquis de Condorcet, "Sur l'admission des femmes au droit de cité" (1789), in *Oeuvres*, 12 vols. (Paris: Didot, 1847), vol. 10, 119-30; Olympe de Gouges, *La declaration des droits de la femme et de la citoyenne* (Paris, 1791).

15. Hippel, *Über die Ehe* (Berlin, Vob, 1793), 239-44, 264.

16. Hull, *Sexuality, State, and Civil Society*, 328-30. Kohnen, Theodor Gottlieb von *Hippel: Eine Zentrale Persönlichkeit*, 178-80. Theodor Gottlieb von Hippel, *Nachlaß über weibliche Bildung* (Berlin: Voß, 1801), 7-8 and passim.

17. Amalie Holst [J.G. Müller, pseud.], *Bemerkungen über die Fehler unserer moderner Erziehung* (Leipzig: Linke, 1791); Amalie Holst, *Über die Bestim-*

mung des Weibes zur höheren Geistesbildung ed. Berta Rahm (Berlin: Fröhlich, 1802; edited new edition, Zurich: Ala, 1984). This edition also contains some relevant primary documents. Carl Wilhelm Otto von Schindel, *Die deutschen Schriftstellerinnen des neunzehnten Jahrhunderts* (Leipzig: Brockhaus, 1823-25), 3:226-27. *Gesamtverzeichnis*, 63:469; 71:143. María Louisa P. Cavana, "Feminism as a Criterion of the True Enlightenment," unpublished paper (1994); and María Louisa P. Cavana, "La 'Aufklärung' en las figuras de Th. G. v. Hippel y Amalia Holst," in *Feminismo e Ilustracion 1988-1992*, Actas del Seminario Permanente (Madrid: Instituto de Investigaciones Feministas Universidad Complutense de Madrid: 1992), 255-65.
18. Holst, *Über die Bestimmung des Weibes*, 41, 75-76.
19. Ibid., 18.
20. Helga Brandes, "Das Frauenzimmer-Journal," 459-67. Ruth Dawson, "'And this shield is called – self reliance': Emerging Feminist Consciousness in the Late Eighteenth Century," in *German Women in the Eighteenth and Nineteenth Centuries: A Social and Literary History* ed. Ruth-Ellen B. Joeres and Mary Jo Maynes (Bloomington: Indiana University, 1986), 160-64. Some of Ehrmann's quotations are taken from Dawson's article and are her translations. Quotations are from an announcement for *Amaliens Erholungsstunden*, as cited in Edith Krull, *Das Wirken der Frau im frühen deutschen Zeitschriftenwesen* (Charlottenburg: Lenz, 1939), 238-39. The successor to *Amaliens Erholungsstunden* was *Die Einsiedlerinn aus den Alpen*. Weckel, *Zwischen Häuslichkeit und Öffentlichkeit*, 115-41. See also Sabine Schumann, "Das 'lesende Frauenzimmer': Frauenzeitschriften im 18. Jahrhundert," in *Die Frau von der Reformation zur Romantik: Die Situation der Frau vor dem Hintergrund der Literatur- und Sozialgeschichte*, ed. Barbara Becker-Cantarino, 2nd ed., Modern German Studies, vol. 7 (Bonn: Bouvier Verlag Herbert Grundmann, 1985), 156-58.
21. Berlepsch's quotations are from Emilie von Berlepsch, "Ueber einige zum Glück der Ehe notwendige Eigenschaften und Grundsätze," *Teutscher Merkur* (1791), 2, 75-76, 100-101. I have taken them from Dawson, "'And this shield is called – self reliance.'" 164-67. The translations are Dawson's.
22. Spittler, *Vorlesungen über Politik*, 51-52.
23. Ibid., 52.
24. Wegele, "Ludwig Timotheus Freiherr von Spittler," *Allgemeine Deutsche Biographie* 35 (1893), 212-16. Hanns Hubert Hoffmann, "Ludwig Timotheus Spittler (1806 Freiherr von)," in *Biographisches Wörterbuch zur deutschen Geschichte*, ed. Helmut Rössler and Günther Franz, revised by Karl Bosl, et al. (Munich: Francke, 1973-75), vol. 3, 2714-15.
25. Wilhelm von Humboldt, "Über den Geschlechtsunterschied und dessen Einfluß auf die organische Natur" (1794), "Über die männliche und weibliche Form" (1795), and "Plan einer vergleichenden Anthropologie" (1795), all in *Gesammelte Schriften*, ed. Königliche Preußische Akademie der Wis-

senschaften (Berlin: Behr, 1903-36; repr. Berlin: de Gruyter, 1968), vol. 1, 311-34, 335-69, 377-410; quotations from 311, 312, 314, 319, 336, 346, 347, 351, 406, 408. Paul Kluckhohn, *Die Auffassung der Liebe in der Literatur des 18. Jahrhunderts und in der deutschen Romantik* (Halle: Niemeyer, 1922), 258-59, 305-306. Rasch, *"Mensch, Bürger, Weib,"* 25-28. Grenz, *Mädchenliteratur*, 25-29. Hertz, *Jewish High Society*, 272.
26. Rasch, *"Mensch, Bürger, Weib,"* 25.
27. Johann Gottlieb Fichte, *Grundlage des Naturrechts nach Prinzipien der Wissenschaftslehre* (1796), vol. 2 of *Werke in sechs Bänden*, ed. Fritz Medicus, Philosophische Bibliothek, vol. 128 (Leipzig: Meiner, n.d.), 2: 306-332, quotations, 311, 312, 317, 319, 332. See also Fichte's *System der Sittenlehre nach den Prinzipien der Wissenschaftslehre* (Jena: Gnobloch, 1798), ibid., 322-37. (The edition has double pagination, 395-759 and 1-369.) Anthony J. La Vopa, "The Revolutionary Moment: Fichte and the French Revolution," *Central European History* 22 (1989): 130-50. Isabel V. Hull, "'Sexualität' und Bürgerliche Gesellschaft," in Frevert, *Bürgerinnen und Bürger*, 62-63 and passim. Hull, *Sexuality, State and Civil Society*, 314-18.
28. Fichte, *Grundlage des Naturrechts*, 320-24.
29. Ibid., 327-28.
30. Ibid., 345-47.
31. Carl Friedrich Pockels, *Versuch einer Charakteristik des weiblichen Geschlechts: Eine Sittengemälde des Menschen, des Zeitalters und des geselligen Lebens* (Hanover: Ritscher, 1797-1802), vol. 1, 18-19. P. Zimmermann, "Karl Friedrich Pockels," *Allgemeine Deutsche Biographie*, vol. 26 (1888), 338-39.
32. [Jakob Mauvillon], *Mann und Weib nach ihren gegenseitigen Verhältnissen geschildert: Ein Gegenstück zu der Schrift: Ueber die Weiber* (Leipzig: Dykische Buchhandlung, 1791), 37, 141, 519. Jochen Hoffmann, "Jacob Mauvillon," *Neue Deutsche Biographie*, vol.16 (1990), 455-57. Duden, "Das schöne Eigentum," 131-40. Honniger, *Die Ordnung der Geschlechter*, 54-58, 63-65.
33. Ernst Brandes, *Ueber die Weiber* (Vienna: Trattern, 1788). Ernst Brandes, *Betrachtungen über das weibliche Geschlecht*. Ernst Brandes, *Betrachtungen über den Zeitgeist in Deutschland in den letzten Decennien des vorigen Jahrhunderts* (Hanover: Hahn, 1808).
34. Helga Brandes, "Die 'Literarische Damen-Gesellschaft,'" 442-46. Helga Brandes, "'Ueber die Revolutionssucht deutscher Weiber': Frauenbilder in der deutschen Publizistik um 1800," in *"Der Menschheit Hälfte blieb noch ohne Recht": Frauen und die Französische Revolution* ed. Helga Brandes (Wiesbaden: Deutscher Universitäts-Verlag, 1991), 146-63. Ulrike Böhmel Fichera, "Das Frauen*zimmer* und die Manns*person*: Politik in literarischen Frauenzeitschriften des ausgehenden 18. Jahrhunderts," in ibid., 133-45.
35. Elisabeth Fehrenbach, *Traditionelle Gesellschaft und revolutionäres Recht: Die Einführung des Code Napoléon in den Rheinbundstaaten*, Kritische Studien

zur Geschichtswissenschaft, vol. 13, 2nd ed. (Göttingen: Vandenhoeck & Ruprecht, 1978), 16-24, 37-56. Barbara Dölemeyer, "Die Einführung und Geltung des Code civil in Deutschland (1804-1814)," in Coing, *Handbuch*, vol. 3, no. 2, 1440-1471.

36. *Civil Gesetzbuch der Französischen Republik*, trans. F. Lassaulx (Koblenz: Lassaulix, 1802-04), 13, 19, 99-156. See especially articles 12, 17, 188, 207, 208, 211. See Werner Schubert, *Französisches Recht in Deutschland zu Beginn des 19. Jahrhunderts: Zivilrecht, Gerichtsverfassungsrecht und Zivilprozeßrecht*, Forschungen zur neueren Privatrechtsgeschichte, vol. 24 (Cologne: Böhlau, 1977), 61-69.

37. *Civil Gesetzbuch der Französischen Republik*, 156-204, esp. articles 223-24. Bavaria's version of the code created an exception, giving wives more equal right to sue for divorce in cases of their husbands' infidelity. Schubert, *Französisches Recht*, 442-44.

38. *Civil Gesetzbuch der Französischen Republik*, 156-83, 205-329, esp. articles 222, 367, 387, 394. Fehrenbach, *Traditionelle Gesellschaft*, 23. Conrad, "Rechtsstellung der Ehefrau," 265-70, emphasizes the "conservative" nature of the French code, as opposed to the "Enlightenment-inspired" codes of Bavaria, Prussia, and Austria.

39. Gerhard Wesenberg, *Neuere deutsche Privatrechtsgeschichte im Rahmen der europäischen Rechtsentwicklung*, 4th ed., revised by Gunter Wesener (Vienna: Böhlau, 1985), 163-64, 168-69. Gerhard Dahlmann, "Österreich," in Coing, *Handbuch*, vol. 3, no. 2: 2699-2709. Conrad, "Rechtsstellung der Frau," 262-63.

40. *Allgemeines bürgerliches Gesetzbuch für die gesammten Deutschen Erbländer der Oesterreichischen Monarchie* (Vienna: Hof- und Staatsdruckerey, 1811), §44, §93-136 in vol.1, 17, 33-53.

41. Ibid., §89-92, in vol.1, 32-33.

42. Ibid., §139, §141, §148, §163-67, §192, §198, in vol. 1, 54-55, 57, 64-65, 75, 77.

43. Ibid., §1219, §1242, §1243 in vol. 2, 350, 358-59.

44. Andreas Kaiser, "Preußisches und französisches Recht der Revolutionszeit: Zur Genesis der bürgerlichen Gesellschaft im Spiegel von Allgemeinem Landrecht (1794) und Code civil (1804)," in Herzig, Stephan, and Winter, *"Sie und nicht Wir,"* 745-48. Gray, *Prussia in Transition*, 99-121.

45. *Ordnung für sämtliche Städte der preußischen Monarchie mit dazu gehöriger Instruktion behufs der Geschäftsordnung der Stadtverordneten bei ihren ordnungsmäßigen Versammlungen*, Königsberg, 19 Nov. 1808, in Heinrich Friedrich Karl vom und zum Stein, *Briefe und amtliche Schriften*, ed. Erich Botzenhart, Walther Hubatsch, et al. (Stuttgart: Kohlhammer, 1957-74), vol. 2 part 2, 947-79 (No. 902).

46. Ibid. §18, §23, §74 on pp. 950, 956. Richard Dietrich, "Verfassung und Verwaltung," in *Berlin und die Provinz Brandenburg im 19. und 20. Jahrhundert*, ed. Hans Herzfeld and Gerd Heinrich, Geschichte von Brandenburg und Berlin, vol. 3, Veröffentlichung der Historischen Kommission zu Berlin, vol. 25 (Berlin: de Gruyter,1968), 216-26.
47. Gause, *Geschichte der Stadt Königsberg*, 2:336. Carl Schulz and Kurt Tiesler, eds., *Das älteste Bürgerbuch der Stadt Königsberg (Pr.) (1746-1809)*, Sonderschriften des Vereins für Familienforschung in Ost- und Westpreußen, vol. 36 (Königsberg, 1939; repr. Hamburg: Verein für Familienforschung in Ost- und Westpreußen, 1978), iii-x, 1-227. For every hundred male applicants in 1809, 5.4 women applied. The average over the previous twenty years was less than one women per two hundred men.
48. Karl-Ernst Jeismann, *Das preußische Gymnasium in Staat und Gesellschaft: Die Entstehung des Gymnasiums als Schule des Staats und der Gebildeten, 1787-1817*, Industrielle Welt, vol. 15 (Stuttgart: Klett, 1974), 215-398. Sigrid Bormann-Heischkeil and Karl-Ernst Jeismann, "Abitur, Staatsdienst und Sozialstruktur: Rekruitierung und Differenzierung der Schicht der Gebildeten am Beispiel der sozialen Herkunft und beruflichen Zukunft von Abiturienten preußischer Gymnasien im Vormärz," in *Bildung, Staat, Gesellschaft im 19. Jahrhundert: Mobilisierung und Disziplinierung*, Nassauer Gespräche der Freiherr-vom-Stein Gesellschaft, vol. 2, ed. Jeismann (Stuttgart: Steiner, 1989), 155-86. Margaret Kraul, "Normierung und Emanzipation: Die Berufung auf den Geschlechtskarakter bei der Institutionalsierung der höheren Mädchenbildung," in ibid., 219-31. Vierhaus, "Bildung," 528-31. Wilhelm von Humboldt, "Über die innere und äussere Organisation der höheren wissenschaftlichen Anstalten in Berlin" (1810),in *Gesammelte Schriften*, ed. Königliche Preubische Akademie der Wissenschaften (Berlin: Behr, 1903-06; repr. de Gruyter, 1968), vol. 10, 250-60; and Humboldt, "Über Reformen in Unterrichtswesen" (1810), ibid., 299-302.
49. Rasch, *"Mensch, Bürger, Weib,"* 28-31.
50. Betty Gleim, *Erziehung und Unterricht des weiblichen Geschlechts: Ein Buch für Eltern und Erzieher* ed. Ruth Bleckwenn, Quellen und Schriften zur Geschichte der Frauenbildung, vol. 4 (Leipzig: Goschen, 1810; repr. Paderborn: Hüttemann, 1989), vol.1, 5-7; vol. 2, 3, 9.
51. Ibid. 1:60, 104-106.
52. Ibid., 1:58-62, 103, 114-16.
53. Ibid., 2:132-35.
54. *Handbuch für Mädchen von reifem Alter; mit moralischen Erzählungen und ökonomischen Kenntnissen* (Munich: Lentner, 1791), 2-3, 31-36, 190-94.
55. Ibid., 2:151-53.
56. Betty Gleim, *Bremisches Kochbuch, nebst einem Anhange wichtiger Haushaltungsregalien* (Bremen: Heyse, 1808). I am indebted to Prof. Klaus Rudolf

Primacy of Public Sphere

of Göttingen, originally of Bremen, who allowed me to use a copy of a late edition that had belonged to one of his foremothers. See Weber, *Handbuch der Ökonomischen Literatur,* 7:325; and *Gesamtverzeichnis,* 48 (1982), 12-13.

57. This is a major conceptual transition, but no linguistic shift is completely tidy. Authors who emphasized the comprehensive role and the traditional moral calling of women continued to use the word *Hausmutter* into the nineteenth century. Even Gleim could not avoid it: "Moreover, the educated woman is especially obligated, as *Hausmutter,* to raise the [female responsibilities] to a type of master craft." Gleim, *Erziehung und Unterricht,* 2:133. See also the following chapter. On the emerging importance of the notion of profession, see Konrad H. Jarausch, "The German Professions in History and Theory," in *German Professions 1800-1950,* ed. Jarausch and Geoffrey Cocks (New York: Oxford University, 1990), 9-12; Werner Conze, "Beruf," in *Geschichtliche Grundbegriffe,* 1 (1972), 496-503. On the professions as a middle-class phenomenon, see Jürgen Kocka, ed. *Das Bildungsbürgertum im 19. Jahrhundert,* Part 4, *Politischer Einfluß und gesellschaftliche Formation* (Stuttgart: Klett, 1989), 16-20.

Chapter Eight

"Scientific Agriculture" and the Sexual Division of Labor (1810-1830)

In 1830 Friedrich Benedict Weber, a professor of Cameral Sciences at Breslau, published an economic assessment of his times. It was clear to Weber that the shape of the economy had changed dramatically during his prolific career of three decades. Weber's book was a response to an anonymous work by an author who described himself as a "nonpartisan friend of the truth." The difference between the two writers was that Weber considered the changes to be positive, while the other, a conservative, viewed them with alarm. There was no doubt in either mind that conditions had been transformed. Like almost all of his contemporaries, Weber understood that Germany had experienced an economic revolution that had established free markets in trade and labor.[1]

Both material conditions and norms were in transition. One of the most important sets of ideas to find footing in Germany during the revolutionary period was that articulated by Adam Smith (1723-1790) in his *Wealth of Nations* in 1776. The Scottish

Notes for this section begin on page 291.

philosopher and economist had a number of enthusiastic interpreters throughout the Germanies. By the turn of the century, his ideals – sometimes loosely explicated – were standard features in the Cameralist university curricula. Georg Sartorius (1765-1828) at Göttingen, Ludwig Heinrich Jakob (1759-1827) at Halle, Christian Jakob Kraus (1753-1807) at Königsberg, and August Ferdinand Lueder (1760-1819) at Braunschweig (later Göttingen) rewrote their lectures, closely following Smith. Lueder, for example, published his *Ueber Nationalindustrie und Staatswirthschaft, nach Adam Smith bearbeitet* (On National Industry and State Economy Based on Adam Smith, 1800-1804). Kraus, a teacher and close acquaintance of several of the men who became members of the Prussian reform ministry after 1807, extracted material from *Wealth of Nations* for his lectures, modifying it to address Prussian conditions. While Smith's emphasis was on manufacture, Kraus gave greater consideration to agriculture, as was appropriate for East-Elbian circumstances. Free trade and a market economy were his guideposts, like they were for other German academics of his generation who concerned themselves with the economy.[2]

The restructuring of the economy resulted in a transformed division of labor accompanied by a new notion of professionalism, and contemporaries often associated these changes with the growth of an urban, bourgeois, commercial society. However, novel conditions were not confined to cities; they also affected the lives and identities of the agrarian populace. German society remained predominantly rural until far into the nineteenth century, and under the new market conditions there developed an agricultural bourgeoisie, a class of nonaristocratic entrepreneurial estate owners.[3]

The concept *Hausvater* was falling out of use. Economists were describing the male proprietor in agriculture as a professional. They were also inventing new norms for the agricultural wife. Some assigned her a "professional" role, but no one envisioned her as a partner in the newly conceptualized productive spheres of the economy.

Albrecht Thaer and Scientific Agriculture

Germany's encounters with Napoleon seemed to offer opportunities for change in agriculture, just as they did in the realms of government and law. Among those who wished to put German agriculture on a completely modern footing was Albrecht Thaer (1752-1828). Trained as a medical doctor, Thaer was town and court physician of the small town of Celle, near Hanover. Out of personal inclination, he developed a passion for agricultural improvement. He joined the Celle Agricultural Society in 1784, purchased an estate of his own, and, in an attempt to turn it into an exemplary farming enterprise, undertook a systematic study of agriculture as he became the leading figure in the Celle Society. Turning to writers of Great Britain who were recording the results of their society's agrarian revolution, Thaer became a partisan of new techniques such as crop rotation and stall-feeding. In 1791 he began publishing his findings. His first work was a practical manual on stall-feeding and the cultivation of clover. Before the end of the decade, he had established his own agricultural teaching institute in Celle, published the first volume of his *Einleitung zur Kenntnib der englischen Landwirthschaft* (Introduction to the Science of English Agriculture), and founded an agricultural journal.[4]

In 1803 Napoleonic forces occupied Thaer's state of Hanover. A few months later King Frederick William III of Prussia invited Thaer to enter the service of the Hohenzollern government as an agricultural specialist. The king offered Thaer the estate of Möglin near the Oder River on which to develop an experimental farm and a modern agricultural training institute.[5] Thaer accepted the king's invitation and left his besieged homeland. Once in Prussia, Thaer participated in the discussions of agrarian reforms set in motion by Prussia's defeat in 1806-1807. In 1810 he became a professor of Cameral Sciences at Berlin's new university, founded by Humboldt and his colleagues. As an author, editor, and translator, Thaer published more than sixty-five volumes and countless articles, establishing himself, by a wide margin, as Germany's most famous expert in agricultural affairs. Thaer's most well-known and systematic work, his four-volume *Grundsätze der rationellen Landwirthschaft* (Principles of Efficient Agriculture, 1809-1812), was reprinted throughout the nineteenth century and often translated, both in Europe and beyond.[6] So formative were his research and publications that agrarian historians often refer to the early nineteenth century as the "Age of Thaer." Within half a century after his death, there were prominent statues of Thaer in Berlin, Leipzig, and Celle, and the popular novelist Theodor Fontane had published a seventy-page tribute to him. Thaer was known as the "Father of Scientific Agriculture" and a great patriot of the Fatherland. Even in the late twentieth century, there is widespread interest in Thaer. Not only historians but also agricultural economists, crop scientists, and animal scientists in Germany, Eastern Europe, Great Britain, Japan and elsewhere continue to study his work.[7]

A product of the age of Enlightenment, Thaer declared agriculture to be a "science" resting on empirical principles and rational methodology. He advocated the systematic collection of data and the use of hypothesis, experimentation, and observation. He rejected the ideal expounded in the old economic literature that tradition or folk custom could contribute to sound farming practices. He strove to make farmers "rational agriculturists," whom he likened to marine navigators using scientific knowledge and instruments to sail uncharted waters. Guided by science, they would far outdistance the ordinary "coastal travelers," the farmers whose knowledge was based merely on experience and who dared not venture out of sight of land.[8]

Thaer praised Arthur Young (1741-1820), Britain's foremost proponent of enclosure, crop rotation, and scientific fertilization. He compared Young's contribution to world culture with that of the British philosophers Bacon, Newton, and Locke. Thaer championed new technology, highly productive crops, and innovative methods of plowing, planting, cultivating, fertilizing, and threshing.[9]

Thaer's conception of the economy was entwined with his emphasis on new plows, threshers, and hay rakes, and on novel means of agricultural production, and this set him apart from his predecessors and some contemporaries who wrote about agriculture. While some partisans of the old school still used the word "economics" *(Wirtschaft)* as a synonym for agriculture, Thaer insisted on a much broader understanding of the concept. In agreement with Smith, Thaer held that the economy encompassed a wide range of human enterprises, not agriculture alone. He suggested reviving an ancient Roman ideal, according to which economics consisted of many branches: procurement of natural resources, farming, state enterprises, and above all, business *(Gewerbe)*. Working with this broad definition of economics, Thaer pursued his lifelong goal of making agriculture a profitable and expanding enterprise in the still preindustrial setting of the early nineteenth century.[10]

Three aspects of Thaer's prescriptions for agricultural life were especially consequential in the formulation of new social norms: privatization of land, creation of a free rural labor market, and establishment of agriculture as an exchange-oriented business. These ideals were not original with him; they were widely shared by contemporaries. Thaer, however, was important for his systematic expression of the new economic precepts in a language accessible to a broad cross section of the educated public. He had a talent for articulating economic goals in a manner that made them seem natural and unquestionable. It is reasonable to assume that many who read his books for the technical information absorbed the new economics with little consciousness of doing so.

In regard to the establishment of modern private property, Thaer participated enthusiastically in discussions of the Prussian government regarding agrarian reforms following Napoleonic defeats. A series of royal Prussian edicts between 1807 and 1821 broke the semifeudal bonds tying rural workers to specific estates under the *Gutsherrschaft* system. They also continued a process, begun in the eighteenth century, of transferring the state-owned farms, the so-called royal domains, to private ownership. The purpose of these initiatives was the creation of a modern real estate system with single-party ownership and freedom to buy and sell at will. The reformers intensely debated the question of ownership of land occupied by peasants within manorial estates: Should the small farmers gain titles to it, or should it belong to the aristocratic proprietors? Thaer and other reformers were less concerned with the fate of landlords and peasants than with the goal of placing farmland in the hands of private individuals who had the unfettered freedom to utilize it and to exchange it on the market. The Prussian reforms made it possible for the urban middle classes, heretofore largely excluded from ownership of agrarian lands, to invest their capital in agriculture. The new measures divided the lands of former estates between the aristocratic owners and well-off peasants. The innovations ultimately affected all classes: many nobles increased their holdings and their dominance of agriculture; some bourgeois entrepreneurs moved to the countryside and undertook farming; some fortunate peasants secured their holdings and became a class of mid-size landowners; multitudes of peasants lost their traditional place on the land, becoming day laborers or leaving the countryside entirely and forming a new preindustrial proletariat.[11]

Thaer was certain that the reforms would bring positive results, for they would effect the establishment of outright owner-

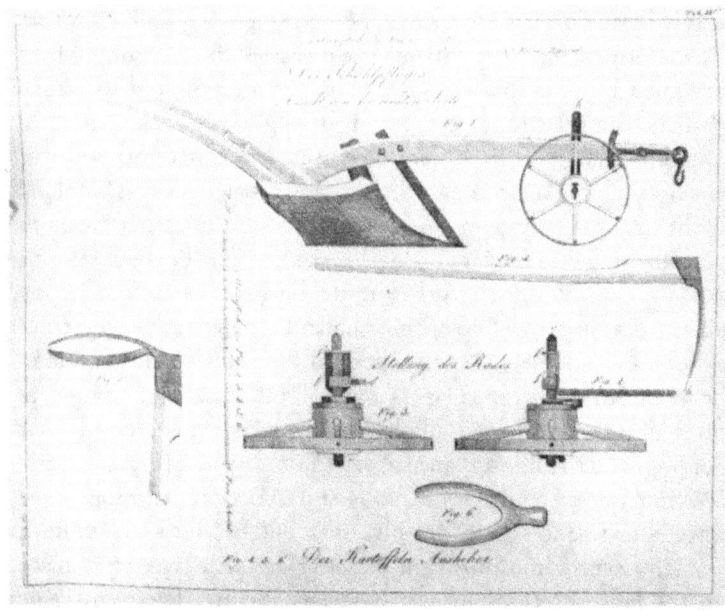

Figures 8.1a and 8.1b Unlike their forbears, Thaer and his generation of agricultural reformers were more interested in farm technology than in people and their relationships. These illustrations of plows and their use come from Thaer's *Beschreibung der nutzbarsten neuen Ackergeräthe* (Description of the most useful newest farming implements, 1803-1806).

ship of property in the modern sense. In Thaer's view, an owner would always take a long-term perspective, strive for profits, and reinvest a part of the earnings. He was highly optimistic about the potential consequences:

> Because most governments currently recognize the great disadvantage arising from limitations in the ownership [and use] of real estate, there is a great emphasis on abolishing the restrictions and making all property free .... Through such measures some nearly worthless [estates] will regain their natural value, and the wealth of the nation will greatly increase.[12]

One of Thaer's basic assumptions – already articulated a half century earlier by the Cameralists – was that individuals who possessed land had the right, even the obligation, to extract the greatest yield possible. This represented a final break with the old notions of the moral household economy and household necessity *(Hausnotdurft)*. Thaer's goal of realizing the greatest profit in order to increase output in future years envisioned humans in command of natural resources, not as stewards of the land. Emphasis in agrarian norms had shifted from maintenance of households to exploitation of the soil for material gain.

A second objective of the agrarian reforms was the establishment of modern wage labor to replace the servant system *(Gesindeordnung)*, a remnant of the household economy. In Thaer's vision, this old arrangement represented fundamental inefficiency, because it hampered the proprietor's freedom. Hence, wage labor was inextricably tied to the concept of free ownership. In his delineation of seven "essential requirements" for a "productive economy," Thaer listed as number one: "complete ownership and free use of the fields, an absence of all servitude and claims that others might have upon the land."[13] He meant the "claims" which peasants under the traditional system could make to livelihood, expressed in their contractual or hereditary right to use common meadows and forests. Thaer declared it "urgent ... for the master, the worker, and the general welfare that [unfree labor systems] be abolished." He regarded labor as a vital component of the agrarian economy and rejected the Physiocratic doctrine, still sometimes emphasized in his day in the economic and patriotic societies, that land was the source of wealth. This doctrine had been important in the late eighteenth century for those who wished to counteract the Cameralist teaching that the source of human prosperity lay in urban trade and commerce. Thaer, however, could move beyond this position, for the reform governments of the Napoleonic era had illustrated commitment to the agrarian economy. It was clear that those who planned for the future understood that Germany was a rural society and that agriculture would play a central role in the economy. What Thaer wished to emphasize was the simple doctrine: "Labor [is] the source of all wealth .... It is through labor that humans obtain, or have obtained, everything they consume and enjoy."[14]

In response to those who expressed concern about the rising cost of agrarian labor, as Germershausen had done some twenty years earlier, Thaer urged a market-oriented perspective. He explained that a network of economic factors determined the level of wages, including food prices, intensity of business activity, local customs, and natural disasters. The recent rise of wages was a normal economic phenomenon balanced by a surge in worker productivity, stimulated by abolition of obligatory labor. Day laborers were more industrious than peasants who worked under semifeudal conditions, "because they must feed themselves and their families and hence must guard against being fired on account of poor work." Hence the increase in wages was a nominal one only; on balance, employers had gained, rather than lost, from the recent developments.[15]

The economics of labor was one side of a coin, and the science of the soil was the other. Only when the two were used together would the desired maximization of production be achieved. The practice of fertilization allowed scientific farmers to enhance the vegetative powers of the land. Crop rotation enabled them to cultivate a great percentage of their property almost perpetually, in contrast to the traditional three-field rotation in which some land was always fallow and meadows for grazing were never put under plow. With extensive scientific data about how plants utilized the earth's nutrients and fertilizers replaced them, Thaer reinforced the notion that agriculture's purpose was intensive cultivation. For the same reason he championed the practice of stall-feeding, which he defined as "sustaining animals primarily with fodder that has been cut and brought to them. Only very little, ... or not at all, do they graze." This system allowed the farmer to turn meadows into productive croplands, to utilize animal manure more efficiently for fertilizer, and to rotate crops more productively. The rational agriculturist carefully orchestrated the conditions of human labor, plant production, animal husbandry, and soil use to allow the most scientifically and economically productive yield. Successful agriculture required a "correct relationship between labor and fertilization."[16]

Finally, Thaer asserted that agriculture was a business *(Gewerbe)* – a relatively new word in application to rural life in Germany, although Justi had used it in the 1760s. Until the mid-eighteenth century and later, *Gewerbe* had meant handwork or artisanship, but the word was taking on its modern definition with Thaer, as is clear from his assertion that the agrarian proprietor was a manager *(Wirthschafts-Direktor)* whose tasks included the hiring, supervision, and maintenance of the work force, the keeping of livestock, and the production of crops, all with the larger goals of reinvesting capital and expanding operations. Absolute freedom in the disposition of capital was essential to successful agricultural enterprise. The very opening sentence of Thaer's *Principles of Efficient Agriculture* made it clear that the yield of products was a means, not an end: "Agriculture is a business that has the purpose … of producing a profit or earning money."[17]

In the enterprise of farming, according to Thaer, there were three types of resources: basic capital, or the worth of the estate itself; standing capital, or the buildings, livestock, and equipment; and operating capital, or liquid assets. Operating capital was the "motivating force of the whole operation" and should constitute the largest percentage of each enterprise's resources. "The true yield of the business is determined less by the size of the estate than by the sum of the [investment]." Informed managers knew that it was best to plan for the long range rather than to attempt to produce great earnings with a single year's produce.[18]

The ideals of Albrecht Thaer represent a post-Enlightenment redefinition of economics and a reconceptualization of human ecology. Rejecting the view of the household economy that held humans to be a part of Nature and that strove to recycle the human-Nature relationship from one generation to the next, Thaer was enthusiastic about people bridling the earth's resources to produce ever-increasing yields. In place of common lands of the estate, private property was the means to extract maximum gain from the soil. In place of the household economy's emphasis on people's consumption of locally produced commodities, Thaer championed the exchange economy, which transported goods from one region to another and led to crop specialization, not only in Germany but in other regions as well. The reformer etched into German agrarian ideals the impersonal laws of science; the market had replaced tradition and religion as guiding principles for agriculture.

Far removed from the seventeenth-century ideals of the morally based household economy, Thaer postulated units of production that would constantly adjust the number of personnel needed on the basis of market conditions. Business managers, unlike the old household masters, had no obligation to their workers; their objective was capital gains, and the relationship between employer and employee was based on the profitability of the latter's labor. Thaer's generation sought to dissociate the mass of the peasantry from the land and to erase the remnants of the notion – insofar as it still existed – that the economy was centered in self-perpetuating households that took from the land just what they needed to sustain themselves and prepare for the next generation.

Thaer's work incorporated less explicit, but no less consequential, ideals about gender. In contrast to the doctrines of the household books, the new science of agricultural economics focused on process rather than people. Thaer advocated that the impersonal market, not a moral philosophy, should determine people's place. His language reflected a diminishing of the female economic role and an expansion of the authority of the male. He emphasized, for example, the importance of systematic, institutional schooling for estate managers, as opposed to the handed-down traditions so important to the master and mistress of the household under the old ideals. Thaer envisioned that the sons – but not the daughters – of estate managers would attend the new institutes to learn scientific agriculture. He used masculine words when writing about educating the young for the profession: "the rational (male) farmer," "the young (male) agriculturist," "men of special talent."[19] The professionalization of agriculture was leading to its becoming a strictly male enterprise.

It is not that women had disappeared entirely in Thaer's writing about agriculture, however, for he still described certain roles as female. For example, he discussed the work of dairymaids *(Hof-Mägde)* in milking and cheese production. Garden workers were also "maids," and certain tasks were performed by "women and youths." In the harvest, men cut the grain while women and youths raked and bound the stalks. Both sexes worked side by side to load the sheaths on wagons and bring them to the barns.[20]

What had vanished was the notion of women as managers of productive economic operations. Thaer described no female counterpart to the agricultural business proprietor. He did regard it as desirable to have a "woman overseer ... for ... the dairy, the internal household, and all work done exclusively by women." But this was a subordinate position, in no way a shared one. It was the role of an employee, not the wife of the estate. Thus, possibly without much thought on the subject, Thaer envisioned a continuation of gendered work in farming, but with female roles subordinated in every way to the (male) management of the enterprise.[21]

As a contemporary of Betty Gleim, Thaer was writing when the bourgeois ideal of the true female "profession" of wife-mother-housekeeper was striking deep roots. He may have assumed, like Gleim, that motherhood would be a primary occupation of women; but if this was his view, he did not comment on it, for Thaer did not discuss reproduction as a part of the agrarian economy. Rather than to bear, nurture, educate, and sustain successive generations, Thaer's business managers were to sustain and enhance their operations by saving, reinvesting, and expanding. Ironically, he knew and admired at least one aristocratic woman, Helene Charlotte von Lesewitz, Frau von Friedland, who single-handedly managed her expansive estates with great expertise.[22] Apparently he could view this situation from the old-regime perspective, in which a woman stepped into a male role when no man was present. But this did not lead him to call into question the patriarchal norm of male proprietorship or to postulate a significant productive role for women in marriage.

Thaer regarded his work in agriculture as a contribution to the emancipatory process of constructing a civil society, a strong "nation." He declared his trust in the positive outcome of the economic, political, and educational reforms of which he was a part. In 1809 he wrote to Theodor von Schön, who a year earlier had been a member of the inner circle of the Stein ministry in Prussia and had played a central role in drafting the agrarian reforms:

> I am very pleased that you have faith in the nation as I do ... . I understand the nation to be those who can read and write. The others must first become part of the civil society ... . [The peasantry has much potential,] but under previous conditions [of servile labor] things were *bound* to go badly.[23]

Thaer, active in the drafting of legislation to transform semifeudal estates into a modern private property system,[24] combined the eighteenth-century notion of "patriot" as improver of agriculture and economy with the nineteenth-century idea of "the nation." In his vision, education led to efficient farming and at the same time was the essential basis for citizenship, a quality reserved for bright and industrious male proprietors. The nation would prosper with good schooling, scientific farming, and a modern market economy, all fostered by the increasingly powerful state. When Thaer wrote of the economy, he meant what had come to be called the "National Economy" *(National-Ökonomie)*, the male dominion where women's work was not significant. For Thaer, the sexual division of labor was a given of nature that did not require elaboration.

Separate Spheres in Agriculture

Acknowledging his own cursory treatment of the role of the household in the economy, Thaer recommended Friedrich Karl

Gericke's "very good instructions regarding the interior household." He referred readers to the second edition of Gericke's *Praktische Anleitung zur Führung der Wirthschafts-Geschäffte für angehende Landwirthe* (Practical Introduction to Agricultural Management). Like Thaer, Gericke (1755-1817), founded and directed an agricultural institute. The Duke of Braunschweig-Lüneburg made available to him a secularized cloister, St. Lüdgeri, to use as a teaching academy, similar to Thaer's in Möglin. For Gericke, it was important that this was near the University of Helmstedt so that young men in his institute could easily study agriculture's "related disciplines," chemistry, botany, mathematics, physics, languages, veterinary medicine, and forestry.[25] Scientific training belonged to the professionalization of agriculture.

Gericke delineated three spheres in the new agrarian economy. One was the realm of the fields *(Acker und Feldpolizei)*; the second was the "exterior household" *(Polizei des äußeren Haushalts)*, which included barnyard, stalls, swine operations, grain storage and brewery; the third consisted of the "interior household" *(Polizei des inneren Haushalts)*. The fields were the age-old realm of male work and remained so in Gericke's scheme. The "exterior household" included many productive activities that the old economists had specified as female in nature; Gericke indicated that these were now to be supervised by the *Hausherr* or, in his absence, a manager *(Ober-Verwalter)* or clerk *(Schreiber)*. The old-regime idea that a wife took over her husband's responsibilities in his absence did not survive the era of the French Revolution and Napoleon in many of the revised law codes, nor did it do so in the ideals of the agrarian reformers. Leaving the wife a remnant of the responsibilities earlier economists would have delegated to her, Gericke gave her prescriptive instructions but not the kind of technical information he presented to her husband. Referring to her by the modern designation, housewife *(Hausfrau)*, Gericke specified that she "oversees safety, cleanliness and order in the kitchen, the cellar, and the dairy stalls." (In the absence of the housewife, the housekeeper *[Haushälterin]* could perform these roles). Seemingly as an afterthought, Gericke added: "One could also assign to [the housewife] the supervision of the geese, ducks, turkeys, chickens, and pigeon house, if one wanted to describe this realm in its entirety." This was distinct, however, from the farmyard operations, the "external household," under male supervision.[26]

Gericke stressed the importance of strict lines of command within the household: "A good agricultural business must have a monarchical structure ... . The housewife is the highest authority over the female servants, but in a well-ordered estate [she] stands below the master and must willingly subordinate herself to his transcendent role." She should refrain from giving orders to male servants, except to those who worked in the inner household, and to the coachmen. In other ways as well, delineated paths of control must always be observed. If the common workers on the estate should have complaints, these must reach the master only via the foreman *(Groß-Knecht)* and never come from individuals. Unambiguous written contracts were important, even for servants of the lower order. Contracts alone, were not sufficient, for servants were not to be trusted. The *Hausherr* must take precautions, for example, to prevent them from stealing household items.[27] Like Thaer, Gericke unquestioningly accepted the ideals of dominance and subordination traditional in their society for centuries, as applied to both social status and gender. Combining these with the ideals of capitalist economy and separate spheres, they created new norms of exclusion and dependence for women.

Most economists of the early nineteenth century – those in academic positions continued to refer to themselves as "Cameralists" – simply ignored women in agriculture. Friedrich Benedict Weber published a handbook, *Ueber die Kameralwissenschaft* (On Cameral Science) hoping to revive interest in what he feared was a field in decline. An intellectual heir of both Justi and Adam Smith, Weber saw economics as a public affair of the state in which agriculture played a small but significant role; hence he gave an important place to farm management in his proposed curriculum in Cameral Sciences. Practically his only mention of women was in his formulaic phrase, "male and female agriculturist" *(Landwirt und Landwirtin*; significantly not *Hausvater* and *Hausmutter)*. He never identified a role for the *Landwirtin*. Regarding the garden, one specifically female realm of the traditional economy, he remarked: "Because of insufficient time, nothing at all can be offered on garden cultivation in these lectures, and due to lack of interest in the subject the previously scheduled special lectures have almost never taken place."[28]

Ironically, twenty-five years earlier Weber had been one of the academicians who had given scholarly recognition to Christian Friedrich Germershausen's *Die Hausmutter* by devoting a separate section of his bibliographical *Handbuch der ökonomischen Literatur* (Handbook of Economic Literature) to "the female agriculturist and *Hausmutter*." As he updated the work every few years, he retained the section, and in 1832 he still listed 136 new publications for female agriculturists. Weber knew that women worked in farming and that there was plentiful literature describing their activities. However, he changed with the times, and by the late 1820s he simply depicted the economy *(National-Ökonomie)* as a male responsibility, possibly not even realizing the transition in his own language and thinking. Weber's modernized Cameralist curriculum simply ignored women. The female role in the economy was insufficiently important to warrant the professor's or the students' attention. The conceptual change in women's role is illustrated by the fact that in the titles he cited for women in agriculture over a span of four decades, the term *Hausfrau* gradually replaced *Hausmutter*.[29] The rural housewife had replaced the mistress of the household.

The female activity of gardening production apparently was of little interest to the new economists; they focused their attention largely on field crops. The garden, always essential to maintenance of the household, sank from consideration. The early nineteenth-century prescriptive writers did not envision garden produce taking on the role they forecast for grain, which could be mass-produced, stored with relative ease, and shipped to distant regions for profit. Their continued use of the traditional term "kitchen garden" is indication that economists considered its products for home consumption, not market sales. Neither kitchen nor consumption belonged to "the economy." Thaer excluded the kitchen garden from his discussion of scientific agriculture because, he said, its production was influenced only by the labor *(Industrie)* put into it, not by the balance of soil conditions, fertilization, and management. Perhaps it was difficult for him to imagine female-produced crops as scientific. Maybe his perspective was influenced by the connotation of garden left from its etymological origins as fenced or hedged property, as opposed to open fields. The concept of garden was traditionally so bound with the notion of house that the two were sometimes used as synonyms. The garden was not important to those who thought in terms of transforming agriculture into a modern enterprise.[30]

A contemporary of Gericke and Thaer, Justus Ludwig Günther Leopold (1761-1823), agreed with many of his generation that agriculture was "the art of producing as much as possible from the land and the soil." A pastor who published several agricultural manuals, Leopold might have been expected to follow the tradition of old-regime authors such as Germershausen who emphasized the moral economy. Instead, a member of the illustrious Celle Agricultural Society, he sought to bring his readers up to date with the latest scientific information which he intertwined with market economics. Excited about the new knowledge of his day, he promised his readers "information that Germershausen ... could not have known." Leopold regretted that the University of Göttingen, where he had studied, did not maintain connections to two large ecclesiastical estates nearby, which would have provided the students with excellent opportunities to practice the latest scientific methods. He called his age the "golden era of economics," and he joined what he characterized as a "loud and emphatic chorus" demanding "economic schools and summer farm institutes" to match the good schools for business that were growing in the cities.[31]

Leopold stressed stall-feeding, field enclosure, crop rotation, and fertilizer production. On some topics he referred his readers to Thaer for further information, and he dedicated a portion of one of his books to the pioneer agriculturist in the same year Thaer moved to Prussia. Leopold advocated that not only traditional field crops, but also garden produce, should be raised for market earnings. He explained that "garden" simply meant a fenced or hedged field for the production of a specified crop, and this was no reason to exclude it from the economic advantage of the new agriculture. The exception, however, was the "kitchen garden" operated by women. This was different:

> [It] must ... not be too large, because it would be much too costly to throw away the kitchen crops if there were no regular market for them ... . In mid-size households, [the kitchen garden] must be the responsibility of the *Hausmutter* and under her supervision ... . [Here] she can keep the maids, hired workers, and growing children busy in slack times with weeding, hoeing, watering, and the like.

In "small households" the kitchen garden was under the direction of the *Hausmutter* and represented an opportunity for her to put to work the children and servants "in their spare time, and on the side." In the modern agricultural household, the husband's responsibility was to employ contemporary methods in production of crops for market sales in order to sustain and expand the operation. The agricultural job of the wife – Leopold called her the *Hausmutter*, but his usage was far from the prototype – was one to be kept small because it was for consumption and not for market purposes. It was a time-filler for servants, maids, and children, and if something productive came out of it, the wife could feel good about this and regard the produce as a "true profit."[32] The new agrarian norms increasingly constructed the kitchen and the market as separate spheres. Leopold, who was focused on farming for profit, patronizingly implied that the farm wife could be pleased if some of her produce actually made it to market. It clearly was not his expectation that this would constitute a significant part of the farm economy.

A decade later, Blasius Merrem (1761-1824), a professor of economics, cameral sciences, and botany in Marburg, pursued the discussion of male and female economic roles. A scholar with the widest ranging accomplishments, Merrem researched and wrote in the fields of physics, botany, ornithology, mathematics, and natural history. He also published travel books and poetic translations of Psalms. When he turned to the subject of "middle-class economics and householding" in 1817, Merrem specified that the household was an economic unit and a business. The goal of the household business was to recognize, preserve and increase its wealth. Inconsistent in his terminology, Merrem introduced his description of the gender realms with the traditional words *"Hausvater"* and *"Hausmutter,"* while in most of his text he used the newer terms *Hausherr* and *Hausfrau*. Merrem explained the differences in male and female roles: The husband should "take over all of those activities that are necessary for the preservation and increase of the wealth." Women could not do this, even though there may be a few who "do not lack the capabilities":

> Their normal ... physical weakness, their propensity to pregnancy, childbearing, nursing, and early education of children ... are serious hindrances to ... the administration of property ... . The above-named characteristics and a certain unique inclination destine women to domesticity and to overseeing the household ... . Thus through God's wise design, the woman is the indispensable helper of the man when he assumes the management of a business.[33]

Merrem stressed that a good housewife would not lead a life of leisure. "She would prefer to patch children's clothing than to read a novel, or to write in her household ledger than to compose letters ... . Making butter is a more enjoyable activity than writing poetry." The wife's first calling was motherhood, for "the highest aspiration and first fruits of a happy marriage between healthy and virtuous partners are children." Up to the fourth or fifth year, they belonged solely to the care of the mother. After that the father would take charge of sons, but the mother would continue to look after daughters. Merrem offered the wife prolific prescriptive advice about rearing children, preparing food, washing, bleaching, and ironing, as well as about caring for domesticated animals raised for home consumption. (Animals raised for business [*Gewerbe*] were under male supervision.) Merrem drafted a model budget for the housewife that made it clear she was a consumer rather than a producer. Her greatest virtue was "thrift."[34]

Prescriptive economic literature for agricultural families was flourishing. The concept "housewife," *(Hausfrau)* was continuing to replace the notion *Hausmutter*; and new terms also appeared in place of *Hausvater*, but these were more varied than their female counterparts. The language was often purposeful. Matthias Eigl (1789-1858), an Austrian author of family guidebooks with a pronounced religious perspective, chose the unusual combination of *Hausfrau* and *Hausvater*, the new word for the wife and the old for the husband. In this interesting formulation, the traditional name for master of the house allowed him to stress the all-encompassing paternal authority. Essentially a conservative, he was not interested in business but in rural patriarchal household. The newer feminine designation allowed him to accentuate the wife's subordination but leave aside the strong economic role normatively ascribed to the *Hausmutter*.

> The German *Hausfrau* is trained as a woman – as mother, spouse, and friend in the strictest sense of the word ... . Above all she imposes on her daughters those female virtues, called modesty ... [and] grace, which are today ... far too uncommon qualities in many *Frauenzimmer* ... . The *Hausvater*, as the highest authority, presides over everything in the house and field, and completely directs the education of the children ... . Only the female education ... does he leave largely to the woman.[35]

Friedrich Röver (d. 1822), a pastor in Calvörde in the Duchy of Braunschweig, published his two-volume *Hausfreund* (Household Friend) in 1820 and shortly thereafter, his three-volume *Hausfreundinn auf dem Lande* (Female Country Household Friend). He composed both for "the rural middle classes." Claiming that wives in agricultural settings had to work harder than their counterparts in cities because they had fewer servants and fewer specialized shops such as bakeries, Röver presented practical information on such topics as barometers, textile fibers, household medicines, hygiene, home brewing, foods, and recipes, including a forty-page article on potatoes. The pastor made it explicit that he was not writing for "delicate ladies, of whom there are more in the countryside than thirty years ago," but rather for "industrious and true household managers." He said he received help in his writing from "some experienced housewives and cooks." Röver viewed the female "manager" as a consumer, a cook, a gardener, and a cleaner; she was not a businesswoman or a producer for the agricultural market. He applied economic terminology to the wife but made the terminology vacuous.[36]

Gender norms of the German-speaking countryside were in transition. Agrarian writers increasingly depicted males as businessmen who competed in the ever-expanding marketplace and females as housewives who worked in the family in roles that were not regarded as belonging to the economy.

"Amalie" and a Female Profession in Agriculture

During the transitional era of the French Revolution and the Napoleonic occupation, one writer made a career of disseminating knowledge for women about the "female economy," by which she meant the "profession" of agrarian wife. Between 1790 and 1811, often using the pen name Amalie, Christine Dorothea Henschel Gürnth (1749-1813) of Silesia published twenty-two books on a wide-range of topics, including gardening, household maintenance, forestry *(weibliche Forstökonomie)*, and needlework. In addition to her Silesian cookbook, she authored specialized culinary and dietary guides. For a short period she was coeditor of an economic journal for women. At an early age she had experienced hardships following the death of her father, and she assumed the mission of helping women find their place and perform their jobs well. She explained to her readers that Sophie von La Roche had inspired her to take up the pen. Gürnth did not write fiction like La Roche; she saw herself as a successor to Germershausen, whose "splendid" *Die Hausmutter* unfortunately was "too expensive ... and a little dull." And furthermore, she said, "the man talks only about thrift and hard work and old-fashioned virtues such as our grandmothers must have liked." While she herself extolled traditional female knowledge and practices, she could make herself look modern by describing Germershausen as outmoded. Gürnth was the self-proclaimed authority on the "female economy." Women needed instruction, and they would benefit from having it from a woman's perspective. It was hard to believe, Amalie said, that many good women knew their profession only superficially. Some had nothing more to work with than just a few notes inherited from their grandmothers! She insisted that her readers should not equate the female economy with cooking alone and appeared defensive that so much of her work consisted of recipes.[37]

In 1807, during the crisis of the Napoleonic wars, Gürnth published her *Rath für junge Hausmütter des Mittelstandes bei theuren Zeiten wohlfeil hauszuhalten* (Advice for Young, Middle-Class Householders in Austere Times), one of her many works on the female economy. Her purpose was to assist her readers in managing their households, despite hardships resulting from the military conflict.[38]

Artful with language, Amalie made use of the changing terminology of her era her to emphasize various connotations of the female profession. When stressing the all-encompassing "female economy," she referred to her subjects and readers as *Hausmütter*, implicitly suggesting the older ideal that gave women managerial roles in the productive and reproductive economy. When she emphasized the virtues of frugality, cleanliness, and order, she

Figure 8.2 By the 1820s gender-specific advice literature for women was proliferating. It invariably depicted women in the domestic sphere, as in this illustration from the *Neues Nürnberger Kochbuch für Hausmütter und Köchinnen* (New Nuremberg Cookbook for *Hausmütter* and Cooks. 1820).

often called them *Hausfrauen,* incorporating into her message the bourgeois values that were becoming pervasive in the era and that would fatefully define women's lives in the century to come. She also frequently used the term *Frauenzimmer,* a term of flattery when applied to middle-class women, certainly designed to gain attention and readership.

She informed her readers that her wartime "economic emergency plan" *(ökonomische Nöth- und Hülfstafel)* fell under two rubrics: Procurement of goods *(Erwerb)* and consumption *(gute Anwendung).* Under procurement, she named two "sources," the first of which was the housewife's own industriousness *(Fleiß),* or work.

> I know, certainly, that the readers of these pages do not belong to the common laboring and wage-earning classes and that female sources

of income flow very sparsely and with great restrictions. Nevertheless I urge young *Hausmütter* to produce the fruits of their own labor by making products that they otherwise might order from milliners, tailors, seamstresses, and other professionals.

The other source of procurement, Gürnth continued, was the garden, the traditional female realm of productive agriculture, which male economists of her day devalued. The *Hausmutter* must work the soil and cultivate plants with great diligence. She must carefully select which varieties to grow in order to use her resources wisely. She must utilize the homegrown produce to the fullest extent, for example by distilling vinegar from overripe fruit and by grinding grain of low quality into meal. "Thus we will procure our household needs more cheaply and at the same time enhance the value of our harvested products and even earn more money ... from them." The goal was thrift: "If we save tiny amounts daily through our attentiveness, diligence, and skill, this will add up to significant sums by the year's end." Many other means of saving were available to the householder: entertaining guests less frequently; wearing clothes for long periods instead of being bound by "the iron yoke of the all-powerful goddess, fashion," and purchasing necessary products directly from the farmer, gardener, or artisan rather than from a retailer.[39]

Regarding the second rubric of the economic emergency plan, consumption, Amalie stipulated the first principle as "punctual orderliness" *(pünktliche Ordnung)*. This was to be a virtue of the *Hausmutter* in all times, but in austere times it was doubly necessary.

> If we organize all of our tasks according to a well-ordered program, we will save time not only for ourselves – but even more for our subordinates – time that can be put to productive use .... Our domestic servants can accomplish much more when our household activity resembles a clock in which every hour has its own purpose .... This love of order helps us fulfill an obligation of our domestic profession, the strict control over our householding .... Even our grand-

mothers sought to express this housewifely duty through a well-known saying: "The woman's eye makes the cow fat."[40]

Gürnth devoted the bulk of her book to the "female economist's" second responsibility, consumption. She presented wartime recipes and offered many concrete suggestions about inexpensive cooking. She advocated the use of products otherwise grown for animal feed and the fruits of wild plants of the forests and meadows. She stressed the importance of cooking with crops that could be cultivated locally in order to avoid dependence on imported foods. She suggested cornbread in place of costly rye; poppy seed oil rather than olive oil; sweeteners from fruit rather than sugar; and ersatz coffee from roasted wild cherries and peanuts.[41]

In an era when professions were increasingly defining individual identities of middle-class men, Amalie sought to undergird the foundations of *the* female profession. Her vocabulary reflected the changing role of women. However, like her intellectual predecessor, Germershausen, she sought to retain the old notion of woman as producer, and unlike her contemporaries Thaer and Gericke, she insisted that women did have a role in the economy – the female economy. What was apparently impossible for Gürnth to envision was women involved in production for market.

She stressed that it was women's civic duty to uphold the households through thrift, ingenuity, and hard work. In her era, men were called upon to build a civil society, together the state by military and diplomatic means, and apply their skills in the marketplace. Women's contribution was to help preserve social order in hard times by being effective housewives – good procurers and primarily good consumers. Gürnth believed in women's destiny to serve society by practicing with excellence their one true profession – a profession not in the market or the public sphere. To stress the importance of her gender, she kept alive the old word *Ökonomie* and employed it as it had been used two centuries earlier, denoting agriculture, not city professions or a nexus of trade.

Apparently untenable in her day was a normative connection of females with the *new* concept of economy, *National-Ökonomie*.

In pursuit of her ideal of creating a profession for women, Amalie advocated that girls, like boys, should be educated formally in schools: "There are in our enlightened age movements to improve ... the education and schooling of youth. However, these advancements are more concerned with boys than with girls," she protested. And even the curricula of the girls' schools that did exist, lacked "the most essential of all female knowledge, economics." No one taught economics to girls because of the widely held prejudice that women needed only know rudiments of cooking, baking, washing, and spinning, skills they could learn from their mothers. Women had little opportunity to gain the scientific and technical knowledge equivalent to that which "young men learn in the Cameralist lecture halls and the forestry and economic academies."[42]

"The female art of householding and agriculture" was a profession that deserved to be taken seriously and studied systematically:

> Several prerequisite skills and auxiliary subjects are more useful for girls' future careers than are the fine arts and sciences, even though the latter should by no means be neglected ... . I regard *natural science, natural history,* and *chemistry,* as well as *technology* and *merchandizing,* as the primary subjects for the female economy. Without these, it is not possible to become an enlightened *Hausmutter.* All of these are ... tightly bound together with the household and the agricultural economy ... . In addition, for the sake of her family's well-being and for the benefit of the household, every *Hausmutter* should understand *dietetics, nursing,* and, yes, even *veterinary medicine.* And finally, in order to keep the domestic machine functioning smoothly, several other sciences seldom associated with the female economy ... are required, for example, *mathematics* and *household bookkeeping.* [There must be instruction in] *the new discoveries, inventions,* and *improvements* ... . The new responsibilities of the *Hausmutter* require, finally, a specific *moral philosophy for Hausmütter.*[43]

Gürnth used the symbolic conceptualization of the old household economy – but often modernized with nineteenth-century terminology such as "veterinary medicine" – to try to sustain the honor of the *Hausmutter*. But "mistress of the household" was an anachronistic concept in her era, and there is a tension in her combination of old and new concepts. She envisioned women becoming society's veterinarians, if only they could gain the necessary professional training for this role. Yet unlike the authors of the old household books, she could present no concrete instructions on animal husbandry. In contrast to Germershausen's volumes devoted to the care of swine and cattle in his *Hausmutter* manuals, Gürnth pled with male authorities – in a single sentence – for schools to teach women animal science. She understood the erosion of women's status in her era, but there was no substance with which she could replace it.

Seeking to keep women from being left out of the mainstream changes of her day, especially the professionalization of work, Gürnth ironically joined writers separating women from men and thus excluding them from "the economy" that was remaking the world. She wanted women to be experts at domesticity, emphasizing the very set of skills that kept them in inferior status in the increasingly bourgeois culture. Women were not the economic producers who supported their families and society; they were the housekeepers, consumers, and nurturers:

> It is indisputable that the happiness of entire families often depends upon the *Hausmutter*. The husband must, of course, earn the living, but in order to enjoy the benefits of it, there must be good patterns of consumption [*gute Anwendung*] in the household. If we examine many households, we will often find that where there are great riches, there is little pleasure in life, yet [sometimes] in the simplest circumstances, prosperity and comfort are present. These situations are the result of ... practices of the profession of *Hausmutter*.

The husband made the living; the wife made the home. Not just individual families, but, indeed, the "well-being of humanity," depended upon the professionalization of housewives. Thus it was essential to establish public "economic training institutes for girls." "Primarily parents of the middle classes, and especially in the country – estate owners, pastors, etc. – should have the opportunity to have their daughters trained to perfection as *Hausmütter*."[44]

Gürnth's *Oeconomische Unterhaltungen für Frauenzimmer* (Economic Conversations for Ladies, 1810) suggests her ideal vision of the female profession. Always romanticizing country life, she led her readers, along with an imaginary upper-class female companion, "Auguste," to the rural estate of "Sophie ... a wise and contemplative agriculturist and *Hausmutter*." Auguste was at first skeptical, believing that the lessons would be irrelevant to her, a person of high status, but Amalie set her straight. Even a noble lady must know her profession:

> I admit that your status, your wealth, etc., set you free from domestic and agricultural work. You have delegated these to your assistant. She is your right hand. [Nevertheless, unless you are actively engaged in household operations] all of the efforts of your husband, who is known as the best agriculturist of the whole region, will come to nothing. They will wear only half a crown if you do not do your part in the female economy.[45]

Auguste was convinced, and she joined Amalie in studying the clever and efficient performance of Sophie. Taking their breakfast in the garden, they discovered that Sophie had brewed the coffee from a mixture of coffee beans and peanuts, the latter a product that could be raised on the estate rather than imported. Impressed, they asked: "Is it patriotism or thrift that leads you to this?" Sophie modestly replied: "It is neither. I do it because I like the taste." This led the three into the garden, where Sophie demonstrated the cultivation of peanuts and discussed their many uses, including the production of good oil and superb brandy. "Yes, we can even use peanuts as a cosmetic, a beauty product. The wild people of Florida crush the raw nuts and rub [the oil] on their bodies. It is supposed to make wrinkled skin firmer."[46]

In this manner they discussed every aspect of the female economy, gaining valuable information on cooking; washing and bleaching; cultivation of flax; baking bread; churning butter; making cheese; harvesting and preparing wild greens, roots, and seeds; spinning; cultivating potatoes ("the manna of the countryman"); fattening calves; managing the house apothecary; and raising turkeys ("the most noble fowl"). Gürnth chose to depict the learners, Amalie and Auguste, as full of wonderment at what they were experiencing and a little helpless but eager to master their profession and engaged in the task. Like Sophie when she refused to claim either patriotism or thrift as her guiding principle, they were unpretentious, but at the same time they were intensely proud of their growing feminine economic expertise.

A leitmotif of Amalie's message was female friendship. The women delighted in one another's company and benefited mutually from their "pleasant intellectual discussions." Gürnth claimed that her friendship with her readers was her reward for the laborious task of writing the book.[47]

Amalie never forgot that, even though the female profession was a noble calling and crucial for the well being of society, it was the only sphere in which women were entitled to be occupied. Challenged by a question from the discerning Sophie – "You must at least admit that writing books does not belong to our profession" – Amalie provided a justification for her role as an author, which, by her own admission, required meticulous research and long hours at her desk:

> Of course you are right, dear friend! But if we ... arrange our time so that our domestic responsibilities do not suffer, I do not agree that [writing] conflicts with our profession ... . [I rise early in the morning and write], and the rest of the day I devote to my professional activities. And is it not true, my dear, that every *Hausmutter* has the right to recuperate from the responsibilities of her profession through sociable pleasure or rest? ... So if I write instead of idling my time ... or playing games, I am by no means culpable.

Asked by Sophie, "Are you not afraid of being criticized?" Amalie explained that she was on safe ground because "I never dare to venture out of my sphere, ... economics and domestic ethics."[48]

The New Female Virtues

The anonymous author of the advice book *Die Hausmutter als Köchin* (The *Hausmutter* as Cook), published two years later than Gürnth's *Advice for Austere Times*, identified herself as a grandmother who wished to record the "ABC's" of the household profession for her granddaughter, Julie. She compiled a series of lessons outlining the female economic sphere *(weibliche Geschäfften)*. Woman's work centered in the kitchen, "the only place in the house ... that is completely under the supervision and management of the female sex." Managing the kitchen was an "art and a science." In 430 pages of practical instructions, the grandmother-author wove careful threads, emphasizing the virtues of the agricultural housewife: circumspection (because of your "great responsibilities") orderliness; cleanliness ("the greatest asset of a cook") and thrift ("the crown of all virtues for the supervisor of a kitchen").[49]

These familiar female virtues were older than the household books of the seventeenth century, and they comprised an almost immutable theme in the prescriptive literature of the early-modern period and right into the nineteenth century. But while the words were constant for centuries, the values associated with them had become something qualitatively different by the time "Julie's Grandmother" brought them before her nineteenth-century reading public. Once applied to aristocratic women who were partners with their husbands – and directed to the husbands as well – the economic virtues now were imperatives for the housewives of men who were citizens and agrarian business managers. The women of the post-Napoleonic era, for whom the female virtues were iterated thousands of times over, belonged, according to the norms of their day, to the kitchen, the nursery, and the kitchen garden, but not to the productive realm of the economy as they had been in earlier eras. "The virtues" had become almost exclusively feminine.

Auguste Gerike (no relation to Friedrich Gericke) made this clear in her *Praktisches Haushaltungs- und Kochbuch* (Practical Household- and Cookbook, 1827). The work enjoyed wide popularity, for her Hanover publisher, Hahn – the publisher of Thaer's early works and Leopold's handbooks – reissued it in 1834, 1839, and 1847, and again in a "greatly expanded" version in 1859. It consisted of two parts, one devoted to householding and one containing primarily recipes. This was analogous to Gürnth's division of the female economy into "procurement" and "consumption." "Householding" included brewing; cheese production; butchering and preservation of meat, poultry and fish; vegetable gardening; pickling and storing of vegetables; soap making; washing; and bleaching. It is clear that these were activities intended for home consumption, not market production.[50]

The theme of her book was the trilogy of housewifely virtues: diligence, frugality, and order *(Fleiß, Sparsamkeit, Ordnung)*. In the preface to her second edition, she restated her case, at the same time revealing that she shared the traditional stereotype of females as vain, lacking focus, and overly concerned about appearance:

> I have written in the first edition about the values of diligence, orderliness, and frugality, but I feel obligated to say another important word about the value of domesticity *(Häuslichkeit)*. If [the housewife] is easily distracted, vain, or addicted to beauty, then twice, or even ten times, what is saved with the right hand will be lost by the left ... . A wise housewife will seek diversity and pleasure in her domestic work. She truly has a broad field before her, which will allow her to extend her effectiveness in the most useful manner.[51]

Gerike stressed that householding and cooking were symbiotic skills. She imbued the term "householding" [*Haushaltung*] with multiple meanings: it was not only a synonym for "barnyard operations" but also for "frugality." The thrifty householder, Gerike wrote, was often more valuable than a great cook who was wasteful, "for even the wealthiest masters are pleased when wise economy and correct organization are practiced in the kitchen."[52] "Householding," "economy," and "thrift" were becoming interchangeable. While "economy" had a meaning outside the household, when used to indicate frugality it was usually applied to a female situation. While Gerike's recipes – typically northern German and expanded in number in each edition – were in many ways unique to her popular handbook, her prescriptive advice, emphasizing the domestic virtues, was familiar. Her norms for female behavior were almost identical with those articulated by members of the dominant male culture.[53]

The market-oriented economy fostered specialization of labor and professionalization of work in rural German society. Joining civil servants, lawyers, businessmen, and medical doctors, the entrepreneurial *Herrschaften* of middle-class agriculture also took on new professional roles. Their wives, the daughters and granddaughters of the *Hausmütter* who had managed estates in partnership with their husbands, were written out of the market sphere of the economy and confined to the "interior household." They were consumers. Their world increasingly revolved around the duties of motherhood. Male and female economic writers prescribed for them in a limitless variety of ways – but with complete predictability – the bourgeois virtues that were to shape their professional existence: cleanliness, order, diligence, and frugality.[54]

Agrarian Norms and Bourgeois Society

The notion of virtue had become more feminine than masculine, and it was associated with women more than men. What was the male counterpart of the constellation, cleanliness, orderliness, and thrift? Thaer, Leopold, Friedrich Gericke, Weber and other economic and agricultural writers clearly had certain ideals in mind that they associated with the new business class of farmers. These included rationality, competitiveness, individuality, authoritativeness, and the ability to draft long-term plans and follow through until they were realized. These were the substance of which professions were made.

Thaer, Gürnth, and their contemporaries may have had little idea that their construction of gender roles would constitute a foundation for subsequent generations' idealization of female domesticity and the creation of an almost completely male-dominated economy. Male writers were captivated by the ideals of scientific methods and the market economy. Meanwhile Gürnth and Auguste Gerike sought to strengthen what was fast becoming the one profession that the normative literature allowed women.

Economics, once the property of aristocratic thinkers who strove to shore up the ideals of the patriarchal household, now belonged to the middle classes, and it rested on the idea of the free market operating in a wide realm. A generation of innovators contributed to a worldview that prized exploitation rather than cooperation and stewardship. Maximizing the output of the soil would enhance productivity; manipulation of labor would lead to greater profits; alteration of gender norms would allow the maintenance of the family. Corollary to these developments was the creation of spheres of the economy.

No one, not even Gürnth, the strongest advocate of professional roles for females in agriculture, conceived of women producing for market. Pervasively, yet without clear articulation on anyone's part, the constructed household functions had changed. The male role was to earn for market, reinvest, and realize a profit. This yielded income but was not sustaining the household in the old connotation; it was managing a business. The woman did not engage in business; she was still sustaining the household in the moral, emotional, and now outmoded economic sense. The little income she earned through gardening surplus and dairy products was in the tradition of the early-modern ideal of sustenance and reproduction.

The transition to capitalism, scientific farming, and ideals of citizenship placed women and men in entirely new positions of subordination and domination, respectively. Modern bourgeois norms rested on the view that women were helpers rather than producers. While reproduction – the bearing of children and the nurturing of families – remained important in the market-oriented society, as an ideal it no longer belonged to the economy. The new social ideals emancipated bourgeois men by placing them in the market and granting them new identities in the form of professions; the same ideals confined women by creating "one true" profession for them, a profession that guaranteed their exclusion from the public sphere.

Notes

1. Friedrich Benedict Weber, *Blicke in die Zeit, in Hinsicht auf National-Industrie und Staatswirthschaft, mit besonderer Berücksichtigung Deutschlands, und vornehmlich des Preußischen Staats* (Berlin: Nicolai, 1830). *Gedanken, Ansichten und Betrachtungen über die Noth und Klage der Zeit, in Staats- und Nationalwirthschaftlicher Hinsicht, von einem unparteiischen Freund der Wahrheit* (Berlin: Duncker und Humblot, 1826).
2. Tribe, "Cameralism and the Science of Government," 277-84. Treue, "Adam Smith in Deutschland," 101-33. Wilhelm Treue, *Wirtschafts- und Technikgeschichte Preußens*, Veröffentlichung der Historischen Kommission zu Berlin, vol. 56 (Berlin: de Gruyter, 1984), 213-18. Fritz Milkowski, "Christian Jacob Kraus: Eine längst fällige Korrektur zur Geschichte der Volkswirtschaftlehre," *Schmollers Jahrbuch für Wirtschafts- und Sozialwissenschaften* 88 (1968): 257-97. Lueder, *Ueber Nationalindustrie*. Christian Jakob Kraus, *Staatswirthschaft*, ed. Hans von Auerswald (Königsberg: Nicolovius, 1808-11).
3. Reinhard Rürup, *Deutschland im 19. Jahrhundert 1815-1871*, Deutsche Geschichte, vol. 8 (Göttingen: Vandenhoeck & Ruprecht, 1984), 87. Rudolf Berthold, "Die Veränderung im Bodeneigentum und in der Zahl der Bauernstellen, der Kleinstellen und der Rittergüter in den preußischen Provinzen Sachsen, Brandenburg und Pommern während der Durchführung der Agrarreformen des 19. Jahrhunderts," in *Studien zu den Agrar-*

reformen des 19. Jahrhunderts in Preußen und Rußland, Sonderband des Jahrbuchs für Wirtschaftsgeschichte (1978), 7-116. Felix Escher, Berlin und sein Umland: Zur Genese der Berliner Stadtlandschaft bis zum Beginn des 20. Jahrhunderts, Veröffentlichungen der Historischen Kommission zu Berlin, vol. 47; Publikationen der Sektion für die Geschichte Berlins, vol. 1 (Berlin: Colloquium, 1985), compare the data on the maps, pp. 70 and 181, and corresponding information in tables I and II in the appendix, 339-44.

4. Albrecht Thaer, *Unterricht über den Kleebau und Stallfütterung für den lüneburgischen Landmann* (Hanover: Hahn, 1791). Albrecht Thaer, *Einleitung zur Kenntniß der englischen Landwirthschaft und ihrer neuen practischen und theoretischen Fortschritte in Rücksicht auf Vervollkommung deutscher Landwirthschaft für denkende Landwirthe und Cameralisten* (Hanover: Hahn, 1800-1801). Albrecht Thaer, ed., *Annalen der niedersächsischen Landwirthschaft* (Hanover: Hahn, 1799-1804).

5. Frederick William to Thaer, Berlin, 19 March 1804, in Wilhelm Körte, *Albrecht Thaer: Sein Leben und Wirken, als Arzt und Landwirth* (Leipzig: Brockhaus, 1839; repr. Walluf: Sändig, 1967), 627-69. Albrecht Thaer, *Geschichte meiner Wirthschaft zu Möglin* (Berlin: Reimer, 1815).

6. Albrecht Thaer, *Grundsätze der rationellen Landwirthschaft* (Berlin: Reimer 1804-12); citations from 2nd ed. (Berlin: Realschulbuchhandlung, 1809-12).

7. Volker Klemm, "Eine 'THAER-Renaissance'? Anmerkung zum Stand und zur zukünftigen Thaer-Forschung," *Zeitschrift für Agrargeschichte und Agrarsoziologie* 42 (1994): 1-9. Volker Klemm und Günther Meyer, *Albrecht Daniel Thaer: Pioneer der Landwirthschaftswissenschaften in Deutschland* (Halle: Niemeier, 1968). Peter Bloch, et al., *Denkmal Albrecht Thaers*, Dahlemer Materialien, vol. 3 (Berlin: Domäne Dahlem, 1992). Abel, *Geschichte der deutschen Landwirtschaft*, 310, 320.

8. Thaer, *Grundsätze*, 1:9-13.

9. Thaer, *Einleitung zur englischen Landwirthschaft*, 1 4-16. H. Higgs, "Arthur Young" in *Dictionary of National Biography*, vol. 21 (1909), 1272-78. Thaer, *Grundsätze*. See also Thaer's *Beschreibung der nutzbarsten neuen Ackergeräthe* (Hanover: Hahn, 1803-1806).

10. Thaer, *Grundsätze*, 1:97-102. Albrecht Thaer, *Leitfaden zur allgemeinen landwirthschaftlichen Gewerbslehre* (Berlin: Realschulbuchhandlung, 1815).

11. Gray, *Prussia in Transition*, 122-30, 150-53. Hartmut Harnisch, "Die Bedeutung der kapitalistischen Agrarreform für die Herausbildung des inneren Markts und die industrielle Revolution in den östlichen Provinzen Preußens in der ersten Hälfte des 19. Jahrhunderts," *Jahrbuch für Wirtschaftsgeschichte*, 1970, no. 4, 63-82. Schissler, *Preußische Agrargesellschaft im Wandel*, 168-73. Hainer Plaul, "The Rural Proletariat: The Everyday Life of Rural Labourers in the Magdeburg Region, 1830-1880," in *The German Peasantry: Conflict and Community in Rural Society from the Eighteenth to the*

Twentieth Centuries ed. Richard J. Evans and W. R. Lee (New York: St. Martin's, 1986), 102-28.
12. Thaer, *Grundsätze*, 1:78, see also 80-94.
13. Ibid., 1:357-58.
14. Ibid., 1:79-101; quotation, 99.
15. Ibid., 1:102-12, 142. Thaer, *Leitfaden*, 4-14. On this theme see Abel, *Geschichte der deutschen Landwirtschaft*, 335. See also the anonymous article with an introduction by Thaer, "Versuch zur Bestimmung des Werthes der Frohndienste," *Möglinsche Annalen der deutschen Landwirthschaft* 1 (1817): 174-99.
16. Thaer, *Grundsätze*, 1:233-356; quotations, 233, 285, 364.
17. Ibid., 1:3. Thaer, *Leitfaden*, passim. On the evolution of the word "Gewerbe," see Dietrich Hilger and Lucian Hölscher, "Industrie, Gewerbe," *Geschichtliche Grundbegriffe*, vol. 3 (1982), 242-49, 262-64. Johann Gottlob von Justi, "Über die Haupthindernisse für den Landwirtschaftlichen Betrieb (1767)," in *Quellen zur Geschichte der deutschen Bauernbefreiung*, ed. Werner Conze, Quellensammlung zur Kulturgeschichte, vol. 12 (Göttingen: Musterschmidt, 1967), 46-52
18. Thaer, *Grundsätze*, 1:24-31; quotations, 26, 28. Thaer, *Leitfaden*, 14-33.
19. Thaer, *Grundsätze*, 1:16-23.
20. Ibid., 1:141-50.
21. Ibid., 1:193. Thaer, *Leitfaden*, 170.
22. Heinrich Kaak, "Vermittelte, selbsttätige und maternale Herrschaft: Formen gutsherrlicher Durchsetzung, Behauptung und Gestaltung in Quidlitz-Friedland (Lebus/Oberbarnim) im 18. Jahrhundert," in *Konflikt und Kontrolle in Gutsherrschaftsgesellschaften: Über Resistenz- und Herrschaftsverhalten in ländlichen Sozialgebilden der Frühen Neuzeit*, ed. Jan Peters, Veröffentlichungen des Max-Planck-Instituts für Geschichte, vol. 120 (Göttingen: Vandenhoeck & Ruprecht, 1995), 90-101, esp. 92. Thaer dedicated the third volume of *Einleitung zur Kenntniß der englischen Landwirthschaft* to Frau von Friedland.
23. Thaer to Schön, Möglin, 3 May 1809, Staatsarchiv Königsberg, Rep. 300 v. Brünneck 1, Nachlaß Theodor von Schön, Nr. 6 in Geheimes Staatsarchiv Berlin-Dahlem. See also Thaer to Schön, 4 April 1810, and other correspondence in this file.
24. Walter Simons, *Albrecht Thaer: Nach amtlichen und privaten Dokumenten aus einer großen Zeit* (Berlin: Parey, 1929), 130-73.
25. Thaer, *Grundsätze*, 1:195. Friedrich Karl Gustav Gericke, *Praktische Anleitung zur Führung der Wirthschafts-Geschäfte für angehende Landwirthe* (Berlin: Realschulbuchhandlung, 1804-1806), 3: Anhang [n.p.]. Löbe, "Friedrich Karl Gustav Gericke," *Allgemeine Deutsche Biographie*, vol. 8 (1878), 785.

26. Gericke, *Praktische Anleitung*, 2nd. ed. (1808-11), 1:iii-xx, 90-91.
27. Ibid., 1: 122-30; quotations,122, 124. Thaer, *Leitfaden*, 170.
28. Friedrich Benedict Weber, *Ueber die Cameralwissenschaft, und das Cameralstudium auf Universitäten; nebst einem Plan zu einem cameralistischen Cursus auf der Universität Breslau, und dem Grundriß der dazu gehörigen einzelnen Vorlesungen selbst* (Breslau: Kupfer, 1828), 1-43; quotations 31, 37.
29. Friedrich Benedict Weber, *Handbuch der ökonomischen Literatur* (Berlin: Fröhlich, 1803-42), vol. 2, 263-82, vol. 3, 286-304, vol. 4, 201-21, vol. 5, 218-35, vol. 6, 280-93, vol. 7, 317-19.
30. Heide Inhetveen, "Die Landfrau und ihr Garten: Zur Soziologie der Hortikultur," in *Zeitschrift für Agrargeschichte und Agrarsoziologie* 42 (1994): 45-47. Thaer, *Gründsätze*, 1:59. Grimm, "Garten," *Deutsches Wörterbuch*, vol. 4 (1878), 1390-91.
31. Justus Ludwig Günther Leopold, *Handwörterbuch des Gemeinnützigsten und Neuesten aus der Oekonomie und Haushaltungskunde*, 2nd ed. (Hanover: Hahn, 1805 [1st ed., Leipzig, 1801]), Vorrede [n.p.]; pp. ii-iii; and the article "Landwirthschaft," 331-32. Justus Ludwig Günther Leopold, *Agricola, oder Belehrung über alle Gegenstände der Landwirthschaft* (Hanover: Hahn, 1804), vol 1, 16. Hamberger and Meusel, *Das gelehrte Deutschland*, 5th ed., vol. 14 (1810), 399-404. Güntz, *Handbuch der landwirtschaftlichen Literatur*, 2:154.
32. Leopold, *Handwörterbuch*, articles, "Garten," 234; "Küchengarten," 324-25; and on the male realm, articles like "Landwirthschaft," 331-32; "Administration eines Gutes," supplement, 1; "Stallfutterung," supplement, 42-45 and passim. Leopold, *Agricola*, vol. 2: n.p., following p. 202.
33. Blasius Merrem, *Allgemeine Grundsätze der bürgerlichen Wirthschaft und Haushaltung* (Göttingen: Röwer, 1817), 42-43, 216-17. Johann Stephan Pütter, *Versuch einer academischen Gelehrten-Geschichte von der Georg-Augustus-Universität zu Göttingen*, 4 vols. (Göttingen: Vandenhoeck & Ruprecht, 1765-1838), vol. 3; excerpt reprinted in *Deutsches Biographisches Archiv*, fiche 830, frames 208-23.
34. Merrem, *Allgemeine Grundsätze*, 262-88.
35. Matthias Eigl, *Die würdige deutsche Hausfrau im täglichen Leben* (Klagenfurth: Gelb, 1822), 16, 27, 57. Matthias Eigl, *Der christliche Hausvater im Krise seiner Angehörigen, und im Umgange mit der Welt: Ein Ebenbild Gottes nach dem Geiste der katholischen Kirche, als Heirathsgeschenk für angehende Ehemänner zur Grhndung und Bef rderung der guten Sitten und der Fürsten- und Vaterlandsliebe bestimmt vom Verfasser der würdigen deutschen Hausfrau* (Klagenfurth: Gelb, 1822). Karl F. Stock, Rudolf Heilinger, and Margelene Stock, "Matthias Eigl," in *Personalbibliographien österreichischer Persönlichkeiten*, Bibliographie österreichischer Bibliographien, Sammelbibli-

ographien, und Nachschlagwerke, section 3 (Graz: Stock und Stock, 1988), vol. 3, 976.
36. Friedrich Röver, *Die Hausfreundin auf dem Lande; oder möglichst vollständige Anweisung für Frauenzimmer, die ihrem ländlichen Haushalt mit Ehren und Vortheil vorstehen, die Geschäfte der Küche des Kellers und der Vorraths-Behältnisse selbst besorgen, und dabey zugleich ihre und der Ihrigen Gesundheit berücksichtigen wollen: Eine ökonomisch-encyclopädischer Unterricht in alphabetischer Ordnung*, 3 vols. (Magdeburg: Heinrichshofen, 1822-23), passim; quotations from Vorrede: viii, x. I was not able to locate Röver's *Hausfreund*. My evidence concerning it is from Röver's reference to it in *Die Hausfreundinn*, title page; and introduction, v.
37. [Christine Dorothea Gürnth], *Gartenökonomie für Frauenzimmer: Oder Anweisung der Produkte des Blumen- Küchen- und Obstgartens in der Haushatung aufs manigfältigste zu benutzen* (Züllichau: Fromann, 1790), vol.1, 2, vol. 2, 5-6, 9. [Christine Dorothea Gürnth], *Oekonomische Unterhaltungen für Frauenzimmer: Eine belehrende Lektüre für Damen auf dem Lande, die ihrer Wirthschaft selbst vorstehen wollen* (Berlin: Duncker und Humblot, 1810), xv. Schindel, *Die deutschen Schriftstellerinnen*, 1:178-183; 3:142. Weckel, *Zwischen Häuslichkeit und Öffentlichkeit*, 162-64, 418-19. Weckel states that no copies of Gürnth's journal, *Oekonomische, moralische und gemeinnützige Journal für Frauenzimmer* exist in German libraries. I was unable to find it outside of Germany.
38. [Christine Dorothea Gürnth], *Rath für junge Hausmütter des Mittelstandes bei theuren Zeiten wohlfeil hauszuhalten: Eine Sammlung von Haushaltungsvortheilen* (Leipzig: Fleischer, 1807), 3-4.
39. Ibid., 5-7.
40. Ibid., 15-16.
41. Ibid., passim.
43. Ibid., 547-48; emphasis in original.
44. Ibid., 548-50.
45. [Gürnth], *Oekonomische Unterhaltungen für Frauenzimmer*, 1-4.
46. Ibid., 15-29.
47. [Christine Dorothea Gürnth], *Unterhaltungen für denkende Hausmütter über allerley Gegenstände der weiblichen Ökonomie* (Breslau: Korn, 1801), xiii.
48. Ibid., xiii-xvi.
49. *Die Hausmutter als Köchin, oder Unterricht in den ersten Grundregeln und Handgriffen beim Kochen, welche junge Mädchen zu wissen nöthig sind, ehe sie zur ausübenden Kochkunst selbst schreiten können* (Leipzig: Eurich, 1809), iii-viii, 5-12, and passim. See also the following work, which stresses the four virtues, orderliness, cleanliness, diligence, and thrift: *Die gelehrige Hauswirthin: Ein Handbuch für Frauenzimmer, welches die ganze Kochkunst sowohl Tafel-Fasten-als Civilspeisen, alle Arten Backwerk, des Eingemachten, Geräuchten,*

Liquers, Sommer- und Winter-Getränke, Sulzen, Geleen, uc., von einer Freundin der Kochkunst (Rutlingen: Erdzinger, 1807), 241-50.
50. Auguste Gerike, *Praktisches Haushaltungs- und Kochbuch oder die wohlerfahrene Lehrerinn im Haushalten und in der Küche* (Hanover: Hahn, 1827-1859). I used the fourth edition, which includes the preface from the first three as well as its own, each explaining the revisions over previous editions. See *Gesamtverzeichnis 1700-1910*, 45:318.
51. A. Gerike, *Praktisches Haushaltungs- und Kochbuch*, ix.
52. Ibid., vi.
53. Ibid., passim.
54. See Münch, *Ordnung, Fleiß und Sparsamkeit*, 32-38.

Conclusion

—∞—

"Every Man is King in His House"

During more than two centuries of change, the economic vocabulary of the household remained relatively constant, yet the *meanings* of pivotal terms were completely transformed. In the post-Enlightenment context of the market economy, the ancient language of patterned work and gender hierarchy had unprecedented reverberations, forming the cultural dichotomy of modern separate spheres.

The continuity of the language is more conspicuous than its changed meanings. Decade after decade economists proclaimed the transcendent role of the husband and father. In 1593 when theologian-economist Johann Coler asserted that "the economy is a monarchy," he did not need to explain that he saw the *Hausvater* as the sovereign. One hundred twenty-three years later, in 1716, the Cameralist Julius Bernhard von Rohr restated the old axiom: "every man is king in his house." After almost another century, in 1808, the scientifically minded agrarian reformer Friedrich Gericke reiterated the accepted wisdom for his own generation: "A good agricultural business must have a monarchical structure." For clarity, he specified: "The housewife stands below the master."[1] This constancy of the metaphor would lead an observer to conclude that

Notes for this section begin on page 303.

patriarchy in the household was rigid and remained unchanged. It seems that regardless of context, husbands ruled and wives obeyed, while masters and mistresses presided over servants and children.

The appearance of continuity, moreover, is intensified by the seemingly immutable patterns of gender-specific agricultural work. Men were always responsible for production in the fields, while women's tasks were centered in the household, kitchen, garden, and dairy. These configurations of daily life, in place centuries before Coler wrote his household book, prevailed long after Thaer and Gericke described the practices of scientific agriculture. The divided work of the farm household appeared to be eternal.

Appearance is not always reality, however. While the language remained the same, the subjective definition of the household-as-monarchy metaphor evolved over time. This was because of the transformation of the economic, cultural, and political circumstances in which the household existed. New generations recast the meanings of old words. The changes were incremental, but the ultimate consequences were revolutionary.

When the household was the normative center of the economy, men and women labored interdependently in production, reproduction, and consumption. In the early-modern vocabulary, women's work with cows, poultry, vegetables, herbs, fibers, and food amounted to material support for the household. Maternal responsibilities – the imparting of cultural values to the young – meant preserving the household heritage and the linear family for posterity. Men's labor with grain, legumes, grasses, bridges, buildings, and horses also equated to nurturing the household; and males participated in the reproductive functions within the gendered structure of patriarchy. All of this collectively amounted to the work of "the economy" – the *oikos*. Householding in the early modern era was a social responsibility with private and public ramifications that absolutely depended upon male and female cooperation.

As a reformed notion of the economy emerged, centered in the state and driven by the market, the idea of distinct, separated roles replaced that of interdependence. By the nineteenth century, women's responsibilities – gardening, dairying, cooking, preserving, sewing, and mothering – did not belong to the economy. Women supported the household – now called the family[2] – but this was now the center of a private and subordinated sphere of life no longer equivalent to the productive realm. If rural women earned a little cash from their garden vegetables, eggs, or cheese, this was good because it supplemented the real income of the estate. However, the standard source of earnings came from products grown, processed, and marketed by the scientific and rational farmer, the *Landwirt*, the husband.

Gürnth (Amalie) understood that the meaning of gendered work had changed, and she strove to restore dignity to the "female economy" in gardening, forestry, the household, and even veterinary medicine. She wanted women to be able to share in the new situations men were experiencing: professionalization of work, increased use of technology, and enhanced productivity. She disliked the widening gender gap. But her pleas rang hollow, because the ideal of professionalization had put the economy in the hands of husbands and sons. Fervently, she argued that women should be allowed to learn science, technology, and merchandizing, yet she filled her books largely with recipes and moral lessons. She had no vocabulary with which she could meaningfully put women back into the productive economy. Men controlled the language; the nouns and the verbs associated with the economy were implicitly masculine. Thus, against her own will she contributed to the construction of woman as consumer, not producer. Using the old terminology of the household – *Ökonomie, Hausmutter* – she essentially prescribed women's role as that of the bourgeois rural housewife. The bourgeois family was a location of reproduction and had become ever more separate from the fields of production.

Meanwhile the recast notion of the economy opened new vistas for ambitious, capable males. The logic of rationality placed education, technology, property, and authority at men's disposal. As the ideal of increased yields gained predominance over older systems based on morals and tradition, only hopeless conservatives defended the archetype of the household, the hierarchical estate with interdependent components, the paternalism of enforced labor, the Christian economy. The doctrines of scientific agriculture and capitalist farming came to be accepted as obvious truths based on common sense. No one could muster an argument against the powerful lure of economic growth. No one doubted that extraction of profit from the soil was a specialized male responsibility, separate from the duties of the home.

Agriculture's revised objectives required a remodeling of the old constructed household through such measures as peasant "emancipation," differentiated labor tasks, geographic mobility of the rural population, and market freedoms. These innovations, while on the one hand exciting to those who planned them, on the other posed the possibility of disorder, and reformers rushed to maintain social stability by promulgating new master-servant codes *(Gesindeordnungen)*[3] to ensure that the world was not turned upside down. These laws, empowering employers to punish workers for leaving hired positions, nevertheless confirmed estate owners' new authority to dismiss workers when their labor was not deemed profitable. In the context of the perceived continuities of everyday life, capitalist farmers never questioned their right to control the destinies of the lower classes living near them, even if the relationships were increasingly determined by the market rather than by the traditional contracts of the household economy.

In times of transition, many also must have taken comfort in the seemingly eternal hierarchy of gender and the sex-specific patterns of daily life. The idea that every man was king in his own house enjoyed the privilege of unquestioned rhetoric and thus appeared as natural as the concept of maximization of profits through rational farming. So men created new economic models for themselves and left women out of the new order by assuming – and insisting on – permanence for the female place. Yet what seemed eternal was, in fact, momentous change.

The old household virtues of efficiency and conservation appeared particularly suited for the new domestic realm. The tradition-steeped concepts of order, thrift, cleanliness, and diligence became defining characteristics of the new female partner.[4] The implications of these middle-class virtues of domesticity resulted from the widened gulf between male and female spheres, but the novelty was obscured by the ageless language used to depict the female roles. The gendered division of labor, thought by the authors of the "household books" to be divinely ordained and after the Enlightenment considered to be rooted in Nature, was social construction accepted as fact. In this idea were anchored the domination and subordination of the modern gender systems.

Largely unnoticed, the meaning of domesticity *(Häuslichkeit)* had gradually but fundamentally changed. While Martin Luther and his sixteenth-century contemporaries had emphasized separation of the domestic virtues from those of the productive life,[5] within a century this notion had been largely eclipsed by the postulate that the household *was* the economy. In the age when the household was the economy, domesticity was a virtue shared by males and females, a shorthand term for thrift, hard work, and order, all qualities designed to sustain people and the inherited culture. Florinus, at the turn between the seventeenth and eighteenth centuries, urged the master and the mistress of the organic household to practice domesticity by being diligent, careful, and moderate in fulfilling their respective daily duties. A century later, domesticity had tumbled out of the constellation of masculine virtues. While Thaer was teaching male farmers to be scientific, rational, managerial and profit-oriented, he gave little consideration to the home. The new head of the household was enterprising, assertive, rational, and acquisitive, qualities almost opposites of those associated with the "domestic" *Hausvater*. Thaer's contemporaries, Gericke, Weber, Leopold, and Merrem, admonished women to uphold the old virtues of domesticity, increasingly identified as frugality, orderliness, cleanliness, and industriousness, while they repeated the formulas of older generations about female modesty and subordination. Wives were good helpmates. They were overseers of domestic responsibilities, which now represented the private and economically nonproductive side of life. But wives were always subject to the authority of their husbands.

The economic values of the nineteenth century formed the basis for a new cultural production of gender. Ever since Cameralists had striven to redefine the economy, the separation of tasks had been part of the unquestioned vocabulary and was equated with efficiency. The notion of division of labor lay behind the rejection of the organic household model and its system of interdependencies. For the sake of profitability, a more flexible arrangement replaced it.[6] Instead of the system of obligations and immutable rights, which kept peasants tied to the estate, the division-of-labor paradigm placed authority in the hands of the master to employ workers when they were profitable and refrain from hiring them when the cost outweighed the benefits – indeed required him to do so. Similarly, the old economic language's emphasis on gender-specific work made an easy transition into the new vocabulary and replaced the emphasis on mutual responsibility. In a world that held the laws of Nature as the ultimate authority, the division of labor and the rule of men over women appeared to be defined by Nature and needed no defense. Enlightenment philosophers had declared this to be so, and lone protesters such as Hippel and Holst were silenced.

The gendered division of labor was most evident in the cities, where workplaces were literally moving away from the household. It was a bourgeois ideal that urban working classes would seek to emulate. In the agrarian sector of society – itself made into a secondary branch of the economy by Cameralists' ideals of specialization – the new gender patterns were less obvious, because work and household remained physically united, as they had been "forever." Yet even here the bourgeois ideals shaped the language of the constructed economy.

Decades before the Industrial Revolution, modern constructions of gender had become a part of the cultural fabric of German-speaking Europe. In a complex weaving of old and new language, the new norms set the stage for subsequent developments that increased the physical and economic distance between the female and male spheres, making the transition to a breadwinner-homemaker dichotomy appear natural and orderly. Masculine dominance and feminine subservience, by no means new, gained unprecedented implications as these patterns established the cleavage between the public, male, productive economy and the private, female, reproductive household. According to the value system of the nineteenth century, the success of agriculture, like the fortune of all economics, depended on the skills of men in the public realm and the confinement of women to the private realm.

Notes

1. Coler, Oeconomia, 3. Rohr, *Vollständiges Hauß-Haltungs Recht*, 169. Gericke, *Praktische Anleitung*, 1:122, 124.
2. Schwab, "Familie," 271-99.
3. Koselleck, *Preußen zwischen Reform und Revolution*, 488, 635, 647-52. Harnisch, "Die Bedeutung der kapitalistischen Agrarreform," 63-82. Hans Mottek, *Wirtschaftsgeschichte Deutschlands: Ein Grundriss* (Berlin: VEB Deutscher Verlag der Wissenschaften, 1974), vol. 2, 38-39.
4. Münch, *Ordnung, Fleiß und Sparsamkeit*, 9-38.
5. Ibid., 32. Münch implies a continuity between the sixteenth-century religious writers and the nineteenth-century prescribers of separate spheres that I do not believe can be supported.
6. Karin Hausen, "Wirtschaften mit der Geschlechterordnung: Ein Essay," in Hausen, *Geschlechterhierarchie und Arbeitsteilung*, 40-42.

Works Cited

Archival Sources

Staatsarchiv Königsberg, Rep 300, Dep. Brünneck, Nachlaß Theodor von Schön. Geheimes Staatsarchiv Preußischer Kulturbesitz, Berlin-Dahlem.

Published Primary Sources

Allgemeines bürgerliches Gesetzbuch für die gesammten Deutschen Erbländer der Oesterreichischen Monarchie. Vienna: k. k. Hof- und Staatsdruckerey, 1811.
Allgemeines Landrecht für die preußischen Staaten von 1794, ed. Hans Hattenhauer and Günther Bernert. Frankfurt am Main and Berlin: Alfred Metzler, 1970.
Amaranthes [Gottlieb Siegmund Corvinus]. *Nutzbares, galantes und curiöses Frauenzimmerlexicon*, 2nd ed. Leipzig: Johann Friedrich Gleditsch und Sohn, 1739.
"Antwort auf die Frage des Münchnerischen Intelligenzblatts Nro. 38." *Baierischer Ökonomischer Hausvater oder gesammelte Schriften der Kurfürstlichen Gesellschaft sittlich- und landwirtschaftlicher Wissenschaften in Burghausen.* Vol. 1 (1780), 190-92.
"Auszug aus eines Freundes, und adelichen Landwirths sehr nützlichen, und praktischen Anmerkungen, über die Wirtschaft eines edelichen gutes." *Baierischer Ökonomischer Hausvater oder*

gesammelte Schriften der Kurfürstlichen Gesellschaft sittlich- und landwirtschaftlicher Wissenschaften in Burghausen. Vol. 2 (1780), 593-603.

Azendorff, Solomon Fischer von. *Unterrichteter Hauß-Vater und kluger Gärtner, nebst dem verständigen Jäger-Meister oder gründliche Anleitung wie die Haußhaltungs-Kunst mit Nutz zu Begreiffen.* Hanover: Nicolaus Förster, 1705.

Baierischer Ökonomischer Hausvater oder gesammelte Schriften der Kurfürstlichen Gesellschaft sittlich- und landwirtschaftlicher Wissenschaften in Burghausen. 8 vols. Munich: Johann Nepomuck Fritz, 1780-1786

Bebel, August. *Die Frau und der Sozialismus.* Stuttgart: Dietz, 1893.

Becher, Johann Joachim. *Politische Diskurs, von den eigentlichen Ursachen, deß Auff- und Abnehmens der Städt, Länder und Repbulicken in Specie, Wie ein Land Volckreich und Nahrhafft zu machen und in eine rechte Societatem civilem zu bringen.* Frankfurt am Main: Johann David Zunner, 1688; repr. Glashütten im Taunus: Detlev Auvermann, 1972.

Becher, Johann Joachim [pseud.]. *Kluger Haus-Vater, verständige Haus-Mutter, vollkommener Land-Medicus, wie auch wohlerfahrner Roß- und Vieh-artzt: Nebenst einem deutlichen und gewissen Handgriff, die Haushaltungs-Kunst innerhalb 24. Stunden zu erlernen ... welchem anietzo noch beygefüget des edlen Weidmanns geheimes Jäger-Cabinet, wie auch einige nützliche und nöthige Rechts- und andere Formularien.* Leipzig: Friedrich Groschuft, 1714.

Becker, Rudolph Zacharias. *Noth- und Hülfbuchlein für Bauersleute, oder lehrreiche Freuden- und Trauer-Geschichte des Dorfes Mildheim.* Ed. Reinhart Siegert. Gotha and Leipzig: Deutsche Zeitung and Georg Joachim Göschen; repr. Dortmund: Harenberg; 1980.

Beckmann, Johann. *Physikalisch-Ökonomische Bibliothek worin von den neuesten Büchern welche die Naturgeschichte, Naturlehre, und die Land- und Staatswirthschaft betreffen, zuverlässige und vollständige Nachrichten ertheilt werden.* 23 vols. Göttingen: Vandenhoeck & Ruprecht, 1770-1808.

"Beschreibung eines Seidenhaspels." *Baierischer Ökonomischer Hausvater oder gesammelte Schriften der Kurfürstlichen Gesellschaft sittlich- und landwirtschaftlicher Wissenschaften in Burghausen* 8 (1785): 246-48.

Brandes, Ernst. *Betrachtungen über das weibliche Geschlecht und dessen Ausbildung in dem geselligen Leben.* 3 vols. 2nd ed. Hanover: Hahn, 1802.

———. *Betrachtungen über den Zeitgeist in Deutschland in den letzten Decennien des vorigen Jahrhunderts.* Hanover: Hahn, 1808.

Brandes, Ernst. *Ueber die Weiber.* Vienna: Johann Thomas von Trattern, 1788.

Campe, Joachim Heinrich. *Über einige verkannte wenigstens ungenützte Mittel zur Beförderung der Industrie, der Bevölkerung und des öffentlichen Wohlstandes.* Wolfenbüttel: Verlag der Schulbuchhandlung. Ed. Gernot Koneffke. 1786; repr. in Series, Paedagogica, Frankfurt am Main: Sauer & Auvermann, 1969.

———. *Väterlicher Rath für meine Tochter: Ein Gegenstuck zum Theophron der erwachsenern weiblichen Jugend gewidmet.* Braunschweig: Verlag der Schulbuchhandlung, 1786, 1790, 1791.

Civil Gesetzbuch der Französischen Republik. Trans. F. Lassaulx. Koblenz: Lassaulx'ischen Buchhandlung, 1802-1804.

Codex Maximilianeus Bavaricus Civilis: Oder neu verbessert und ergänzt Chur-Bayerisches Land-Recht. Munich: Johann Jacob Vötter, 1759.

Colerus, Johannes. *Calendarium oeconomicum & perpetuum: Vor die Haußwirt, Ackerleut, Apotecker und andere gemeine handwerksleut, Kauffleut, Wanderleut, Weinherrn, Gertner und alle diejenige so mit Wirtschafft umbgehen.* Epilogue by Gotthardt Frühsorge. Wittenberg: Christoff Axim, 1591; repr. Weinheim: Acta Humaniora, 1988.

———. *Oeconomia Ruralis et Domestica.* 2 vols. Wittenberg, 1593-1601; Mainz: Nicolaus Hayln, 1645.

Compendieuses und Nutzbarer Haußhaltungs-Lexicon, worinnen Alle beim Feld- Acker- Garten- und Weinbau, Wiesewachs, Holzungen, Jägerei, Fischerey, Bierbrauen, Vieh-Zucht, und sonst bei dem Haußhalten vorkommende Wörter und Redens-Arten gründlich und deutlich erkläret, Auch derer Thiere und Kräuter, Eigenschaft, Natur, Gebrauch und Mißbrauch auf das treulichste untersuchet worden sind; Daß man solcher sowohl in der Stadt, als auf dem Lande, bey allen großen mittleren und kleinen Haushaltungen nützlich gebrauchen kan, In alphabetische Ordnung gebracht, mit sonderbarem Fleiß zusammen getragen von einem Liebhaber Oeconomischer Wissenschaften. Chemnitz: Conrad Stößel und Sohn, 1728.

Condorcet, Marie Jean Antoine Nicholas de Caritat Marquis de. "Sur l'admission des femmes au droit de cité" (1789). In *Oeuvres*. 12 vols. Paris: Didot, 1847.

Conze, Werner, Ed. *Quellen zur Geschichte der deutschen Bauernbefreiung*. Quellensammlung zur Kulturgeschichte, vol. 12. Göttingen, Berlin and Frankfurt: Musterschmidt, 1967.

Döbel, Heinrich Wilhelm. *Geschickter Hausvater und fleissige Hausmutter, oder kurze, doch gründliche Einleitung zur Haushaltung oder Landwirthschaft, nebst einer nützlichen Hausapothecke*. Ed. G.H. Zincke. Leipzig, 1747; rev. ed., 1771.

Eigl, Matthias. *Der christliche Hausvater im Kreise seiner Angehörigen, und im Umgange mit der Welt: Ein Ebenbild Gottes nach dem Geiste der katholischen Kirche, als Heirathsgeschenk für angehende Ehemänner zur Gründung und Beförderung der guten Sitten und der Fürsten- und Vaterlandsliebe bestimmt vom Verfasser der würdigen deutschen Hausfrau*. Klagenfurt: Anton Gelb, 1823.

———. *Die würdige deutsche Hausfrau im täglichen Leben mit ihrer gebildeten Tochter und ihrem edlen Sohne: in drei Sittengemählden dargestellt, zur Beförderung der guten, und zur Verdrängung der schlechten Seite unsers Zeitgeistes als ein belehrendes und erbauendes Geschenck bestimmt für deutsche Mütter, Töchter und Söhne gebildeten Standes*. Klagenfurt: Anton Gelb, 1822.

"Eines alten Freundes, und Gönners der Leipziger Sammlung eingeschickter Beytrag, von der Gesinden oder Ehehalten Noth." *Baierischer Ökonomischer Hausvater oder gesammelte Schriften der Kurfürstlichen Gesellschaft sittlich- und landwirtschaftlicher Wissenschaften in Burghausen* 1 (1780), 120-28.

Enslin, Theodor Christian. *Bibliotheca Oeconomica oder Verzeichnis aller brauchbaren in älterer und neuerer Zeit, bis zur Mitte des Jahres 1824 in Deutschland erschienen Bücher über Land- und Hauswirthschaft*. Berlin and Landsberg a. d. W.: Enslin, 1825.

Fichte, Johann Gottlieb. *Grundlage des Naturrechts nach Prinzipien der Wissenschaftslehre* (1796). Vol 2 of *Werke in Sechs Bänden*, ed. Fritz Medicus. Philosophische Bibliothek, vol. 128. Leipzig: Felix Meiner, n.d.

———. "Reden an die deutsche Nation" (1808). In *Werke in Sechs Bänden*, ed. Fritz Medicus. Vol. 1, 357-64. Philosophische Bibliothek, vol. 128. Leipzig: Felix Meiner, n.d.

_____. *System der Sittenlehre nach den Prinzipien der Wissenschaftslehre*. Jena: Gnobloch, 1798.

Fischer, Heinrich August. *Versuch einer historisch-pragmatischen Beschreibung der alten deutschen Oekonomie und des in der Folge der Zeit, daraus erwachsen deutschen fürstlichen Cammerwesens*. Leipzig: Bernhard Christoph Breitkopf, 1775.

Florinus, Franciscus Philippus. *Oeconomus Prudens et Legalis: Oder Allgemeiner Klug- und Rechtsverständiger Haus-Vater*. 2 vols. Nuremberg, Frankfurt an der Oder, and Leipzig: Christoph Riegels, 1702.

Fontane, Theodor. *Jenny Treibel*. Trans. Ulf Zimmermann, in *Short Novels and Other Writings*, ed. Peter Demetz. The German Library, vol. 48. New York: Continuum, 1982.

Friedrich der Große. "Über die Erziehung." In *Die Werke Friedrichs des Großen in deutscher Übersetzung*. Trans. Friedrich von Oppeln-Bronikowski, ed. Gustav Berthold Volz, vol. 8, 257-62. Berlin: Reimar Hobbing, 1913.

G., E.B.M., and Adam Friedrich Schmelz. *Der sächsische Landwirth in seiner Landwirthschaft, was er jetzt ist und was er seyn könnte, oder: wie ein jeder seine Einkünfte in kurzer Zeit um mehr als die Hälfte sehr leicht erhöhen könne*. 3 vols. Leipzig: Christian Gottlob Hilscher, 1788-1791.

Gasser, Simon Peter. *Einleitung zu den oekonomischen, politischen und Cameralwissenschaften worin für dieses mal die oeconomico-cameralia von den Domainen- oder Cammer- auch andern Gütern, deren Administration und Anschlägen, so wol des Ackerbaues als anderer Pertinentien halber samt den Regalien angezeigt und erläutert werden*. Halle: Verlag des Waysenhauses, 1729; repr. Glashütten im Taunus: Detlev Auvermann, 1970.

Gedanken, Ansichten und Betrachtungen über die Noth und Klage der Zeit in Staats- und Nationalwirthschaftlicher Hinsicht, von einem unparteiischen Freund der Wahrheit. Berlin: Duncker & Humblot, 1826.

Die gelehrige Hauswirthin: Ein Handbuch für Frauenzimmer, welches die ganze Kochkunst sowohl Tafel-Fasten-als Civilspeisen, alle Arten Backwerk, des Eingemachten, Geräuchten, Liquers, Sommer- und Winter-Getränke, Sulzen, Geleen, uc., von einer Freundin der Kochkunst. Rutlingen: Johannes Erdzinger, 1807.

Georgica Bavarica: Oder oeconomische Auszüge und gründliche Nachricht wie sowohl Adeliche Land- als gemeine Bauern-Güther verbessert, und derselben jährlichen Erträgnissen und ein Merkliches vermehrt werden können. Munich: Johann Jacob Vötter, 1752.

Gericke, Friedrich Karl Gustav. *Praktische Anleitung zur Führung der Wirthschafts-Geschäfte für angehende Landwirthe.* Ed. Albrecht Thaer. 4 vols. 2nd ed. Berlin: Realschulbuchhandlung, 1808-1811.

Gerike, Auguste. *Praktisches Haushaltungs- und Kochbuch oder die wohlerfahrene Lehrerinn im Haushalten und in der Küche.* 4th ed. Hannover: Hahn, 1847.

Germershausen, Christian Friedrich. *Das Ganze der Schafzucht aus Beurteilung und Berichtigung älterer und neuerer Theorien nach Gründen und eigener Erfahrung.* 2 vols. bound in 1. Leipzig: Johann Friedrich Junius, 1789-1790.

_____. *Die Hausmutter in allen ihren Geschäfften.* 5 vols. Leipzig: Johann Friedrich Junius, 1777-1781.

_____. *Der Hausvater in systematischer Ordnung.* 5 vols. Leipzig: Junius, 1783-1786.

_____. "Der Mann kann die Frau nicht reich machen, wohl aber die Frau der Mann: Denn der ersparte Pfennig ist besser als der erworbene." In *Nützliche Sammlung von Aufsätzen und Wahrnehmungen über die Witterungen, die Haushaltungskunde, das Gewerbe, die Naturkenntniß, Polizey, und andere damit verknüpfte Wissenschaften, welche die Fortsetzung des Wittenbergschen Wochenblatts ausmachen,* ed. Johann Daniel Titius. Vol. 1, 1-5. Leipzig: Junius, 1782.

_____."Nachricht von Herrn Pastor Germershausens Hausvater." In *Nützliche Sammlung von Aufsätzen und Wahrnehmungen über die Witterungen, die Haushaltskunde, das Gewerbe, die Naturkenntniß, Polizey, und andere damit verknüpfte Wissenschaften, welche die Fortsetzung des Wittenbergschen Wochenblatts ausmachen,* ed. Johann Daniel Titius. Vol. 1, 125-27. Leipzig: Junius, 1782.

_____. *Oekonomisches Reallexikon, worin alles was nach den Theorien und erprobten Erfahrungen der bewährtesten Oekonomen unsrer Zeit zu wissen nöthig ist.* 4 vols. Leipzig: Johann Gottlob Feind, 1795-1799.

Gleim, Betty. *Bremisches Kochbuch.* Bremen and Aurich: Johann Heinrich Müller 1808.

———. *Erziehung und Unterricht des weiblichen Geschlechts: Ein Buch für Eltern und Erzieher*. Ed. Ruth Bleckwenn. 2 vols. Leipzig: Goschen, 1810; repr. Paderborn: M. Hüttemann Verlag für historische Publikationen und Reprints, 1989.

Gouges, Olympe de. *La declaration des droits de la femme et de la citoyenne*. Paris: 1791.

[Gürnth, Christine Dorothea]. *Gartenökonomie für Frauenzimmer: Oder Anweisung der Produkte des Blumen- Küchen- und Obstgartens in der Haushaltung auf's mannichfaltigste zu benutzen*. 4 vols. Züllichau: N. G. Fromann, 1790-1795.

———. *Oekonomische Unterhaltungen für Frauenzimmer: Eine belehrende Lektüre für Damen auf dem Lande, die ihrer Wirtschaft selbst vorstehen wollen*. Berlin: Duncker und Humblot, 1810.

———. "Plan eines ökonomischen Instituts für Mädchen." *Schlesische Provinzblätter* 37 (1803): 546-52.

———. *Rath für junge Hausmütter des Mittelstandes bei theuren Zeiten wohlfeil hauszuhalten: Eine Sammlung von Haushaltungsvortheilen*. Leipzig: Gerhard Fleischer d. J., 1807.

[Gürnth, Christine Dorothea (Amalie, pseud.)]. *Unterhaltungen für denkende Hausmütter über allerley Gegenstände der weiblichen Ökonomie*. Breslau and Leipzig: Wilhelm Gottlieb Korn, 1801.

Hamberger, Georg Christoph and Johann Georg Meusel. *Das gelehrte Deutschland: Oder Lexikon der jetzt lebenden Schriftsteller*. 5th ed. Lemgo, 1796-1834; repr. Hildesheim: Olms, 1966.

Handbuch für Mädchen von reiferm Alter, mit moralischen Erzählungen und ökonomischen Kenntnissen. Munich: Joseph Lentner, 1791.

Das häusliche Glück: Vollständiger Haushaltungsunterricht nebst Anleitung zum Kochen für Arbeiterfrauen, ed. Commission des Verbandes "Arbeiterwohl." 11th ed. Mönchengladbach: A. Reiffarth, 1882.

Die Hausmutter als Köchin, oder Unterricht in den ersten Grundregeln und Handgriffen beim Kochen, welche junge Mädchen zu wissen nöthig sind, ehe sie zur ausübenden Kochkunst schreiten können. Leipzig: J.C. Eurich, 1809.

Hippel, Theodor Gottlieb von. *Nachlaß über weibliche Bildung*. Berlin: Voß, 1801.

———. *On Improving the Status of Women*. Trans. Timothy Sellner. Detroit: Wayne State University, 1979.

———. *Über die bürgerliche Verbesserung der Weiber*. Ed. Ralph-Ranier Wuthenow. Berlin: Voß, 1792, Frankfurt am Main: Syndikat 1977.

———. *Über die Ehe*. Berlin: Voß, 1774.

———. *Über die Ehe*. Berlin: Voß, 1793.

Hohberg, Wolf Helmhard von. *Georgica curiosa aucta, Das ist: Umständlicher Bericht und klarer Unterricht von dem Adelichen Land- und Feldleben, Auf alle in Teutschland übliche Land- und Hauswirtschafften gerichtet ... und in Dreyen absonderlichen Theilen, in Zwölff Büchern bestehende, vorgestetllet; Also und dergestalt, dasz in dem Ersthen Theil Der Land-Güter Zugehörungen und Beobachtungen ... enthalten. Im Andern Theil, wie der gantze Feldbau auf das leichteste, beste und nutzlichste anzuordnen ... abgehandelt wird; Im Dritten Theil ist, was bevorab, in berührten 12 Büchern, gar nicht oder kürzlich enthalten, nunmehro vollständig ausgeführt zu finden; wobey ein bewährtes sehr nützliches Koch-buch ... auch wie die Weinberge, Obst-küchen- Artzney- und Blümen-Gärten auf das beste einzurichten ...* 3 vols. Nuremberg: Michael und Johann Friedrich Endters Erben, 1682, 1695.

Holst, Amalie [J. G. Müller, pseud.]. *Bemerkungen über die Fehler unserer modernen Erziehung*. Leipzig: Linke, 1791.

Holst, Amalie. *Über die Bestimmungen des Weibes zur höheren Geistesbildung*. Ed. Bertha Rahm. Berlin: Fröhlich: 1802; new ed. Zurich: Ala, 1984.

Humboldt, Wilhelm von. "Plan einer vergleichenden Anthropologie" (1794). In *Gesammelte Schriften*. Ed. Königliche Preußische Akademie der Wissenschaften, vol. 1, 377-410. Berlin: B. Behr, 1903-1936; repr. Berlin: Walter de Gruyter, 1968.

———. "Über den Geschlechtsunterschied und dessen Einfluß auf die organische Natur" (1794). In *Gesammelte Schriften*, ed. Königliche Preußische Akademie der Wissenschaften, vol. 1, 311-34. Berlin: B. Behr, 1903-1936; repr. Berlin: Walter de Gruyter, 1968.

———. "Über die innere und äussere Organisation der höheren Wissenschaftlichen Anstalten in Berlin" (1810). In *Gesammelte Schriften*, ed. Königliche Preußische Akademie der Wissenschaften, vol. 10, 250-60. Berlin: B. Behr, 1903-1936; repr. Berlin: Walter de Gruyter, 1968.

———. "Über die männliche und weibliche Form" (1795). In *Gesammelte Schriften*, ed. Königliche Preußische Akademie der

Wissenschaften, vol. 1, 335-69. Berlin: B. Behr, 1903-1936; repr. Berlin: Walter de Gruyter, 1968.

———. "Über Reformen in Unterrichtswesen" (1810). In *Gesammelte Schriften*, ed. Königliche Preußische Akademie der Wissenschaften, vol. 10, 299-302. Berlin: B. Behr, 1903-1936; repr. Berlin: Walter de Gruyter, 1968.

Jablonski, Johann Theodor. *Allgemeines Lexikon der Künste und Wissenschaften, oder: Deutliche Beschreibung des Reichs der Natur, der Himmel, und himmlischen Cörper, der Luft, der Ende, sammt den bekannten Gewächsen, der Thiere, Steine und Erzte, des Meers und der darinne lebenden Geschöpfe; Ingleichen aller menschlichen Handlungen, Staats- Rechts- Kriegs- Policey- Haushaltungs- und Gelehrten Geschäffte, Hanthierungen und Gewerbe, samt einer Erklärung der dabey vorkommender Kunst- Wörter und Redens-Arten*. Revised ed. Königsberg and Leipzig: Johann Heinrich Hartung, 1748.

Jöcher, Christian Gottlieb. "Johann Riem." In *Allgemeines Gelehrten-Lexikon*, continued and expanded by H.W. Rotermund 6 (1819), in *Deutsches Biographisches Archiv*, fiche 1037, frames 284-93.

Justi, Johann Heinrich Gottlob von. *Die Grundfeste der Macht und Glückseligkeit der Staaten; oder ausführliche Vorstellung der gesamten Polizeiwissenschaft*. 2 vols. Königsberg and Leipzig: Johann Heinrich Hartungs Erben, 1760; repr. Aalen: Scienta, 1965.

———. *Grundsätze der Polizeywissenschaft in einem vernünftigen, auf den Endzweck der Polizey gegründeten, Zusammenhänge und zum Gebrauch akademischer Vorlesungen, abgefasset*. 3rd ed. Göttingen: Vandenhoeck & Ruprecht, 1782; repr. Frankfurt: Sauer & Auvermann, 1969.

———. *Staatswirthschaft: oder Systematische Abhandlung aller Oekonomischen und Cameral-Wissenschaften, die zur Regierung eines Landes erfordert werden*. 2nd ed. Leipzig: Bernhard Christoph Breitkopf, 1758; repr. Aalen: Scienta, 1963.

———. "Über die Haupthindernisse für den landwirtschaftlichen Betrieb" (1767). In *Quellen zur Geschichte der deutschen Bauernbefreiung*. Ed. Werner Conze, 46-52. Quellensammlung zur Kulturgeschichte, vol. 12. Göttingen, Berlin, and Frankfurt: Musterschmidt, 1967.

———. "Von Einrichtung der Steuern und Abgaben in einem Staat." In *Gesammelte politische und Finanz-Schriften über wichtige Gegenstände der Staatskunst, der Kriegswissenschaften und des Kameral- und Finanzwesens.* Gesammelte politische und Finanz-Schriften über wichtige Gegenstände der Staatskunst, der Kriegswissenschaften und des Kameral- und Finanzwesens, vol. 1, 365-79. Kopenhagen and Leipzig: Roth, 1761.

[Justi, Johann Heinrich Gottlob von]. "Vorschlag von Einrichtung einer Akademie für das Frauenzimmer." *Ergetzungen der vernüftigen Seele aus der Sittenlehre und der Gelehrsamkeit überhaupt* 5, no. 1 (1747): 312-27.

Kant, Immanuel. *Anthropologie in pragmatischer Hinsicht* (1800). In *Immanuel Kants Werke*, vol. 8, 1-228. Berlin: Bruno Cassirer, 1923.

———. *Anthropology from a Pragmatic Point of View.* Trans. Mary J. Gregor. The Hague: Martinus Nijhoff, 1974.

———. *"Beantwortung der Frage: Was ist Aufklärung?"* (1784). In *Immanuel Kants Werke*, vol. 7, 167-76. Berlin: Bruno Cassirer, 1922.

———. "Die Metaphysik der Sitten" (1797). In *Immanuel Kants Werke*, vol. 7, 1-309. Ed. Ernst Cassirer. Berlin: B. Cassirer, 1922.

———. "Über Pädagogik" (1803). In *Immanuel Kants Werke*, vol. 8, 453-508. Ed. Ernst Cassirer. Berlin: Bruno Cassirer, 1923.

König, Emanuel. *Georgica Helvetica Curiosa, oder neu curioses Eydgenossisch-Schweitzerisches Haus-Buch.* Basel: König, 1706.

Kraus, Christian Jakob. *Staatswirthschaft.* Ed. Hans von Auerswald. 5 vols. Königsberg: Nicolovius, 1808-1811.

Kreittmayr, Wiguläus Xaverius Aloysius. *Anmerkungen über den Codicem Maximilianeum Civilem: Worin derselbe sowohl mit dem Gemein- als ehemalig Chur-Bayrischen Land-Recht genau collationirt, sohin der Unterschied zwischen dem alt- und neueren Recht samt den Urquellen, woraus das letztere geschöpft worden ist, überall angezeigt, und dies dadurch in ein helleres Licht gesetzt wird.* 2nd unchanged ed. Munich: Verlag der Königlichen Central-Verwaltung der Regierungs- und Intelligenzblätter, 1821.

Kreyßig, W.A. *Die Einrichtung der Landgüter nach Bedingungen ihres höchsten nachhaltigen Reinertrages der Volkswohlfahrt und Volksveredelung.* Braunschweig: G. Westermann, 1841.

———. *Wegreiser zum praktischen Studium der Landwirthschaft sowie zum Kaufen und Pachten der Landgüter für angehende Landwirthe und Käufer, die nicht Landwirthe sind*. Braunschweig: G. Westermann, 1840.

Krünitz, Johann Georg. *Oekonomische Encyklopädie oder allgemeines System Staats- Stadt- Haus- und Landwirthschaft in alphabetischer Ordnung*. 242 vols. Rev. ed. Berlin: Joachim Pauli, 1784.

Leonhardi, Friedrich G. *Erdbeschreibung der preußischen Monarchie*. 5 vols. Halle: Schwett und Sohn, 1791-1798.

Leopold, Justus Ludwig Günther. *Agricola, oder Belehrung über alle Gegenstände der Landwirtschaft*. Hanover: Hahn, 1804.

———. *Handwörterbuch des gemeinnützigsten und neuesten aus der Oekonomie und Haushaltungskunde*. 2nd ed. Hanover: Hahn, 1805.

Leopoldt, Johann Georg. *Nützliche und auf die Erfahrung gegründete Einleitung zu der Landwirtschaft*. Berlin and Golgan: Christian Friedrich Günther, 1759.

Liberti, Daniel. *Die in Churfürstenthum Sachsen und angräntzenden Landen approbirte Adeliche Hauß-Wirthschafts-Kunst in welcher diejenigen Sachen, so in einer wichtigen Hauß-Haltung täglich vorkommen, absonderlich was ein rechtschaffener Haußwirth und Verwalther jeden Monat durchs gantze Jahr zuthun und wie er endlich Jahres-Rechnung formieren und schlüssen soll, abgehandelt werden*. Leipzig: Friedrich Groschuff, 1701.

Lueder, August Ferdinand. *Ueber Nationalindustrie und Staatswirthschaft, nach Adam Smith bearbeitet*. Berlin: Fröhlich, 1800-1804.

[Mauvillion, Jakob]. *Mann und Weib nach ihren gegenseitigen Verhältnissen geschildert: Ein Gegenstück zu der Schrift: Ueber der Weiber*. Leipzig: Dykische Buchhandlung, 1791.

Menius, Justus. *Oeconomia Christiana, dat ys, van Christliker hußholdinge*. Wittenberg: Hynrick Ottinger, 1529.

Merrem, Blasius. *Allgemeine Grundsätze der bürgerlichen Wirthschaft und Haushaltung*. Göttingen: Röwer, 1817.

Meusel, Johann. *Lexikon der vom Jahr 1750 bis 1800 verstorbenen teutschen Schriftsteller*. 15 vols. Leipzig: Gebrüder Fleischer, 1802-1816; repr. Hildesheim: Georg Olms Verlagsbuchhandlung, 1968.

Münchhausen, Otto von. *Der freye Kornhandel als das beste Mittel um Mangel und Theuerung zu verhütten; zur Warnung auf künftige Zeiten aus der Erfahrung und aus neuen Gründen erwiesen*. Hanover: Försters Hof-Buchhandlung, 1772.

_____. *Der Hausvater.* 5 vols. Hanover: Nicolaus Försters und Sohns Erben, 1764-1774.

_____. *Der Hausvater.* 5 vols. 3rd. ed. Hanover: Nicolaus Försters und Sohns Erben; Helwingischen Hof-Buchhandlung, 1771-73.

Munther, Friedrich Reinhold. *Die landwirthschaftliche Buchhaltung in einfacher staatswirthschaftlicher Form.* Berlin: F. Rubach, 1838.

Neues Nürnberger Kochbuch für Hausmütter und Köchinnen oder: Geprüfte Vorschriften zur Zubereitung aller in einer Haushaltung vorkommenden Speisen, und der besten und vorzüglichsten Bäckereien. 2nd ed. Nuremberg: C.H. Zeh'schen Buchhandlung, 1820.

Paula Schrank, Franz von. "Gedanken über die Erziehung der Bauernjugend." *Baierischer Ökonomischer Hausvater, oder gesammelte Schriften der Kurfürstlichen Gesellschaft sittlich- und landwirtschaftlicher Wissenschaften in Burghausen,* 5 (1781): 130-175.

Pestalozzi, Johann Heinrich. *Lienhard und Gertrud: Ein Buch für das Volk* (1781). Winkler Dünndruck Ausgabe. Munich: Winkler, 1977.

Pockels, Carl Friedrich. *Versuch einer Charakteristik des weiblichen Geschlechts: Ein Sittengemälde des Menschen, des Zeitalters, und des geselligen Lebens.* 5 vols. Hanover: Christian Ritscher, 1797-1802.

Pütter, Johann Stephen. *Versuch einer academischen Gelehrten-Geschichte von der Georg-Augustus-Universität zu Göttingen.* 4 vols. Göttingen and Hanover: Vandenhoeck & Ruprecht, 1765-1838.

Rau, Karl Heinrich. *Geschichte des deutschen Pfluges.* Heidelberg: Winter, 1845.

Röver, Friedrich. *Die Hausfreundin auf dem Lande; oder möglichst vollständige Anweisung für Frauenzimmer, die ihrem ländlichen Haushalt mit Ehren und Vortheil vorstehen, die Geschäfte der Küche des Kellers und der Vorraths-Behältnisse selbst besorgen, und dabey zugleich ihre und der Ihrigen Gesundheit berücksichtigen wollen: Eine ökonomisch-encyclopädische Unterricht in alphabetischer Ordnung.* 3 vols. Magdeburg: W. Heinrichshofen, 1822-1823.

Rohr, Julius Bernhard von. *Compendieuse Haushaltungsbibliotheck: Darinnen nicht allein die neuesten und besten Autores die sowohl von der Haußhaltung sowohl überhaupt als auch insonderheit vom Ackerbau, Viehzucht, Jägerei, Gärtnerei, Kochen, Bierbrauen, Weinbergen, Wäldern, Bergwercken, usw. geschrieben, recensiret und beurtheilet.* Leipzig: Johann Christian Martini, 1716.

———. *Vollständiges Hauß- Haltungs-Recht, in welchem die nötigsten und nützlichsten Rechts-Lehren welche so wohl bey den Land-Gütern überhaupt, derselben Kauffung, Verkauffung, und Verpachtung als insonderheit bey dem Acker-Bau Gärtnerey, Viehzucht, Jagten, Wäldern, Fischereyen, Mühlen, Weinbergen, Bierbrauen, Vorwercken, Handel und Wandel mit anderen oeconomischen Materien vorkommen, der gesunden Vernunfft, denen Römisch und Teutschen Gesetzen nach ordentlich und ausführlich abgehandelt werden.* Leipzig: Johann Christian Martini, 1716.

———. *Vollständiges Haußwirthschafts-Buch, welches die Hauswirthschaffts-Regeln, die so wohl im Ansehung der Oeconomie überhaupt als insonderheit bey dem Feld-Bau, der Viehzucht, der Gärtnerey, den Jagt- und Först-Sachen, Fischereyen und Teichen, dem Kochen, Confitüren, Wein-Bau, Bierbrauen, und andern nöthigen Materien sich applieren Lassen, ohne Einmischung fremder Sachen gründlich und ordentlich vorträgt.* Leipzig: Johann Friedrich Gleditsch, 1722; rev. ed. 1751.

Rousseau, Jean-Jacques. *Émile* (1762). Trans. Barbara Foxley. London: Dent, 1911.

Rühl, Franz, ed. *Aus der Franzosenzeit: Ergänzungen zu den Briefen und Aktenstücken zur Geschichte Preußens unter Friedrich Wilhelm III., vorzugsweise aus dem Nachlaß von F. A. von Staegemann.* Leipzig: Duncker und Humblot, 1904.

Rulffs, August Friedrich. *Ueber die Preisfrage der königlichen Socieität der Wissenschaften zu Göttingen: von der vortheilhaftesten Einrichtung der Werk- und Zuchthäuser.* Göttingen: Rosenbusch, 1783.

Sächsisch- und Brandenburgisches Land- und Hauß-wirtschaftsbuch. Nuremberg: Christoph Riegeln, 1730.

Der sächsische Landwirth in seiner Landwirthschaft, was er jetzt ist und was er seyn könnte, oder wie ein jeder seine Einkünfte in kurzer Zeit um mehr als die Hälfte sehr leicht erhöhen könne. 3 vols. Leipzig: Christian Gottlob Hilscher, 1788-1791.

Schindel, Carl Wilhelm Otto von. *Die deutschen Schriftstellerinnen des neunzehnten Jahrhunderts.* 3 vols. Leipzig: Brockhaus, 1823-1825.

Schönfeld, Johann Gottlob von. *Die Landwirtschaft und deren Verbesserung nach eigenen Erfahrungen beschrieben.* Leipzig: Bernhard Christoph Breitkopf, 1773.

Schröder, Wilhelm von. *Fürstliche Schatz- und Rent-Cammer.* Leipzig: 1686.

Schulz, Carl, and Kurt Tiesler, eds. *Das älteste Bürgerbuch der Stadt Königsberg (Pr.) (1746-1809).* Sonderschriften des Vereins für Familienforschung in Ost- und Westpreußen Sonderschriften des Vereins für Familienforschung in Ost- und Westpreußen, Vol. 36. Königsberg: 1939; repr. Hamburg: Verein für Familienforschung in Ost- und Westpreußen, 1978.

Seckendorff, Viet Ludwig von. *Teutscher Fürsten-Stat oder: gründliche und kurze Beschreibung welcher Gestalt Fürstenthumer und Graff- und Herrschaften im Heil. Röm. Reich teutscher Nation, welche Landes, Fürstliche und hohe obrigkeitliche Regalia haben von Rechts- und löblicher Gewohnheit wegen beschaffen zu seyn.* 2 vols. Frankfurt: Gotzen, 1665; repr. Glashütten: Detlev Auvermann, 1976.

Sonnenfels, Joseph von. *Grundsätze der Polizey, Handlung und Finanzwissenschaft.* 2nd ed. Vienna: Kurzböck, 1768.

———. *Politische Abhandlungen.* Vienna: Joseph Edlen, 1777; repr. Aalen: Scienta, 1964.

Der Sorgfältige Hauß-Wirthschafts-Verwalter, welcher gründlich zeiget was durchs gantze Jahr so wohl in Wirthschafts-Rechnungen als im Haus-Wesen und Acker-Bau In acht zu nehmen, daß ein guter Nutzen daraus erfolge, Nebst wohl approbirten Vieh- Roß- Artzeneyen und dienlichen Hauß-Mitteln versehen. Leipzig: Michael Rohrlachs Wittib und Erben, 1712.

Sorgfältiger Hauß-Halter, ganz neu vermehrter, betreffend einen nutz- und Lust- bringenden Baum- Küchen- und Blümen-Garten ... sambt einem Dreyfachen Koch- Condir- und Distillier-Buch nebst noch einem zwar kleinen doch auserlesenen Arzney-Büchlein. Osnabrück: J. Wolfgang Distner, 1687.

Spittler, Ludwig Timotheus von. *Vorlesungen über Politik.* Ed. Karl Wächter. Stuttgart and Tübingen: J. G. Cotta, 1828.

Stein, Heinrich Friedrich Karl vom und zum. *Briefe und amtliche Schriften.* Ed. Erich Botzenhart and Walther Hubatsch et. al. 10 vols. Stuttgart: W. Kohlhammer, 1957-1974.

Süßmilch, Johann Peter. *Die göttliche Ordnung in den Veränderungen des menschlichen Geschlechts, aus der Geburt, dem Tode und der Fortpflanzung desselben erwiesen.* 2 vols. 3rd ed. Berlin: Süßmilch, 1756.

———. "On Removing the Obstacles to Population Growth." Trans. Eileen B. Hennessy. *Population and Development Review* 9 (1983): 521-29.

Thaer, Albrecht. *Beschreibung der nutzbarsten neuen Ackergeräthe.* 3 vols. Hanover: Hahn, 1803-1806.

———. *Einleitung zur Kenntniß der englischen Landwirthschaft und ihrer neuen praktischen und theoretischen Fortschritte in Rücksicht auf Vervollkommnung deutscher Landwirthschaft für denkende Landwirthe und Cameralisten.* 2 vols. 2nd ed. Hanover: Hahn, 1800-1801.

———. *Geschichte meiner Wirthschaft zu Möglin.* Berlin: Realschulbuchhandlung; Vienna: Gerold, 1815.

———. *Grundsätze der rationellen Landwirthschaft.* 4 vols. 2nd ed. Berlin: Realschulbuchhandlung, 1809-1812.

———. *Leitfaden zur allgemeinen landwirthschaftlichen Gewerbs-Lehre.* Berlin: Reimer, 1815.

———. *Unterricht über den Kleebau und Stallfütterung für den lüneburgischen Landmann.* Hanover: Hahn, 1793.

———, ed. *Annalen der niedersächsischen Landwirthschaft.* 6 vols. Hanover: Hahn, 1799-1804.

Thieme, Johann Christoph. *Haus-, Feld-, Artzney-, Koch-Kunst und Wunder-Buch, Das ist: Ausführliche Beschreib- und Vorstellung wie ein kluger Haus-Vater und sorgfältige Haus-Mutter wes Standes und Würden sie auch immermehr seyn mögen, mit vortrefflichem Nutzen und ersprießlichem Nahrungs-Aufnehmen ihr Haus-Wesen führen, und, durch Gottes reichen Segen auf ihre Nachkommen höchst glücklich fortpflanzen mögen: Alles um richtiger Ordnung Willen in zwantzig Abtheilungen enthalten.* Nuremberg: Johann Hoffman, 1687.

Titius, Johann Daniel, ed. *Nützliche Sammlung von Aufsätzen und Wahrnehmungen über die Witterungen, die Haushaltskunde, das Gewerbe, die Naturkenntniß, Polizey, und andere damit verknüpfte Wissenschaften, welche die Fortsetzung des Wittenbergschen Wochenblatts ausmachen,* vol. 1. Leipzig: Junius, 1782-1792.

"Versuch zur Bestimmung des Werthes der Frohndienste," introduction by Albrecht Thaer. *Möglinsche Annalen der deutschen Landwirthschaft* 1 (1817): 174-199.

Weber, Friedrich Benedict. *Blicke in die Zeit, in Hinsicht auf National-Industrie und Staatswirthschaft, mit besonderer Berücksichtigung*

Deutschlands, und vornehmlich des Preußischen Staats. Berlin and Stettin: Nicolai, 1830.

———. *Handbuch der ökonomischen Literatur, oder systematische Anleitung zur Kenntniß der deutschen ökonomischen Schriften die sowohl die gesammte Land- und Hauswirthschaft als die mit derselben verbundenen Hülfs- und Nebenwissenschaften angehen.* 8 vols. Berlin: Heinrich Fröhlich; Berlin: Duncker & Humblot; Breslau: Wilibald Aug. Holäufer; Leipzig: C.H.F. Hartman; Breslau: Max; Berlin: Grimma: 1803-1842.

———. *Lehrbuch der politischen Oekonomie.* 2 vols. Breslau: Barth, 1813.

———. *Ueber die Cameralwissenschaft, und das Cameralstudium auf Universitäten; nebst einem Plan zu einem cameralistischen Cursus auf der Universität zu Breslau, und dem Grundriß der dazu gehörigen einzelnen Vorlesungen selbst.* Breslau: Gustav Kupfer, 1828.

Wichmannshausen, J.B. von. *Das Oeconomische Allerley.* Leipzig: Johann Wendler, 1762.

[Wiegand, Johann]. *Der wohlerfahrene Landwirth: oder vorläufige Anleitung wie die Landwirtschaftsökonomie, nämlich der Feldbau, die Waldungen, die Teiche, die Mayerhöfe und die Schäfereyen in einen viel verbesserten Stand gebracht werden könnte.* 2 vols. Vienna: Johann Paul Krauß, 1774-1775.

Winter, Georg, ed. *Die Reorganisation des preußischen Staates unter Stein und Hardenberg: Allgemeine Verwaltungs- und Behördenreformen.* Vol. 1: Vom Beginn des Kampfs gegen die Kabinettsregierung bis zum Wiedereintritt des Ministers vom Stein. Publikationen aus den preußischen Staatsarchiven, vol. 93. Leipzig: Hirzel, 1931.

Wohl unterrichtete Landwirthin, oder Anfangs-Gründe zur Erlernung einer klugen und vernünftigen Haus- und Landwirtschaft zum besten des weiblichen Geschlechts gesammelt. new ed. Nuremberg: Wolfgang Schwarzkopf, 1774.

Wohl unterwiesener Landwirth, oder der Freund des Landmannes. Nuremberg: Wolfgang Schwarzkopf, 1768.

Wolff, Christian. *Vernünftige Gedanken von dem gesellschaftlichen Leben der Menschen: und insonderheit dem gemeinen Wesen oder Buch über die Politik zu Beförderung der Glückseligkeit des menschlichen Geschlechts, den Liebhabern der Wahrheit mitgetheilt.* (1721). Gesammelte Werke, Vol. 5. Frankfurt and Leipzig: Regner, 1756; repr. Hildesheim: Olms, 1975.

Wollstonecraft, Mary. *Vindication of the Rights of Women.* Ed. Carol H. Poston. Norton Critical Editions in the History of Ideas. London: J. Johnson, 1975.

Zedler, Johann Heinrich, ed. *Grosses vollständiges Universal-Lexikon aller Wissenschaften und Künste welche bißhero durch menschlichen Verstand und Witz erfunden worden.* 68 vols. Halle and Leipzig: Johann Heinrich Zedler, 1732-1754; repr. Graz: Akademische Druck- und Verlagsanstalt, 1961-1964.

Zincke, Georg Heinrich. *Allgemeines Oeconomisches Lexicon.* 2 vols. Leipzig: Johann Friedrich Gleditsch, 1731.

Secondary Sources

Abel, Wilhelm. *Agrarkrisen und Agrarkonjunktur: Eine Geschichte der Land- und Ernährungswirtschaft Mitteleuropas seit dem hohen Mittelalter.* 3rd ed. Hamburg and Berlin: Paul Parey, 1978.

———. *Geschichte der deutschen Landwirtschaft vom frühen Mittelalter bis zum 19. Jahrhundert.* Deutsche Agrargeschichte, vol. 2. Stuttgart: Eugen Ulmer, 1962.

———. *Massenarmut und Hungerkrisen im vorindustriellen Deutschland.* Kleine Vandenhoeck Reihe, vol. 1352. Göttingen: Vandenhoeck & Ruprecht, 1986.

Abrams, Lynn. "Concubinage, Cohabitation and the Law: Class and Gender Relations in Nineteenth-Century Germany." *Gender and History* 5 (1993): 82-83.

———. "Martyrs or Matriarchs? Working-Class Women's Experience of Marriage in Germany before the First World War." *Women's History Review* 1 (1992): 357-76.

Adams, Carole Elizabeth. *Women Clerks in Wilhelmine Germany: Issues of Class and Gender.* Cambridge, England: Cambridge University, 1988.

Albrecht, Peter. "Die zunehmende Kleiderpracht der Mägde in den Städten des Herzogtums Braunschweig-Wolfenbüttel in der Mitte des 18. Jahrhunderts." *Braunschweigisches Jahrbuch* 60 (1969): 99-108

Algazi, Gadi. *Herrngewalt und Gewalt der Herrn im späten Mittelalter: Herrschaft, Gegenseitigkeit und Sprachgebrauch.* Historische Studien, vol. 17. Frankfurt am Main and New York: Campus, 1992.

Works Cited

Allen, Ann Taylor. *Feminism and Motherhood in Germany, 1800-1914.* New Brunswick, NJ: Rutgers University, 1991.

Allgemeine Deutsche Biographie, ed. Historische Commission bei der Königlichen Akademie der Wissenschaften. 56 vols. Leipzig: 1875-1912; repr. Berlin: Duncker & Humblot, 1967-1971.

Altpreußische Biographie, ed. Christian Krollman, Kurt Forstreuter, and Fritz Gause. Königsberg and Marburg: Elwert, 1941-1978.

Anderson, Barbara. "State-Building and Bureaucracy in Early Nineteenth-Century Nassau." *Central European History* 24 (1991): 222-47.

Aubin, Hermann, and Wolfgang Zorn. *Handbuch der deutschen Wirtschafts- und Sozialgeschichte.* 2 vols. Union: Klett-Cotta, 1971-1976.

Aumüller, Ursula. "Industrieschule und ursprüngliche Akkumulation in Deutschland: Die Qualifizierung der Arbeitskraft im Übergang von der feudalen in die kapitalistische Produktionsweise." In *Schule und Staat im 18. und 19. Jahrhundert: Zur Sozialgeschichte der Schule in Deutschland,* ed. Klaus L. Hartmann, Hans Waldeyer, and Franz Wenzel, 9-145. Edition Suhrkamp, vol. 694. Frankfurt am Main: Suhrkamp, 1974.

Autorenkollektiv. *Grundlinien des ökonomischen Denken in Deutschland: Von den Anfangen bis zur Mitte des 19. Jahrhunderts.* Ed. Akademie der Wissenschaften der DDR. Schriften des Zentralinstituts für Wirtschaftswissenschaften, vol. 3. Berlin: Akademie, 1977.

Bachmann, Hans-Martin. "Zur Wolffschen Naturrechtslehre." In *Christian Wolff 1679-1754: Interpretationen zu seiner Philosophie und deren Wirkung,* ed. Werner Schneiders, 161-70. Studien zum achtzehnten Jahrhundert, vol. 4. Hamburg: Felix Meiner, 1986.

Baxmann, Inge. "Von der Egalité im Salon zur Citoyenne – Einige Aspekte der Genese des bürgerlichen Frauenbildes." In *Frauen in der Geschichte III,* ed. Anette Kühn and Jörn Russen, 109-37. Düsseldorf: Schwann, 1983.

Beck, Hamilton H.H. *The Elusive "I" in the Novel: Hippel, Sterne, Diderot, Kant.* American University Studies, Series I: Germanic Language and Literature, vol. 46. New York, Bern, Frankfurt am Main, and Paris: Peter Lang, 1987.

_____. "Review of Theodor Gottlieb von Hippel, Über die Ehe and Über die bürgerliche Verbesserung der Weiber." *Lessing Yearbook* 16 (1984): 298-301.

Beechey, Veronica. *Unequal Work*. Questions for Feminism. London: Verso, 1987.

Beer, Ursula, and Ursula Müller. "Coping with a New Reality: Barriers and Possibilities." *Cambridge Journal of Economics* 17 (1993): 281-94.

Benecke, G. *Society and Politics in Germany 1500-1750*. London: Routledge & Kegan Paul, 1974.

Berding, Helmut. "Begriffsgeschichte und Sozialgeschichte." *Historische Zeitschrift* 223 (1976): 98-110.

_____. *Napoleonische Herrschafts- und Gesellschaftspolitik im Königreich Westfalen 1807-1813*. Kritische Studien zur Geschichtswissenschaft, vol. 7. Göttingen: Vandenhoeck & Ruprecht, 1973.

_____, ed. *Soziale Unruhen in Deutschland während der Französischen Revolution*. Special Issue, Geschichte und Gesellschaft, vol. 12 (1988).

Berding, Helmut, and Peter Ullman. *Deutschland zwischen Revolution und Restauration*. Athenäum-Droste Taschenbücher Geschichte, vol. 7240. Königstein-Taunus: Altenäum, 1981.

Berthold, Rudolf. "Die Veränderung im Bodeneigentum und in der Zahl der Bauernstellen, der Kleinstellen und der Rittergüter in den preußischen Provinzen Sachsen, Brandenburg und Pommern während der Durchführung der Agrarreformen des 19. Jahrhunderts." *Studien zu den Agrarreformen des 19. Jahrhunderts in Preußen und Rußland*. Special Issue, Das Jahrbuch für Wirtschaftsgeschichte (1978): 7-116.

Bien, Günther. "Die Wirkungsgeschichte der aristotelischen 'Politik'." In *"Aristoteles 'Politik": Akten des XI. Symposium Aristotelicum Friedrichshafen/Bodensee 25.8.-3.9.1987*, ed. Günther Patzig, 333-51. Göttingen: Vandenhoeck & Ruprecht, 1987.

Biermann, Rudolf. "Erziehungsmittel oder Erziehungsmassnahme? Zur Wandlung der philanthropischen Pädagogik bei Basedow, Campe, und Salzmann." *Paedagogica Historica* 2 (1972): 342-69.

Binder. "Friedrich Eberhard Freiherr von Rochow." In *Allgemeine Deutsche Biographie*, vol. 28 (1889), 727-34.

Birtsch, Günther. "Zum konstitutionellen Charakter des preußischen Allgemeinen Landrechts von 1794." In *Politische Ideologien und nationalstaatliche Ordnung: Studien zur Geschichte des 19. und 20. Jahrhunderts: Festschrift für Theodor Schieder*, ed. Kurt Kluxen and Wolfgang J. Mommsen, 97-115. Munich and Vienna: R. Oldenbourg, 1968.

Blackbourn, David, and Geoff Eley. *The Peculiarities of German History: Bourgeois Society and Politics in Nineteenth-Century Germany.* Oxford, England: Oxford University, 1984.

Blackwell, Jeannine. "Sophie von La Roche." In *German Writers in the Age of Goethe: Sturm und Drang to Classicism*, ed. James Hardin and Christoph E. Schweitzer, 154-61. Dictionary of Literary Biography, vol. 94. Detroit, New York, and London: Gale Research, 1990.

Blasius, Dirk. "Bürgerliche Rechtsgleichheit und die Ungleichheit der Geschlechter: Das Scheidungsrecht im historischen Vergleich." In Frevert, ed., *Bürgerinnen und Bürger*, 67-84.

———. *Ehescheidung in Deutschland 1794-1945: Scheidung und Scheidungsrecht in historische Perspektive.* Kritische Studien zur Geschichtswissenschaft, vol. 74. Göttingen: Vandenhoeck & Ruprecht, 1987.

———. "Familie." In *Geschichtliche Grundbegriffe*, vol. 2 (1975), 253-302.

Bleek, Wilhelm. *Von der Kameralausbildung zum Juristenprivileg: Studium, Prüfung, und Ausbildung der höheren Beamten des allgemeinen Verwaltungsdienstes in Deutschland im 18. und 19. Jahrhundert.* Historische und pädagogische Studien, vol. 3. Berlin: Colloquium, 1972.

Blickle, Peter. *Deutsche Untertanen: Ein Widerspruch.* Munich: C.H. Beck, 1980.

———, ed. *Landgemeinde und Stadtgemeinde im Mitteleuropa: Ein struktureller Vergleich.* Historische Zeitschrift, Supplement, vol.13. 1991.

Blickle, Renate. "From Subsistence to Property: Traces of a Fundamental Change in Early Modern Bavaria." *Central European History* 25 (1992): 377-85

———. "Hausnotdurft: Ein Fundamentalrecht in der altständischen Ordnung Bayerns." In *Grund- und Freiheitsrechte von der ständischen zur spätbürgerlichen Gesellschaft*, ed. Günter Birtsch,

42-62. Veröffentlichungen zur Geschichte der Grund- und Freiheitsrechte, vol 2. Göttingen: Vandenhoeck & Ruprecht, 1987.

———. "Nahrung und Eigentum als Kategorien in der ständischen Gesellschaft." In *Ständische Gesellschaft und soziale Mobilität*, ed. Winfried Schulze, 73-93. Munich: R. Oldenbourg, 1988.

Bloch, Peter, et al. *Denkmal Albrecht Thaers*. Dahlemer Materiellen, vol. 3. Berlin: Domäne Dahlem, 1992.

Bloch, Ruth. "The Gendered Meanings of Virtue in Revolutionary America." *Signs: Journal of Women in Culture and Society* 13 (1987): 38-58.

Blochmann, Elisabeth. *Das "Frauenzimmer" und die "Gelehrsamkeit": Eine Studie über die Anfänge des Mädchenschulwesens in Deutschland.* Anthropologie und Erziehung, vol. 17. Heidelberg: Quelle & Meyer, 1966.

Blossfeld, Hans-Peter. "Labor-Market Entry and the Sexual Segregation of Careers in the Federal Republic of Germany." *American Journal of Sociology* 93 (1987): 89-118.

Bödeker, Hans Erich. "Das staatswissenschaftliche Fächersystem im 18. Jahrhundert." In *Wissenschaften im Zeitalter der Aufklärung: Aus Anlaß des 250jährigen Bestehens des Verlages Vandenhoeck & Ruprecht*, ed. Rudolf Vierhaus, 143-62. Göttingen: Vandenhoeck & Ruprecht, 1985.

Böning, Holger, ed. *Französische Revolution und deutsche Öffentlichkeit: Wandlungen in Presse und Alltagskultur am Ende des achtzehnten Jahrhunderts*. Deutsche Presseforschung, vol. 28. Munich and New York: K. G. Saur, 1992.

Bog, Ingomar. "Mercantilism im Germany." In *Revisions in Mercantilism*, ed. D. C. Coleman, 162-89. Debates in Economic History. London: Metheun, 1969.

Bollnow, Otto Friedrich. "Johann Bernhard Basedow." In *Neue Deutsche Biographie*, vol. 1 (1953), 618-19.

Bormann-Heischkeil, Sigrid, and Karl-Ernst Jeismann. "Abitur, Staatsdienst und Sozialstruktur: Rekrutierung und Differenzierung der Schicht der Gebildeten am Beispiel der sozialen Herkunft und beruflichen Zukunft von Abiturienten preußischer Gymnasien im Vormärz." In *Bildung, Staat, Gesellschaft im 19. Jahrhundert: Mobilisierung und Disziplinierung*, ed. Jeismann, vol. 2, 155-186.

Nassauer Gespräche der Freiherr-vom-Stein Gesellschaft. Stuttgart: Franz Steiner, 1989.

Botzenhart, Erich. "Ernst Brandes." In *Neue Deutsche Biographie*, vol. 2 (1955), 518-19.

Bovenschen, Sylvia. *Die imaginierte Weiblichkeit: Exemplarische Untersuchungen zu kulturgeschichtlichen und literarischen Präsentationsformen des Weiblichen.* Edition Suhrkamp, vol. 921. Frankfurt am Main: Suhrkamp, 1979.

Brandes, Helga. "Das Frauenzimmer-Journal: Zur Herausbildung einer journalistischen Gattung im 18. Jahrhundert." In *Deutsche Literatur von Frauen,* ed. Gisela Brinker-Gabler, vol. 1, 452-68. Munich: C.H. Beck, 1988.

———. "Die 'Literarische Damen-Gesellschaft' Oldenburg zur Zeit der Französischen Revolution." In *Französische Revolution und deutsche Öffentlichkeit: Wandlungen in Presse und Alltagskultur am Ende des achtzehnten Jahrhunderts,* ed. Holger Böning, 439-51. Deutsche Presseforschung, vol. 28. Munich and New York: K.G. Saur, 1992.

———. "'Ueber die Revolutionssucht deutscher Weiber': Frauenbilder in der deutschen Publizistik um 1800." In *"Der Menschheit Hälfte blieb noch ohne Recht": Frauen und die Französische Revolution,* ed. Helga Brandes, 146-63. Wiesbaden: Deutscher Universitäts-Verlag, 1991.

Braun, Hans-Joachim. "Economic Theory and Policy in Germany 1750-1800." *Journal of European Economic History* 4 (1975): 301-322.

———. "Die Sozietäten in Leipzig und Karlsruhe als Vermittler englischer ökonomisch-technischer Innovationen." In Vierhaus, ed. *Deutsche patriotische und gemeinnützige Gesellschaften,* 241-54.

Brenning, E. "Johann Georg Scheffner." In *Allgemeine Deutsche Biographie,* vol. 30 (1890), 685-88.

Bridenthal, Renate, and Claudia Koonz. "Beyond Kinder, Küche, Kirche: Weimar Women in Politics and Work." In *When Biology Became Destiny: Women in Weimar and Nazi Germany,* ed. Renate Bridenthal, Atina Grossmann, and Marion Kaplan, 33-65. New York: Monthly Review, 1984.

Brown, Jane K. "Johann Wolfgang von Goethe." In *German Writers in the Age of Goethe: Sturm und Drang to Classicism,* ed. James Hardin and Chritoph E. Schweitzer. *Dictionary of Literary Biography*, vol. 94. Detroit, New York, and London: Gale Research, Inc., 1990.

Brückner, Jutta. *Staatswissenschaften, Kameralismus und Naturrecht: Ein Beitrag zur Geschichte der Politischen Wissenschaften im Deutschland des späten 17. und frühen 18. Jahrhunderts.* Münchener Studien zur Politik, vol. 27. Munich: C.H. Beck, 1977.

Brunner, Otto. *Adeliges Landleben und europäischer Geist: Leben und Werk Wolf Helmhards von Hohberg, 1612-1688.* Salzburg: Otto Müller, 1949.

_____. "Europäisches Bauerntum." In *Neue Wege der Verfassungs- und Sozialgeschichte*, ed. Brunner, 3rd ed., 199-212. Göttingen: Vandenhoeck & Ruprecht, 1980.

_____. "Das 'ganze Haus' und die altereuropäische 'Ökonomik.'" In *Neue Wege der Verfassungs- und Sozialgeschichte*, 3rd ed.,103-127. Göttingen: Vandenhoeck & Ruprecht, 1980.

_____. "Hausväterliteratur." In *Handwörterbuch der Sozialwissenschaften*, vol. 5, 92-93. Stuttgart: Fischer; Tübingen: J.C.B. Mohr (Paul Siebeck); Göttingen: Vandenhoeck & Ruprecht, 1956-1966.

_____. *Land and Lordship: Structures of Governance in Medieval Austria.* Trans. Howard Kaminsky and James Van Horn Melton. Philadelphia: University of Pennsylvania; 1992.

Brunner, Otto, Werner Conze, and Reinhart Koselleck, eds. *Geschichtliche Grundbegriffe: Historisches Lexikon zur politisch-sozialen Sprache in Deutschland.* 7 vols. Stuttgart: Klett and Klett-Cotta, 1972-1992.

Burkhardt, Johannes, Otto Gerhard Oexle, and Peter Spahn. "Wirtschaft." In *Geschichtliche Grundbegriffe*, vol. 7 (1992), 511-594.

Cavana, María Louisa P. "La 'Aufklärung' en las Figuras de Th. G. v. Hippel Y Amalia Holst." *Feminismo e Ilustracion 1988-1992*, 255-65. Actas del Seminario Permanente. Madrid: Instituto de Investigaciones Feministas, 1992.

_____. "Feminism as a Criterion of True Enlightenment." Unpublished manuscript. presented at International Society for Study of European Ideas, Graz, Austria, 22-27 August 1993.

Cocalis, Susan L. "Der Vormund will Vormund Sein: Zur Problematik der weiblichen Unmündigkeit im 18. Jahrhundert." In *Gestaltet und Gestaltend: Frauen in der deutschen Literatur*, ed. Marianne

Burkhard. 33-55. Special edition of Amsterdamer Beiträge zur Neueren Germanistik, special edition, vol. 10 (1980)

Coing, Helmut. *Europäisches Privatrecht, I: Älteres gemeines Recht (1500 bis 1800)*. Munich: C.H. Beck, 1985.

———, ed. *Handbuch der Quellen und Literatur der neueren europäischen Privatrechtsgeschichte*, 3 vols. 9 parts. Munich: C.H. Beck, 1960-1988.

Conrad, Hermann. "Die Rechtsstellung der Ehefrau in der Privatrechtsgesetzgebung der Aufklärungszeit." In *Aus Mittelalter und Neuzeit: Gerhard Kallen zum 70. Geburtstag*, ed. Josef Engel and Hans Martin Klinkenberg, 253-270. Bonn: Peter Hanstein, 1957.

Conze, Werner. "Beruf." In *Geschichtliche Grundbegriffe*, vol. 1 (1972), 490-507.

———. "Mittelstand." In *Geschichtliche Grundbegriffe*, vol. 4 (1978), 49-92.

Cott, Nancy. *The Bonds of Womanhood: Woman's Sphere in New England, 1780-1835*. New Haven, CT: Yale University, 1977.

———. *Domestic Ideology and Domestic Work*. Munich and New York: Saur, 1992.

Dahlmann, Gerhard. "Österreich." In *Handbuch der Quellen und Literatur der neueren europäischen Privatrechtsgeschichte*, 3 vols. 9 parts, ed. Helmut Coing, vol. 3, part 2, 2669-2709. Munich: C.H. Beck, 1960-1988.

Dann, Otto. *Lesegesellschaften und bürgerliche Emanzipation: Ein europäischer Vergleich*. Munich: Beck, 1981.

———, "Die Lesegesellschaften und die Herausbildung einer modernen bürgerlichen Gesellschaft in Europa." In *Lesegesellschaften und bürgerliche Emanzipation: Ein europäischer Vergleich*, ed. Dann, 9-28. Munich: Beck, 1981.

Davidoff, Leonore, and Catherine Hall. *Family Fortunes: Men and Women of the English Middle Class, 1780-1850*. Women in Culture and Society. Chicago: University of Chicago, 1991.

Dawson, Ruth P. "'And this shield is called – self-reliance': Emerging Feminist Consciousness in the Late Eighteenth Century." In Joeres and Maynes, eds., *German Women in the Eighteenth and Nineteenth Centuries*. 157-74.

———. "The Feminist Manifesto of Theodor Gottlieb von Hippel (1741-96)." In *Gestaltet und Gestaltend: Frauen in der deutschen*

Literatur, ed. Marianne Burkhard. 13-32. Special edition of Amsterdamer Beiträge zur Neueren Germanistik, 10 (1980).

———. "Theodor Gottlieb von Hippel und seine Schrift, 'Über die bürgerliche Verbesserung der Weiber.'" *Jahrbuch für internationale Germanistik* 8 (1980). Akten des VI. Internationalen Germanisten-Kongresses, 65-69.

Deike, Ludwig. "Die Celler Sozietät und Landwirtschaftsgesellschaft von 1764." In Vierhaus, ed., *Deutsche patriotische und gemeinnützige Gesellschaften*, 161-94.

———. *Die Entstehung der Celler Landwirtschaftsgesellschaft: Ökonomische Sozietäten und die Anfänge der modernen Agrarreformen im 18. Jahrhundert*, ed. Ilse Deike and Carl-Hans Hauptmeyer. Quellen und Darstellungen zur Geschichte Niedersachsens, vol. 113. Hanover: Hahn, 1994.

Deutsches Biographisches Archiv: Eine Kumulation aus 254 der wichstigen biographischen Nachschlagwerke für den deutschen Bereich bis zum Ausgang des 19. Jahrhunderts, ed. Bernhard Fabian and Willi Gorzny. Microfiche. Munich: K.G. Sauer, 1982-1985.

Dietrich, Richard. "Verfassung und Verwaltung." In *Berlin und die Provinz Brandenburg im 19. und 20. Jahrhundert*, ed. Hans Herzfeld and Gerd Heinrich, 181-291. Geschichte von Brandenburg und Preußen, vol. 3: Veröffentlichung der Historischen Kommission zu Berlin, vol. 25. Berlin: Walter de Gruyter, 1968.

Dinklage, Karl. "Gründung und Aufbau der theresianischen Ackerbaugesellschaften." *Zeitschrift für Agrargeschichte und Agrarsoziologie* 13 (1965): 200-11.

Dirr, Pius. *Buchwesen und Schrifttum im alten München 1450-1800*. Kultur und Geschichte: Freie Schriftenfolge des Stadtarchivs München, vol. 3. Munich: Knorr & Hirth, 1921.

Dittrich, Erhard. *Die deutschen und österreichischen Kameralisten*. Erträge der Forschung, vol. 23. Darmstadt: Wissenschaftliche Buchgesellschaft, 1974.

———. "Johann Heinrich Gottlob Justi, Cameralist." In *Neue Deutsche Biographie*, vol. 10 (1974), 707-709.

Doege, Michael. *Armut in Preußen und Bayern (1770-1840)*. Miscellanea Bavarica Monacensia, vol. 157. Munich: Kommissionsverlag UNI-Druck, 1991.

Döhring, Erich. "Johann Georg Büsch." In *Neue Deutsche Biographie*, vol. 3 (1957), 3.

Dölemeyer, Barbara. "Die Einführung und Geltung des Code civil in Deutschland (1804-1814)." In *Handbuch der Quellen und Literatur der neueren europäischen Privatrechtsgeschichte*, 3 vols. 9 parts, ed. Helmut Coing, vol. 3, part 2, 1440-71. Munich: C.H. Beck, 1960-1988.

Dreitzel, Horst. *Protestantischer Aristotelismus und Absoluter Staat: Die "Politica" des Henning Arnisaeus (ca. 1575-1636)*. Veröffentlichungen des Instituts für Europäische Geschichte Mainz, vol. 55, Abteilung Universalgeschichte. Wiesbaden: Franz Steiner, 1970.

Duden, Barbara. "Das schöne Eigentum: Zur Herausbildung des bürgerlichen Frauenbildes and der Wende vom 18. zum 19. Jahrhundert." *Kursbuch* 47 (1977): 125-140.

Duden, Barbara, and Karin Hausen. "Gesellschaftliche Arbeit – geschlechtspezifische Arbeitsteilung." In *Frauen in der Geschichte: Frauenrechte und die gesellschaftliche Arbeit der Frauen im Wandel: Fachwissenschaftliche und fachdidaktische Studien zur Geschichte der Frauen*, ed. Annette Kuhn and Gerhard Schneider, 11-33. Geschichtsdidaktik: Studien, Materialen, ed. Klaus Bergmann et al, vol. 6. Düsseldorf: Schwann, 1979.

Dülmen, Richard van. *Enstehung des frühneuzeitlichen Europa 1550-1648*. Fischer Weltgeschichte, vol. 24. Frankfurt am Main: Fischer, 1982.

―――. "Formierung der europäischen Gesellschaft in der frühen Neuzeit." *Geschichte und Gesellschaft* 7 (1981): 5-41.

―――. *Frauen vor Gericht: Kindsmord in der frühen Neuzeit*. Frankfurt am Main: Fischer Taschenbuch Verlag, 1991.

―――. *Die Gesellschaft der Aufklärer: Zur bürgerlichen Emanzipation und aufklärerischen Kultur in Deutschland*. Frankfurt am Main: Fischer Taschenbuch Verlag, 1986.

―――. "Der Infame Mensch." In *Arbeit, Frömmigkeit und Eigensinn*, ed. van Dülmen, 106-40. Studien zur Historischen Kulturforschung, vol. 2. Frankfurt am Main: Fischer Verlag, 1990.

―――. *Kultur und Alltag in der frühen Neuzeit*. 3 vols. Munich: C.H. Beck, 1990-1994.

Dürr, Renate. *Mägde in der Stadt: Das Beispiel Schwäbish Hall in der Frühen Neuzeit.* Geschichte und Geschlechter, vol. 13. Frankfurt and New York: Campus, 1995.

Eberle, Friedrich, and Theo Stamm, eds. *Die Französische Revolution in Deutschland: Zeitgenössische Texte deutscher Autoren.* Universalbibliothek, vol. 8537. Stuttgart: Reklam, 1989.

Eifert, Christiane. "Gesellschaftshierarchie in der Wohlfahrtspflege: Der sozialdemokratische Verband 'Arbeiterwohlfahrt' in den zwanziger Jahren." In Hausen, ed., *Geschlechterhierarchie und Arbeitsteilung,* 193-213.

Ellerkamp, Marlene, and Brigette Jungmann. "Unendliche Arbeit: Frauen in der 'Jutespinnerei und -weberei Bremen' 1888-1914." In *Frauen Suchen ihre Geschichte: Historische Studien zum 19. und 20. Jahrhundert,* ed. Karin Hausen, 128-43. Beck'sche Schwarze Reihe, vol. 276. Munich: C.H. Beck, 1983.

Engelhardt, Ulbrich. "Zum Begriff der Glückseligkeit in der kameralistischen Staatslehre des 18. Jahrhunderts (J.H.G. v. Justi)." *Zeitschrift für Historische Forschung* 8 (1981): 36-79.

Engels, Friederick. *The Origin of the Family, Private Property and the State* (1884), ed. Eleanor Burke Leacock. New York: International Publishers, 1972.

Engelsing, Rolf. *Der Bürger als Leser: Lesergeschichte in Deutschland, 1500-1800.* Stuttgart: Metzler, 1974.

Eulen, Focko. *Vom Gewerbefleiß zur Industrie: Ein Beitrag zur Wirtschaftsgeschichte des 18. Jahrhunderts.* Schriften zur Wirtschafts- und Sozialgeschichte, vol. 11. Berlin: Duncker & Humblot, 1967.

Evans, Richard J. "Liberalism and Society: The Feminist Movement and Social Change." In *Society and Politics in Wilhelmine Germany,* ed. Evans, 186-214. London and New York: Croon Helm and Barnes and Noble, 1978.

Fehrenbach, Elisabeth. *Traditionelle Gesellschaft und revolutionäres Recht: Die Einführung des Code Napoléon in den Rheinbundstaaten.* 2nd ed. Kritische Studien zur Geschichtswissenschaft, vol. 13. Göttingen: Vandenhoeck und Ruprecht, 1978.

Ferber, Marianne A., and Julie A. Nelson, eds. *Beyond Economic Man: Feminist Theory and Economics.* Chicago and London: University of Chicago, 1993.

Fichera, Ulrike Böhmel. "Das Frauenzimmer und die Mannesperson: Politik in literarischen Frauenzeitschriften des ausgehenden 18. Jahrhunderts." In *"Der Menschheit Hälfte blieb noch ohne Recht": Frauen und die Französische Revolution*, ed. Helga Brandes, 133-45. Wiesbaden: Deutscher Universitätsverlag, 1991.

Finley, M.I. "Aristotle and Economic Analysis." *Past and Present: A Journal of Historical Studies* 47 (1970): 3-25.

Fleischer, Manfred P. "The First German Agricultural Manuals." *Agricultural History* 55 (1981): 1-15.

Flockerzie, Lawrence. "State-Building and Nation-Building in the 'Third Germany': Saxony after the Congress of Vienna." *Central European History* 24 (1991): 268-92.

Folbre, Nancy. "The Unproductive Housewife: Her Evolution in Nineteenth-Century Economic Thought." *Signs: Journal of Women in Culture and Society* 17 (1991): 463-84.

Fox-Genovese, Elizabeth. *The Origins of Physiocracy: Economic Revolution and Social Order in Eighteenth-Century France*. Ithaca, NY and London: Cornell University, 1976.

Fraas, Carl Nicholaus. *Geschichte der Landbau und Forstwissenschaft bis zur Gegenwart*. Geschichte der Wissenschaften in Deutschland, vol. 3. Stuttgart: Cotta, 1865; repr. New York: Johnson Reprint, 1965.

Franz, Günther. *Geschichte des deutschen Bauernstandes vom frühen Mittelalter bis zum 19. Jahrhundert*. Deutsche Agrargeschichte, vol. 4. Stuttgart: Eugen Ulmer, 1976.

———. "Pfarrer als Wissenschaftler." In *Das Evangelische Pfarrhaus: Eine kultur- und Sozialgeschichte*, ed. Martin Greiffenhagen, 285-286. Stuttgart: Kreuz, 1984.

Franzoi, Barbara. *At the Very Least She Pays the Rent: Women and German Industrialization, 1871-1914*. Contributions in Women's Studies, vol. 57. Westport, CT.: Greenwood, 1985.

Frauendorfer, Sigmund von. *Ideengeschichte der Agrarwirtschaft und Agrarpolitik im deutschen Sprachgebiet*. 2nd ed. Munich, Basel, Vienna: BLV Verlagsgesellschaft, 1963.

Freckmann, Klaus. "Landwirtschaftliche Umfragen der napoleonischen Zeit und ihre Bedeutung für die Kulturraumforschung Pfalz und Rheinland." *Zeitschrift für Agrargeschichte und Agrarsoziologie* 37 (1989): 126-67.

Freudenberger, Herman. "Government and Economy: Introduction." In *State and Society in Early Modern Austria*, ed. Charles W. Ingrao, 141-53. West Lafayette, IN: Purdue University, 1994.

Frevert, Ute "Bürgerliche Meisterdenker und das Geschlechtsverhältnis: Konzepte, Erfahrungen, Visionen an der Wende vom 18. zum 19. Jahrhundert." In Frevert, ed. *Bürgerinnen und Bürger*, 17-48.

_____. "Frauen und Ärzte im späten 18. und frühen 19. Jahrhundert – zur Sozialgeschichte eines Gewaltverhältnisses." In *Frauen in der Geschichte II*, ed. Annette Kuhn and Jörn Rüsen, 179-182. Düsseldorf: Pädagogischer Verlag Schwann-Bagel, 1983.

_____. *Women in German History: From Bourgeois Emancipation to Sexual Liberation*. Trans. Stuart Evans et al. New York, Oxford, and Munich: Berg, 1989.

_____, ed. *Bürgerinnen und Bürger: Geschlechtsverhältnisse im 19. Jahrhundert*. Kritische Studien zur Geschichtswissenschaft, vol. 77. Göttingen: Vandenhoeck & Ruprecht, 1988.

Frühsorge, Gotthardt. "Die Begründung der 'väterlichen Gesellschaft' in der europäischen oeconomia christiana: Zur Rolle des Vaters in der 'Hausväterliteratur' des 16. bis 18. Jahrhunderts in Deutschland." In *Das Vaterbild in Abendland I: Rom, Frühes Christentum, Mittelalter, Neuzeit, Gegenwart*, ed. Hubertus Tellenbach, 110-23. Stuttgart, Berlin, Cologne, and Mainz: W. Kohlhammer, 1978.

_____. "Die Einheit aller Geschäffte: Tradition und Veränderung des 'Hausmutter'-Bildes in der deutschen Ökonomieliteratur des 18. Jahrhunderts." *Wolfenbüttler Studien zur Aufklärung* 3 (1976): 137-57.

_____. "Die Krise des Herkommens: Zum Wertekanon des Adels im Spiegel alteuropäischer Ökonomieliteratur." In Schulze and Gabel, eds., *Ständische Gesellschaft und soziale Mobilität*, 95-112.

Furet, François. *Interpreting the French Revolution*. Trans. Elborg Forster. Cambridge, New York, and Paris: Cambridge University and Editions de la Maison des Sciences de l'Homme, 1981.

Furet, François, and Mona Ozouf, eds. *A Critical Dictionary of the French Revolution*. Trans. Arthur Goldhammer. Cambridge, MA: Harvard University, 1989.

Gagliardo, John G. *Germany Under the Old Regime, 1600-1790*. Longman History of Germany. London and New York: Longman, 1991.

———. *From Pariah to Patriot: The Changing Image of the German Peasant, 1770-1840*. Lexington: University Press of Kentucky, 1969.
Gassmann, Rita. "Frauen und Gewerkschaften." In *Les Femmes et la Suisse en évolution – Die Frauen im Wandel der Schweiz*, ed. Than-Huyen Ballmer-Cao, 56-70. Aarau, Frankfurt am Main, Salzburg: Sauerländer, 1989.
Gause, Fritz. *Geschichte der Stadt Königsberg in Preußen*. 3 vols. Cologne and Graz: Böhlau, 1965-1971.
Geißler, Rainer. *Die Sozialstruktur Deutschlands: Ein Studienbuch zur gesellschaftlichen Entwicklung im geteilten und vereinten Deutschland.* Bonn: Bundeszentrale für politische Bildung, 1992.
Gesamtverzeichnis des deutschsprachigen Schrifttums 1700-1910, ed. Peter Geils and Willi Gorzny. Microfiche. Munich, New York, London, and Paris: K.G. Saur, 1979-1987.
Gesamtverzeichnis des deutschsprachigen Schrifttums 1911-1965, ed. Peter Geils and Willi Gorzny. 160 vols. Munich, New York, London, and Paris: K.G. Saur, 1976-1981.
Gimpel-Hinteregger, Monika. "Arbeitsplatz Haushalt – Kann die Ehe als materielle Existenzgrundlage dienen?" In *Über Frauenleben Männerleben und Wissenschaft: Österreichische Texte zur Frauenforschung*, ed. Beate Frakele, Elisabeth List, and Gertrude Pauritsch, 240-49. Österreichische Texte zur Gesellschaftskritik, vol. 29. Vienna: Verlag für Gesellschaftskritik, 1987.
Gleixner, Ulrike. *"Das Mensch" und "der Kerl": Die Konstruktion von Geschlecht in Unzuchtsverfahren der frühen Neuzeit (1700-1760)*. Geschichte und Geschlechter, vol. 8. Frankfurt am Main: Campus, 1994.
Göpfert, Herbert G. *Vom Autor zum Leser: Beiträge zur Geschichte des Buchwesens*. Munich: Hanser/VM, 1977.
———. "Bemerkungen über Buchhändler und Buchhandel zur Zeit der Aufklärung in Deutschland." *Wolfenbütteler Studien Zur Aufklärung* 1 (1974): 69-83.
———. "Lesegesellschaften im 18. Jahrhundert." In Kopitzsch, ed., *Aufklärung, Absolutismus und Bürgertum*, 403-11.
Goldfriedrich, Johann. *Geschichte des Deutschen Buchhandels im Auftrag des Börsenvereins der Deutschen Buchhändler*, vol. 3: *Geschichte des Deutschen Buchhandels vom Beginn der klassischen Literaturperiode bis zum Beginn der Fremdherrschaft (1740-1804)*. Leipzig:

Börsenverein der deutschen Buchhändler, 1909; repr. Leipzig: Zentralantiquariat der Deutschen Demokratischen Republik, 1970.

Grab, Walter. *Norddeutsche Jakobiner: Demokratische Bestrebungen zur Zeit der französischen Revolution.* Hamburger Studien zur neueren Geschichte, vol. 8. Frankfurt am Main: Europäische Verlagsanstalt, 1967.

Gray, Marion W. "Educating for Domesticity: Pedagogical Ideals in the Hausmütterliteratur during the Age of Enlightenment." In *Views of Women's Lives in Western Tradition: Frontiers of the Past and the Future,* ed. Frances Richardson Keller, 407-31. Women's Studies, vol. 5. Lewiston, N.Y.: Edwin Mellen, 1990.

_____. "'Modifying the Traditional for the Good of the Whole': Commentary on Statebuilding and Bureaucracy in Nassau, Baden and Saxony in the Early Nineteenth Century." *Central European History* 24 (1991): 293-303.

_____. "Prescriptions for Productive Female Domesticity in a Transitional Era: Germany's Hausmütterliteratur, 1780-1840." *History of European Ideas* 8 (1987): 413-426.

_____. *Prussia in Transition: Society and Politics under the Stein Reform Ministry of 1808.* Transactions of the American Philosophical Society, vol. 76, part 1. Philadelphia: American Philosophical Society, 1986.

Grenz, Dagmar. *Mädchenliteratur: Von den moralisch-belehrenden Schriften im 18. Jahrhundert bis zur Herausbildung der Backfischliteratur im 19. Jahrhundert.* Germanistische Abhandlungen, vol. 52. Stuttgart: Metzler, 1981.

Greven-Aschoff, Barbara. *Die bürgerliche Frauenbewegung in Deutschland 1894-1933.* Kritische Studien zur Geschichtswissenschaft, vol. 46. Göttingen: Vandenhoeck & Ruprecht, 1981.

Grimm, Jakob, and Wilhelm Grimm. *Deutsches Wörterbuch,* ed. Deutsche Akademie der Wissenschaften in cooperation with the Akademie der Wissenschaften zu Göttingen. 16 vols. Leipzig: S. Hirzel, 1854-1956; repr. Munich: Deutscher Taschenbuch Verlag, 1984.

Groebner, Valentin. "Außer Haus: Otto Brunner und die 'alteuropäische Ökonomik.'" in *Geschichte in Wissenschaft und Unterricht* 46 (1995): 69-80.

Groh, Dieter. "Cäserismus, Napoleonismus, Bonapartismus, Führer, Chef, Imperialismus." In *Geschichtliche Grundbegriffe*, vol. 1 (1972): 726-71.
Gruenter, Rainer. "Die Hausmutter in allen ihren Geschäfften." *Euphorion: Zeitschrift für Literaturgeschichte* 57 (1963): 219-26.
———. "Nachtrag zur Hausmutter." *Euphorion: Zeitschrift für Literaturgeschichte* 61 (1967): 155-62.
Güntz, Max. *Handbuch der landwirtschaftlichen Literatur*. 3 vols. Leipzig: Hugo Vogt, 1897-1902; repr. Vaduz, Liechtenstein: Topos, 1977.
Hagemann, Karen. "Ausbildung für die 'weibliche Doppelrolle': Berufswünsche, Berufswahl und Berufschancen von Volksschülerinnen in der Weimarer Republik." In Hausen, ed., *Geschlechterhierarchie und Arbeitsteilung*. 214-36
Hagen, William W. "Seventeenth-Century Crisis in Brandenburg: The Thirty Years' War, the Destabilization of Serfdom, and the Rise of Absolutism." *American Historical Review* 94 (1989): 302-35.
———. "Village Life in East-Elbian Germany and Poland, 1400-1800." In Scott, ed., *The Peasantries of Europe*, 145-90.
———. "Working for the Junker: The Standard of Living of Manorial Laborers in Brandenburg, 1584-1810." *Journal of Modern History* 58 (1986): 143-58.
Hall, A. Rupert. *Philosophers at War. The Quarrel Between Newton and Leibniz*. Cambridge, England: Cambridge University, 1980.
———. *The Revolution in Science 1500-1750*. London: Longman, 1983.
Hall, Catherine. *White, Male and Middle-Class: Explorations in Feminism and History*. Cambridge, England: Polity, 1992.
Hammerstein, Notker. *Aufklärung und katholisches Reich: Untersuchungen zur Universitätsreform und Politik katholischer Territorien des Heiligen Römischen Reichs deutscher Nation im 18. Jahrhundert*. Historische Forschung, vol. 12. Berlin: Duncker & Humblot, 1977.
Hanstein, Adalbert von. *Die Frauen in der Geschichte des deutschen Geisteslebens des 18. und 19. Jahrhunderts*. 2 vols. Leipzig: Freund & Wittig, 1899-1900.
Harding, Sandra, ed. *Feminism and Methodology: Social Science Issues*. Bloomington and Indianapolis: Indiana University Press; Milton Keynes: Open University, 1987.

Harnisch, Hartmut. "Die Bedeutung der kapitalistischen Agrarreform für die Herausbildung des inneren Markts und die industrielle Revolution in den östlichen Provinzen Preußens in der ersten Hälfte des 19. Jahrhunderts." *Jahrbuch für Wirtschaftsgeschichte* 1970, no. 4, 63-82.

———. "Die Gutsherrschaft: Forschungsgeschichte, Entwicklungsgeszusammenhänge und Strukturelemente." *Jahrbuch für die Geschichte des Feudalismus* 9 (1985): 189-240.

———. "Die Landgemeinde der frühen Neuzeit und die Gemeindebauten." *Zeitschrift für Agrargeschichte und Agrarsoziologie* 40 (1992): 168-185.

Harnisch, Hartmut, and Gerhard Heitz, eds. *Deutsche Agrargeschichte des Spätfeudalismus.* Studienbibliothek DDR-Geschichtswissenschaft: Forschungswege, Bilanz, Aufgaben, vol. 6, ed. Akademie der Wissenschaften der DDR, Zentralinstitut für Geschichte (Berlin: Akademie Verlag, 1986).

Harrington, Joel F. "Hausvater and Landesvater: Paternalism and Marriage Reform in Sixteenth-Century Germany." *Central European History* 25 (1992): 57-58.

Hartmann, Heidi I. "The Family as the Locus of Gender, Class, and Political Struggle: The Example of Housework." In Harding, ed., *Feminism and Methodology,* 109-34.

Hartung, Fritz, and Rudolf Vierhaus. *Der Akademiegedanke im 17. und 18. Jahrhundert.* Wolfenbütteler Forschungen, vol. 3. Bremen and Wolfenbüttel: Jacobi, 1977.

Hartwig, Wolfgang. "Verein, Gesellschaft, Geheimgesellschaft, Assoziation, Genossenschaft, Gewerkschaft." In *Geschichtliche Grundbegriffe,* vol. 6 (1990): 789-830.

Hausen, Karin, ed. *Geschlechterhierarchie und Arbeitsteilung: Zur Geschichte ungleicher Erwerbschancen von Männern und Frauen,* Sammlung Vandenhoeck. Göttingen: Vandenhoeck & Ruprecht, 1993.

———. "Die Polarisierung der 'Geschlechtscharaktere' – Eine Spiegelung der Dissozation von Erwerbs- und Familienleben." In *Sozialgeschichte der Neuzeit Europas: Neue Forschungen,* ed. Werner Conze, 363-93. Industrielle Welt, vol. 21. Stuttgart: Ernst Klett, 1976.

———. "Wirtschaften mit der Geschlechterordnung: Ein Essay." In Hausen, ed., *Geschlecherhierarchie und Arbeitsteilung,* 40-67.

Haushofer, Heinz. "Das Problem des Florinus." *Zeitschrift für Agrargeschichte und Agrarsoziologie* 30 (1982): 168-75.
Heindl, Waltraud. *Gehorsame Rebellen: Bürokratie und Beamte in Österreich 1780 bis 1848.* Studien zu Politik und Verwaltung, vol. 36. Vienna, Cologne, and Graz: Böhlau, 1991.
Hendrix, Scott H. "Christianizing Domestic Relations: Women and Marriage in Johann Freder's Dialogus dem Ehestand zu Ehren." *Sixteenth Century Journal* 23 (1992): 251-66.
Henning, Friedrich Wilhelm. "Bestimmungsfaktoren der bäuerlichen Einkommen im 18. Jahrhundert." *Jahrbuch für Wirtschaftsgeschichte* 1970, no. 1, 165-83.
_____. *Dienste und Abgaben der Bauern im 18. Jahrhundert.* Stuttgart: G. Fischer, 1969.
Herrmann, Ulrich. "Aufklärung als pädagogischer Prozeß: Konzeptionen, Hoffnungen und Desillusionierungen im pädagogischen Denken der Spätaufklärung in Deutschland." In Vierhaus, ed., *Aufklärung als Prozeß,* 35-56.
Hertz, Deborah. *Jewish High Society in Old Regime Berlin.* New Haven, CT, and London, England: Yale University, 1988.
Herzig, Arno, Inge Stephan, and Hans G. Winter, eds. *"Sie und nicht wir": Die Französische Revolution und ihre Wirkung auf Norddeutschland und das Reich: Politik und Recht, Literatur und Musik.* Hamburg: Dölling und Galitz, 1989.
Heuer, Uwe-Jens. *Allgemeines Landrecht und Klassenkampf: Die Auseinandersetzung um die Principien des Allgemeinen Landrechts Ende des 18. Jahrhunderts als Ausdruck der Krise des Feudalsystems in Preußen.* Berlin: Deutscher Zentralverlag, 1960.
Higgs, H. "Arthur Young." In *Dictionary of National Biography,* vol. 221 (1909), 1272-78.
Hilger, Dietrich, and Lucian Hölscher. "Industrie, Gewerbe." In *Geschichtliche Grundbegriffe,* vol. 3 (1982), 237-304.
Hinske, Norbert. "Immanuel Kant." In *Neue Deutsche Biographie,* vol. 11 (1977), 110-25.
Hintze, Otto. "Der Beamtenstand." In Hintze, *Regierung und Verwaltung: Gesammelte Abhandlungen zur Staats-, Rechts- und Sozialgeschichte Preußens,* vol. 3 of *Gesammelte Abhandlungen,* ed. Gerhard Oesterreich, 2nd.ed., 66-125. Göttingen: Vandenhoeck & Ruprecht, 1962.

———. "Der österreichische und preußische Beamtenstaat im 17. und 18. Jahrhundert." In Hintze, *Regierung und Verwaltung: Gesammelte Abhandlungen zur Staats-, Rechts- und Sozialgeschichte Preußens*, vol. 3 of *Gesammelte Abhandlungen*, ed. Gerhard Oesterreich, 2nd.ed, 321-58. Göttingen: Vandenhoeck & Ruprecht, 1962.

Hobsbawm, E.J. *The Age of Revolution 1789-1848*. New York: Mentor, 1964.

Hoffman, G.E. "Phillip Ernst Lüders: Ein landwirtschaftlicher Reformer Schleswig-Holsteins im 18. Jahrhundert." *Blätter für Deutsche Landesgeschichte* 89 (1952): 134-52.

Hoffman, Julius. *Die "Hausväterliteratur" und die "Predigten über den christlichen Hausstand": Lehre vom Haus und Bildung für das häusliche Leben im 16., 17., und 18. Jahrhundert*. Göttinger Studien zur Pädagogik, vol. 37. Weinheim: Julius Beltz, 1959.

Hoffmann, Hanns Hubert. "Ludwig Timotheus Spittler (1806 Freiherr von)." In *Biographisches Wörterbuch zur deutschen Geschichte*, ed. Helmut Rössler and Günther Franz; revised by Karl Bosl, et al. Munich: Francke, 1973-1975.

Hoffmann, Jochen. "Jacob Mauvillon." In *Neue Deutsche Biographie*, vol. 16 (1990), 455-57.

Honegger, Claudia. *Die Ordnung der Geschlechter: Die Wissenschaften vom Menschen und das Weib 1750-1850*. Frankfurt: Campus, 1991.

Hübner, Rudolf. *Grundzüge des deutschen Privatrechts*. 2nd ed. Leipzig: Deichert, 1913.

Hull, Isabel V. "'Sexualität' und Bürgerliche Gesellschaft." In Frevert, ed., *Bürgerinnen und Bürger*, 49-66.

———. *Sexuality, State, and Civil Society in Germany, 1700-1815*. Ithaca, NY and London: Cornell University, 1996.

Humphries, Jane. "The Sexual Division of Labor and Social Control: An Interpretation." *Review of Radical Political Economics* 23 (1991): 269-96.

Hungerbühler, Ruth. "Haus und Familienarbeit." In *Les Femmes et la Suisse en évolution – Die Frauen im Wandel der Schweiz*, ed. Than-Huyen Ballmer-Cao. 71-77. Aarau, Frankfurt am Main, Salzburg: Sauerländer, 1989.

Hunt, Lynn. *Politics, Class, and Culture in the French Revolution*. Berkeley, Los Angeles, London: University of California, 1984.

Imhof, Arthur E. *Einführung in die historische Demographie*. Beck'sche Elementarbücher. Munich: C.H. Beck, 1977.
Inama. "Justus Bernhard von Rohr." In *Allgemeine Deutsche Biographie*, vol. 29 (1889), 62-64.
Ingrao, Charles W. *The Hessian Mercenary State: Ideas, Institutions, and Reform Under Frederick II, 1760-1785*. Cambridge, England: Cambridge University, 1987.
———, ed. *State and Society in Early Modern Austria*. West Lafayette, IN: Purdue University, 1994
Inhetveen, Heide. "Die Landfrau und ihr Garten: Zur Soziologie der Hortikultur." *Zeitschrift für Agrargeschichte und Agrarsoziologie* 42 (1994): 41-58.
Jäger, Hans W. "Theodor Gottlieb von Hippel." In *Neue Deutsche Biographie*, vol. 9 (1972), 202-03.
Jarausch, Konrad H. "The German Professions in History and Theory." In *German Professions 1800-1950*, ed. Jarausch and Geoffrey Cocks, 9-24. New York and Oxford: Oxford University, 1990.
Jeismann, Karl-Ernst. *Das preußische Gymnasium in Staat und Gesellschaft: Die Entstehung des Gymnsasiums als Schule des Staats und der Gebildeten, 1787-1817*. Industrielle Welt, vol. 15. Stuttgart: Ernst Klett, 1974.
Jentzsch, Rudolf. *Der deutsch-lateinische Büchermarkt nach den Leipziger Ostermeß-Katalogen von 1740, 1770 und 1800 in seiner Gliederung und Wandlung*. Beiträge zur Kultur- und Universalgeschichte, vol. 22. Leipzig: R. Voigtländer, 1912.
Joeres, Ruth-Ellen B. "'That Girl is an entirely different character!' Yes, but is she a feminist? Observations on Sophie von La Roche's Geschichte des Fräuleins von Sternheim." In Joeres and Maynes, eds., *German Women in the Eighteenth and Nineteenth Centuries*, 137-156.
Joeres, Ruth-Ellen B., and Mary Jo Maynes, eds. *German Women in the Eighteenth and Nineteenth Centuries: A Social and Literary History*. Bloomington: University of Indiana, 1986.
Jones, Garth Stedman. *Languages of Class: Studies in English Working Class History, 1832-1982*. Cambridge, England: Cambridge University, 1983.
Jung, R. "Johann Georg Schlosser." In *Allgemeine Deutsche Biographie*, vol. 31 (1890), 544-47.

Jütte, Robert. *Obrigkeitliche Armenfürsorge in deutschen Reichstädten der frühen Neuzeit.* Cologne: Böhlau, 1984.

Kaak, Heinrich. "Vermittelte, selbsttätige und maternale Herrschaft: Formen gutsherrlicher Durchsetzung, Behauptung und Gestaltung in Quidlitz-Friedland (Lebus/Oberbarnim) im 18. Jahrhundert." In *Konflikt und Kontrolle in Gutsherrschaftsgesellachaften: Über Resistenz- und Herrschaftsverhalten in ländlichen Sozialgebilden der Frühen Neuzeit,* ed. Jan Peters, 54-117. Veröffentlichungen des Max-Planck-Instituts für Geschichte, vol. 120. Göttingen: Vandenhoeck & Ruprecht, 1995.

Kaiser, Andreas. "Preußisches und französisches Recht der Revolutionszeit: Zur Genesis der bürgerlichen Gesellschaft im Spiegel von Allgemeinem Landrecht (1794) und Code Civil (1804)." In *"Sie und nicht wir": Die Französische Revolution und ihre Wirkung auf Norddeutschland und das Reich: Politik und Recht, Literatur und Musik,* ed. Arno Herzig, Inge Stephan, and Hans G. Winter, 743-62. Hamburg: Dölling und Galitz, 1989.

Kaufmann, Claudia. "Die Gleichstellung von Frau und Mann." In *Les Femmes et la Suisse en évolution – Die Frauen im Wandel der Schweiz,* ed. Than-Huyen Ballmer-Cao, 101-106. Aarau, Frankfurt am Main, Salzburg: Sauerländer, 1989.

Kellenbenz, Wolfgang. "Gewerbe und Handel 1500-1648." In Aubin and Zorn, eds., *Handbuch der deutschen Wirtschafts- und Sozialgeschichte,* vol. 1, 414-64.

Kiesel, Helmuth and Paul Münch. *Gesellschaft und Literatur im 18. Jahrhundert: Voraussetzungen und Entstehungen des literarischen Markts in Deutschland.* Beck'sche Elementarbücher. Munich: C.H. Beck, 1977.

Klemm, Volker. "Eine THAER Renaissance? Anmerkungen zum Stand und zur Zukünftigen Thaer-Forschung." *Zeitschrift für Agrargeschichte und Agrarsoziologie* 42 (1994): 1-9.

Klemm, Volker, and Günther Meyer. *Albrecht Daniel Thaer: Pioneer der Landwirthschaftswissenschaften in Deutschland.* Halle: Niemeier, 1966.

Klingenstein, Grete. "Between Mercantilism and Physiocracy: Stages, Modes, and Functions of Economic Theory in the Habsburg Monarchy, 1748-63." In Ingrao, ed., *State and Society in Early Modern Austria,* 181-214.

Klippel, Diethelm. "Von der Aufklärung der Herrscher zur Herrschaft der Aufklärung." In *Aufklärung als Mission: Akzeptanzprobleme und Kommunikationsdefizite/La mission des Lumnières: Accueil réciproque ed difficultées de communication*, ed. Werner Schneiders, 159-74. Das Achtzehnte Jahrhundert, Supplementa, vol. 1; Colloques de Luxembourg, vol. 2. Marburg: Hitzeroth, 1993.

Kluckhohn, Paul. *Die Auffassung der Liebe in der Literatur des 18. Jahrhunderts und in der deutschen Romantik*. Halle: Max Niemeyer, 1922.

Klueting, Harm. "Stadt und Bürgertum: Aspekte einer sozialen Typologisierung der deutschen Städte im 18. Jahrhundert." In *Stadt und Bürger im 18. Jahrhundert*, ed. Gotthardt Frühsorge, Harm Klueting, and Franklin Kopitzsch, 17-39. Das Achtzehnte Jahrhundert, Supplementa, vol. 2. Marburg: Hitzeroth, 1993.

Knemeyer, Franz-Ludwig. "Polizeibegriffe in den Gesetzen des 15. bis 18. Jahrhunderts: Kritische Bemerkungen zur Literatur über die Entwicklung des Polizeibegriffes." *Archiv des öffentlichen Rechts* 92 (1967): 153-80.

Knittler, Herbert. "Between East and West: Lower Austria's Noble Grundherrschaft, 1550-1750." In Ingrao, ed., *State and Society in Early Modern Austria*, 154-80.

Kocka, Jürgen. *Das Bildungsbürgertum im 19. Jahrhundert*. Politischer Einfluß und gesellschaftliche Formation, Part 4. Stuttgart: Klett, 1989.

⎯⎯⎯. "Stand – Klasse – Organization: Strukturen sozialer Ungleichheit in Deutschland vom späten bis zum frühen 20. Jahrhundert im Aufriß." In *Klassen in der europäischen Sozialgeschichte*, ed. Hans-Ulrich Wehler. Kleine Vandenhoeck Reihe, vol. 1456. Göttingen: Vandenhoeck & Ruprecht, 1979.

Kohnen, Joseph. "Aspekte der Frankreich-Rezeption in Königsberg." *Aufklärung als Mission: Akzeptanzprobleme und Kommunikationsdefizite/La mission des Lumnières: Accueil réciproque ed difficultées de communication*, ed. Werner Schneiders. 279-94. Das Achtzehnte Jahrhundert, Supplementa, vol. 1; Colloques de Luxembourg, vol. 2. Marburg: Hitzeroth, 1993.

⎯⎯⎯. *Theodor Gottlieb von Hippel 1741-1796: L'homme et l'oeuvre*. 2 vols. Publications Universitaires Européenes: Series I, Langue et litterature allemandes, vol. 727. Bern, Frankfurt am Main, New York, Nancy: Peter Lang, 1983.

———. *Theodor Gottlieb von Hippel: Eine zentrale Persönlichkeit der Königsberger Geistesgeschichte: Biographie und Bibliographie.* Lüneburg: Verlag Nordostdeutsches Kulturwerk, 1987.

König, Helmut. *Zur Geschichte der Nationalerziehung in Deutschland im letzten Drittel des 18. Jahrhunderts.* Monumenta Paedogogica, vol. 1. Berlin: Akademie, 1960.

Koonz, Claudia. *Mothers in the Fatherland: Women, the Family, and Nazi Policy.* New York: St. Martin's, 1987.

Kopitzsch, Franklin. "Einleitung: Die Sozialgeschichte der deutschen Aufklärung als Forschungsaufgabe." In Kopitzsch, ed., *Aufklärung, Absolutismus, und Bürgertum,* 1-167.

———. "Die Hamburgische Gesellschaft zur Beförderung der Künste und nützlichen Gewerbe (Patriotische Gesellschaft von 1765) im Zeitalter der Aufklärung: Ein Überblick." In Vierhaus, ed., *Deutsche patriotische und gemeinnützige Gesellschaften,* 71-118.

———, ed. *Aufklärung, Absolutismus, und Bürgertum in Deutschland: Zwölf Aufsätze.* Nymphenburger Texte zur Wissenschaft, vol. 24. Munich: Nymphenburger Verlagsbuchhandlung, 1976.

Körte, Wilhelm. *Albrecht Thaer: Sein Leben und Wirken, als Arzt und Landwirth.* Leipzig: Brockhaus, 1839; repr. Walluf: Sändig, 1967.

Koselleck, Reinhart. *Futures Past: On the Semantics of Historical Time.* Trans. Keith Tribe. Studies in Contemporary German Social Thought. Cambridge, MA, and London: MIT, 1979.

———. *Preußen zwischen Reform und Revolution: Allgemeines Landrecht, Verwaltung und soziale Bewegung von 1791 bis 1848.* Industrielle Welt, vol. 7. Stuttgart: Ernst Klett, 1967.

———. "Sprachwandel und sozialer Wandel im ausgehenden Ancien Régime." In *Deutschlands kulturelle Entfaltung: Die Neubestimmung des Menschen,* ed. Bernhard Fabian, Wilhelm Schmidt-Biggemann, and Rudolf Vierhaus, 15-30. Studien zum achtzehnten Jahrhundert, vol. 2, part 3. Munich: Kraus, 1980.

———. "Volk, Nation, Nationalismus, Masse." In *Geschichtliche Grundbegriffe.* vol. 7 (1992), 141-431.

Kraul, Maragret. "Normierung und Emanzipation: Die Berufung auf den Geschlechtskarakter bei der Institutionalisierung der höheren

Mädchenbildung." In *Bildung, Staat, Gesellschaft im 19. Jahrhundert: Mobilisierung und Disziplinierung*, ed. Karl-Ernst Jeismann, vol. 2, 219-31. Nassauer Gespräche der Freiherr-vom-Stein Gesellschaft. Stuttgart: Franz Steiner, 1989.

Krauth, Wolf-Hagen. *Wirtschaftsstruktur und Semantik: Wissenssoziologische Studien zum wirtschaftlichen Denken in Deutschland zwischen dem 13. und 17. Jahrhundert.* Berlin: Duncker und Humblot, 1984.

Kriedte, Peter. *Spätfeudalismus und Handelskapital: Grundlinien der europäischen Wirtschaftsgeschichte vom 16. bis zum Ausgang des 18. Jahrhunderts.* Kleine Vandenhoeck Reihe, vol. 1459. Göttingen: Vandenhoeck & Ruprecht, 1980.

Kriedte, Peter, Hans Medick, and Jürgen Schlumbohm. *Industrialization before Industrialization: Rural Industry in the Genesis of Capitalism.* Trans. Beate Schempp. Studies in Modern Capitalism. Cambridge, London, New York: Cambridge University; Paris: Editions de la Maison des Sciences de l'Homme, 1981.

Krüger, Sabine. "Zum Verständnis der Oeconomica Konrads von Megenberg: Griechische Ursprünge der spätmittelalterlichen Lehre vom Hause." *Deutsches Archiv für Erforschung des Mittelalters* 20 (1964): 475-561.

Krull, Edith. *Das Wirken der Frau im frühen deutschen Zeitschriftenwesen.* Charlottenburg: Rudolf Lenz, 1939.

Kuhn, Annette. "Das Geschlecht – eine Historische Kategorie?" In *Frauen in der Geschichte IV: "wissen heißt leben ... ." Beiträge zur Bildungsgeschichte von Frauen im 18. und 19. Jahrhundert*, ed. Ilse Brehmer, Juliane Jacobi-Dittrich, Elke Kleinau, and Annette Kuhn, 34-50. Geschichtsdidaktik: Studien, Materialien, ed. Klaus Bergmann, et al, vol. 18. Düsseldorf: Schwann, 1983.

Küther, Carsten. *Räuber und Gauner in Deutschland: Bandenwesen im 18. und frühen 19. Jahrhundert.* Kritische Studien zur Geschichtswissenschaft, vol. 20. Göttingen: Vandenhoeck & Ruprecht, 1976.

La Vopa, Anthony J. *Prussian Schoolteachers: Profession and Office, 1763-1848.* Chapel Hill: University of North Carolina, 1980.

―――. "The Revolutionary Moment: Fichte and the French Revolution." *Central European History* 22 (1989): 130-50.

Lange, Hermann. *Schulaufbau und Schulverfassung der frühen Neuzeit: Zur Entstehung und Problematik des modernen Schulwesens.* Pädagogische Studien, vol. 12. Weinheim and Berlin: Beltz, 1967.
Lee, Loyd E. "Baden Between Revolutions: State-Building and Citizenship, 1800-1848." *Central European History* 24 (1991): 258-67.
⸺. *The Politics of Harmony: Civil Service, Liberalism, and Social Reform in Baden, 1800-1850.* Newark: University of Delaware, 1980.
Leisewitz, C. "Albrecht Daniel Theodor Thaer." In *Allgemeine Deutsche Biographie,* vol. 37 (1894), 636-41.
⸺. "Otto von Münchhausen." In *Allgemeine deutsche Biographie,* vol. 23 (1886), 7-8.
⸺. "W.A. Kreyßig." In *Allgemeine Deutsche Biographie,* vol. 17 (1883), 158-160.
Lenthe, Gebhard von, and Hans Mehrenholtz. *Stammtafeln der Familie von Münchhausen.* Schaumburger Studien, vol. 36. Rinteln: C. Bösendahl, 1976.
Lesemann, Silke. *Arbeit, Ehre, Geschlechterbeziehungen: Zur sozialen und wirtschaftlichen Stellung von Frauen im frühneuzeitlichen Hildesheim.* Schriftenreihe des Stadtarchivs und der Stadtbibliothek Hildesheim, vol. 23. Hildesheim: Bernward, 1994.
Liebel, Helen P. *Enlightened Bureaucracy versus Enlightened Despotism in Baden, 1750-1792.* Transactions of the American Philosophical Society, New Series, vol. 55, no. 5. Philadelphia: American Philosophical Society, 1965.
Lies-Schindler, Ingrid. "Die Ehe als Gottgewollter Stand: Die Bedeutung der Ehe- und Hausstandslehre Martin Luthers für die Entwicklung bürgerlicher Familienleitbilder vom 16. bis 18. Jahrhundert." In *Martin Luther, 1483-1983: Ringvorlesung der Philosophischen Fakultät Sommersemester 1983,* 203-41. Saarbrücken: Universität des Saarlandes, 1983.
Lindemann, Mary. *Patriots and Paupers: Hamburg 1712-1830.* New York and Oxford: Oxford University, 1990.
Lindenfeld, David F. *The Practical Imagination: The German Sciences of the State in the Nineteenth Century.* Chicago and London: University of Chicago, 1997.
Link, Christopher. "Rechtswissenschaft." In Vierhaus, ed., *Wissenschaften im Zeitalter der Aufklärung,* 120-42.

Löbe. "Friedrich Karl Gustav Gericke." In *Allgemeine Deutsche Biographie*, vol. 8 (1878), 785.
Lütge, Friedrich. *Deutsche Sozial- und Wirtschaftsgeschichte: Ein Überblick*. 3rd ed. Enzyklopädie der Rechts- und Staatswissenschaft. Berlin and Heidelberg: Springer, 1966.
———. *Geschichte der deutschen Agrarverfassung vom frühen Mittelalter bis zum 19. Jahrhundert*. 2nd ed. Deutsche Agrargeschichte, vol. 3. Stuttgart: Eugen Ulmer, 1967.
Maas, Barbara. "Idealisierung und Domestikation: Das bürgerliche Frauenbild in der frühviktorianischen Publizistik." In *Frauen in der Geschichte III: Fachwissenschaftliche und fachdidaktische Beiträge zur Geschichte der Weiblichkeit vom frühen Mittelalter bis zur Gegenwart mit geeigneten Materialen für den Unterricht*, ed. Annette Kuhn and Jörn Rüsen, 139-66. Geschichtsdidaktik: Studien, Materialien, vol. 13. Düsseldorf: Schwann, 1983.
Mager, Wolfgang. "Republik." In *Geschichtliche Grundbegriffe*. vol. 5 (1984), 571-618.
Mahrer, Isabell. "Die Frau im Erwerbsleben." *Les Femmes et la Suisse en évolution – Die Frauen im Wandel der Schweiz*, ed. Than-Huyen Ballmer-Cao, 57-65. Aarau, Frankfurt am Main, Salzburg: Sauerländer, 1989.
Maier, Friederike. "The Labor Market for Women and Employment Perspectives in the Aftermath of German Unification." *Cambridge Journal of Economics* 17 (1993): 281-94.
Martens, Wolfgang. *Die Botschaft der Tugend: Die Aufklärung im Spiegel der deutschen Moralischen Wochenschriften*. Stuttgart: Metzler, 1971.
Mayhew, Alan. *Rural Settlement and Farming in Germany*. New York: Barnes and Noble, 1973.
Maynes, Mary Jo. *Schooling for the People: Comparative Local Studies of Schooling History in France and Germany, 1750-1850*. New York and London: Holmes & Meier, 1985.
Medick, Hans, and David Sabean. "Emotionen und materielle Interessen in Familie und Verwandtschaft: Überlegungen zu neuen Wegen und Bereichen einer historischen und sozialanthropologischen Familienforschung." In *Emotionen und Materielle Interessen: Sozialanthropologische und historische Beiträge zur Familienforschung*, ed. Hans Medick and David Sabean, 27-54. Göttingen: Vandenhoeck & Ruprecht, 1984.

Meikle, Scott. "Aristotle and Exchange Value." In *A Companion to Aristotle's "Politics,"* ed. David Keyt and Fred D. Miller, 156-81. Oxford and Cambridge, MA: Blackwell, 1991.
———. "Aristotle and the Political Economy of the Polis." *Journal of Hellenistic Studies* 99 (1979): 57-73.
———. *Aristotle's Economic Thought*. Oxford: Clarendon; 1995
Merchant, Carolyn. *The Death of Nature: Women, Ecology and the Scientific Revolution*. New York: Harper Collins, 1989.
Milkowski, Fritz. "Christian Jakob Kraus: Eine längst fällige Korrektur zur Geschichte der Volkswirthschaftlehre." *Schmollers Jahrbuch für Wirtschafts- und Sozialwissenschaften* 88 (1968): 257-97.
Mittenzwei, Ingrid. "Die Agrarfrage und der Kameralismus." In Harnisch and Heitz, eds., *Deutsche Agrargeschichte des Spätfeudalismus*, 146-85.
Mitterauer, Michael. "Gesindedienst und Jugendphase im europäischen Vergleich." *Geschichte und Gesellschaft* 11 (1985): 177-204.
———. "Vorindustrielle Familienformen: Zur Funktionsentlastung des 'ganzen' Hauses im 17. und 18. Jahrhunderts." In *Grundtypen alteuropäischen Sozialformen: Haus und Gemeinde in vorindustriellen Gesellschaften*, ed. Mitterauer, 35-97. Kultur und Gesellschaft: Neue historische Forschungen, vol. 5. Stuttgart: Fromann-Holzboog, 1979.
Mitterauer, Michael, and Reinhard Sieder. *Vom Patriarchat zur Partnerschaft: Zum Strukturwandel der Familie*. 2nd ed. Beck'sche Schwarze Reihe, vol. 158. Munich: C.H. Beck, 1980.
Moeller, Robert G. *Protecting Motherhood: Women and the Family in the Politics of Postwar West Germany*. Berkeley: University of California, 1993.
Mohrmann, Ruth-E. "Die Stellung der Frau im bäuerlichen Ehe- und Erbrecht: Ein historisch-volkskundlicher Vergleich." *Zeitschrift für Agrargeschichte und Agrarsoziologie* 40 (1992): 248-58.
Moore, Cornelia Niekus. *The Maiden's Mirror: Reading Material for German Girls in the Sixteenth and Seventeenth Centuries*. Wolfenbütteler Forschungen, vol. 36. Wiesbaden: Otto Harrassowitz, 1987.
Mooser, Josef. *Ländliche Klassengesellschaft 1770-1848: Bauern und Unterschichten, Landwirtschaft und Gewerbe im östlichen Westfalen.*

Kritische Studien zur Geschichtswissenschaft, vol. 64. Göttingen: Vandenhoeck & Ruprecht, 1984.

Motteck, Hans. *Wirtschaftsgeschichte Deutschlands: Ein Grundriss.* 5th ed. Berlin: Deutscher Verlag der Wissenschaften, 1974.

Müller, Hans-Heinrich. "Der agrarische Fortschritt und die Bauern in Brandenburg vor den Reformen von 1807." *Zeitschrift für Geschichtswissenschaft* 12 (1964): 636-48.

———. "Bauern, Pächter und Adel im alten Preußen." *Jahrbuch für Wirtschaftsgeschichte* 1966, no. 1, 259-277.

Münch, Paul. *Ordnung, Fleiß und Sparsamkeit: Texte und Dokumente zur Entstehung der "bürgerlichen Tugenden."* DTV Dokumente, vol. 2940. Munich: Deutscher Taschenbuch Verlag, 1984.

Natali, Carlo. "Aristote et la chrématistique." In *Aristotles' "Politik": Akten des XI. Symposium Aristotelicum, Friedrichshafen/Bodensee, 25.8.-3.9. 1987,* ed. Günther Patzig, 296-324. Göttingen: Vandenhoeck & Ruprecht, 1990.

Netting, Robert McC. *Balancing on an Alp: Ecological Change and Continuity in a Swiss Mountain Community.* Cambridge, England: Cambridge University, 1981.

Neue Deutsche Biographie, ed. Historische Kommission bei der Bayerischen Akademie der Wissenschaften. 18 vols. Berlin: Duncker und Humblot, 1953-1997.

O'Brien, Mary. *The Politics of Reproduction.* Boston: Routledge & Kegan Paul, 1981.

Oakley, Anne. *Woman's Work: The Housewife, Past and Present.* New York: Random House, 1976.

Oexle, Otto Gerhard. "Die funktionale Dreiteilung als Deutungsschema der sozialen Wirklichkeit in der ständischen Gesellschaft des Mittelalters." In Schulze and Gabel, eds., *Ständische Gesellschaft und soziale Mobilität,* 19-51.

———. "Haus und Ökonomie im frühen Mittelalter." In *Person und Gemeinschaft im Mittelalter,* ed. Gerd Althoff et al. Sigmaringen: Jan Thorbecke, 1988.

Ogilvie, Sheilagh. "Germany and the Seventeenth-Century Crisis." In *The General Crisis of the Seventeenth Century,* 2nd ed., ed. Geoffrey Parker and Leslie M. Smith, 57-86. London and New York: Routledge, 1997.

Okin, Susan B. *Justice, Gender and the Family*. New York: Basic Books, 1989.
Opitz, Claudia. "Neue Wege der Sozialgeschichte? Ein Kritischer Blick auf Otto Brunners Konzept des Ganzen Hauses." In *Geschichte und Gesellschaft* 20 (1994): 88-98.
Ortner, Sherry B., and Harriet Whitehead. *Sexual Meanings: The Cultural Construction of Gender and Sexuality*. New York: Cambridge University, 1981.
Ozment, Steven. *When Fathers Ruled: Family Life in Reformation Europe*. Cambridge, MA, and London: Harvard University, 1983.
Paul, Hermann. *Deutsches Wörterbuch*, ed. Werner Betz. 6th ed. Tübingen: Max Niemeyer, 1966.
Peterken, Paul. *Gesellschaftliche und fiktionale Identität: Eine Studie zu Theodor Gottlieb von Hippels Roman "Lebensläufe nach aufsteigender Linie nebst Beilagen A, B, C."* Stuttgarter Arbeiten zur Germanistik, no. 106. Stuttgart: Akademischer Verlag Hans-Dieter Heinz, 1981.
Peters, Jan. "Gutsherrschaftgeschichte in historisch-anthropologischer Perspektive." In *Gutsherrschaft als soziales Modell: Vergleichende Betrachtungen zur Funktionsweise frühneuzeitlicher Agrargesellschaften*, ed. Peters, Historische Zeitschrift Supplement, 1995, 2-21.
_____. "Ostelbische Landarmut – sozialökonomisches über landlose und landarme Agrarproduzenten im Spätfeudalismus." In Harnisch and Heitz, eds., *Deutsche Agrargeschichte des Spätfeudalismus*, 213-44.
_____. "Ostelbische Landarmut: Statistisches über landlose und landarme Agrarproduzenten im Spätfeudalismus," *Jahrbuch für Wirtschaftsgeschichte* 1970, no. 1, 97-126.
Plaul, Hainer. "The Rural Proletariat: The Everyday Life of Rural Labourers in the Magdeburg Region, 1830-1880." In *The German Peasantry: Conflict and Community in Rural Society from the Eighteenth to the Twentieth Centuries*, ed. Richard J. Evans and W.R. Lee. New York: St. Martin's, 1986.
Prokop, Ulrike. *Die Illusion vom großen Paar*, vol. 1: *Weibliche Lebensentwürfe im deutschen Bildungsbürgertum 1750-1770* Psychoanalytische Studien zur Kultur. Frankfurt am Main: Fischer Taschenbuch Verlag, 1991.

Prüsener, Marlies. "Lesegesellschaften im achtzehnten Jahrhundert: Ein Beitrag zur Lesergeschichte" *Archiv für Geschichte des Buchwesens*, special issue, vol. 13 (1972), 370-594. Frankfurt am Main: Buchhandler-Vereinigung, 1972.

Puhlmann, Angelika. *Mädchenerziehung in der bürgerlichen Gesellschaft: Klassenspezifische Unterschiede in der Vergesellschaftung der Mädchenerziehung*. 2nd ed. Pahl-Rugenstein-Hochschulschriften, Gesellschafts- und Naturwissenschaften 13: Series Studien zu Bildung und Erziehung. Cologne: Pahl-Rugenstein, 1980.

Pujol, Michèle. *Feminism and Anti-Feminism in Early Economic Thought*. Hants: Edgar Elgar, 1992.

Quataert, Jean. *Reluctant Feminist in German Social Democracy 1885-1917*. Princeton, NJ: Princeton University, 1979.

Rabuzzi, Daniel A. "Women as Merchants in Eighteenth-Century Northern Germany: The Case of Stralsund, 1750-1830." *Central European History* 28 (1995): 435-56.

Rall, Hans. "Wiguläus Xaverius Aloysius Freiherr von Kreittmayr." In *Neue Deutsche Biographie*, vol. 12 (1980), 741-43.

Rasch, William. "*Mensch, Bürger, Weib*: Gender and the Limitations of Late 18th-Century Neohumanist Discourse." *The German Quarterly* 66 (1993): 20-33.

Rebel, Hermann. "Peasantries under the Austrian Empire, 1300-1800." In Tom Scott, ed., *Peasantries of Europe*, 191-226.

———. "Reimagining the Oikos: Austrian Cameralism in its Social Formation." In *Golden Ages, Dark Ages: Imagining the Past in Anthropology and History*, ed. Jay O'Brien and William Roseberry, 61-62. Berkeley, Los Angeles, Oxford: University of California, 1991.

Reichardt, Rolf, and Eberhard Schmitt, eds. *Handbuch politisch-sozialer Grundbegriffe in Frankreich 1680-1820*. 35 vols. Vol. 10: Ancien Régime. Munich: R. Oldenbourg, 1985-1998.

Reif, Heinz. *Westfälischer Adel: Vom Herschaftsstand zur regionalen Elite*. Kritische Studien zur Geschichtswissenschaft, vol. 35. Göttingen: Vandenhoeck & Ruprecht, 1979.

Richarz, Irmintraut. *Herrschaftliche Haushalte in vorindustrieller Zeit im Weserraum*. Beiträge zur Ökonomie von Haushalt und Verbrauch, vol. 6. Berlin: Duncker & Humblot, 1971.

———. *Oikos, Haus und Haushalt: Ursprung und Geschichte der Haushaltsökonomik*. Vandenhoeck & Ruprecht, 1991.

Riedel, Manfred. "Bürger, Staatsbürger, Bürgertum." In *Geschichtliche Grundbegriffe*, vol. 1 (1972), 672-725.

———. "Gesellschaft, bürgerliche." In *Geschichtliche Grundbegriffe*, vol. 2 (1975), 719-800.

———. "Gesellschaft, Gemeinschaft." In *Geschichtliche Grundbegriffe*, vol. 2 (1975), 801-62.

Riehl, Wilhelm Heinrich. *The Natural History of the German People*. Ed. and trans. David J. Diephouse. Studies in German Thought and History, vol. 13. Lewiston, NY: Edwin Mellen, 1990.

Rigler, Edith. *Frauenleitbild und Frauenarbeit in Österreich vom ausgehenden 19. Jahrhundert bis zum Zweiten Weltkrieg*. Sozial- und wirtschaftshistorische Studien, vol. 8. Munich: R. Oldenbourg, 1976.

Robisheaux, Thomas. "The Peasantries of Western Germany, 1300-1750. In Tom Scott, *Peasantries of Europe*, 111-44.

———. *Rural Society and the Search for Order in Early Modern Germany*. Cambridge, England: Cambridge University, 1989.

Rösener, Werner. *Bauern im Mittelalter*. Munich: R. Oldenbourg, 1991.

Rössler, Dietrich. "Pfarrhaus und Medizin." In *Das evangelische Pfarrhaus: Eine Kultur- und Sozialgeschichte*, ed. Martin Greiffenhagen, 243-246. Stuttgart: Kreuz, 1984.

Roper, Lyndal. *The Holy Household: Women and Morals in Reformation Augsburg*. Oxford Studies in Social History. Oxford: Oxford University, 1989.

Roscher, Wilhelm. *Geschichte der National-Oekonomie in Deutschland*. Geschichte der Wissenschaften in Deutschland: Neue Zeit, vol. 14. Munich: R. Oldenbourg, 1874; repr. New York and London: Johnson Reprint., 1965.

Rosenbaum, Heidi. *Formen der Familie: Untersuchungen zum Zusammenhang von Familienverhältnissen, Sozialstruktur und sozialem Wandel in der deutschen Gesellschaft des 19. Jahrhunderts*. Suhrkamp Taschenbuch Wissenschaft, vol. 374. Frankfurt am Main: Suhrkamp, 1982.

Rosenberg, Dorothy J. "Shock Therapy: GDR Women in Transition from a Socialist Welfare State to a Social Market Economy." *Signs: Journal of Women in Culture and Society* 17 (1991): 129-51.

Rosenberg, Hans. *Bureaucracy, Aristocracy and Autocracy: The Prussian Experience, 1660-1815*. Harvard Historical Monographs, vol. 34. Cambridge, MA: Harvard University, 1958.

_____. "The Rise of the Junkers in Brandenburg-Prussia, 1410-1653." *American Historical Review* 49 (1943-1944): 228-39.

Rürup, Reinhard. *Deutschland im 19. Jahrhundert 1815-1871*. Deutsche Geschichte, vol. 8. Göttingen: Vandenhoeck & Ruprecht, 1984.

Saalfeld, Dietrich. "Ländliche Bevölkerung und Landwirtschaft Deutschlands am Vorabend der Französischen Revolution." *Zeitschrift für Agrargeschichte und Agrarsoziologie* 37 (1989): 102-10.

Sabean, David Warren. *Property, Production, and Family in Neckarhausen, 1700-1870*. Cambridge Studies in Social and Cultural Anthropology, vol. 73. Cambridge, New York, Melbourne: Cambridge University, 1990.

Sachße, Christoph, and Florian Tennstedt. *Geschichte der Armenfürsorge in Deutschland*. Stuttgart: W. Kohlhammer, 1980.

Scheel, Heinrich. *Die Begegnung deutscher Aufklärer mit der Revolution*. Sitzungsberichte des Plenums und der Klassen der Akademie der Wissenschaften der DDR, 1972, no. 7. Berlin: Akademie Verlag, 1973.

_____. *Süddeutsche Jakobiner: Klassenkämpfe und republikanische Bestrebung im deutschen Süden Ende des 18. Jahrhunderts*. 2nd ed. Schriften des Zentralinstituts für Geschichte, Series I: Allgemeine und deutsche Geschichte, vol. 13. Berlin: Akademie, 1962.

Schenda, Rudolf. *Volk ohne Buch: Studien zur Sozialgeschichte der populären Lesestoffe 1770-1910*. Studien zur Philosophie und Literatur des neunzehnten Jahrhunderts, vol. 5. Frankfurt am Main: Klostermann, 1970.

Schilling, Renate. *Schwedisch-Pommern um 1700: Studien zur Agrarstruktur eines Territoriums extremer Gutsherrschaft, untersucht auf der Grundlage des schwedischen Matrikelwerkes 1692-1698*. Abhandlung zur Handels- und Sozialgeschichte, vol. 27. Weimar: Hermann Böhlaus Nachfolger, 1989.

Schindler, Norbert, and Wolfgang Bonß. "Praktische Aufklärung – Ökonomische Sozietäten in Süddeutschland und Österreich im 18. Jahrhundert." In Vierhaus, ed., *Deutsche patriotische und gemeinnützige Gesellschaften*, 255-353.

Schissler, Hanna. *Preußische Agrargesellschaft im Wandel: Wirtschaftliche, gesellschaftliche und politische Transformationsprozesse von 1763 bis 1847*. Kritische Studien zur Geschichtswissenschaft, vol. 33. Göttingen: Vandenhoeck & Ruprecht, 1978.

Schlosser, Hans. "Der Gesetzgeber Kreittmayr und die Aufklärung in Kurbayern." In *Wigläus Xaver Aloys Freiherr von Kreittmayr: Ein Leben für Recht, Staat und Politik, Festschrift zum 200. Todestag*, ed. Richard Bauer and Hans Schlosser, 3-36. Munich: Beck, 1991.

Schlumbohm, Jürgen. *Freiheit – die Anfänge der bürgerlichen Emanzipationsbewegung in Deutschland im Spiegel ihres Leitworts (ca. 1760-ca. 1800)*. Geschichte und Gesellschaft: Bochumer Historische Studien, vol. 12. Düsseldorf: Schwann, 1975.

———. "'Traditional' Collectivity and 'Modern' Individuality: Some Questions and Suggestions for the Historical Study of Socialization: The Examples of the German Lower and Upper Bourgeosies around 1800." *Social History* 5 (1980): 74-89.

Schmidlechner, Karin Maria. "Frauen in Österreich seit 1945." In *Über Frauenleben, Männerleben und Wissenschaft: Österreichische Texte zur Frauenforschung*, ed. Beate Frakele, Elisabeth List, and Gertrude Pauritsch, 213-24. Österreichische Texte zur Gesellschaftskritik, vol. 29. Vienna: Verlag für Gesellschaftskritik, 1987.

Schmidlin, Heinrich. *Arbeit und Stellung der Frau in der Landgutswirtschaft der Hausväter*. Heidelberg: Winter, 1941.

Schneiders, Werner. *Aufklärung und Vorurteilskritik: Studien zur Geschichte der Vorurteilstheorie*. Forschungen und Materialien zur deutschen Aufklärung, Abteilung II: Monographien, vol. 2. Stuttgart-Bad Cannstatt: Fromann-Holzboog, 1983.

———. *Die wahre Aufklärung: Zum Selbstverständnis der deutschen Aufklärung*. Freiburg: Alber, 1974.

Schröder, Richard. *Geschichte des ehelichen Güterrechts in Deutschland.* 2 vols., 4 sections. Stettin: Saunier, 1967.

Schröder-Lembke, Gertrud. "Englische Einflüsse auf die deutsche Gutswirtschaft im 18. Jahrhundert." *Zeitschrift für Agrargeschichte und Agrarsoziologie* 12 (1964): 29-36.

———. "Oeconomische Gesellschaften im 18. Jahrhundert." *Zeitschrift für Agrargeschichte und Agrarsoziologie* 38 (1990): 15-23.

———. "Protestantische Pastoren als Landwirtschaftsreformer." *Zeitschrift für Agrargeschichte und Agrarsoziologie* 27 (1979): 94-104.

Schubert, Werner. *Französisches Recht in Deutschland zu Beginn des 19. Jahrhunderts: Zivilrecht, Gerichtsverfassungsrecht und Zivilprozeßrecht.* Forschungen zur neueren Privatrechtsgeschichte, vol. 24. Cologne and Vienna: Böhlau, 1977.

Schulze, Winfried. "Vom Gemeinnutz zum Eigennutz: Über den Normenwandel in der ständischen Gesellschaft der frühen Neuzeit." *Historische Zeitschrift* 243 (1986): 591-626.

Schulze, Winfried, and Helmut Gabel, eds. *Ständische Gesellschaft und soziale Mobilität.* Schriften des Historischen Kollegs: Kolloquien, vol. 12. Munich: R. Oldenbourg, 1988.

Schumann, Sabine. "Das 'lesende Frauenzimmer': Frauenzeitschriften im 18. Jahrhundert." In *Die Frau von der Reformation zur Romantik: Die Situation der Frau vor dem Hintergrund der Literatur- und Sozialgeschichte*, ed. Barbara Becker-Cantarino, 138-69. 2nd ed. Modern German Studies, vol. 7. Bonn: Bouvier, 1985.

Schumpeter, Joseph. *History of Economic Analysis.* New York: Oxford University, 1954.

Schuurmans, Frank. "Economic Liberalization, Honour and Perfectibility: Karl Sigmund Altenstein and the Spiritualization of Liberalism." *German History* 16 (1998) 165-84.

Schuurmans, Frank T.W.C. "State, Society, and the Market: Karl Sigmund Altenstein and the Language of Reform 1770-1807." Ph.D. diss. University of Wisconsin-Madison, 1995.

Schwab, Dieter. "Eheschliessungsrecht und nichteheliche Lebensgemeinschaft – eine rechtsgeschichtliche Skizze." *Zeitschrift für das gesamte Familienrecht* 28 (1981): 1151-56.

_____. "Familie." In *Geschichtliche Grundbegriffe*, vol. 2 (1975), 253-302.

_____. *Grundlagen und Gestalt der staatlichen Ehegesetzgebung in der Neuzeit bis zu Beginn des 19. Jahrhunderts.* Schriften zum deutschen und europäischen Zivil-, Handels- und Prozessrecht, 45. Bielefeld: Ernst und Werner Gieseking, 1967.

Schwartz, Paul. *Der Erste Kulturkampf in Preußen um Kirche und Schule (1788-1798).* Monumenta Germaniae Paedagogica, vol. 58. Berlin: Weidmann, 1925.

Scott, Joan Wallach. "Gender: A Useful Category of Historical Analysis." In Joan Scott, ed., *Gender and the Politics of History*, 28-50.

_____. *Gender and the Politics of History.* Gender and Culture. New York: Columbia University, 1988.

———. "On Language, Gender, and Working-Class History." In Joan Scott, ed., *Gender and the Politics of History*, 53-67.

Scott, Tom, ed. *The Peasantries of Europe From the Fourteenth to the Eighteenth Centuries*. London and New York: Longman, 1998.

Secomb, Wally. "The Housewife and Her Labor under Capitalism." *New Left Review* 83 (1974): 3-24.

Seiz, Janet. "Feminism and the History of Economic Thought." *History of Political Economy* 25 (1993): 185-201.

Sellner, Timothy F. "Introduction." In Theodor Gottlieb von Hippel, *On Improving the Status of Women*. Trans. and ed. Sellner. Detroit: Wayne State University, 1979.

Sewell, William H. *Work and Revolution in France: The Language of Labor from the Old Regime to 1848*. Cambridge, England: Cambridge University, 1980.

Shaffer, John W. *Family and Farm: Agrarian Change and Household Organization in the Loire Valley, 1500-1900*. SUNY Series on European Social History. Albany: State University of New York, 1982.

Sheehan, James J. *German History 1770-1866*. Oxford History of Modern Europe. Oxford: Clarendon, 1989.

Simmel, Monika. *Erziehung zum Weibe: Mädchenbildung im 19. Jahrhundert*. Campus Paperbacks: Pädagogik. Frankfurt am Main: Campus, 1980.

Simons, Walter. *Albrecht Thaer: Nach amtlichen und privaten Dokumentation aus einer großen Zeit*. Berlin: P. Parey, 1929.

Smith, Bonnie. *Ladies of the Leisure Class: The Bourgeoises of Northern France in the Nineteenth Century*. Princeton: Princeton University, 1981.

Spittler, Gerd. "Abstraktes Wissen als Herschaftsbasis: Zur Entstehungsgeschichte bürokratisicher Herrschaft im Bauernstaat Preußen." *Kölner Zeitschrift für Soziologie und Sozialpsychologie* 32 (1980): 574-604.

Stavenhagen, Gerhard. *Geschichte der Wirtschaftstheorie*. Grundriss der Sozialwissenschaft, vol. 2. Göttingen, Vandenhoeck & Ruprecht, 1969.

Stock, Karl F., Rudolf Heilinger, and Margelene Stock. "Matthias Eigl." In *Personalbibliographien österreichischer Persönlichkeiten*. Bibliographie österreichischer Bibliographien,

Sammelbibliographien, und Nachschlagwerke, section 3, vol. 3, 976. Graz: Stock und Stock, 1988.

Stolleis, Michael. *Geschichte des öffentlichen Rechts in Deutschland.* 3 vols. Munich: C.H. Beck, 1988-1992.

Strassmann, Diana. "The Stories of Economics and the Power of the Storyteller." *History of Political Economy* 25 (1993): 147-165.

Strauss, Gerald. *Luther's House of Learning: Indoctrination of the Young in the German Reformation.* Baltimore and London: Johns Hopkins, 1978.

Stucke, Horst. "Aufklärung." In *Geschichtliche Grundbegriffe*, vol. 1(1972), 243-342.

Stürmer, Michael. *Herbst des alten Handwerks: Quellen zur Sozialgeschichte des 18. Jahrhunderts.* Munich: Deutscher Taschenbuch Verlag, 1979.

Suchier, Wolfram. "Die Mitglieder der Deutschen Gesellschaft in Göttingen von 1738 bis Anfang 1755." *Zeitschrift des historischen Vereins für Niedersachsen* 81 (1916): 44-124.

Tautscher, Anton. *Staatswirtschaftslehre des Kameralismus.* Bern: A. Francke, 1947.

Teich, Mikulás. "Interdisciplinarity in J.J. Becher's Thought." *History of European Ideas* 9 (1988): 145-60.

Thomas, Janet. "Women and Capitalism: Oppresion or Emancipation? A Review Article." *Comparative Studies in Society and History* 30 (1988): 534-49.

Tracy, James D., ed. *Luther and the Modern State in Germany.* Sixteenth Century Essays and Studies, vol. 7. Kirksville, MO: Sixteenth Century Journal Publishers, 1986.

Treue, Wilhelm. "Adam Smith in Deutschland: Zum Problem des 'politischen Professors' zwischen 1776 und 1810." In *Deutschland und Europa: Historische Studien zur Völker- und Staatenordnung des Abendlandes*, ed. Werner Conze, 101-33. Düsseldorf: Droste, 1951.

———. *Wirtschafts- und Technikgeschichte Deutschlands.* Veröffentlichung der historischen Kommission zu Berlin, 56. Berlin and New York: Walter de Gruyter, 1984.

Tribe, Keith. "Cameralism and the Science of Government." *Journal of Modern History* 56 (1984): 263-84.

———. *Governing Economy: The Reformation of German Economic Discourse 1750-1840*. Cambridge, England: Cambridge University, 1988.

Troitzsch, Ulrich. "Die Schriften von Johann Beckmann (1739-1811) unter dem Aspekt der 'Gemeinnützigkeit': Ein Diskussionsbeitrag ed., Vierhaus, *Deutsche patriotische und gemeinnützige Gesellschaften*, 355-69.

Trossbach, Werner. "Das 'Ganze Haus' – Basiskategorie für das Verständnis der ländlichen Gesellschaft deutscher Territorien in der Frühen Neuzeit?" In *Blätter für deutsche Landesgeschichte* 129 (1993): 277-314.

Ulrich, Silvia. "Die Bedeutung des Gleichheitsgrundsatzes für die rechtliche und faktische Gleichstellung von Frau und Mann in Österreich." In *Über Frauenleben, Männerleben und Wissenschaft: Österreichische Texte zur Frauenforschung*, ed. Beate Frakele, Elisabeth List, and Gertrude Pauritsch, 225-39. Österreichische Texte zur Gesellschaftskritik, vol. 29. Vienna: Verlag für Gesellschaftskritik, 1987.

Ungern-Sternberg, Wolfgang von. "Schriftsteller und literarischer Markt." In *Hansers Sozialgeschichte der deutschen Literatur*, vol 3: *Deutsche Aufklärung bis zur Französischen Revolution, 1680-1789,*: ed. Rolf Grimminger, 2nd ed., part 1, 133-85. Munich: Deutscher Taschenbuch Verlag, 1980.

Vickery, Amanda. "Golden Age to Separate Spheres? A Review of the Categories and Chronologies of English Women's History." *The Historical Journal* 36 (1993): 383-414.

Vierhaus, Rudolf. "Aufklärung als Emanzipationsprozeß." In Vierhaus, ed., *Aufklärung als Prozeß*, 3-18.

———. "Aufklärung und Freimaurerei in Deutschland." In *Das Vergangene und die Geschichte: Festschrift für Reinhard Wittram zum 70. Geburtstag*, ed. Rudolf von Thadden, Gert von Postohlkors, and Helmuth Weiss, 23-41. Göttingen: Vandenhoeck & Ruprecht, 1973.

———. "Bildung." In *Geschichtliche Grundbegriffe*, vol. 1 (1972), 508-51.

———. "Deutschland im 18. Jahrhundert: Soziales Gefüge, politische Verfassung, geistige Bewegung." In Kopitzsch, ed., *Aufklärung, Absolutismus und, Bürgertum*, 173-91.

_____. *Deutschland im Zeitalter des Absolutismus (1648-1763).* Deutsche Geschichte, vol. 6; Kleine Vandenhoeck Reihe, vol. 1431. Göttingen: Vandenhoeck & Ruprecht, 1984.

_____. "'Patriotismus' – Begriff und Realität einer moralisch-politischen Haltung." In Vierhaus, ed., *Deutsche patriotische und gemeinnützige Gesellschaften,* 9-29.

_____, ed. *Aufklärung als Prozeß.* Aufklärung: Interdisziplinäre Halbjahresschrift zur Erforschung des 18. Jahrhunderts und seiner Wirkungsgeschichte, vol. 2, part 2. Hamburg: Felix Meiner, 1987.

_____, ed. *Deutsche patriotische und gemeinnützige Gesellschaften.* Wolfenbüttler Forschungen, vol. 8. Munich: Kraus, 1980.

_____, ed. *Wissenschaften im Zeitalter der Aufklärung.* Göttingen: Vandenhoeck & Ruprecht, 1985.

Viet-Brause, Irmline. "A Note on Begriffsgeschichte." *History and Theory* 20 (1981): 61-67.

Vogel, Barbara. *Allgemeine Gewerbefreiheit: Die Reformpolitik des preubischen Staatskanzlers Hardenberg (1810-1820).* Kritische Studien zur Geschichtswissenschaft, vol. 57. Göttingen: Vandenhoeck & Ruprecht, 1983.

Vogel, Ursula. "Property Rights and the Status of Women in Germany and England." In *Bourgeois Society in Nineteenth-Century Europe,* ed. Jürgen Kocka and Alan Mitchell. Oxford and Providence, RI: Berg, 1993.

Vogler, Günther. "Dorfgemeinde und Stadtgemeinde zwischen Feudalsimus and Kapitalismus." In *Landgemeinde und Stadtgemeinde im Mitteleuropa: Ein struktureller Vergleich,* ed. Peter Blickle, 39-64. Historische Zeitschrift, supplement 13. Munich: R. Oldenbourg, 1991.

Voss, Jürgen. "Deutsche und französische Enzyklopädien des 18. Jahrhunderts." In *Aufklärung als Mission: Akzeptanzprobleme und Kommunikationsdefizite/La mission des Lumières: Accueil réciproque ed difficultées de communication,* ed. Werner Schneiders, 238-47. Das Achtzehnte Jahrhundert, Supplementa, vol. 1; Colloques de Luxembourg, vol. 2. Marburg: Hitzeroth, 1993.

_____, ed. *Deutschland und die französische Revolution: 17. Deutsch-französisches Historikerkolliquium des Deutschen Historischen Instituts Paris (Bad Homburg 29. September-2. Oktober 1981).* Francia, vol. 12. Munich and Zurich: Artemis, 1983.

Walker, Mack. *German Home Towns: Community, State, and General Estates, 1648-1871.* Ithaca, NY: Cornell University, 1971.

———. "Rights and Functions: The Social Categories of Eighteenth-Century Jurists and Cameralists." *Journal of Modern History* 50 (1978): 241-43.

Wangermann, Ernst. "Joseph von Sonnenfels und die Vaterlandsliebe der Aufklärung." In *Joseph von Sonnenfels,* ed. Helmut Reinalter, 157-69. Veröffentlichung der Kommission für die Geschichte Österreichs, vol. 13. Vienna: Verlag der österreichischen Akademie der Wissenschaften, 1988.

Weber, Marianne. *Ehefrau und Mutter in der Rechtsentwicklung: Eine Einführung.* Tübingen: J.C.B. Mohr (Paul Siebeck), 1907.

Weber, Wolfhard. "Johann Georg Krünitz, Enzyklopädist." In *Neue Deutsche Biographie,* vol. 3 (1982), 110-11.

Weckel, Ulrike. *Zwischen Häuslichkeit und Öffentlichkeit: Die ersten deutschen Frauenzeitschriften im späten 18. Jahrhundert und ihr Publikum.* Studien und Texte zur Sozialgeschichte der Literatur, vol. 61. Tübingen: Max Niemeyer, 1998.

Wegele. "Ludwig Timotheus Freiherr von Spittler." In *Allgemeine Deutsche Biographie,* vol. 35 (1893), 212-16.

Wehler, Hans-Ulrich. *Deutsche Gesellschaftsgeschichte: Vom Feudalismus des Alten Reiches bis zur defensiven Modernisierung der Reformära: 1700-1815,* vol. 1. Munich: C.H. Beck, 1987.

Weis, Eberhard. *Monteglas.* 2 vols. Munich: C.H. Beck, 1988-1989.

Weis, Eberhard, and Elisabeth Müller-Luckner, eds. *Reformen im rheinbündischen Deutschland.* Schriften des Historischen Kollegs, Kolloquien 4. Munich: R. Oldenbourg, 1984.

Wesenberg, Gerhard. *Neuere deutsche Privatrechtsgeschichte im Rahmen der europäischen Rechtsentwicklung.* Revised by Gunther Wesener. 4th ed. Vienna, Cologne, and Graz: Böhlau, 1985.

Wierling, Dorothee. "'Ich hab meine Arbeit gemacht – was wollte sie mehr?' Dienstmädchen im städtischen Haushalt der Jahrhundertwende." *Frauen Suchen ihre Geschichte: Historische Studien zum 19. und 20. Jahrhundert,* ed. Karin Hausen, 144-71. Beck'sche Schwarze Reihe, vol. 276. Munich: C.H. Beck, 1983.

Wiesner, Merry E. "Beyond Women and the Family: Towards a Gender Analysis of the Reformation." *Sixteenth Century Journal* 18 (1987): 311-21.

———. "Luther and Women: The Death of Two Marys." In *Disciplines of Faith: Studies in Religion, Politics, and Patriarchy*, ed. Jim Obelkevich, Lyndal Roper, and Raphael Samuel. History Workshop Series. London: Routledge and Kegan Paul, 1987.
———. *Women and Gender in Early Modern Europe*. Cambridge, England: Cambridge University, 1993.
———. *Working Women in Renaissance Germany*. Douglas Series on Women's Lives and the Meaning of Gender. New Brunswick, NJ: Rutgers University, 1986.
Wild, Reiner. "Stadtkultur, Bidlungswesen und Aufklärungsgesellschaften." In *Hansers Sozialgeschichte der deutschen Literatur*, vol. 3: *Deutsche Aufklärung bis zur Französischen Revolution, 1680-1789*, ed. Rolf Grimminger, 2nd ed., part 1, 103-32. Munich: Deutscher Taschenbuch Verlag, 1980.
Woodtli, Susanna. *Gleichberechtigung: Der Kampf um die politischen Rechte der Frau in der Schweiz*. Frauenfeld: Huber, 1975.
Worster, Donald. *Nature's Economy: A History of Ecological Ideas*. Cambridge, England: Cambridge University, 1994.
Wunder, Bernd. *Priviligierung und Disziplinierung: Die Entstehung des Berufsbeamtentums in Bayern und Württemberg*. Studien zur modernen Geschichte, vol. 21. Munich: R. Oldenbourg, 1978.
Wunder, Heide. *Die Bäuerliche Gemeinde in Deutschland*. Kleine Vandenhoeck Reihe, vol. 1483. Göttingen: Vandenhoeck & Ruprecht, 1986.
———. *'Er ist die Sonn, sie ist der Mond': Frauen in der frühen Neuzeit*. Munich: C.H. Beck, 1992.
———. "Gender Norms and their Enforcement in Early Modern Germany." In *Gender Relations in German History: Power, Agency and Experience from the Sixteenth to the Twentieth Century*, ed. Lynn Abrams and Elizabeth Harvey, 39-56. Durham, NC: Duke University, 1993.
———. "Die ländliche Gemeinde als Strukturprinzip der spätmittelalterlich-frühneuzeitlichen Geschichte Mitteleuropas." In *Landgemeinde und Stadtgemeinde im Mitteleuropa: Ein struktureller Vergleich*, ed. Peter Blickle. Historische Zeitschrift, supplement 13. Munich: R. Oldenbourg, 1991.
Zachmann, Karin. "Männer arbeiten, Frauen helfen: Geschlechtsspezifische Arbeitsteilung und Maschinisierung in der Textilindustrie

des 19. Jahrhunderts." In Hausen, ed., *Geschlechterhierarchie und Arbeitsteilung:* 71-96

Zimmermann, P. "Georg Heinrich Zincke." In *Allgemeine Deutsche Biographie,* vol. 45 (1900), 313-15.

———. "Karl Friedrich Pockels." In *Allgemeine Deutsche Biographie,* vol. 26 (1888), 338-39.

Zorn, Wolfgang. "Gewerbe und Handel 1648-1800." In Aubin and Zorn, eds., *Handbuch der deutschen Wirtschafts- und Sozialgeschichte,* vol. 1, 531-73.

———. "Handwerk und Verlagswesen im 18. Jahrhundert." In Aubin and Zorn, eds., *Handbuch der deutschen Wirtschafts- und Sozialgeschichte,* vol 1, 536-41.

———. "Sozialgeschichte 1500-1648." In Aubin and Zorn, eds., *Handbuch der deutschen Wirtschafts- und Sozialgeschichte,* in vol. 1, 465-94.

———. "Sozialgeschichte 1648-1800." In Aubin and Zorn, eds., *Handbuch der deutschen Wirtschafts- und Sozialgeschichte,* vol. 1, 574-607.

Index

A

absolutism, 92
Academy of Commerce (Hamburg), 134
agriculture
    as a science, 103
    early-modern ideal, 49-80
    agriculture
    eighteenth-century crisis of, 173-207
    Justi on, 102-04
    scientific, 258-91 passim
Allgemeines Landrecht. *See* Prussian General Lawcode
Allgemeines Oeconomisches Lexicon, 97
Amalie. *See* Gürnth, Christine Dorothea Henschel
Amaliens Erholungsstunden, 225
Anthropologie in Pragmatischer Hinsicht, 152-54
aristocracy, 26-29
    and household books, 76-78, 98
    culture of, 125
Aristotle, 50, 54, 70, 90, 94, 95, 125
Arnisaeus, Henning, 92
Aufklärung. *See* Enlightenment
Augsburg, 128

Austria, 5, 55, 99, 179, 216, 217, 237-40

B

Bürger, Bürgertum. *See* townspeople, middle classes, and civil society
bürgerliche Gesellschaft. *See* civil society
Büsch, Johann Georg, 134-35
Bacon, Francis, 261
Baden, Grand Duchy, 219, 220
Baierischer Ökonomischer Hausvater, 181-82
Basedow, Johann Bernhard, 137
Bavaria, 159, 181-82, 217
Bavarian Academy of Sciences, 131, 159
Becher, Johann Joachim, 90, 93
Beckmann, Johann, 193, 201
Begriffsgeschichte, 10-12
Behr, Burchard Christian von, 179
Bemerkungen über die Fehler unserer moderner Erziehung, 224
Berlepsch, Emilie, 226, 233, 249
Berlin,
    city, 127, 132, 150, 229
    University, 243, 260
Betrachtungen über das weibliche Geschlecht und dessen Ausbildung in dem geselligen Leben, 234

Bildungsbürgertum, 127
Bonaparte, Jerome, 215-16
Bonaparte, Napoleon, 215-16
    See also Napoleonic era
Bonn,
    city, 128
    University, 93
bourgeoisie. *See* townspeople, middle classes
Brandes, Ernst, 154, 224, 234
breadwinner (concept), 10
Bremen, 244
Bremisches Kochbuch, 248-49
Brentano, Clemens, 150
Burke, Edmund, 154-55

C

calendar
    agricultural, 58
    economic, 54
    Gregorian, 78
Cameral Sciences. *See* Cameralism
Cameralism, 89-114, 133, 156, 163, 173, 174, 178, 180, 217, 260, 265, 272, 302
Campe, Johann Heinrich, 137, 138-39, 155-56, 157, 224, 234, 243, 247
Canon Law, 29
Carl Friedrich of Baden, 175, 176, 219
Carmer, Johann Heinrich Casimir von, 161, 166
Cato, 50
Celle Society and Agricultural Organization, 180, 183, 260, 276
Chotek, Rudolf von, 179
chrematistics, 90
Christian VII of Denmark, 179
Christianity
    and Enlightenment, 122
    Justi on, 100-101
church, Catholic, 39-40, 238
church, Protestant, 39-40, 238

cities, Justi on, 101. *See also* townspepole
Civil Code of Austria, 238-40
Civil Code of France, 217, 235-37
civil servants (*Beamtenstand*), 127
civil society (*bürgerliche Gesellschaft*), 123-26, 235, 242
civil society, 95
clergy, 40
    Catholic, 58
    Protestant, 58
Codex Maximilianeus bavaricus civilis, 159-61, 164, 237
Coler, Jakob, 53-79-passim
Coler, Johann, 52-79 passim, 90, 113, 297, 298
Collumella, 50
Condorcet, Marquis de, 223
Confederation of the Rhine, 215-16, 234
Congress of Vienna, 220
Copernicus, Nicolaus, 121
Corvinus, Siegmund, 40-41

D

Döbel, Heinrich Wilhelm von, 97
Denmark, 178
depression (economic). *See* Great Depression
divorce, 2, 163, 236, 238
domesticity (concept), 1, 4, 6
    early-modern, 74
    modern, 288
Dutch Republic, 92

E

East Germany. *See* German Democratic Republic
economic societies, 174-80
economy, economics
    Cameralist concept of, 89-114
    "Christian," 50, 52-54, 58, 76, 113, 184, 300
    early-modern, 8, 15

Index

Greek concept of, 50, 52, 58, 90, 95, 113
household, 10, 14, 15, 49-79, 102-3, 173-207, 297-303
key word, 13
modern, 15
moral (*See* economy, household)
Thaer on, 262, 267-68
theory vs. practice 80n 1
"women's economy" (Gürnth), 278-82
education
and separate spheres, 243-49
and the Enlightenment, 135-39, 155-58
Bildung, (concept), 136
Erziehung (concept), 136
Humboldt on, 243-44, 247
in household economy, 63-65
Industrie-Schulen, 138
of women (Germershausen), 199-200
of women (Gleim), 244-49
of women (Hippel), 147, 222-23
of women (Hohberg), 69-70, 96
of women (Holst), 224-25
of women (Justi), 107-9
of women (Kant), 153-54
Ehrmann, Marianne, 225, 233, 234, 249
Einleitung zur Kenntnis der englischen Landwirtschaft, 260
Einsiedel, Detlev von, 220
Die Einsiedlerinn aus den Alpen, 225-26
Elbe River, 27, 128
Emile, 136-37
Enlightenment, 17, 107, 120-40, 145-68, 174, 182, 214-50 passim, 261

Enslin, Friedrich, 201
Erlangen, University, 93
Erziehung und Unterricht des weiblichen Geschlechts, 244

F

Familie. See family
family (concept)
bourgeois, 164
Justi on, 102
Prussian General Lawcode on, 163-64
Roman, 51
See also Geschlecht
Federal Republic of Germany, 5
female (cultural construct), 15, 152. *See also* gender
feminism, 4, 6, 221-28, 252n 13
Fichte, Johann Gottlob, 150, 230-33, 234
First World War, 5
Fischer, Heinrich August, 113-14
Fleiß (concept), 124, 138-39, 189, 206
Florinus, Franz Philipp, 52-79, 89, 91, 98, 113,184, 301
Flurzwang, 31
Fontane, Theodor, 18n, 261
Frankfurt am Main, 37, 128, 165
Frankfurt an der Oder, University, 53, 91
Frauenzimmer (concept), 148, 151, 188, 202-03, 226, 248, 280
Frauenzimmerlexikon, 41
Frederick II (the Great) of Prussia, 99, 139, 146, 161, 163, 175, 176
Frederick II of Hesse-Cassel, 175
Frederick William I of Prussia, 91-92
Frederick William III of Prussia, 216, 260
Frederik V of Denmark, 99
freedom (concept), 12-13, 42, 56
Freemasons, 130, 131, 146

Index

French Revolution, 15, 50, 214-21, 221-50 passim
Der Freye Kornhandel als das beste Mittel um Mangel und Theuerung zu verhütten, 187
Friedrich of Württemberg, 228

G

Galileo Galilei, 121
ganzes Haus. *See* "whole house"
Gemeinde. *See* peasants, community
gender
  bourgeois construct, 16
  social construct, 9
gender norms (modern, bourgeois), 1-7, 14, 290-91
gender systems, early modern, 7
George III of Great Britain, 179
Georgica curiosa aucta, 52-79 passim
Gericke, Friedrich Karl, 270-72, 282, 289, 297, 298, 301
Gerike, Auguste, 288-289
German Confederation, 220
German Democratic Republic, 5
German Society of Göttingen, 132
Germershausen, Christian Friedrich, 191-201, 204, 206, 266, 274, 279, 282
Geschichte des Fräulein von Sternheim, 148-49, 151
Geschickter Hausvater and fleissige Hausmutter, 97
Geschlecht (concept), 41-42, 68, 110, 152
Gewerbe (concept), 262, 266
Gießen, University, 92
Gleim, Betty, 244-49, 269
Glückseligkeit (concept), 110. 114
Goethe, Cornelia, 165-76
Goethe, Johann Caspar, 165
Goethe, Johann Wolfgang von, 165-67
Göttingen
  city, 99, 128
  University, 93, 184, 216, 227, 259, 274
Göttliche Ordnung in den Veränderungen des menschlichen Geschlechts, 94
"Götz von Berlingen," 167
Gottsched, Johann Christoph, 145
Gouges, Olympe de, 223
Great Britain, 176, 179
Great Depression, 5
Grubin, Charlotte Albertina, 242
Grundfeste der Macht und Glückseligkeit der Staaten, 110, 123-24
Grundherrschaft, 26-27, 101
Grundsätze der Polizey, Handlung, und Finanzwissenschaft, 111
Grundsätze der rationellen Landwirtschaft, 261, 266
Gürnth, Christine Dorothea Henschel, 278-87, 290, 299
guilds, 10, 12, 37-38, 39, 101
Gutsherrschaft, 27, 30, 32, 77, 101, 262

H

Habsburg Monarchy. *See* Austria
Hall, Catherine, 11
Halle, University, 91, 93, 94, 259
Hamburg Patriotic Society, 131, 134, 135
Hamburg, 128-29, 131, 134, 135, 151, 216, 224
Handbuch der Ökonomischen Literatur, 201
Handbuch für Mädchen vom reifem Alter, 247
Hanover, 179, 182-91
Hardenberg, Karl August von, 217-18
Haus (concept). *See* household.
Haus- Feld- Artzney-, Koch-Kunst und Wunder-Buch 60, 70-79 passim

Index

Haus- und Feldwirtschaft (concept).
See economy, household
Hausfrau (concept), 13, 188, 191, 246-47, 271-73, 277
Der Hausfreund, 277-78
Die Hausfreundin auf dem Lande, 278
Hausherr (concept), 271-72
Hausmutter (concept), 13, 51-79 passim, 97, 106-7, 113, 151, 188, 191, 191-201 passim, 206, 250, 259-91 passim
Die Hausmutter in allen ihren Geschäfften 192-202, 204, 279, 299
Hausnotdurft (domestic necessity), 30, 73, 114, 265
Hausvater (concept), 13, 51-79 passim, 97, 107, 113, 183-91, 250, 259-91 passim, 297
Der Hausvater, 182-91
Der Hausvater in systematischer Ordnung, 191-201 passim, 204
Hauswirt. See Hausvater (concept)
Heidelberg, University, 92
Helmstedt, University, 271
Herz, Henriette, 150, 150, 229
Hesiod, 54
Hinüber, Jobst Anton von, 179
Hippel, Theodor Gottlieb von, 146-49, 150, 151, 153, 216, 221-24, 230, 233, 249
Hohberg, Wolf Helmhard von, 52-79, passim, 90, 95-96, 98, 113, 184
Hohenzollern Monarchy. See Prussia
Holst, Amalie, 224-25, 233, 246, 249
Holst, Ludolf, 224
Holstein, 77
Holy Roman Empire, 25, 128, 219
  grain tariffs of, 187
  population of, 32
  Protestant population of, 78

Home, Francis, 176
household
  as economy (*See* economy, household)
  bourgeois, 63
  concept, 13-15
  urban, 39
household books, 51-59, 83-85n
household economy. *See* economy, household
housewife (concept) 1, 9-10. *See also Hausfrau*
Hoym, Karl Georg Heinrich von, 176
Humboldt, Wilhelm von, 215, 229, 230, 243-44

I

individualism (concept), 33, 42
Industrial Revolution, 9-10, 14, 302
Industrie. See industry
industry, industriousness (concept), 13, 124, 138-39, 182, 185, 205-06, 274
inheritance patterns, 33-34

J

Jacobin Clubs, 217
Jakob, Ludwig Heinrich, 259
Jews, 40, 41, 238
Joseph II of Austria, 175
Justi, Johann Heinrich Gottlob, 98-104, 105-12, 120, 123-26, 133-34, 174

K

Kaiserslautern, Univeristy, 92
Kaiserslautern. *See* Lautern
Kant, Immanuel, 122, 135-36, 147, 150, 152-54, 215, 229, 230, 238
Karl August of Weimar, 175
Karl Theodor of Bavaria, 175

Karl Wilhelm Ferdinand, Duke of Braunschweig-Wolfenbüttel, 137, 259, 271
Kepler, Johannes, 77
Klein, Ernst Ferdinand, 161
Königsberg
   city, 128, 146, 150, 242
   University, 146, 259
Kraus, Jakob, 259
Kreittmayr, Wiguläus Xaverius Aloysius von, 159-61
Krünitz, Johann Georg, 201-03
Küstrin (prison), 99

L

La Roche, Sophie von, 149-50
Landesvater (concept), 78, 96, 123
Landwirt (concept), 13,106, 273
Landwirtin (concept), 106-7, 273
Landwirtschaft (concept), 14, 102-3, 106
Lautern (Kaiserslautern), 179
Leibnitz, Gottfried Wilhelm, 77
Die Leiden des jungen Werthers, 167
Leinhard und Gertrud, 137
Leipzig Economic Society, 178, 179
Leipzig
   city, 129
   University, 94
Leopold of Austria, 55
Leopold Friedrich Franz of Anhalt-Dessau, 137
Leopold, Justus Ludwig Günther, 274-76, 289, 301
Lesewitz, Helene Charoltte, Frau von Friedland, 269
Levin, Rahel, 150, 229
Levy, Sara, 150
Literary Ladies Society of Oldenburg, 216, 234
Locke, John, 261
Louis XIV of France, 92
Louis XVI of France, 216
Lower Saxony, 182

Ludwig Eugen of Württemberg, 228
Lueder, Ferdinand, 259
Lüders, Philipp Ernst, 178
Luther, Martin, 52-54, 76, 301

M

Möglin, 260, 271
male (cultural construct), 15, 152. *See also* gender
Mann und Weib nach ihren gegenseitigen Verhältnissen geschildert, 233
Manorial Jurisdiction. *See Grundherrschaft*
Maria Theresa of Austria, 99, 175
marriage
   and Civil Code of Austria, 239-40
   and Civil Code of France, 236-37
   and Codex Maximilianeus bavaricus, 159-61
   and Prussian General Lawcode, 161-64
   early-modern aristocratic, 28-29, 34
   early-modern peasant, 31, 34, 35
   Fichte on, 231-33
   Germershausen on, 195, 206
   Hippel on, 146-49
   Hohberg on, 71-73
   Holst on, 224-25
   Humboldt on, 229-30
   Kant on, 230
Marschall von Bieberstein, Ernst Franz Ludwig, 219
Masons, Masonic Order. *See* Freemasons
materfamilias. See Hausmutter
Mauvillon, Jakob, 233
Maximilian Joseph III of Bavaria, 159
Mecklenburg, 27

Menius, Justus, 52, 54, 76, 90
Menschenfreund, 151
mercantilism, 92, 178
Merrem, Blasius, 276-77, 301
"Metaphysik der Sitten," 154
Mevius, David, 27
middle classes
    and agriculture (Germershausen) 193-94, 199
    and cameralist thought, 112
    and era of French Revolution, 214-15
    and new gender norms, 290-91
    new, 126-32
Miller, Philip, 176
Mills, John, 176
moral weeklies, 129
Münchhausen, Otto von, 182-91, 203
Munich, University, 93

N

Napoleonic Code. *See* Civil Code of France
Napoleonic era, 17, 214-21, 221-50 passim, 260-70 passim
Nassau, 219, 220
National Socialism, 5
National-Ökonomie (concept), 270, 273, 282
Natural Law, 121-23, 139, 159-61, 238
Nature (concept), 125, 148, 151-52, 203, 221-22, 229, 233, 302
Newton, Isaac, 77, 185, 261
nobility. *See* aristocracy
norms, social, 8, 14

O

Oeconomia Christiana. See economy, "Christian"
Oeconomia Ruralis et Domestica, 52-79 passim

Oeconomische Unterhaltungen für Frauenzimmer, 285
Oeconomisches Magazin, 178
Oeconomus Prudens et Legalis, 52-79, 89
Ökonomie. *See* economy
Oekonomische Encyklopaedie, 199-200
Oekonomisch-technische Encyklopaedie, 200
oikos, 50, 77, 111, 298

P

Palladius, 50
Passau (civil code of), 28
paterfamilias. *See* Hausvater (concept)
patrimonial jurisdiction 31
Patriot (publication), 129
"patriotic and public interest societies," 130-31
peasants, 29-36, 216
    community (*Gemeinde*), 31, 33
Pestalozzi, Johann Heinrich, 137, 156-57, 244, 248
Philanthropinists, 137-39, 156
Physiocracy, 177-78
Pockels, Carl Friedrich, 224, 233, 234
police sciences. *See* Polizei, Polizeiwissenschaft
polis (concept), 91
Politische Abhandlungen, 111
Polizei, Polizeiwissenschaft, 91, 93, 110, 124, 132, 271
Pomona fhr Teutschlands Töchter, 150
population growth, 32, 109, 174. *See also* Holy Roman Empire, population of
poverty, 132-35
Praktische Anleitung zur Führung der Wirthschafts-Geschäffte für angehende Landwirthe, 271

Index

Praktisches Haushaltungs- und Kochbuch, 288-89
protoindustrialization, 27, 35
Prussia, 26, 127, 146-47, 159, 161-64, 174, 216, 217, 223, 240-43, 260-70 passim
Prussian General Lawcode, 147, 159, 161-64, 166, 237, 240
Psalm 127, 53
Pufendorf, Samuel von, 92

Q

Quesnay, François, 177-78

R

Rath für junge Hausmütter des Mittelstandes bei theuren Zeiten wohlfeil hauszuhalten, 279-82
reading societies, 129-31, 216
Reformation, 34
Renaissance, 50
Riehl, Wilhelm Heinrich, 81n
Riem, Johann, 179
Rinckin, Regina, 242
Rist, Johann, 77
Rochow, Friedrich Eberhard von, 139
Röver, Friedrich, 277-78
Rohr, Julius Bernhard von, 28, 94, 98, 104-5, 297
Rohrbach, Anna Margaretha (Marusch) von, 55
Roman law, 222
Rousseau, Jean-Jacques, 136-37, 156, 224
Royal Danish Agricultural Society, 178
Royal Society of Sciences (Göttingen), 134

S

Sachsenspiegel (lawcode), 28
Salons, 150-51, 229
Sartorius, Georg, 259
Saxony, Electoral, 179
Saxony, Kingdom, 220
Saxony-Weimar, 167
Scheffner, Johann Georg, 147, 150
Schlesische Volkszeitung, 176
Schleswig, 178
Schlosser, Johann Georg, 166
Schön, Theodor von, 270
Scholastics, 50, 90
schoolmasters, 38
schoolteachers, 4
Schröder, Wilhelm von, 90
Scott, Joan, 11
Seckendorff, Viet Ludwig von, 90, 92
Second World War, 5
separate spheres, 4, 155-58, 165-67, 243-49, 249-50, 270-78
servants
   domestic, 3
   Gericke on, 272
   Germershausen on, 195-97
   Leopold on, 275
   rural, 181
   Thaer on, , 265, 269
   urban, 36, 38
Silesia, 32, 176
Silesian Economic-Patriotic Society, 176
Smith, Adam, 14, 134, 258-59
Sonnenfels, Joseph von, 111, 120, 126
Spectator (of London), 129
Spittler, Ludwig Timotheus, 216, 227-29
St. Lüdgerei, 271
Staatswissenschaften. See State Sciences
Staegemann, Elisabeth, 150
Staegemann, Friedrich, 217
State Sciences, 92-114 passim
statistics, science of, 94
Stein, Heinrich Friedrich Karl vom, 240-41, 243
Stettin, 128

Stuttgart, University, 93
sub-peasant class, 32
Süßmilch, Johann Peter, 94, 109, 174
Sulzbach, Christian August von, 56
Svarez, Carl Gottlieb, 161, 162
Switzerland, 6

T

Tableau économique, 177-78
Teutscher Fürsten-Stat, 91
Teutscher Merkur, 226
Thaer, Albrecht, 12, 260-70, 271, 274, 282, 289, 290, 298, 301
Thieme, Johann Christoph, 60, 70-79 passim
Thirty Years War, 27, 54, 76, 177
Thomasius, Christian, 92, 121
Tilsit, Peace of, 217
Townspeople, early-modern, 36-39
Tull, Jethro, 176

U

Über die Bestimmung des Weibes zur höheren Geistesbildung, 224-25
Über die bürgerliche Verbesserung der Weiber, 221-24
Über die Ehe, 146-49, 223
Über die Weiber, 154, 234
Ueber die Kameralwissenschaft, 272
Ueber Nationalindustrie und Staatswirthschaft, nach Adam Smith Bearbeitet, 259

U

Universal Lexicon, 189
Urfaust, 167

V

Väterlicher Rath für meine Tochter, 155-56, 247
Varnhagen, Rahel Levin, 150
Varro, 50
Die Vernünftigin Tadlerinnen, 145
Versuch einer Charakteristik des weiblichen Geschlechts, 233
Vienna
 city, 128, 216
 University, 92
village communities
 Justi on, 101
 See also peasants, community
Vindication of the Rights of Women, 223
Virgil, 50
virtues
 and household economy, 74, 190
 civic, 124-25
 economic, 198
 middle-class, 301
 new female, 287-89
Voß, Christian Friedrich, 146, 147, 220
Vollständiges Haußwirthschafts-Buch, 98

W

Württemberg, University, 92
Wagemann, Arnold, 139
Wagemann, Ludwig Gerhard, 138
Wealth of Nations, 11, 134, 258-59
Weber, Friedrich Benedict, 201, 272, 289, 301
Weimar Republic, 5
West Germany. *See* Federal Republic of Germany
Westphalia (area), 183
Westphalia, Kingdom, 215-16, 217
"whole house," 81-82n
widowers, 34, 237
widows, 34, 39, 133, 149, 237
Wirt. *See* Hausvater
Wirtschaft (concept). *See* economy, household
Wolff, Christian, 121, 160
Wollstonecraft, Mary, 223, 224
work
 among peasants, 34

    as key word, 13
    reproductive, 7
workhouses, 133-34
working classes, 2-4
    rural, 16
    urban. *See* servants

X

Xenophon, 50, 54, 90

Y

Young, Arthur, 261

Z

Zedler, Johann Heinrich, 41-42, 189
Zeiller, Franz A. Elder, 238-40
Zincke, Georg Heinrich, 96-97

www.ingramcontent.com/pod-product-compliance
Lightning Source LLC
Chambersburg PA
CBHW071146070526
44584CB00019B/2678